MEXICO CITY, PUEBLA
& CUERNAVACA

1ST EDITION

MEXICO CITY, PUEBLA & CUERNAVACA

Zain Deane

The Countryman Press
Woodstock, Vermont

ISBN 978-1-58157-105-9

Interior photos by the author unless otherwise specified
Book design by Bodenweber Design
Composition by PerfecType, Nashville, TN
Maps by Erin Greb Cartography, © The Countryman Press
Mexico City subway map courtesy of AdvantageMexico.com

Published by The Countryman Press, P.O. Box 748, Woodstock, Vermont 05091

Distributed by W. W. Norton & Company, Inc., 500 Fifth Avenue, New York, NY 10110

Manufactured in the United States of America

10 9 8 7 6 5 4 3 2 1

Recommended by *National Geographic Traveler* and *Travel + Leisure* magazines

A crisp and critical approach, for travelers who want to live like locals.
—*USA Today*

Great Destinations™ guidebooks are known for their comprehensive, critical coverage of regions of extraordinary cultural interest and natural beauty. Each title in this series is continuously updated with each printing to ensure accurate and timely information. All the books contain more than one hundred photographs and maps.

Current titles available:

The Adirondack Book

The Alaska Panhandle

Atlanta

Austin, San Antonio
  & the Texas Hill Country

Baltimore, Annapolis & the Chesapeake Bay

The Berkshire Book

Big Sur, Monterey Bay
  & Gold Coast Wine Country

Cape Canaveral, Cocoa Beach
  & Florida's Space Coast

The Charleston, Savannah
  & Coastal Islands Book

The Coast of Maine Book

Colorado's Classic Mountain Towns

Costa Rica

Dominican Republic

The Erie Canal

The Finger Lakes Book

The Four Corners Region

Galveston, South Padre Island
  & the Texas Gulf Coast

Glacier National Park & the Canadian Rockies

Guatemala

The Hamptons Book

Hawaii's Big Island

Honolulu & Oahu

The Jersey Shore: Atlantic City to Cape May

Kauai

Lake Tahoe & Reno

Las Vegas

Los Cabos & Baja California Sur

Maui

Memphis and the Delta Blues Trail

Mexico City, Puebla & Cuernavaca

Michigan's Upper Peninsula

Montreal & Quebec City

The Nantucket Book

The Napa & Sonoma Book

North Carolina's Outer Banks
  & the Crystal Coast

Nova Scotia & Prince Edward Island

Oaxaca

Oregon Wine Country

Palm Beach, Fort Lauderdale, Miami
  & the Florida Keys

Palm Springs & Desert Resorts

Philadelphia, Brandywine Valley
  & Bucks County

Phoenix, Scottsdale, Sedona
  & Central Arizona

Playa del Carmen, Tulum & the Riviera Maya

Salt Lake City, Park City, Provo
  & Utah's High Country Resorts

San Diego & Tijuana

San Juan, Vieques & Culebra

San Miguel de Allende & Guanajuato

The Santa Fe & Taos Book

Santa Barbara and California's Central Coast

The Sarasota, Sanibel Island & Naples Book

The Seattle & Vancouver Book

The Shenandoah Valley Book

Touring East Coast Wine Country

Tucson

Virginia Beach, Richmond & Tidewater Virginia

Washington, D.C., and Northern Virginia

Yellowstone & Grand Teton National Parks
  & Jackson Hole

Yosemite & the Southern Sierra Nevada

The authors in this series are professional travel writers who have lived for many years in the regions they describe. Honest and painstakingly critical, full of information only a local can provide, Great Destinations guidebooks give you all the practical knowledge you need to enjoy the best of each region.

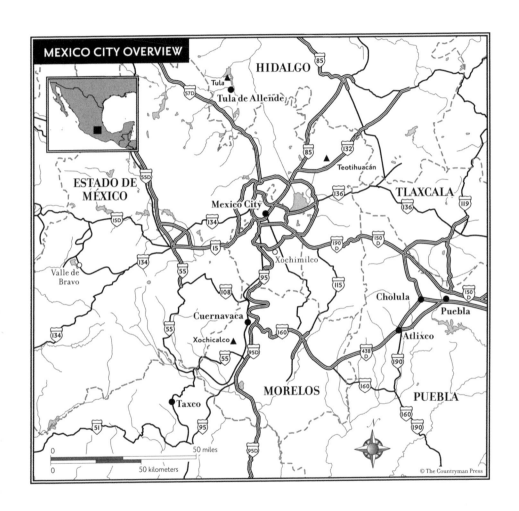

MEXICO CITY OVERVIEW

HIDALGO

Tula
Tula de Allende

ESTADO DE
MÉXICO

Teotihuacán

TLAXCALA

Mexico City

Valle de
Bravo

Xochimilco

Cuernavaca

Cholula
Puebla

Xochicalco

Atlixco

MORELOS

PUEBLA

Taxco

0   50 miles

0   50 kilometers

© The Countryman Press

CONTENTS

PUEBLA & CUERNAVACA

Acknowledgments

This book was a labor of love, but one that never would have been feasible without the help and support of the many people who made me feel at home in Mexico and let me experience it as both a tourist and a local. At the top of this list is my sister, who was the first person to convince me of Mexico's beauty and who blazed the first trails for me.

I must thank Kim Grant, who supported the idea of this book, and Kermit Hummel, who commissioned it. Yusfia Jimenez was a tremendous help in my initial research. Once I reached Mexico, I had the support and friendship of a vast number of people who showed me what Mexican hospitality is all about. While I can't mention them all, I have to give special thanks to José Carlos Gutiérrez Margáin at Apporta and Patricia Quintana at Izote, my ambassadors of Mexican fine dining; Sylvie Laitre at the outstanding Mexico Boutique Hotels; and my friends Sebastian Fitje, Gonzalo Serrano, Gerardo (and Mom!), Maria Cristina, Javier, José Luis, and the gang. In Puebla, Denise and Mercedes organized a wonderful stay, and Erica Perez was a great help in Cholula. Eleonora García Ferrel, Karina Aguilar Corona, and Rubén Cortés were amazing hosts who made Cuernavaca feel like home. Without them, and without the hundreds of people who extended their hands to help me, I'd never have been able to write about the Mexico I know and love.

Finally, to my parents, thanks for letting me continue to live a dream, and thanks to Saira, who gets to hear about my adventures ad nauseam after the fact but hasn't yet been able to come with me. I hope to change that.

Introduction

Mexico City gets a bad rap: while tourists flood Mexico's well-known, footloose-and-fancy-free resort centers in Cancún, Acapulco, and the Mayan Riviera, many visitors avoid Mexico City because its reputation has preceded it. Rumors of pollution, overpopulation, high crime, and a bustling, dangerous, angry urban sprawl keep travelers away.

This is unfortunate, because by skirting Mexico City, tourists who love this country are missing out on its most exciting urban center and one of the most fascinating cities in the world. There's no doubt that this can be a daunting destination; as you fly into Benito Juárez International Airport and look out over the unending expanse of the metropolis, you can't help but notice how overwhelming Mexico City is.

Not to worry: once you get acclimated, it's more likely that you will be fascinated by the sights, sounds, tastes, and charm of this city, and that you'll fall in love with its mix of ancient empire and modern, sophisticated society. The oldest city in the Americas, Mexico City was both the Aztec and Spanish capital, and it has preserved its pre-Hispanic and colonial heritage so well that two of its areas (not buildings . . . *areas*) have been designated World Heritage Sites by the United Nations Educational, Scientific, and Cultural Organization (UNESCO).

Within a few hours' ride of Mexico City's continuously expanding borders lie magnificent temples, ritzy retreats, volcanoes, and historic towns. Puebla, the first Spanish city that was not built on the rubble of an Indian settlement, is a colonial gem and a worthy second city of central Mexico. (Incidentally, Puebla's city center is also a World Heritage Site.) Cuernavaca, known for its climate, ecotourism, spas, and million-dollar vacation homes, has been a holiday destination for Mexicans since the Aztecs; it's also a useful base from which to explore surrounding points of interest. Puebla and Cuernavaca are just two of the many nearby communities that draw millions of local and international tourists from the city each year.

Mexico City will challenge you. It's not a destination that immediately bowls you over with its beauty; rather, you have to venture out and discover its pockets of splendor, color, and undeniable character. A basic understanding of Spanish is essential if you want to explore beyond the guided tours and hotels, but the people here are hospitable and kind. Crime, congestion, and the sheer logistics of navigating through Mexico City's various neighborhoods are not to be ignored. But if you're willing to brave its gruff and often misunderstood exterior, you'll be rewarded by a city that has been fascinating adventurers, wanderers, and explorers for thousands of years.

—Zain Deane

How to Use This Book

Mexico City can be a daunting destination. It's massive, crowded, and generally non-English-speaking. Enough travelers have returned with unhappy stories to drown out those who come back touting its many advantages.

In writing this book I had to take into account the difficulties that come with visiting Mexico, or else I'd be painting a false picture. You can have an unforgettable vacation here, but if you walk in unprepared, you can also be in for a rough time. Those preparations range from the very basic—don't drink the water—to the essential—how to call a taxi.

I'm not trying to scare you away from Mexico City and its surrounding areas. On the contrary, I want to make your experience in the region as enjoyable as possible. A secondary aim of this book is to help travelers appreciate why Mexico is such a fascinating destination. Its culture spans millennia, includes some of the world's great ancient treasures, and preserves the saga of the conquistadores in the New World better than any other nation. One of its best attributes is its ability to honor both the legacy of the Spanish (especially the Catholic Church) and its Native heritage.

You will find that this book dwells on the history of the destinations covered; this is only because these accounts are so fascinating, filled with such intrigue, tragedy, and romantic heroism, that to not focus on them would be to do these places an injustice. I firmly believe that to appreciate this country, one has to embrace its turbulent history. Mexico, and central Mexico in particular, is a sacred land, a place of power that has been fought over for centuries. This is where some of the world's great idealists have made a stand or found a home. And it is a civilization born of strife. When you visit one of Mexico City's incredible museums; tour the churches of Puebla and Cholula; or follow in the footsteps of the freedom fighter Emiliano Zapata, you'll find ample evidence of Mexico's conflicted past. The ruins of ancient empires lie juxtaposed with or directly beneath marvelous new symbols of the strength and power of the country's conquerors. The capital's evocative murals relate the near-continuous struggle of the have-nots against the haves, the majority against the minority.

So where does that leave the tourist? I would say squarely in the pages of history, in the telling of an incredible legend, and in the pulsating heart of Mexico. This is not the book, or the destination, for those who want the beachfront resort experience. Rather, it is a guide for those who want to immerse themselves in Latin America's greatest metropolis and its surrounding communities. To include every attraction, museum, and point of interest would have been impractical for a book of this size. Thus in these pages I've singled out places and activities that I feel are worth the effort and the money. These include the popular, the quirky, and the surprising. I'm willing to bet Mexico will surprise you . . . even if you think you know all about it.

Once you leave Mexico City for other points of interest in central Mexico, you'll find that the landscape, the people, the very essence of your experience changes. Some of the country's most important pre-Hispanic ruins, religious structures, and natural wonders are found in this region, and I've endeavored to show you the best of them in Puebla, Cuernavaca, and the state of Morelos.

It seems the people of Mexico have suffered from the same reputation as their country. Mexicans, especially from the American point of view, are not exactly held in the highest regard, and this truth isn't lost on them. It's a shame, because in my travels through Mexico, I've met wonderful people who have welcomed me to their country and cities with open arms. Of course, there is an unfriendly element, and Mexicans' opinions of gringos vary greatly . . . but we'll get to that. Suffice it to say that, if you are willing to speak a little Spanish and can show an honest appreciation for their country, you'll find Mexico's people to be gracious hosts.

Tourists also have access to ample resources to help them plan their trip. The **Mexico Tourism Board**'s portal, www.visitmexico.com, is a comprehensive online directory that provides information, recommendations, and tips on every part of the country. **Mexico Boutique Hotels** (www.mexicoboutiquehotels.com) is a resource I highly recommend, not only for having the finest small hotels under its umbrella, but also for its terrific customer service, which begins even before you arrive in the country. And finally, look for the **Tesoros de Mexico** brand of reputable hotels and restaurants, many of which are included in this guide.

In general, Mexico offers a completely different experience from what you'll find in the United States, even the *Mexican* parts of the U.S. However, there are examples of Americana around if you're so inclined. American fast-food chains can be found in abundance. Some restaurants carry English-language menus and some (by no means all) museums and galleries have information available in English. But by and large, Mexico is a world away from its neighbor. That's part of its allure.

Prices

The interesting thing about Mexico is that you can enjoy it on a pauper's budget or spend a fortune, depending on your preference and resources. I can say without exception that every museum I visited in Mexico is a bargain by American standards. Your dining options range from under-a-dollar tacos to restaurants that cost as much as New York's finest. And hotels range from remarkably cheap hostels to elite, lavish properties.

Because of the range of prices that travelers will encounter, I've used the following chart to help you decide where to go, what to eat, and what to see and do. Central Mexico is a region with a very agreeable climate year-round and, as a result, is not subject to seasonal fluctuations in its tourist pricing. There are peak periods, of course, coinciding with major holidays. But generally speaking, prices tend to be relatively static throughout the year.

Please note that these prices do not include taxes or gratuities. Tipping follows its own customs in Mexico. A taxi driver does not generally expect a tip but will appreciate one all the same. Porters and other hotel staff should be tipped for their services, and at restaurants, a 10 to 15 percent tip is standard. Make sure to check your bill at restaurants, as some include the service charge.

Price Guide

Code	Lodging (double occupancy)	Restaurants (per entrée)	Attractions (per adult)
$	Up to $100	Up to $10	Up to $10
$$	$101–$200	$11–$25	$11–$25
$$$	$201–$300	$26–$35	$26–$50
$$$$	More than $300	More than $35	More than $50

The Aztecs battle the conquistadores in a scene from Diego Rivera's History of Cuernavaca and Morelos, Conquest and Revolution

THE HISTORY OF CENTRAL MEXICO

A Clash of Civilizations

Mexico's history is a fascinating chronicle of high drama, global intrigue, and human struggle on a massive scale. It is a history forged in the heat of battle and conquest, and it is no coincidence that practically every Mexican hero has died a violent death. For thousands of years, Mexico City has always been center stage, a hotly contested prize for indigenous tribes, Spanish conquistadores, American troops, French emperors, and the embattled Mexicans who rose up and wrested it free. Its roots run deep, beginning with the tribes who once ruled in Mesoamerica.

Most of the world knows ancient Mexico as the land of the Aztecs and the Mayas. While this is true, it is also incomplete. In fact, the Aztecs were latecomers to the pre-Columbian stage; and although they made Mexico City the heart of their empire, they weren't the first to settle in the region. Their predecessors, whose traces can be seen today, laid the groundwork for the mighty civilizations that would come.

Mexico's pre-Columbian history is usually broken down into distinct eras. The first is the **archaic period**, which stretches from 8000 B.C. to 1500 B.C. and marks the arrival of humans to the area and the establishment of primitive agricultural settlements. At around 2000 B.C., settlements began to arise on Mexico's Pacific coast, evidence of an early culture known as the Mokaya. The Mokayas, or People of the Corn, were the ancestors of two of Mexico's great societies: the Olmec, whose history dominates the **pre-classic period** (1500 B.C. to A.D. 300), and the Maya.

The Olmecs settled on Mexico's Gulf coast in present-day Veracruz and Tabasco. Considered the forerunners of many Mesoamerican cultures, they excelled in astronomy, architecture, urban planning, and arts and crafts. Among their achievements were a rudimentary calendar, pyramids, sculptures (most notably their famous megalithic stone heads, easily identifiable today for their rounded shape), and the origins of the cult of the jaguar. The Olmecs flourished from approximately 1200 B.C. to 600 B.C. and vanished by around 400 B.C., but other societies began to emerge throughout Mexico during the pre-classic period.

THE RISE OF TEOTIHUACÁN AND THE MAYAN EMPIRE

From around 100 B.C. to A.D. 700, a period that stretches from the pre-classic to the **classic**, a new and enigmatic civilization arose just north of present-day Mexico City. Today, **Teotihuacán** is among Mexico's most magnificent archaeological sites, yet much about its people remains a mystery. A remarkably advanced settlement, Teotihuacán became the largest pre-Columbian city in the Americas, boasting a population of as many as 200,000 people and serving as the economic and cultural center of all Mesoamerica. As quickly as it flourished, the mighty city was abandoned under unknown circumstances.

The Mayan civilization reached its height between A.D. 250 and 900. The Mayas perfected the Olmec calendar, built elaborate edifices and cosmopolitan cities, and developed a sophisticated social and religious order. Among their most significant and far-reaching achievements were the development of a hieroglyphic writing system that was soon adopted throughout Mesoamerica; complex architectural styles; and advanced mathematics.

Who were the Mayas? The answer to that question could fill a book. They were not a homogeneous people but rather an amalgamation of ethnic groups, languages, and cultures. The Mayan empire at one point occupied over 186,000 square miles over parts of present-day Mexico, Guatemala, Belize, Honduras, and El Salvador.

The classic period (A.D. 250–900) was defined by the intellectual and physical growth of the Mayan empire. While its city-states multiplied and prospered, giving rise to some of its greatest monuments, this was not a time of peace; excavated tombs are replete with evidence of sacrifices, and stelae from the era recount the numerous conquests and infighting among the different ruling dynasties. Frequent warring among Mayan rulers eventually debilitated their most powerful city-states.

After A.D. 900, the center of Mayan power shifted to the coastal cities and the Yucatán Peninsula. This was the **post-classic period** of the empire, which lasted until the Spanish conquerors arrived in the 15th century and changed Mexico forever. But in central Mexico, new tribes would settle in and around Mexico City, and would have dominion over great cities and vast empires.

FROM TOLTEC TO AZTEC

For all their reputation for barbarism, the early civilizations of Mexico and Mesoamerica were primarily based on agriculture and trade. However, two peoples emerging in the post-classic period made a name for themselves through their bloody rituals, tribal warfare, and brutal conquests: the Toltecs and the Aztecs.

The Toltecs were one of several bands of invading tribes from the north who migrated into the area at around the time of the fall of Teotihuacán. In the 10th century, they built the imposing city of Tula, near present-day Mexico City. The Toltecs were a hardened militaristic society, spawning the elite warrior classes of the jaguar and the eagle. They also had a healthy appetite for ritual human sacrifice. In fact, it is possible that the practice of mass sacrifice began in Tula. Despite their fierce nature, or perhaps because of it, the Toltecs did not last long. Tula was sacked and looted in the 12th century.

For the next 100 years or so, the central region was home to numerous and disparate city-states. The period heralded the arrival of a nomadic tribe who claimed to have come from a land called Aztlan: they called themselves the Azteca, but later took the name

Ruins of the Toltec capital at Tula

Mexica. It was the Mexica who would found the last great indigenous civilization of the New World, while the term "Aztec" applies in a larger context to the period, and to various ethnic groups who spoke the Nahuatl language. But history and popular culture has made the Aztec name synonymous with the Mexica tribe that dominated Mesoamerica for two centuries. This book follows popular norms while recognizing that "Aztec," strictly speaking, is a broader term.

Two gods in particular guided the fate of the Mexica. The first and most important was Huitzilopochtli (which means "left-handed hummingbird"), a war god and a sun god. The other was Quetzalcoatl, the Feathered Serpent. It was one of Huitzilopochtli's priests, Tenoch, who after a long migration settled his people in the valley of present-day Mexico City in the 13th century. When the Mexica came to a large island on Lake Texcoco, they witnessed a sight foretold in tribal prophecy: an eagle perched on a cactus and devouring a snake. Heeding the omen, they settled the area and founded a new capital called Tenochtitlán in 1325. It would become a metropolis unrivaled in ancient Mexico, whose aqueducts and canals, vibrant plazas and markets, extraordinary architecture, and grand scale made it one of the wonders of its time.

It was also a city ruled by a sophisticated society. The Aztecs were blessed with a succession of able leaders, including Montezuma I (spelled "Motecuhzoma" in Nahuatl), Tizoc, Ahuizotl, and Montezuma II. Its nobility was comprised of priests and tax collectors, and it boasted a prosperous merchant class and, of course, a powerful warrior class.

Through conquest, the Aztecs exacted tribute that fed the economy, and also fed the gods. Human sacrifice was one highly glorified component of a fantastically complex religious order and was a practice tied directly to the rising of the sun. The Aztecs believed the sun that rose daily above them was in fact the fifth sun of their world; the previous four

The Legacy of the Feathered Serpent

One of the most powerful and enigmatic deities in the Mesoamerican pantheon, **Quetzalcoatl,** the Feathered Serpent, has played a key role in Mexican history. Quetzalcoatl's influence stretched across Mesoamerica, and across the centuries. The Mayas' respect for the god is evident in the great city of Chichén Itzá. And Quetzalcoatl would later be honored as one of the chief gods of the Toltecs and Aztecs. However, as we will see, legend has it that the god was partly responsible for the fall of the Aztecs to the Spaniards.

had been destroyed. As a result, keeping Huitzilopochtli satisfied was a main objective of the Aztec priests, and the best way to do so, apparently, was to offer the god a steady diet of human hearts. This belief in nourishing their gods with human victims led the Aztecs to practice human sacrifice on a massive scale.

They were also proficient astronomers, following calendars adopted from their predecessors. Time, and the cyclical nature of time, was important to the Aztecs. Each day was controlled by two gods, who provided a divine yin-yang balance to life. Their years were measured by a solar calendar as well as a ritual one, the former lasting 365 days and the latter 260 days. The two calendars would synchronize every 52 years, which meant the Aztecs lived according to continuous 52-year cycles, and the end of each of these periods was a potentially apocalyptic date. It is one of the world's amazing and prophetic coincidences that the end of one such cycle heralded the arrival of a stranger from a foreign land named Hernán Cortés.

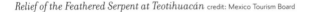

Relief of the Feathered Serpent at Teotihuacán credit: Mexico Tourism Board

The Aztecs ruled through military supremacy. In the 15th century, three of their city-states joined forces in a formidable triple alliance that quickly and decisively subdued neighboring rivals and cemented what would become the strongest of all Mesoamerican empires. Eventually the empire governed a population of roughly 5 million subjects, who lived in self-sustaining units called calpulli, each of which paid tribute to the supreme ruler. During the reign of Montezuma II, this dominion extended throughout central and southern Mexico and reached both the Pacific and Gulf coasts.

THE SPANISH CONQUEST AND NUEVA ESPAÑA

They say history is written by the winners, and for the most part this is true. However, in writing this guide and compiling my historical research on the clash of New World versus Old, I have relied on a remarkable book called *Visión de los Vencidos* (Vision of the Vanquished), which documents the Spanish conquest from the Native perspective. According to this text, the Aztecs foresaw a coming doom as early as ten years before the arrival of the Spanish, and recorded numerous portents of the end of their days. Among these harbingers were a comet spotted in 1517, the spontaneous burning of the temple of Huitzilopochtli, repeated apparitions of two-headed men, and, one of the most puzzling, a bird brought to Montezuma which had a mirror sticking out of its head, through which the king saw an approaching force.

But the Spanish alone were not responsible for the demise of the Aztecs. Despite its tremendous achievements, the empire had begun to crack by the 16th century. Dissension and revolt had spread in the land, and into this volatile environment stepped the expeditioner Hernán Cortés in 1519. A popular (and highly disputed) legend says that when Montezuma received reports of bearded white men reaching the shores of the Gulf of Mexico (in present-day Veracruz), he believed the new arrivals marked the return of Quetzalcoatl from the east, as foretold in ancient Aztec lore.

Cortés didn't simply rampage through Mexico with his brave conquistadores until the Natives were subdued, however. For one thing, he had brought only 550 soldiers with him from Spain, nowhere near enough to defeat the hordes of Aztec warriors. For another, he was invited to Tenochtitlán by Montezuma, a diplomatic gesture with catastrophic consequences. Moreover, the Spanish mandate never called for an invasion. In moving against the Aztecs, Cortés acted on his own, chasing dreams of silver and gold.

Most important to his ambitions were indigenous allies. As Cortés marched toward the Aztec capital, he realized that his host ruled over a fractured nation, with numerous disgruntled tribes who paid tribute to Tenochtitlán (considering that this tribute was partly in the form of human sacrifices, one can understand their resentment). The conquistador made alliances with those who were willing to join him, most notably the people of Tlaxcala, who were bitter enemies of the Aztecs. By the time he reached the capital, Cortés was at the head of a Spanish *and* Native army.

Still, all that force would not have availed the Spanish if it had not been for Montezuma's gracious welcome. Inviting Cortés into his city and meeting the conquistador's demands, the Aztec king sealed his fate. Montezuma was imprisoned and his nobles massacred by the Spanish. While Montezuma was in captivity, a new development threatened Cortés's plans: Spain had sent a force to the New World to intercept and replace its maverick explorer, who had disobeyed the crown by embarking on his quest for riches.

Cortés left the city to meet this new contingent and ended up converting many of the soldiers to his cause; but while he was gone, the people of Tenochtitlán revolted under the leadership of a new ruler, Cuitláhuac, whose reign lasted a mere 80 days. Their rebellion came about as the result of a massacre of some 10,000 Aztec nobles at the hands of Pedro de Alvarado, Cortés's second in command and a man known for his cruelty to the indigenous people of the New World.

Cortés returned to find the Aztec capital in turmoil. He and his allies were routed and forced to flee the island city after suffering such heavy casualties that, upon reaching the mainland, the conquistador rested by a great tree and wept for the loss of his people. This moment in Mexican history has come to be known as *la noche triste* (the sad night), and the stump of that very tree still stands in Mexico City.

The Spanish soon returned to the Aztec capital and laid siege to Tenochtitlán. In May 1521, after 75 days of bitter fighting, Cortés defeated the stiff Aztec resistance led by Cuauhtémoc, the last of the Aztec emperors, and took control of the city. Over its ashes, the Spanish laid the foundations for modern-day Mexico City. Their rule would span three centuries.

After the fall of Tenochtitlán, Cortés set about systematically colonizing the area until, by 1574, the majority of the Aztec empire had been brought under Spanish control and most of its people were enslaved to the conquistadores. Although the Indians fought bravely and bitterly, they were overmatched not just by superior weapons, armor, and training (the Aztecs had never learned or practiced the art of organized warfare on a mass scale), but by two other, equally decisive, factors: disease and religion.

The Spanish brought their illnesses from the Old World to the New. As the indigenous people of Mexico had never been exposed to these diseases (most notably smallpox, which decimated their numbers), they had no immunity against them, and the effects were devastating. It is believed that approximately 24 million people died of sickness between 1521 and 1605, a staggering loss to the Native population.

In its own way, the Catholic Church was just as effective at subduing the indigenous people of Mexico as war and disease. Missionaries from Spain first arrived in Mexico in 1523. They built monasteries and churches throughout Mexico. Aztec religious beliefs and learning were banned, and new churches were built directly over razed temples. This prac-

Mexico's Pocahontas

It is arguable that Cortés could never have achieved his victory without the aid of a Native woman who has come to be known as la Malinche (she is also called Malintzin, and Cortés referred to her as Doña Marina). An Aztec noble who was enslaved by the Mayas, la Malinche proved invaluable as a translator for the conquistadores, as she spoke both Mayan and Nahuatl, the language of the Aztecs. Cortés had found a Spaniard named Gerónimo de Aguilar, who spoke the Mayan language. Between Aguilar and la Malinche, Cortés had found a direct channel of communication to the Aztec people.

La Malinche eventually became Cortés's mistress and learned enough Spanish to translate directly for him. However, unlike the heroine of Disney's feel-good parable *Pocahontas*, la Malinche hasn't fared well in history. In Mexico, her name has come to be associated with treachery, and to be called *malinchista* today is no compliment.

Church built on site of indigenous temple, Mexico City's Plaza de las Tres Culturas

tice achieved two goals. First, it demonstrated convincingly the dominance of the Catholic God over the Aztec ones. After all, the new deity quite literally sat on the remains of the old ones, a powerful image for the vanquished. Second, it showed the Aztecs that their daily practices need not change. They would still go to the same place to worship; they would find visual elements that enabled them to relate to their new god; and finally, they found in Catholicism a figure whom they could revere above the pantheon of their gods: Mary.

To understand the crucial importance of the Virgin Mother, it is important to note that the Aztecs had great reverence for the feminine. Reproduction and birth were sacred, and in Mary, the locals found divinity with which they could relate. The church understood this and used Mary to its advantage, so much so that, to this day, Mexico is alive with myriad representations of *la Virgen.*

The defeat of the Aztecs entrenched the Spanish in the New World and signified the beginning of *Nueva España,* or New Spain. It was a new paradigm, and, like with any con- quered land, produced an uneasy marriage between the colonizers and the colonized. The Spanish took over where the tributary system of the Aztecs left off, and also introduced their own brand of feudalism, called the encomienda. Under this system, Spanish lords built huge colonial estates and prospered while the vast majority of the Native population fell under a type of serfdom that was more like slavery. During the colonial period, this harsh treatment, coupled with sickness and warfare, reduced the Native population of Mexico by more than 90 percent.

Given his victories, Cortés's disobedience was forgiven by the crown and he returned to Spain as a conquering hero. In his place, the governance of New Spain fell under the office of the viceroy, which lasted to the end of the colonial era. Under the viceroy, a new caste system developed in Mexico. At the top were the *peninsulares,* the elite class of colonialists who had come directly from the mother country. Beneath them were the *criollos,* or those of mixed Spanish and Native heritage who formed a tenuous (and increasingly bitter) middle class. Next in line were the *mestizos,* people of mixed ethnicity economically and politically worse off than the criollos. Not surprisingly, the lowest of the lot were the indigenous people and the imported African slaves. These class distinctions are important, as they shaped the future of Mexico. The revolution that would liberate Mexico from Spain was sparked by the criollos and their resentment of the peninsulares and the mother country. However, it is mestizo blood that flows in most Mexicans today and attests to their indigenous heritage.

While the class struggles were brewing, the Spanish were growing fat off the land they had conquered. The colony expanded beyond the borders of present-day Mexico, gold and silver were sent back by the shiploads, and Spain became the richest nation in Europe. Things went well for the Spanish for close to three hundred years. And then Napoleon invaded.

INDEPENDENCE, TYRANNY, AND REVOLUTION

Napoleon I's invasion of Spain in 1808 was the beginning of the end of the colonial empire. In Mexico, it would trigger the march for independence. Unfortunately, it also began a period of political instability, bloody uprisings, and national turmoil that would last for more than a century. Surprisingly, the movement for independence began with an unlikely alliance between conservative landowners and the liberal class of criollos who pushed for a democratic Mexico. Both parties agreed on two fundamental beliefs: Mexico would not bow to France, and the time for independence had arrived.

A Catholic priest named Miguel Hidalgo set the wheels in motion: on September 16, 1810, he issued his famous *grito,* or cry, for independence in the town of Dolores in Guanajuato. (To this day, a patriotic *grito* is repeated every year on September 15, the eve of Independence Day, throughout Mexico.) Hidalgo led a peasant army against Guanajuato and achieved the first victory of the rebellion. As he and Ignacio Allende (a captain of the Spanish army in Mexico who switched allegiances) marched toward Mexico City, the revolt gathered momentum. However, they failed to take the capital, and were chased across Mexico until they were finally captured and executed for treason. While he never lived to see his dream realized, Hidalgo is commemorated today as the father of Mexican independence.

After his death, another priest, José María Morelos, became the leader of the revolt. In 1813, at the Congress of Chilpancingo, Morelos formally declared independence from Spain and ratified what would become the first national constitution of Mexico. Morelos harried the Spanish troops until he, too, was captured and killed in 1815. After Morelos's death, the cause was taken up by Vicente Guerrero.

Still, the death of its two principal architects dealt a profound blow to the movement, and it might have collapsed had it not been for General Agustín de Iturbide, a commander of the Spanish army who sympathized with the Mexican cause. Iturbide met in secret with Guerrero and proposed joining forces under the banner of what he called the Army of the

Three Guarantees. Those guarantees were for an independent Mexico under a constitutional monarchy, the abolition of class segregation, and the appointment of Catholicism as the new state's official religion. Guerrero agreed, and the combined army marched into Mexico City in 1821. Eleven years after Hidalgo's *grito*, the Spanish viceroy capitulated, ending three hundred years of Spanish rule in Mexico.

Following his victory, Iturbide made the questionable move of anointing himself the first emperor of Mexico. His empire, the first of two in the country, lasted less than a year; under mounting opposition, Iturbide was forced to abdicate in 1823. He fled the country but returned in 1824, where, following in history's footsteps, he was promptly arrested and executed. The "empire" was dissolved and in its place a republic was proclaimed, with Guadalupe Victoria becoming Mexico's first president (the aforementioned Vicente Guerrero would be its second).

The fledgling republic struggled mightily. It was economically bankrupt and politically in a state of near-constant turmoil. And it didn't help that it went to war against another nation immediately to the north. The architect of much of this chaos was the infamous Antonio López de Santa Anna. A hero of the war of independence, Santa Anna became president in 1833 and would lead his nation a remarkable eleven times, blithely switching political allegiances along the way. During his first term, Santa Anna managed to disband the congress and abrogate the constitution, causing insurgencies to spring up throughout Mexico; some of the rebelling states formed their own government, and Santa Anna crushed every one of these uprisings, save one: Tejas—Texas.

The state of Texas declared independence from Mexico in 1836, and Santa Anna marched against its defenders, winning battles at Goliad and the Alamo. He was brought down and captured at the battle of San Jacinto in April of that year, and in exchange for his release, granted Texas its independence. As it turns out, the loss of Texas was only a preview of things to come for Santa Anna and Mexico. After the state was annexed to the U.S. in 1845, the two nations went to war over Mexico's northern territory in 1847.

History paints the Mexican-American War in different lights, depending on which side of the border one stands. For the Americans, it was an answer to Mexican aggression and repeated warnings that the annexation of Texas would lead to war. For the Mexicans it was nothing short of an invasion. (It is telling that there were many in the U.S. who shared the Mexican viewpoint, including a congressman named Abraham Lincoln.)

However you look at it, the Mexican-American War, which lasted two years, ended catastrophically for Mexico. American troops won battle after battle against the Santa Anna—led opposition, eventually reaching and occupying Mexico City. The battle of Chapultepec proved the decisive conflict for control of the city, with both sides giving no quarter and suffering heavy casualties. A lasting and poignant memory in Mexican lore comes from this campaign: after the retreat had been sounded, six young cadets decided to fight to the death rather than surrender. The last of them wrapped his body in a Mexican flag and threw himself from Chapultepec Castle to his death. The six *Niños Héroes* (Child Heroes) are remembered with great honor today.

By 1848, Mexico was forced to surrender. Under the terms of the Treaty of Guadalupe Hidalgo, the government ceded roughly half its territory to the United States, comprising present-day California, Nevada, Utah, and parts of Colorado, Arizona, New Mexico, and Wyoming; all in all, more than 500,000 square miles. If you throw Texas into the mix, Mexico had lost more than two-thirds of its land to the Americans.

Mural depicting the fate of the last of the Niños Héroes, at Chapultepec Castle.

The aftermath of the war was bleak for Mexico. Santa Anna was ousted for the last time in 1855, and a civil war ensued which ended with the appointment as president of Benito Juárez, a man who would become one of the most beloved figures in Mexican history. But Juárez's first term came on the footsteps of yet another bloody conflict. Because Napoleon invaded. Again. Sort of.

Napoleon III orchestrated a bizarre interlude in Mexican history. Supported by conservatives in Mexico and the Catholic Church, the French invaded Mexico in 1862. In what has become a globally well-known date for all the wrong reasons, the highly disciplined French army initially suffered a humiliating defeat in the town of Puebla on May 5, or Cinco de Mayo. But they eventually took the capital in 1863, and Napoleon installed an Austrian, Archduke Maximilian of the Hapsburgs, as emperor of Mexico in 1864.

For all of Maximilian's progressive ideas and attempts to reform his new nation, the second Mexican empire fared little better than the first. After three years of war, the Republican army, led by Benito Juárez, retook Mexico City in 1867. Maximilian was captured and, naturally, executed. (In a rather gruesome aside, the emperor was known for his brilliant blue eyes, and after he was killed, someone decided to take them.) Benito Juárez was restored to the presidency and the republic was reestablished. Juárez would serve as president until his death in 1872, and perhaps no one did more to unify Mexico and institute needed reforms than he did. Unfortunately, his efforts were blunted when a general named Porfirio Díaz led a coup following Juárez's death and assumed power.

Díaz controlled Mexico from 1877 to 1911, and his rule has come to be known as the Porfiriato. A dictator who is still reviled for selling out his country to foreign interests, Díaz ushered in a period of relative calm and modernization in the nation. But the Porfiriato was also a time of rampant social inequality, and the nation's working classes suffered. Díaz was a harsh leader who courted U.S. businesses, manipulated the electoral process, and supported the increasing wealth and influence of Mexico's hacendados, or landowners. It is no surprise that he made himself unpopular with the average Mexican, who resented the American invasion, the repressive measures of the regime, and the gradual encroachment of the established nobility.

Things came to a head in 1910, when Díaz ran for reelection against an academic named Francisco Madero. Despite Madero's huge popularity, the election results showed Díaz winning in a landslide, with Madero garnering a minuscule number of votes. It was the last straw, and Madero called for a rebellion. The Mexican Revolution was under way.

Like the War of Independence, the revolution was a protracted affair, replete with valiant heroes who sacrificed their lives for their nation. Two of the most revered figures in Mexico emerged during this time: the daring Pancho Villa in the north, and the idealistic Emiliano Zapata in the south. Both fought alongside Madero, but while Madero became president in 1911 and brought the Porfiriato to an end, he also failed to institute the land reforms Zapata had championed. Zapata broke ranks and drafted the Plan de Ayala, which called for the return of hacendado lands to the peasants and revolt against the government. (For his ideals, more than his military achievements, Zapata remains a romantic national hero unrivaled in the annals of Mexican folklore.)

In 1913, following a conspiracy in which the U.S. ambassador took part, Madero was betrayed and killed by Victoriano Huerta, and the country again descended into war. Zapata, Villa, Álvaro Obregón, and Venustiano Carranza led the revolution, and nearly all of them paid with their lives. Zapata was tricked and ambushed in 1919; Villa was shot in

Statue of revolutionary hero Emiliano Zapata, Cuautla, Morelos

1923; and Carranza, who succeeded Huerta and drafted the Constitution of 1917, which applies to this day, was assassinated in 1920. It was a chaotic time for Mexico. The warring armies became practically autonomous entities, in some cases printing their own money to pay for their supplies and housing. The revolution dragged on until 1920, when Obregón took over after Carranza's death (Obregón was himself killed a few years later). In nine years of fighting, the conflict claimed close to a million lives.

In 1929 Obregón's successor, General Plutarco Elías Calles, formed the Partido Nacional Revolucionario (PNR), or National Mexican Party, which combined the fractious Mexican forces to create a unified Mexican army, a resounding move that some herald as the true end of the revolution. The PNR would become the Partido Revolucionario Institucional (Institutional Revolutionary Party), or PRI (pronounced PREE), and would dominate the political landscape of Mexico for the rest of the 20th century.

Even with the foundation of the PNR, Mexico's situation was unclear until Lázaro Cárdenas was elected president in 1934. Cárdenas promptly exiled Calles and set about doing what Zapata had fought for all along: land redistribution. He also removed the army from power, nationalized the oil industry, and solidified the PRI for the future. His focus on social reform, education, and greater equality transformed Mexico, and Cárdenas is justly revered today for his efforts.

MODERN MEXICO

Following Cárdenas's sweeping reforms, the PRI presided over a period of sustained economic growth that was called *el milagro mexicano,* or the Mexican miracle. While there were setbacks, the Mexican economy prospered until the 1970s. The revolution proved to be the last military campaign for the governance of Mexico, but it wasn't the end to the violence and tragedy that befell the nation.

Two incidents in particular remain fresh in the mind of Mexico City residents. In 1968, just ten days before Mexico City would host the summer Olympics, a student protest was brutally put down by the government. The protest was the result of increasing political unrest, and the student body at the Universidad Nacional Autónoma de Mexico (UNAM) was a vocal proponent for change. The police surrounded the campus, arresting and beating students; in response, a mass demonstration was held, with more than 15,000 students marching across Mexico City. In the Plaza de Las Tres Culturas in the Tlatelolco neighborhood, 5,000 students gathered for what was intended to be a peaceful rally. The police and the army moved in at sunset and began firing into the crowd. The body count rose as the killing continued through the night. The number of deaths is still unknown, but estimates range from a few hundred to several thousand. The people have never forgotten it.

Far more devastating for the city was the earthquake of 1985, one of the worst in the history of the continent. The earthquake struck the neighboring state of Michoacán, but its greatest damage was done in Mexico City, where many of the city's buildings collapsed, due in part to a corrupt administration that turned a blind eye to faulty construction. The death toll was enormous, with estimates ranging from 9,000 to up to 100,000 (many Mexicans believe the government, in addition to responding poorly to the crisis, downplayed the true statistics). Much of the fabled Centro Histórico, or Historic Center, was brought down, and evidence of the earthquake can still be seen in numerous buildings. Today, it is not uncommon for Mexico City residents to ask one another: "Where were you during the earthquake?"

The 1990s finally saw the PRI begin to lose its hegemony in Mexican politics, as opposition parties emerged and took on a more prominent role. Despite Mexico's joining the North American Free Trade Agreement (NAFTA) in 1994, economic mismanagement led to the country ringing up an unprecedented budget deficit by the end of the year. Political tensions boiled over when PRI presidential candidate Luis Donaldo Colosio was assassinated. In 1994 Ernesto Zedillo took the reins and quickly moved to stabilize the economy and introduce electoral reforms, helping to set the stage for the possibility of another political party coming into power.

This happened in the very next election, when Vicente Fox, the candidate of the Partido Acción Nacional (National Action Party or PAN), won the presidency in 2000. It was the first time a member of another party had held the office in over 70 years, a clear sign of a new political balance of power among Mexico's three ruling political parties: the PRI, the PAN, and the PRD, or Partido de la Revolución Democrática (Democratic Revolution Party). The PRD was in a great position to assume the mantle of leadership in 2006. It had a dynamic candidate in Mexico City mayor Andrés Manuel López Obrador, who also went by the acronym AMLO. A Rudy Giuliani–type figure (he even hired Giuliani to help him install a zero-tolerance crime policy) noted for his reforms, he seemed like a shoo-in for the next president.

But it was not to be. The PAN candidate, Felipe Calderón, won the election by the slimmest of margins (about 0.5%). The results were so close that it took more than a month to tally the votes. AMLO immediately declared foul play and demanded a recount. His case was dismissed, but Obrador would not go quietly. He staged a series of protests in the congested downtown, the most notorious of which was a blockade in July 2006 of over 7 miles of Paseo de la Reforma, a vital central artery through the city and home to Mexico's stock market. Nevertheless, the presidency remained in the hands of Calderón.

The Calderón administration has been forced to deal with two major crises since coming to power, the first being the rapidly escalating drug war that has besieged the northern states bordering the U.S. in particular. Calderón declared war on Mexico's powerful drug cartels shortly after becoming president, deploying over 45,000 troops and 5,000 federal police across 18 states. Since 2007 close to 10,000 people have died as a result of the conflict, which in mid-2009 continued to rage across Mexico and into the United States. The U.S. Department of Justice National Drug Intelligence Center has called the Mexican drug trade "the greatest drug trafficking threat to the United States."

The second challenge faced by the Calderón administration is the H1N1, or swine flu, pandemic, which originated in Mexico in spring 2009. As of this publication, the new strain of flu had killed over 300 people worldwide and infected more than 77,000, according to the World Health Organization. The disease caused global panic and brought Mexico, particularly Mexico City, to its knees economically during the government-ordered five-day shutdown of businesses and nonessential public services. The situation in Mexico has improved greatly, and the fears of a flu pandemic seem almost a distant memory in the capital today. But new cases continue to be reported around the world, and the virus remains a global concern to health officials.

If Calderón's presidency is to be measured based on these developments, his record is a mixed one. Initially he received widespread local and American support for his crackdown on the drug trade, even if many Mexicans doubted his ability to curtail the problem. This support had begun to wane by 2009, as the war took its toll. And although the government eventually won praise for its measures to combat the flu crisis, it was soundly criticized initially for not acting fast enough to report on and curtail the spread of the disease.

It remains to be seen how Calderón, and the country, emerge from this latest chapter of Mexico's complex history.

Mexico City at night

2

Planning Your Trip

The Checklist

You hear a lot about Mexico in the news, and unfortunately much of it is downright scary. As of this writing, the drug wars in the border state of Chihuahua raged unchecked despite a massive effort by the government to crack down on the cartels. Traveling to certain parts of the country these days is not merely inadvisable, but practically asking for trouble. Then there's the N1H1 flu, which originated in Mexico in 2009 and became a global pandemic.

None of these are trivial issues, and travelers should take every precaution when visiting Mexico. But I mention the bad before the good only because a negative news update can sometimes shine a frightening spotlight, when the reality is far less intimidating. Is Mexico still in the grip of a deadly disease? Fortunately, by summer 2009 the swine flu pandemic was largely under control and Mexico City had returned to normal. New flu cases were still being reported, and some officials and residents continued to wear the surgical masks that were ubiquitous in the initial stages of the outbreak, but the near-total shutdown of the city is a thing of the past. Many countries have lifted their travel bans to Mexico, and there is a concerted effort under way to galvanize the country's tourism industry. Tourists planning a trip to Mexico City should check the World Health Organization's updates (www.who.int/csr/en/) as well as the advisories posted by the U.S. Centers for Disease Control and Prevention (CDC) (wwwn.cdc.gov/travel/content/novel-h1n1-flu.aspx).

No matter where you go in Mexico, you need to travel smart; there are ways for tourists to safeguard against crime, sickness, and even getting ripped off (although this will be, to some extent, unavoidable). Visitors can take steps to ensure their experience in Mexico is positive and rewarding. That's what this chapter is all about.

ENTERING MEXICO

All travelers to Mexico are required to present original **photo identification** and **proof of citizenship.** All U.S. travelers to Mexico are required to present a **valid passport** at the airport and upon reentry to the United States. If you have a foreign passport but are a legal resident of the U.S., bring your green card as well. Always treat these documents as your most precious commodities when traveling abroad. In case you lose your passport, contact your country's embassy or consulate immediately.

Citizens (and legal residents) of the U.S., Canada, and several other countries around the world do not need a visa to enter Mexico but are required to have a **Mexican Tourist**

Permit (FMT), which serves the same purpose. If you are flying to Mexico, your airline should provide you with this absolutely critical document, but in case you don't get one on board, it is available upon arrival at the airport. The FMT card can be issued for up to 180 days, and will be given a stamped time limit by immigration officials. Often, officials will arbitrarily assign an exit date, so if you are planning to stay a long time (say, more than 60 days), make sure to ask for the full time limit. Just say, "Ciento ochenta días por favor" (180 days, please). After the FMT card is stamped, it will be handed back to you. **Do not discard it!** Visitors are required to present the card upon exiting Mexico. Failure to produce it will result in fines and bureaucratic hurdle-jumping that will have you cursing the country before you leave. Just ask my mother.

Customs

After immigration, you will pass through customs. You must have a completed **Customs Declaration Form**; air travelers will receive this document too from the airline. You will then punch a button to find out if you have a green light (cleared to proceed) or a red light (need to have your luggage checked). It is truly arbitrary.

Customs officials are lenient when it comes to what you can bring into Mexico duty-free. Technically, the list is quite specific: no more than two cameras, five toys, three speedboats . . . it goes on. In practice, however, officials are mainly concerned with people trying to bring in items for resale. Obviously, drugs and firearms are not allowed. Tourists traveling by air are allowed to bring in gifts and permitted goods up to a value of $300 (by land, the amount is $50, except for alcohol and tobacco). If you exceed this amount, you have to pay a flat 15 percent tax on the amount exceeding the exemption. You can also bring in a computer with peripherals worth up to $4,000 duty-free, but you will be required to hire a customs broker if its value exceeds this amount. If you are carrying in excess of $10,000, you must declare it on the customs form but you won't be required to pay tax on it. For the latest customs information in English, visit www.aduanas.sat.gob.mx/aduana_mexico/2008/ pasajeros/139_10134.html, or call 800-463-6728 toll-free in Mexico.

Embassies in Mexico City
Canada
55-5724-7900
www.canadainternational.gc.ca/mexico-mexique/index.aspx
Schiller 529, Col. Bosque de Chapultepec, Mexico, D.F.

United Kingdom
55-5207-2449
http://ukinmexico.fco.gov.uk
Río Lerma 71, Col. Cuauhtémoc, Mexico, D.F.

United States
55-5080-2000
www.usembassy-mexico.gov
Paseo de la Reforma 305, Col. Cuauhtémoc, Mexico, D.F. (Mexico address)
American Embassy Mexico, P.O. Box 9000, Brownsville, TX 78520-9000 (U.S. address)

When leaving Mexico, U.S. citizens who have been in the country for at least 48 hours can take back $800 worth of goods duty-free. (Note that close to 3,000 items, including all Mexican handicrafts, are exempt from U.S. customs duties.) There is a flat rate of duty on anything above this amount. Lottery tickets, drugs, fireworks, and many food products are among the items that cannot be brought back into the U.S. from Mexico. Also on the list are Cuban cigars, which are available in the country (although not all "Cubans" sold in Mexico are really Cuban). For the full list of what is permissible and duty fees, visit the U.S. Customs and Border Protection Web site at www.cbp.gov, or call 877-287-8667.

Climate

Central Mexico, which includes Mexico City, Puebla, and Cuernavaca, is an elevated, mountainous region that enjoys pleasant weather for most of the year. There is a rainy season, which runs from April to October, although Cuernavaca has a more subtropical environment. Rain is sporadic, and many times of the flash-flood variety: strong downpours that appear suddenly and vanish after a short but thorough soaking. The rainy season also overlaps with the hottest months of the year in April and May. The dry season runs from mid-October to April, and includes a mild winter from December to February, when it's brisk enough to require warm clothes but is certainly not extreme. Mexico has a hurricane season in the fall, but while storms and rough winds might batter the coasts, the most

Overcast skies are common during the rainy season

you'll experience in central Mexico is overcast days and strong rains, with occasional flooding.

Altitude plays a major role in influencing the weather. Mexico City is at an elevation of over 7,000 feet above sea level, and most of the rest of the central region is above 5,000 feet. Throughout the year, the higher areas like Mexico City can see any number of cool nights, but this makes for a pleasant contrast to the very agreeable weather during the day.

So when should you go, and what should you pack? Mexico has two travel seasons. High season runs from December to the end of March, and low season from April to December. However, while the coastal resort towns have seasonal fluctuations in prices depending on the time of year, don't expect these variations in central Mexico. Also, there are spikes in travel during major holidays, especially Easter and Christmas. Personally, I love traveling to this part of the country during the winter months, when the weather is perfect during the day and cold but not unbearable at night, and when some of Mexico's best annual festivals take place.

Regardless of when you go, check the weather forecast beforehand. It's not uncommon for travelers to walk around in a T-shirt and jeans during the day and change into a nice pair of trousers and a warm sweater for evening. Part of this is owing to the weather and part to style. Mexicans dress well and conform to a certain standard when stepping out at night. At most restaurants, the shorts-and-Hawaiian-shirt getup will have you sticking out like the worst kind of gringo. In fact, it's rare to see Mexico City men and women wearing shorts, even on the hottest days.

While I recommend variety when it comes to your suitcase, my other piece of advice is to leave the valuables at home. It's no secret that there is crime in Mexico City (although it is less prevalent in Puebla and Cuernavaca), and wearing flashy jewelry isn't the wisest move when you're out on the town.

GETTING TO MEXICO CITY, CUERNAVACA, AND PUEBLA

For the purposes of this book, your entry point into Mexico will most likely be the well-appointed Benito Juárez International Airport in Mexico City, although some international carriers fly to Puebla as well. There is also excellent bus service from the airport directly to Cuernavaca and Puebla.

As of this printing, the airport has recently opened a new terminal, which is still being filled with the requisite gift shops, restaurants, and other services. Terminal One has plenty of places to shop and eat, as well as all the major services for tourists. Both terminals are linked by a monorail, and international flights arrive at either one, depending on the airline. The monorail can be useful especially for travelers coming into the newer terminal. Sometimes there are no taxis waiting here, while a short hop on the free monorail will take you to Terminal One, where a long line of taxis stands ready. The airport has an excellent bilingual Web site (www.aicm.com.mx), or you can call 55-2482-2424 or 2482-2400 for information.

Of course, you can also travel to Mexico by car, but I would advise against it. For one, you'll have to go through the Mexico-U.S. border, which can be a nightmare, especially on the return trip. For another, it's a lengthy drive from the border to central Mexico, and while driving is a great way to see the country, taking a car into Mexico is only advisable for those who are planning a long stay.

By Air

Virtually every major American and international carrier flies into Mexico through Benito
Juárez International Airport. In addition, a host of regional and national airlines operate
here. Here is just a sample of the major foreign carriers serving the airport from U.S. cities,
as well as Mexican airlines with international routes. As with any international flight, make
sure to arrive at your departure airport at least two hours prior to the flight time.

Mexican Airlines
AeroMexico
800-237-6639 (U.S.)
55-5133-4000 (Mexico City)
800-021-4000 (toll-free in Mexico)
www.aeromexico.com
A member of the Sky Team alliance, AeroMexico serves more than 40 destinations around
Mexico and has direct flights to seven U.S. cities.

Aviacsa
866-246-0961 (U.S.)
55-5482-8280 (Mexico City)
800-AVIACSA (toll-free in Mexico)
www.aviacsa.com.mx
Primarily a local airline, Aviacsa has one cross-border route to Las Vegas.

Mexicana
800-531-7921 (U.S.)
55-5998-5998 (Mexico City)
800-801-2010 (toll free in Mexico)
www.mexicana.com
The airline with the fourth-longest tradition in the world, Mexicana also has the most
extensive international coverage from Mexico.

U.S. Airlines
Alaska Airlines
800-252-7522 (U.S.)
www.alaskaair.com

American Airlines
800-433-7300 (U.S)
55-5209-1400 (Mexico City)
800-904-6000 (toll-free in Mexico)
www.aa.com

Continental Airlines
800-523-3273 (U.S.)
55-5283-5500 (Mexico City)
800-900-5000 (toll-free in Mexico)
www.continental.com
Continental flies to Mexico City and also has direct flights to Aeropuerto Internacional de
Puebla.

Delta Air Lines

800-221-1212 (U.S.)

55-5279-0909 (Mexico City)

800-123-4710 (toll-free in Mexico)

www.delta.com

Northwest Airlines/KLM

800-225-2525 (U.S.)

55-5279-5390 (Mexico City)

800-907-4700 (toll-free in Mexico)

www.nwa.com

Northwest flies into Mexico City and Puebla.

United Airlines

800-864-8331 (U.S.)

55-5627-0222 (Mexico City)

800-003-0777 (toll-free in Mexico)

www.ual.com

US Airways

800-428-4322 (U.S.)

www.airways.com

International Airlines

Air Canada

888-247-2262 (U.S. and Canada)

55-5208-1883 (Mexico City)

www.aircanada.com

Air France

800-992-3932 (U.S.)

55-5627-6060 (Mexico City)

www.airfrance.com.mx

British Airways

800-247-9297 (U.S.)

866-835-4133 (toll-free in Mexico)

www.britishairways.com

Iberia

800-772-4642 (U.S.)

55-1101-1515 (Mexico)

www.iberia.com

Japan Air Lines

800-525-3663 (U.S.)

55-5242-0150 (Mexico)

www.jal.com

Lufthansa
800-399-5838 (U.S.)
55-5230-0000 (Mexico)
www.lufthansa.com

Qantas
800-227-4500 (U.S.)
800-892-9761 (toll-free in Mexico)
www.qantas.com.au

Taca
800-400-TACA (U.S.)
55-5553-3366 (Mexico City)
800-400-8222 (toll-free in Mexico)
www.taca.com

By Land

Again, I urge tourists not to travel by car from outside the country to Mexico City, Puebla, or Cuernavaca unless they are coming here for a long stay and plan to tour the country extensively. Why am I so adamant? Let's start with the paperwork. At the border checkpoint, travelers are required to present the original and two copies of the following documents:

· Valid proof of citizenship (passport or birth certificate).
· The Mexican Tourist Permit (FMT).
· A valid vehicle-registration certificate, or a document, like the vehicle's title, that certifies legal ownership by the driver.
· A leasing contract, if the vehicle is leased or rented, in the name of the renter. If the vehicle belongs to a company, you must have documentation that certifies your employment with that company.
· A valid driver's license.
· An international credit card in the name of the driver of the vehicle.

Drivers also need a temporary car-importation permit. To acquire this, you have to bring all these documents to the customs office at the border. Go through the Declarations Lane and look for the MODULO DE CONTROL VEHICULAR sign. You'll be in for a much easier time if you have a credit card, which you can use to post the required "return guarantee" bond. If you don't have a credit card, you'll have to leave a guarantee deposit based on the model year of the vehicle. In Texas, California, and Illinois, drivers can arrange for the certificate and payments in advance from the Mexican consulate. **Note: The owner of the car or a relative must be in the car at all times while it's being driven in Mexico.** Drivers must also get their vehicle insured in Mexico, as liability insurance is mandatory and U.S. coverage is invalid. U.S. companies that provide insurance in Mexico are located at the border.

Then there is the driving time, which can vary from 12 to 48 hours from the border. For example, the drive from the border city of Juárez to Mexico City will take you roughly 23 hours. From Tijuana to Mexico, it's about 33 hours. And that's not counting how long it will take you to get from your point of departure to the border. And finally, there is the simple fact that rentals are readily available once you get to Mexico, and bus travel within the country is excellent.

Getting to and from the Airport

Rental Car

If you want to rent a car after arriving in Mexico, the following car-rental agencies are available in the international section of Mexico City's airport, in Concourse E.

Alamo
55-5786-9214
www.alamo.com
Open 24/7

Avis
55-5786-9452
www.avis.com
Open 24/7 except Monday

Budget
55-5762-0900
www.budget.com
Open daily 7 AM–11 PM

Economóvil Rent
55-2599-0148
Open Monday to Friday 8 AM–10 PM, Saturday 8 AM–6 PM

Europcar
55-5786-8265
www.europcar.com
Open 24/7

Gold Car Rental
55-2599-0090
Open 24/7

Hertz
55-5762-8977, 5784-7400, 5784-7628
www.hertz.com
Open daily 7 AM–10:30 PM

Kim Car Rent
55-2599-0267
Open daily 7 AM–11 PM

Royal Rent-a-Car
55-5802-8000, 5802-8398
Open daily 7 AM–10 PM

Thrifty
55-5786-9486, 5786-9487, 5786-8268
www.thrifty.com
Open daily 7 AM–11 PM

Bus

Surprisingly, there is no bus service from the airport to Mexico City; unless you rent a car, you will have to rely on the metro or take a taxi. However, there is convenient and comfortable bus service directly from the terminal to Cuernavaca and Puebla.

Autobuses Estrella Roja

55-5786-9341, 5786-9358, 5786-9338, 5786-9342
Ground Terminal, International Section
Service runs 24 hours a day, bound for Puebla. $$.

Autobuses Pullman de Morelos

55-5786-9341, 5786-9358, 5786-9338, 5786-9342
Ground Terminal, International Section
Service runs 24 hours a day, bound for Cuernavaca. $$.

Metro

The Terminal Area Station on Line 5 takes you into the city. It is open Monday to Friday 5 AM–1 AM, Saturday 6 AM–midnight, Sunday 7 AM–10 PM. It's a bit of a hassle, but by far the cheapest way to travel. $.

Taxi

Taxis are the most convenient way to get to Mexico City. Travelers should use only authorized airport taxis, available directly from the terminal. Follow the GROUND TRANSPORTATION signs to the end of the terminal, where you'll see taxi counters. Buy your ticket at the window (make sure to request a regular sedan; the large vans are more expensive). The rates are based on zones, which are displayed at the counter. You can take a taxi from the airport directly to Cuernavaca or Puebla, but this will be significantly more expensive than the bus.

Protaxi Ejecutivo

55-2599-0333
Operates 24/7. $$–$$$.

Sitio Taxi

55-2482-2424, 55-5571-9344
www.taxisdelaeropuerto.com.mx
Operates 24/7. $$–$$$.

THE MYTHS AND REALITIES OF MEXICO TRAVEL

Negative preconceptions of Mexico travel abound, fueled by horror stories about near-death illnesses after consuming the local food, ripoffs everywhere, kidnappings, and worse. Unfortunately, these stories often have more than a grain of truth to them. At the same time, a little bit of common sense will enable you to avoid many of the pitfalls that snare the less-savvy tourist.

Safety

Safety is a major concern for most Americans traveling to Mexico. I don't think I've ever said "I'm going to Mexico" without getting a raised eyebrow or a "Be careful!" But the basic fact is that millions of U.S. citizens visit Mexico every year without incident. For every horror story, there are many more tales of wonderful vacations.

It goes without saying that tourists should always exercise caution in any foreign country. The most frequent incidents in Mexico City are mugging, armed robbery, and kidnapping. A common practice with respect to the latter involves taxis, especially green-and-white Volkswagen Beetles. The way the scam works is as follows: a taxi picks up an unsuspecting passenger and follows a predetermined route. At a prearranged intersection, armed individuals jump in the cab and mug or kidnap the victim. For this reason, it cannot be stressed enough that while in Mexico tourists rely on *sitio* or radio taxis (these are taxis located at designated taxi stands; alternatively, a pickup can be arranged over the phone).

If you are the victim of a robbery or mugging, don't resist. But you can also lessen your chances of being targeted by not wearing valuables, and limiting the cash and credit cards you carry. A basic rule of traveling abroad is to lock your extra cash, valuables, and passport in a hotel safe. Here are a few other simple precautions to follow while in Mexico:

For safety's sake, avoid the free-ranging green-and-white VW Beetle taxis

- When driving, use main roads whenever possible; when driving longer distances, especially at night, use toll roads.
- If possible, carry a cell phone with international coverage. If you don't have one of these, buy a phone card, which are widely available.
- Remember three numbers:
    - 060 for reporting crime
    - 065 for the Red Cross and ambulance service
    - 078 for tourist assistance
- Try to stay in well-lit areas at night, and keep to secure neighborhoods.
- At night, take a *sitio* taxi to and from your destination.
- Always keep the phone number and address of your hotel handy. Many hotel key-cards have this information printed on them.
- Before your trip, check the latest U.S. State Department travel advisories for Mexico at www.travel.state.gov.

Montezuma's Revenge

"Montezuma's Revenge" is the popular term among foreigners for the potent and unpleasant causes of consuming unhygienic food or drinking unclean water. The Mexicans call it *turista*. The symptoms include nausea, diarrhea, stomach cramps, and fever. If your condition is severe, visit a doctor.

Can you avoid it? Yes and no. Some tourists, especially those traveling abroad for the first time, will have an adverse reaction to foreign foods. It's impossible to predict exactly how your digestive system will respond, but there are ways to keep Montezuma's vengeful spirit at bay. The easiest and most important is to never drink tap water. Many hotels and restaurants serve purified water, but to play it safe, always order bottled water.

Also, take your gastronomic tour of Mexico in gradual steps. Heading from the airport directly to the nearest taco stand isn't the wisest move if this is your first trip. Try to avoid spices and raw vegetables until you're completely acclimated. Practically every restaurant in Mexico has fresh limes on the table for seasoning. Make liberal use of these, which can help keep you healthy. Your body has to adjust to its new environment, and that includes adjusting to new foods. It takes time, but even if Montezuma wags his finger in your direction, leaving your stomach a little unsettled, I'd encourage you to persevere. Mexican food is worth the initial trouble.

Altitude and Pollution

For the purposes of this book, we'll discuss pollution as strictly a Mexico City issue—the air in Cuernavaca and Puebla is fine. So how bad is it in the capital? The truth is that Mexico City's air had long been considered very clean. In the last few decades, however, pollution became a serious problem, so much so that it was a health risk for animals as well as people.

The good news is that things have gotten better. Sure, there is still a layer of smog to contend with, and pollution limits often exceed acceptable levels as measured by Mexico's Metropolitan Index of Air Quality (IMECA). But the city is in the midst of an ambitious environmental cleanup program targeting air quality and emissions. I wouldn't embark on a five-mile jog the day after I land in Mexico, but that has as much to do with the altitude as with the air quality. If you want to know how clean the air is on any given day, check the Web site of the Atmospheric Monitoring System of the City of Mexico at www.sma.df.gob .mx/simat/. The IMECA scale is as follows:

- o–50: Good
- 51–100: Regular
- 101–150: Bad
- 151–200: Very Bad
- Over 201: Extremely Bad

As long as the numbers fall between o and 150, the vast majority of people—locals and tourists alike—need not worry. As you can imagine, numbers over 150 do not signal good levels of air quality, and if the levels push beyond 201, the city is likely to take action.

As for altitude, most of central Mexico is at an elevation of above 5,000 feet. Altitude sickness affects some travelers more than others. Many people won't notice much of a change; some may find the air a little thin; still others might experience headaches, dizziness, shortness of breath, and fatigue. Travelers with heart- or lung-related medical problems should consult with a doctor before flying to Mexico City. If you do experience any of the above symptoms, do not exercise, drink plenty of fluids but stay away from alcohol, and wait it out. As with the food, your body will adjust.

A (Positive) Word about Mexicans

Over drinks one night, a Mexican friend of mine turned to me and asked, "What do you think of us?" The question wasn't directed at me specifically, but rather at Americans in general. Many Mexicans have something of a complex when it comes to their gringo neigh-

Like Tepoztlán, south of Mexico City, most of central Mexico is at an altitude above 5,000 feet

The Basílica de Guadalupe in Mexico City is Mexico's holiest shrine Credit: Mexico Tourism Board

bors, and it's not surprising why. Mexicans are well aware that the sentiment across the border isn't always positive. Whether it's because of illegal immigration, crime, or a general misconception, the people of this country have long been viewed in a negative light by their neighbors to the north.

Anyone who visits Mexico City with these prejudices will not just be pleasantly surprised, but quite possibly stunned. I have to admit, the first time I came here, it happened to me. I never expected an urban center of such sophistication, culture, and elegance. And I was moved by the kindness that so many strangers showed me. Once people understand that you don't think negatively of them and their country, they will open up to you, and you'll find them to be friendly and helpful. But if you're condescending, expect no warmth in return.

Family is very important in Mexico, but so is friendship. Expect a Mexican man to defend his friend at all costs in any bar spat, no matter who's at fault. You'll also find

Mexicans to be generally very polite. Men are addressed as *señor*, women as *señora*, and young women or girls as *señorita*. Another common prefix you'll hear is *licensiado/a*, a title of respect referring to college graduates.

Mexicans love their food and drink—the latter a bit too much, sometimes. They also love their heritage, both the colonial and the indigenous side of it; Mexican people have a strong identity and are proud of their nation's role as an intellectual and artistic center in Latin America. And they especially love the Virgin Mary. Mexico is the largest Roman Catholic nation in the world after Brazil, a remarkable testament to the Spanish missionaries who came here at the dawn of the New World. About 90 percent of the population is Catholic, and *la Virgen,* in her many forms, is the most revered figure in Mexico. There are hundreds of representations of the virgin, but the most beloved is *la Virgen de Guadalupe* (the Virgin of Guadalupe). More than a religious icon, she is a national symbol.

MONEY MATTERS

The currency of Mexico is the peso. It is indicated by the $ symbol and the code MXN. As of this printing, $1 USD was the equivalent of about $13 MXN. While there are some businesses that will take payment in dollars, expect to pay in pesos everywhere you go.

Changing money is easy and convenient in Mexico. Banks and/or *casas de cambio* (money-changing booths) are usually a short walk away. If the line at the bank is long (always the case on Fridays), *casas de cambio* are almost always quick and they're open later than banks. Cash in Spanish is known as *efectivo.* When it comes to your *efectivo,* a useful tip is to horde your change. Buses, taxis, and taquerías all crave or require it, and you'll need plenty for tips.

Credit cards are widely accepted, Mastercard and Visa more than American Express. Cards are called *tarjetas de crédito.* Some establishments will add a small surcharge (3 to 6 percent) to your bill if you're paying by card. Your local bank ATM will not work here (international ATMs do), but if you're in a pinch, a bank will issue a cash advance on a credit card account.

Determining a budget is a tough thing to do in Mexico, because your expenses can range from minimal to exorbitant. The good news is, you can tailor your vacation to just about any budget you set . . . even if it means a steady diet of street food (not a terrible way to go).

A 10 percent tip is customary and expected at restaurants and hotels, and at the end of organized tours, but not at taco stands, inexpensive eateries, or for taxis. Still, a tip is always appreciated. A 15 percent value-added tax, known as *impuesto al valor agregado* (IVA) is added to all goods and services purchased in Mexico. Hotels add an additional 2 percent lodging tax.

MEXICAN FOOD, MEXICAN DRINK

Mexican food has been as misrepresented as the land it comes from. The tacos, burritos, and enchiladas so widely available throughout the U.S. can scarcely be found once you cross the border . . . at least, not in the way they are presented stateside. But the cuisine here goes much further than the street food we know and love. Its roots span millennia and incorporate ingredients, recipes, and techniques from the Aztecs, the Spanish, the French, and the U.S. (when McDonald's first opened in Mexico City, there was a line around the block to get in).

The pre-Hispanic tribes are responsible for the nation's most essential foods—tortillas and tamales, for example—as well as some of its most flavorful ingredients. Some are well known to us, like cocoa, corn, and chile; others are more exotic, and include a great variety of flora. *Flor de calabaza* (squash blossom), *nopales* (the fleshy pads of the cactus), and *cuitlacoche* (a truffle-like fungus found on corn) are three staples of classic Mexican cooking.

The Spanish brought other essentials, including beef, pork, rice, garlic, and oil. Their influence, along with later contributions by other cultures (including African, Asian, and other European nations), greatly expanded Mexican gastronomy. This diverse legacy has produced a broad range of cuisine, from strips of meat slapped together between a tortilla to refined dishes that use techniques and flavors subtle enough to please the most discriminating gourmand.

Sampling all of these flavors and delicacies is one of the joys of traveling to Mexico, but to really savor the experience, be a bit adventurous. Some of the delicacies available to you will range from eyebrow-raising to run-for-the-door. I always take a bring-it-on attitude with me to any eatery in Mexico, and for the most part, it has served me well. Then there's the language. Even if you know Spanish, you'll be dumbfounded by many items on the menu, either because they are in Nahautl or because they use unfamiliar Mexicanisms.

To help you navigate through this new culinary world, I've included a Traveler's Dictionary that includes popular Mexican ingredients and foods at the end of this book. But don't let the drawbacks of language and exotic ingredients deter you from branching out where your palate is concerned. Even if you're not the adventurous type, you can't leave Mexico without visiting at least one taquería. I believe it's in the constitution. Or at least, it should be.

Nopales *from cacti are a popular food all over Mexico*

As for what to drink, alcohol goes back to the pre-Columbian tribes, but they went about things a little differently. The Aztecs only allowed the priest class and the elderly to drink; everyone else faced capital punishment for imbibing. Modern Mexicans have both more variety in their spirits and more lenient rules. The locals love their *cerveza,* or beer, which is available just about everywhere. Then there's a smorgasbord of local liquor, starting with the world-famous tequila, which has been around for over 400 years, and of which there are over 700 brands. Tequila is made from the blue agave plant and is generally found in two categories: 100 percent blue agave and *tequila mixto* (mixed). Within these categories, there are finer distinctions:

- *tequila blanco* (white tequila). The purest form of the blue agave, this spirit is clear and unaged.
- *tequila joven abocado* (young, smooth tequila). A gold-colored, young, and relatively inexpensive formulation.
- *tequila reposado* ("rested" tequila). A popular golden variety aged between two and 11 months.
- *tequila añejo* (aged tequila). A refined, rich, and smooth spirit that must be aged for at least one year.
- *tequila extra añejo* (extra-aged tequila). A classification given to tequilas aged more than three years, this variety has a darker hue than regular *añejo.*

After tequila comes a parade of Mexican liquors. *Mezcal* is a cousin of tequila, a strong liquor made from different types of maguey plants. Pulque, the fermented sap of the agave

Pulkata, in Cholula, is a classic pulquería

plant, has a nutty flavor; the best place to enjoy it, both for variety and local ambience, is at a *pulquería*. *Pasita* is a liquor made from raisins. And *aguardiente,* which is typically made from sugarcane, begins at around 75 proof. It's not called firewater for nothing. There are also several other regional brews.

Finally, a host of other alcoholic beverages are popular here: brandy, Kahlua, Cointreau, wine (specified as *vino de uva,* or grape wine), and a variety of mixed drinks and cocktails. The most famous of these, of course, is the margarita.

MAJOR HAPPENINGS THROUGHOUT THE YEAR

The last thing on your checklist is when to go. This is not merely a weather-based decision; it also depends on what's going on in Mexico throughout the year. Because there are literally thousands of festivals, parades, and parties in the country, I've focused on the biggest and the most beloved national events, or those specific to Mexico City, Puebla, and Cuernavaca.

January 1: New Year's Day. *Año Nuevo* is a national holiday, a day when many a hangover is nursed back to health.

January 6: Three Kings Day. *Día de Los Reyes* marks the end of the Christmas season. It is the most important day of the season, when gifts are traditionally exchanged and families eat a special cake called *rosca de reyes* ("kings' wreath"), a large doughnut-shaped fruitcake into which is baked a small figure of a baby. The person who gets the slice with the baby has the responsibility of throwing a party on (or before) Candlemas, or *Candelaria*.

February 2: Candlemas. *Día de Candelaria* is a nationwide celebration marking the end of winter and honoring the rebirth and fertility of the land.

February 5: Constitution Day. *Día de la Constitución* is a national holiday commemorating the ratification of the Mexican constitution in 1917.

February: Carnaval. The exact date of Carnaval varies, but it takes place during the week leading up to Lent and involves all the color, noise, and pageantry of Mardi Gras.

February 24: Flag Day. On this nationwide holiday, public figures outdo one another in their efforts to proclaim their patriotism.

March 21: Benito Juárez's Birthday. A national holiday to honor one of Mexico's most revered leaders.

March/April: Easter. *Semana Santa* (Holy Week) is the most popular religious celebration in Mexico, marked by pilgrimages, huge masses, and parades.

May 1: Labor Day. A national holiday, called *Día del Trabajo.*

May 5: Cinco de Mayo. Mayo 5 is celebrated around the U.S. as a time to get drunk. Most people don't know that the holiday marks a historic battle between French and Mexican troops in Puebla.

May 10: Mother's Day. As mentioned, the maternal figure has long been sacred in Mexico. It's little surprise, then, that *Día de la Madre,* or Mother's Day, is given serious attention here.

September 1: Presidential "State of the Nation." A great time to be in Mexico City's Zócalo, or central square, to hear the president wax poetic . . . or passionate . . . or loquacious.

September 15–16: Independence Day. Celebrated in every nook and cranny of Mexico, these two days honor the end of Spanish rule in Mexico. Millions cram into Mexico City's Zócalo to hear the president give *el grito* (the cry), echoing Miguel Hidalgo's proclamation of independence in 1810.

November 1–2: Day of the Dead. *Día de los Muertos* is my favorite holiday in Mexico. All Saints' Day is November 1, while the official Day of the Dead is November 2. Skeleton costumes abound, parades are held, and thousands of people throw open their homes to strangers bearing offerings for the dead.

November 20: Revolution Day. *Día de la Revolución* is another national holiday where politicians take center stage and launch patriotic speeches.

December 12: Feast of the Virgin of Guadalupe. One of the most important religious holidays in the country, December 12 brings an annual horde of people to *la Virgen*'s shrine in Mexico City.

December 16: Beginning of the Christmas season. The Christmas season stretches from December 16 to January 6, and includes parades, processions, and parties. Beginning December 16 there are nine days of *posadas*—candlelight processions that travel to a com-

Day of the Dead decoration Credit: Mexico Tourism Board

munity's nativity scene or a neighbor's home, reenacting Joseph and Mary's search for lodging.

December 24–25: Christmas Eve and Christmas Day. On Christmas Eve (*Nochebuena*) a midnight mass called *Misa del Gallo*, or Rooster's Mass, is held, with masses continuing throughout Christmas Day.

December 28: Day of the Innocents. *Día de los Inocentes* is Mexico's April Fool's Day.

December 31: New Year's Eve. A night of revelry and partying, to close the chapter on the old and welcome the new. In Mexico it's called *Nochevieja*, or Old Night.

Mexico City today

3

MEXICO CITY TODAY

The Supermetropolis

Modern Mexico City, or the Distrito Federal (Federal District), or simply, el D.F. (pronounced el deh-EH-feh) is a dynamic, crowded, jumbled, historic, and exuberant metropolis. It is the crucible in which modern Mexico was, and continues to be, forged. And it is one of the world's oldest cities, which has its faults, but also many advantages. Over time, it has come to celebrate its diverse roots.

INTRODUCING THE LARGEST CITY IN THE AMERICAS

The D.F. is not a single city so much as it is a vast network of towns and suburbs that have been gradually incorporated into a massive urban sprawl. It is a place of continuous discovery: you could travel here half a dozen times and never see the same thing twice. Because the D.F. is so diverse, and so immense, it would be highly confusing to try to tackle the city's many attractions and points of interest as a whole—there's just too much ground to cover. This book breaks Mexico City down into its distinct neighborhoods, while skirting those areas tourists should avoid no matter how adventurous they are.

Mexico City is full of surprises. This is a place of parks; of world-class museums and fantastic displays of public art; of a staggering diversity of dining and entertainment options. It's also a city of stark contrasts: Latin America's tallest skyscraper overlooks a park that predates the 16th-century Spanish conquest. The hungriest visitor can feast for a pittance or spend a fortune at one of the city's finer restaurants (and enjoy a delicious meal either way). The Aztec and the Catholic are comfortably and simultaneously embraced. Streets are named after revolutionaries and saints, pacifists and communist world leaders, with equal honor. And you'll be amazed, once you get familiar with the place, at how a city with a population representing about one-fifth of all Mexico can function so seamlessly.

A Proud Heritage

A great divide separates Mexicans from the D.F.—known as *chilangos*—and those from the rest of the country. Outside the D.F., *chilangos* are considered gruff, rude, and generally unpleasant. I equate it to many outsiders' feelings of New Yorkers. *Chilangos* are street-smart and city-slick, but when you live in one of the largest cities in the world, you have to be. They're also a bit more formal in social customs, particularly wardrobe. But whatever else they are, Mexico City's residents are intensely proud of their city. This was where

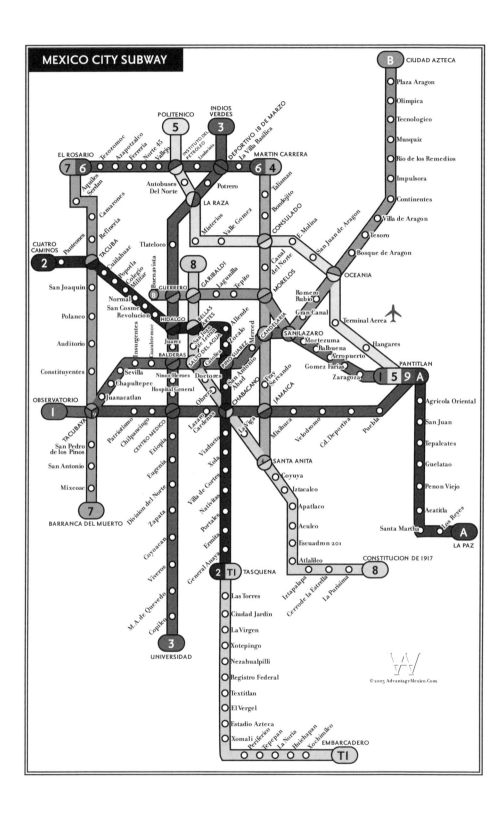

MEXICO CITY SUBWAY

Cortés subdued an empire. It was here that the *Niños Heroes* fought and died for their country. And it is here that the nation's leaders, from Cuauhtémoc to Benito Juárez, are commemorated with reverence.

With Mexico City's embarrassment of riches, it is small surprise that *chilangos* love to experience what their city has to offer. Museums, theaters, and ancient ruins are invariably packed on weekends and during special events; the sprawling Chapultepec Park draws droves of people; and the D.F.'s vaunted restaurants, bars, and clubs enjoy a roaring business.

An Emphasis on Art

One of Mexico City's most pleasing attributes is its astounding number of museums. From the world-class centers of art and culture to niche, boutique museums focusing on such esoteric themes as caricature and stamps, you'll find a dizzying variety of artistic expression. The gorgeous **Palacio de Bellas Artes** in the city center is testament to Mexico City's focus on, and appreciation of, the arts. In my opinion, the D.F.'s many artistic and cultural institutions rival those of any of the world's great cities.

But nowhere is Mexico City's art as poignantly and passionately expressed as it is through murals. Mural art is a storied tradition in Mexico, begun as an egalitarian effort to bring art to the masses. Along the way, it also offered a powerful chronicle of the times, of Mexico's conflicted and violent history, and its vibrant culture. With the city as its canvas, Mexico's premier artists went to work . . . and created an incredible legacy.

The Palacio de Bellas Artes

Some Mexican artists have carved a place for themselves among the country's most respected sons and daughters. Thanks to Hollywood, **Frida Kahlo** hardly needs an introduction. Her vibrant, colorful paintings, many of them self-portraits and studies in symbolism and suffering, have made her an international icon. Many Mexicans believe her talent and fame are owed to her husband, **Diego Rivera**, one of the principal architects of the muralist movement. Other prominent artists include **Davíd Alfaro Siqueiros, José Clemente Orozco,** and **Rufino Tamayo,** and authors **Octavio Paz** and **Carlos Fuentes.**

As rich and varied as the arts in Mexico is the architecture. Not for nothing is Mexico City known as the City of Palaces. From baroque and neoclassic masterpieces to the remnants of ancient Aztec civilization to the spires of modern skyscrapers, the buildings, churches, and monuments of the city are part of its treasured cultural heritage.

Far, Far Beyond Tacos: World-Class Dining

Don't get me wrong; if it's tacos you're looking for, there are thousands of places to get them (burritos, on the other hand, are not so ubiquitous; that particular dish comes from the North). But if you think the menu ends with the Tex-Mex platters you find at your local "South of the Border" eatery, Mexico City respectfully begs to differ.

The most innovative cuisine in the D.F. goes beyond the marriage of indigenous and Spanish cooking. It's deeply rooted in the past while exploring new techniques, presentations, and flavor combinations. Nouveau Mexican cuisine, as it's known, continues to evolve, and its manner of evolution is a matter of debate among its champions. I spoke with three of Mexico City's top chefs at the vanguard of refined Mexican gastronomy, about their views of nouveau Mexican cuisine.

Chef **Patricia Quintana**, owner of the famed **Izote**, follows a guiding philosophy that honors tradition while making subtle changes to boost flavor and offer a more distinguished presentation of the classics. Chef **Enrique Olivera** takes a different, almost maverick, approach to Mexican cuisine. His restaurant, **Pujol**, brings cutting-edge techniques, wildly innovative compositions, and unique plates that reinvent, and in some cases completely transform, the classics. The chef is charting his own culinary course, but he also understands the importance of tradition. Taking the middle road is Chef **Daniel Ovadía.**

The Taco-Chain Experience

In my review of Mexico City's neighborhoods, I've included a "Taco Corner" listing the best taquerías each one has to offer. In addition to these, the city is full of taquería chains that are, for the most part, reliable and hygienic enough to warrant your business. Most of these open early and close late, making them ideal for a quick meal or a late-night snack:

El Farolito
www.taqueriaselfarolito.com.mx

El Fogoncito
www.fogoncito.com.mx

El Tizoncito
www.eltizonzito.com.mx

Taco Inn
www.tacoinn.com

Chef Enrique Olivera is among the most innovative practitioners of nouveau Mexican cuisine

His restaurant, **Paxia**, remains grounded in tradition while offering specials that Ovadía calls *nuevas locuras* (new crazies)—dishes that take what is well known and modify it with what is new and unexpected.

While these and other chefs continue to push the envelope of Mexican cuisine, many others stay firmly rooted in the recipes of the past. Whichever is your preference, I can promise one thing: if you starve in Mexico City, it won't be for a lack of options.

The Mexican Chain-Diner Experience

While Mexican cuisine can be highly refined, that doesn't mean you can't have your down-home comfort food. There are national chains that offer up basic Mexican staples in a casual atmosphere. While they're not the best options as far as taste and talent go, they tend to be clean, decent, and cheap:

Los Bisquets Bisquets Obregón

www.bisquetsobregon.com.mx

There's an interesting historical context to this restaurant. *Bisquets* or *café chinos* were restaurants operated by Chinese families in the '40s and '50s. Over time they have faded away, but this chain, which has its roots in the Mexico City neighborhood of Colonia Roma, is still flourishing. The food isn't bad, and of course the biscuits are a must.

Sanborns

www.sanborns.com.mx/sanborns

It seems you can't throw a stone in Mexico City without hitting a Sanborns, the franchise owned by telecommunications mogul Carlos Slim. They're everywhere, and range in personality from a basic diner to a fancy eatery (especially the one in the Casa de los Azulejos, covered in chapter 4). However, the food wherever you go remains the same . . . uninventive but true to the Mexican basics. Sanborns is known more for its all-in-one experience: restaurant, minimall, bookstore, electronics, pharmacy, and just about anything else can be found at most branches.

Toks
www.toks.com.mx
The most diner-like of them all, Toks offers a large menu that runs from waffles to burgers to enchiladas.

Vips
www.vips.com.mx
This simple eatery, in its bright setting similar to fast-food chains, serves a large variety of dishes, none of which may leave your taste buds begging for more but that can make for a passable meal. It's so formulaic that it even has one of those "If the waiter doesn't smile at least once at you, the bill's on us" disclaimers.

Sushi Itto
www.sushi-itto.com.mx
A surprising corollary to the chain diner is the chain sushi eatery. This popular franchise specializes in creative Mexican-Japanese sushi rolls and bento box lunches. While the quality varies branch to branch, and I wasn't all that impressed with the food, the chain has invaded the D.F.

Seat of Empire

Mexico City is, and has long been, the economic, legislative, and cultural heart of the country. Today it is one of Latin America's most important economic centers, producing over one-fifth of the country's gross domestic product. The country's largest financial institutions are headquartered here, with the relatively new Santa Fe suburb a futuristic gathering of modern towers and sleek architecture. It is the home of Mexico's World Trade Center and stock exchange, and its telecommunications industry has made Carlos Slim one of the richest people in the world. Other industries include construction, cement, iron and steelworks, textiles, and plastics, as well as tourism.

Mexico is a democratic republic with a government similar to the U.S. congressional system. A president is elected every six years in a multiparty election dominated by the nation's three primary political parties. Mexico's government has an executive, legislative, and judicial branch and follows its constitution, which was ratified in 1917. Mexico (officially the United Mexican States) is a federation of 31 states, which are in turn divided into municipalities. The presidency and federal branches of government are based in Mexico City, which, as a federal district, follows the same mold as Washington, D.C. The D.F. is bordered by the states of México and Morelos.

Unlike D.C., Mexico's capital city is the most populated city in the country and among the largest cities in the world. The most recent figures show a population of between 18 and 20 million. The crowds and the great divide between the city's rich and poor are ideal conditions for a thriving underworld. While the government has clamped down on crime in recent years, tourists should exercise caution even in the most posh neighborhoods.

The neighborhood of Santa Fe has a distinctly modern vibe

Some areas—notably the Centro Histórico—are generally safe during the day but wandering around them at night is not advisable.

Getting Around

There is no shortage of transportation options to help you get around Mexico City. In general, I'd avoid driving, recommend only certain types of taxis, and highly advocate making full use of the public transportation system, which may look daunting but is the most convenient and cheapest way to get around. Finally, for all its vastness, this is a walking city, and many parts of it are best enjoyed on foot.

Taxis

In Mexico City, there are taxis, and there are taxis. When I first visited, my sister, who had been living in the D.F. for years, gave me the rundown.

- Always carry the number of a reliable taxi service, and call it whenever you need transportation. *Sitio* taxis are the safest form of transportation. You'll need to speak passable Spanish to communicate where you are and how the driver will be able to identify you, and the operator will tell you, in Spanish, what model and color of car will be picking you up. *Sitios* are expensive, but they offer the most peace of mind. Below are a few reliable operators. You can also find *sitio* taxis at designated taxi stands throughout the city.
- Your hotel can arrange a taxi for you, and while this is very safe, it is also the most expensive option. Better to call a *sitio* directly and have it pick you up.
- If you do not have a radio-taxi-service's number and you're in a pinch, you can flag

down a red-and-gold checkered taxi. These metered cabs are generally considered safe, although you may end up taking the "scenic route" to your destination once the driver realizes you're not from around these parts

- Your last resort is the green-and-white taxi, especially the classic VW Beetles. These have been almost completely phased out, but in case you see one, know that they are considered the least reliable option

Radio Elite
55-5660-1122

Radio Taxi
55-5552-1376

Servicio Elite
55-5660-1060

Servitaxi
55-5516-6020

Taxi Mex
55-5519-7690

If you do plan on taking something other than a *sitio* taxi, your Spanish should be good enough that you're able to hold a conversation. Also make sure the license number and ID of the driver is prominently displayed on a license card. And finally, whether you're booking a taxi via the phone or hailing one on the street, always ask what the fare will be, even if it's an approximation. After one or two rides, you'll know when you're getting ripped off.

Metro

Mexico City's metro system has to be one of the most ridiculously cheap bargains in urban-transportation history. The cost for a one-way ticket? Two pesos. At press time, this is approximately 14 cents! The metro is also very efficient and extensive. There are 11 color-coded lines, labeled 1 through 9 and then A and B, that cover the majority of the city, getting you to, at most, ten or fifteen minutes from almost every destination. The trains and stations are generally clean and well lit, and some have beautiful murals and works of art displayed inside. Visitors are sometimes wary of what they feel is an unsafe trip underground, but the metro's main hazards are pickpockets, and tourists should keep their eyes on their valuables at all times.

During the morning and evening rush hour, an army of commuters descends on the trains (the metro moves about 5 million people per day), and you'll be best served by avoiding traveling during these hours, unless you enjoy being squashed in the press. Also during peak periods, authorities will designate some cabins for women only. Women can choose to travel here or with their families and friends in the other cabins. The other interesting, and unofficial, bit of segregation that occurs is more social. At night, it is common for the last two cars on the train to be occupied by gay men and women. The metro runs weekdays 5 AM–midnight, Saturday 6 AM–midnight, Sundays and holidays 7 AM–midnight. For more information call 55-5709-1133, or visit www.metro.df.gob.mx

Beyond the metro, there is the *tren ligero* (light rail) that extends farther south from Tasqueña to Xochimilco. These trains require another ticket, but are also quite cheap.

Bus

The bus system here is terrific, whether you're enjoying coach-class service to destinations outside the D.F. or heading a few blocks down the road. To get around the city, your best bet is the *pesero*. This is the name for the small, rickety buses that careen around the city streets on routes that are impossible to find on a map but will get you where you want to go. To this day, I've been unable to unearth a bus map of the vast and complex network, but look at the posted final destinations on the window and ask the driver if he or she is passing your stop. The bus is extremely cheap, with a maximum fare of about 50 cents. *Peseros* can be hailed at stops and can be found at the end of each metro line; they also have a tendency to stop just about anywhere, so if you see your destination pass by, ask the driver to drop you off.

Peseros might scare off tourists even more than the metro, but besides the usual threat of pickpockets and getting lost, they're great fun. There are some *peseros* that switch on disco lights and loud club music at night, making them the cheapest mobile nightlife options around. In addition to the *pesero,* there is a **Metrobús** line that runs along Avenida Insurgentes, one of the main roads through the city. This cleaner, newer bus runs in an exclusive lane in the middle of the road, with frequent stops along the way. There are no *peseros* on Insurgentes, so this is the only bus service here. It can get crowded during rush hour, but it's consistent and reliable. To use the Metrobús, you'll need to purchase a card, on which you can then add money. Swipe the card at the turnstile at the bus station to get on. You can buy cards at any Metrobús station.

Beyond the city, Mexico has a fabulous bus system that offers luxury first-class service and comfortable second-class service to virtually anywhere in the country. There are four major bus terminals around the city:

- **Terminal Central del Norte (Northern Terminal)**
  55-5133-2444
  Avenida de los Cien Metros 1907
  Metro Line 5 (yellow) to Autobuses del Norte
  Bus service to northern Mexico and the U.S., including Guanajuato, Puebla, Oaxaca, Querétaro, San Miguel de Allende, and Veracruz.

- **Terminal Central del Sur (Southern Terminal)**
  55-5689-9745
  Avenida Tasqueña 1320
  Metro Line 2 (blue) to Tasqueña
  Also known as Terminal Tasqueña. Bus service to Cuernavaca, Morelos, Puebla, Oaxaca, and Taxco and other destinations.

- **Terminal Oriente (Eastern Terminal)**
  55-5542-0400
  Calz. Ignacio Zaragoza 200
  Metro Line 1 (pink) or B to San Lázaro
  Also known as the TAPO. Bus service to Campeche, Cancún, Puebla, Oaxaca, Tlaxcala, and Tabasco, among other destinations.

- **Terminal Poniente (Western Terminal)**
  55-5271-0038

Mexico City's bus terminals are clean and efficient

Avenida Sur 122

Metro Line 1 (pink) to Observatorio

Bus service to Guerrero, Jalisco, Morelia, Toluca, and Valle de Bravo, among other
destinations.

As for bus lines, there are tons of them. Buses to Puebla, Cuernavaca, and other day-
trip destinations are covered in later chapters. A helpful central resource is **Ticket Bus**
(www.ticketbus.com, 55-5133-2424; 800-702-8000), which lists all the major lines operating in Mexico. For many destinations, you can choose between first-class and second-
class service. The former has more comfortable seats, follows a more express route, and
plays movies (sometimes in Spanish, sometimes in English), even if they're obscure 1980s
flicks you never thought you'd see again.

Driving

Driving around Mexico City is an aggravating, road-rage-inducing, panic-causing,
exhausting experience . . . and that's on a good day. The main cause of the city's infamous
pollution is its absolutely awful traffic, and many residents will leave their cars at home
during the week at all costs. I recommend following their lead.

It seems every Mexican in the city went to aggressive-driving school and graduated with
top honors, but getting cut off, making lanes where none exist, and generally making other
motorists' lives miserable is only part of the story. Traffic jams will often clog up half your
day. It's easy to get lost when you're driving around. If you're renting a car, buy a Guía Roji
street map, an indispensable tool for any motorist, and familiarize yourself with the major
arteries through the city. Also do everything in your power to avoid rush hour, from 8–10
AM and 5–8 PM on weekdays. In addition, look out for *Hoy No Circula* (Don't Drive Today)

days—designated days when cars are banned from the street according to the ending number of the license plate. Finally, as of September 1, 2008, cars with foreign plates are banned from 5 AM—11 AM.

If you want to rent a car in Mexico City, you'll find all the major chains have offices here, and many have branches at the bigger hotels. However, be prepared to spend more than you would on a rental in the U.S. While it's not always the case, local rental agencies can be cheaper than foreign ones, and many offer discounts. Among these are:

Casanova Renta de Automóviles
800-227-26682
55-5514-0449 (Chapultepec location)
www.casanovarent.com.mx
Several locations in the city, the most central of which is Avenida Chapultepec 442, Col. Roma, Mexico, D.F.

Eclipse Rent a Car
55-5564-6489
www.eclipserent.com
Avenida Baja California 111, Col. Roma Sur, Mexico, D.F.

Fácil Car Rental
55-5511-7641, 5533-4716, 5514-1869
www.rentafacil.com.mx
Río Lerma 157, Col. Cuauhtémoc, Mexico, D.F.

Hit Car Rental
55-5310-5436
www.hitcarrental.com
At the Holiday Inn Oriente, Avenida Javier Rojo Gomez, 630, Col. Leyes de Reforma, Mexico, D.F.

Parking
Good luck finding a spot in major tourist areas, and be prepared to deal with a cottage industry of flag-waving "parking attendants." These are unofficial claimants of an empty stretch of road who wave a flag to catch the attention of a passing car and guide the vehicle into "their" spot. Then they'll ask you for a tip in exchange for looking out for your car. In truth, if you want to drive, you'd be well advised to work with them, as they are all over the city and can make your life easier. But there is no guarantee that your paid "attendant" will actually stick around to watch over your vehicle. I've seen enough heated discussions between my friends and the flagmen to know that it's a racket, but it does buy you a parking spot for a minimal fee. One trick that has proven useful is to promise a good tip when you return, thereby ensuring your car is looked after in your absence.

Estacionamientos, or parking garages, are all over the city but not always near where you want to be. A very small number of Mexico City's streets have parking meters. If you park at such a spot, make sure the meter stays fed. If it expires, you may find a clamp on your car when you return. Finally, wherever you park, never leave any valuables inside your car.

In Puebla and Cuernavaca, you might consider renting a car. In both cities, driving is easier than in Mexico City, although traffic can be an issue. Plus, if you want to explore the surrounding area, a car is a good idea if you're not with a guide. The main highways are well labeled and well maintained. Many routes give you the option of taking a toll (*cuota*) road, which isn't too expensive and affords you the luxury of traveling on a much less-trafficked road. The toll roads are also safer for motorists at night.

EMERGENCY INFORMATION

Emergency and Police	060 (911 will work from cell phones)
Red Cross	065
Fire Department	068
LOCATEL (missing persons)	52-5658-1111
National 24-Hour Tourist Helpline	800-987-8224(from within Mexico)
	55-5089-7500 (in Mexico City)
Tourist Security	800-007-7100 (from within Mexico)
	55-5250-0123/0493/0027/0151/0292/0589
Tourist-Aid Police	52-5250-8221
Tourist Legal Assistance	55-5625-8153
Federal Highway Police	52-5677-2227

PRACTICAL INFORMATION

Country Code	52
Mexico City Area Code	55 (Note: all phone numbers in Mexico City are 8 digits long, beginning with 5. If you see a 7-digit number, add the 5 before it when dialing)
Operator-assistance	020 (domestic long distance)
	040 (domestic directory assistance)
	090 (international long distance)
Altitude	7,240 feet above sea level
Climate	Annual average of 64°F
Time Zone	Mexico City is at GMT -6, or 1 hour behind Eastern Standard Time (dial 030 for the official time)
Hours of Operation (General)	Shopping centers and other commecial businesses open daily 9 AM–8 PM
	Banks open Monday to Friday 9 AM–4 PM
	Museums open Tuesday to Sunday 9 AM–5 PM, with free admission on Sundays
	Public transportation operates from 5 AM–midnight

TOURIST INFORMATION

Infotur

Offers maps, information, and literature in English and Spanish by the Ministry of Tourism

888-401-3880 (from the U.S.)

800-987-8244 (within Mexico)

55-5208-1030 (in Mexico City)

Presidente Masaryk 172, ground floor, Chapultepec
Morales, Miguel Hidalgo, Mexico City
Open Monday to Friday 8–6, Saturday 10–3

Sectur (Ministry of Tourism)

Mexico's Tourism Board has an excellent national portal for tourists called **www.visitmexico.com**, or you can call 800-44-MEXICO from the U.S. Mexico City's Ministry of Tourism also has a useful and detailed online resource at **www.mexicocity.gob.mx**, and can be reached at 800-008-9090 (from within Mexico). In addition, the ministry operates tourist-information booths throughout the city, including these prominent locations:

Benito Juárez International Airport
55-5786-9002
National Arrivals Terminal
Open daily 7–9

TAPO Bus Terminal
55-5784-3077
Open daily 9–6

Terminal Central Del Sur (Tasqueña Bus Terminal)
55-5336-2321
Open daily 9–6

Centro Histórico
55-5518-2799
At the Alameda Central in front of the Palacio de Bellas Artes
Open daily 9–6
55-5518-1003
At the Zócalo by the Metropolitan Cathedral
Open daily 9–6

Chapultepec-Polanco
55-5286-3850
Paseo de la Reforma in front of the Museo Nacional de Antropología
Open daily 9–6
55-5208-1030
Paseo de la Reforma at the Angel de la Independencia Plaza
Open daily 9–6

Other useful Web sites:
www.tiempolibre.com.mx
www.mexicofile.com
www.inside-mexico.com
www.mexicocitylife.com

Useful magazines:
Dónde Ir (Spanish)
Chilango (Spanish)
Explore México (Bilingual)

TEN BEST . . .

ve breakdown of what I feel are the best lodging, dining, and attractions
ıas to offer. I compiled this list as a means to help you organize your time
and provide you with an easy reference to the city's premier destinations. I also took into
consideration the value for your money, location/accessibility (the neighborhood appears
in parentheses), and (for hotels) amenities. Detailed information on the places listed here
can be found in chapter 4.

Hotels
Four Seasons Mexico (Reforma)
W Hotel Mexico City (Polanco)
Condesa DF (Condesa)
Hábita Hotel (Polanco)
Presidente Intercontinental (Polanco)
La Casona (Roma)
Gran Meliá Mexico Reforma (Reforma)
JW Marriott (Polanco)
Camino Real Mexico Polanco México (Polanco)
Casa Vieja (Polanco)

Restaurants
Pujol (Polanco)
Izote (Polanco)
Paxia (San Ángel/Santa Fe)
Jaso (Polanco)
Les Moustaches (Reforma)
Tezka (Zona Rosa)
Zhen Shanghai (Polanco)
Puerto Madero (Polanco)
La Casa de Las Sirenas (Centro Histórico)
Ligaya (Condesa)

Creative dishes put Tezka in the top ten

Museums
Museo Nacional de Antropología
(Chapultepec)
Museo Templo Mayor (Centro Histórico)
Museo de Arte Popular (Centro Histórico)
Museo Frida Kahlo (Coyoacán)
Castillo de Chapultepec/National Museum
of History (Chapultepec)
Museo Mural Diego Rivera (Centro
Histórico)
Museo Franz Mayer (Centro Histórico)
Museo Soumaya (San Ángel)
Museo San Carlos (Reforma)
Museo Rufino Tamayo (Chapultepec)

Sights and Activities

The Zócalo, including the
Catedral Metropolitana,
Templo Mayor, and Palacio
Nacional (Centro Histórico)

Alameda Central (Centro
Histórico)

Ruins of Teotihuacán (north of
Mexico City)

Basílica de Guadalupe (north of
Mexico City)

Floating Islands of Xochimilco
(south of Mexico City)

Ballet Folklórico (Centro
Histórico)

Lucha Libre (Centro Histórico)

Taxco (southwest of Mexico
City)

Bazar Sábado (San Ángel)

Visit a Mercado/Tianguis
(throughout Mexico City)

The Museo Nacional de Antropología is one of the best museums of its kind in the world

Taxco makes for a lovely day trip

4

MEXICO CITY

Getting to Know the Neighborhoods

Mexico City is a tapestry of distinct *colonias,* or neighborhoods, sorted into 16 *delegaciones,* or boroughs. As a tourist, it's wise to organize your time and your itinerary with these areas in mind. What follows is the breakdown of the main sections of the city, sometimes in groups of two neighboring communities that it makes sense to visit together. Beyond the neighborhoods, I've also mentioned other noteworthy destinations around the D.F.

CENTRO HISTÓRICO

Mexico City's Centro Histórico, or Historic Center (commonly referred to simply as the Centro) is the cradle of the city, the nation, and before that, the empire. It was the ancient Aztec capital of Tenochtitlán, and later, the heart of New Spain. It is, in other words, a city center that has been a thriving, dominant force for over 700 years. The entire area has been designated a World Heritage Site by UNESCO.

The Centro Histórico revolves around the **Zócalo,** a huge open plaza also known as the Plaza de la Constitución. (Most Mexican cities feature a *zócalo,* or central square. I follow tradition here in capitalizing Mexico City's). Here you'll find some of the country's most important and historic landmarks, surrounding what has to be one of the biggest flags you'll ever see. The Zócalo alone can easily occupy two full days of touring, between the **Catedral Metropolitana** (Metropolitan Cathedral), the ruins and museum of the **Templo Mayor,** and the murals and gorgeous architecture of the surrounding

Street performers are a common sight in the Centro Histórico

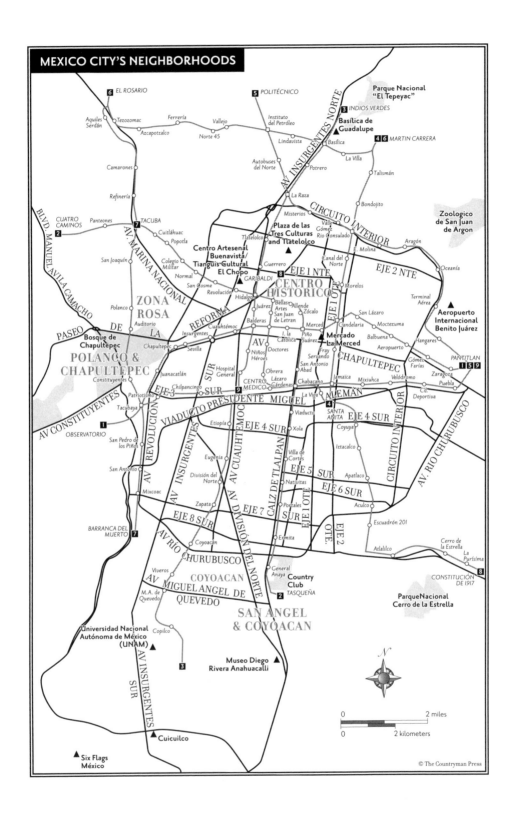

MEXICO CITY'S NEIGHBORHOODS

buildings. From the main plaza, a network of streets fans out to the rest of the city center. A walk down Calle Tacuba, 5 de Mayo, or Francisco Madero presents you with the magnificent architecture of the old city and leads to the **Alameda Central**—a large green plaza dotted with fountains, street performers, monuments, and food vendors. (It's worth the few pesos' tip to listen to the wandering organ grinders, an old custom in the city.) North of the Alameda along the broad Eje Central Lázaro Cárdenas Norte you'll come to the famous **Plaza Garibaldi**, known for its abundance of mariachis, the colorful troupes of street musicians outfitted in silver-studded *charro* (cowboy) costumes and wide-brimmed hats. And surrounding this nexus, in what is called the Colonia Centro, are plenty of destinations worth visiting.

In short, the Centro Histórico is a sightseers' paradise, and also offers some fine restaurants, a surprising number of budget hotels, and a fair choice of nightlife. It's extremely accessible by bus and metro (there are ten metro stops that place you within walking distance of the main tourist areas), but can be an expensive taxi ride through lots of traffic.

The Centro also boasts an active security force highlighted by a mounted police unit in the Alameda, who are courteous, helpful, knowledgeable, and in their sombreros and full regalia, quite happy to pose for a photo. Even so, at night during the week, it tends to be deserted, and visitors should be cautious about venturing out to explore after sundown. Where possible, always stay on crowded streets or take a *sitio* taxi from your hotel at night.

In addition to its tourist sights, the city center is a thriving commercial and business district, and tourists will be particularly happy with the choice souvenir and arts and crafts shops and markets.

The Zócalo and the Catedral Metropolitana Credit: Mexico Tourism Board

LODGING

BEST WESTERN HOTEL MAJESTIC
55-5521-8600
www.bestwestern.com
Avenida Madero 73, Col. Centro, Mexico,
D.F.
Metro: Zócalo

One of the most prominent hotels in the
city center has an enviable location right on
the Zócalo, in a lovely seven-story colonial
building with an ornate, baroque-style
lobby. Its rooftop restaurant is popular for
its terrific views, but you'll be sneered at if
you try to take in the sights without ordering anything. I wish the grandeur of the
lobby carried through to the rooms, but for
the price they're not a bad deal. The hotel
does not offer Internet access, but on a
positive note, children under 12 stay for
free. $–$$.

FIESTA INN
55-5130-2900
www.fiestainn.com
Avenida Juárez 76/José Azueta 27 C, Col.
Centro, Mexico, D.F.
Metro: Juárez

Compared to its neighbor, the sleek and
shiny Sheraton, the Fiesta Inn seems
almost drab, but consider that it shares
prime location on the Alameda Central at
far cheaper prices, and includes plenty of
amenities (24-hour room service, gym,
free wireless Internet service, and plenty
of meeting space). $.

HOLIDAY INN ZÓCALO
55-5130-5130
www.holidayinn.com
Avenida Cinco de Mayo 61, Col. Centro,
Mexico, D.F.
Metro: Zócalo

Located in a colonial building next to the
Zócalo, the Holiday Inn has 105 minimal

but clean and well-kept rooms (the old-
fashioned photos of the city in the rooms
are a nice touch). At these prices, they're
quite reasonable, and the suites are a bargain, given the extra space and large bathrooms. The hotel also has plenty of meeting
space and a business center for business
travelers, a rooftop restaurant with lovely
views, a sauna, and—a highly convenient
feature—on-site washers and dryers for
guest use. $–$$.

HOSTAL MONEDA
55-5522-5803
www.hostalmoneda.com.mx
Calle Moneda 8, Col. Centro, Mexico, D.F.

A perennial favorite with backpackers and
budget travelers from all over the world,
the Hostal Moneda can house you for as little as $10 U.S. if you're willing to share, and
not much more if you want a private room

Organ grinder in the Centro Histórico

CENTRO HISTÓRICO

PASEO DE LA REFORMA

VALERIO TRUJANO

AVENIDA HIDALGO

Gran Meliá México Reforma

Museo Franz Mayer

Museo Nacional de La Estampa

Plaza de la Santa Veracruz

Museo Mural Diego Rivera

Hidalgo

Hemiciclo a Benito Juárez

Alameda Central

Bellas Artes

Palacio de Bellas Artes

Sheraton Centro Histórico

Fiesta Inn

Museo de Arte Popular

Juárez

JUÁREZ

AVENIDA

EJE CENTRAL LÁZARO CÁRDENAS

Plaza Garibaldi

Garibaldi

Plaza Manuel Tolsá

Museo Nacional de Arte

Palacio de Correos

Templo de San Francisco

Torre Latinoamericana

INDEPENDENCIA

ARTÍCULO 123

DOLORES

VICTORIA

LUIS MOYA

AYUNTAMIENTO

BUEN TONO

Mercado de Artesanías de San Juan

REVILLAGIGEDO

ARCOS DE BELÉN

BALDERAS

Mercado de Artesanías La Ciudadela

Balderas

REP. DE PERÚ

REP. DE CHILE

REPÚBLICA DE CUBA

BELISARIO DOMÍNGUEZ

REPÚBLICA DE BOLIVIA

REPÚBLICA DE COLOMBIA

REPÚBLICA DE VENEZUELA

REPÚBLICA DE ARGENTINA

SAN ILDEFONSO

BRASIL

DE

PALMA

DONCELES

Arena Coliseo

Portales de los Evangelistas

Templo de Santa Domingo

Antiguo Palacio de la Inquisición

Plaza de Santo Domingo

Secretaría de Educación Pública

Antiguo Colegio de San Ildefonso

Museo José Luis Cuevas

CARRANZO

Allende

5 DE MAYO

Casa de los Azulejos

Palacio de Iturbide

16 DE SEPTIEMBRE

FRANCISCO I. MADERO

Hotel Gillow

TACUBA

REP. DE CHILE

Mexico City Hostel

Hotel Catedral

Hostal Catedral

Catedral Metropolitana y Sagrario

Nacional Monte de Piedad

Holiday Inn Zócalo

Best Western Hotel Majestic

Templo Mayor

Hostal Moneda

Museo Nacional de las Culturas

Palacio Nacional

Zócalo

Plaza de la Constitución (El Zócalo)

NH Centro Histórico

PALMA

REPÚBLICA

ISABEL LA CATÓLICA

BOLÍVAR

Isabel la Católica

San Juan de Letrán

Salto del Agua

EJE CENTRAL LÁZARO CÁRDENAS

VENUSTIANO

DE

URUGUAY

JOSÉ MA. PINO SUÁREZ

DE

20 DE NOVIEMBRE

REPÚBLICA

Museo de la Ciudad de México

EL SALVADOR

JOSÉ MA. IZAZAGA

Pino Suárez

© The Countryman Press

(and these rates include breakfast and Internet access). Throw in a great location a block away from the Zócalo, the terrace bar, a tour company on premises, and inexpensive airport pickup service, among other amenities, and it's easy to see why this hostel stays busy. $.

HOSTEL CATEDRAL

55-5518-1726; 800-823-2410
www.hostelcatedral.com
República de Guatemala 4, Col. Centro, Mexico, D.F.
Metro: Zócalo

Let's see: lodging starts at prices cheaper than lunch at many restaurants, if you don't mind a bunk bed, and the cost is not much more for a private room. Amenities including an on-site cyber café, rooftop bar with awesome views of the Centro Histórico, breakfast included, free daily walking tours, and a host of activities from poker to movie nights. There's an on-site cheap and reliable tour company. And its location right behind the Metropolitan Cathedral is ideal. What more can you ask for from one of the best-run hostels in the city? This is a lively, convivial place that attracts a young crowd, has a great staff, and is the ideal haven for the college or budget traveler. $.

HOTEL CATEDRAL

55-5518-5232, 5521-6183; 800-701-8340
www.hotelcatedral.com
Donceles 95, Col. Centro, Mexico D.F
Metro: Zócalo

Sister to the Hotel Gillow, the Hotel Catedral offers a similar package of bargain prices and great value. True to its name, it overlooks the Metropolitan Cathedral (ask for a top-floor room if you want a good view), which makes it ideal for sightseeing in the city center. Rooms are comfortable and modern, even if they lack the polish of the marble-floored lobby. But it's the little

extras that make this such a convenient and economical choice—like the purified drinking water from the taps in each room; the free local calls and Internet access; and the seventh-floor terrace with panoramic views. The hotel also has a travel agency and a reliable restaurant and bar. $.

HOTEL GILLOW

www.hotelgillow.com
55-5510-0791, 5510-8585, 5518-1440
Isabel la Católica 17, Col. Centro, Mexico, D.F.
Metro: Zócalo

Hotel Gillow was built in 1875 by an English jeweler. Now, with that introduction, the elegant building and fancy lobby might give you the impression that you're walking into a far more expensive establishment, but the Gillow is a terrific bargain. Its rooms are colorful, and if they're not as opulent as the lobby, they're at least carpeted, clean, and offer all the basic amenities (plus free high-speed Internet access, always a plus). The suites are a great value, spacious and equipped with Jacuzzi bathtubs, and the prices are a lot less than you'd expect from Mexico City's second-oldest hotel. $

MEXICO CITY HOSTEL

55-5512-3666, 5512-7731
www.mexicocityhostel.com
República de Brasil 8, Col. Centro, Mexico, D.F.
Metro: Zócalo

One of the newest and prettiest of the city center's many hostels, Mexico City Hostel offers basic rooms in a clean, white colonial building with arches and wrought-iron railings. Backpackers and budget travelers can choose from shared or private accommodations; both include breakfast. Electronic key cards are a welcome safety feature here. There is a communal kitchen, tour services, airport pickup, and laundry service, among other facilities. $.

NH CENTRO HISTÓRICO

55-5130-1850
www.nh-hotels.com
Palma 42, Col. Centro, Mexico, D.F.
Metro: Zócalo

One of my favorite places to stay in the city
center, the NH, located just a block away
from the Zócalo, offers plenty of value for
the money. Its minimalist Asian-themed
décor, with dark wood furniture and contemporary accents, is unpretentious and
comfortable; and its amenities, which
include a business center, meeting rooms,
gym, and restaurant with daily buffet
breakfast, make it a great choice for business or leisure travelers. You'll be hard-
pressed to find better lodgings in a more
central location at these prices. $–$$.

SHERATON CENTROL HISTÓRICO

55-5130-5300
www.starwoodhotels.com
Avenida Juarez 70, Col. Centro, Mexico,
D.F.
Metro: Juárez

Boasting a prime location off the Alameda
Central and five-star status, the tall, sleek
tower that is the Sheraton Centro Histórico
is the city center's most exclusive address.
The beautiful and airy lobby has an ample
reception area, a great Mexican restaurant,
and a funky corner bar. The hotel's 457
rooms and suites are furnished in a modern
style that may be somewhat generic in
appearance but certainly doesn't lack for
comfort. They all come with a kitchenette,
flat-screen TV, and work desk, among
other amenities, although the charge for
high-speed Internet is a little grating
(you'll find this in many of Mexico's finest
hotels, however). Many have outstanding
views of the city. The hotel is particularly
popular among business travelers, thanks
to its plush business center, fully equipped
gym, and meeting space—all among the best
in the city—and the fact that it is the only

The Sheraton Centro Histórico

hotel in the city with an in-house convention center. There's even a heliport for the
executive types. $$–$$$$.

DINING

CAFÉ TACUBA

55-5521-2948
Calle Tacuba 28, Col. Centro, Mexico, D.F.
Metro: Allende

By all accounts, the standards at this once-
hallowed restaurant on Tacuba Street have
fallen, and the uneven service hasn't
helped. Still, it's one of the city center's
iconic eateries, housed in a 17th-century
colonial gem of a building and running
strong since 1912. One of Mexico's most
popular rock bands is even named after it.

The menu is traditional Mexican, with a trio of chicken enchiladas served fresh from the oven and the *cuatro cositas* ("four small things")—a great sampler of tamale and enchilada with sides—as the highlights. For all its faults, it does have an undeniable ambience, with oil paintings, a mural of nuns working in the kitchen, and live music every night. Come between Wednesday and Sunday evenings, when medieval-costumed singers provide the entertainment. Open daily 8 AM–11 PM. $–$$$.

CHURRERÍA EL MORO

55-5512-0896
Eje Central 42, Col. Centro, Mexico, D.F.
Metro: San Juan de Letrán

El Moro draws a happy crowd for one main reason: its crispy, sugary churros. You can watch them being cranked out in the open kitchen, and either go straight for the kill or enjoy a *taco al pastor* (made outside on, and carved off, a spit) before sampling the specialty here. For the full experience, dip your churro in hot chocolate before crunching into it. Open 24/7. $.

DANUBIO

55-5512-0912
www.danubio.com
Uruguay 3, Col. Centro, Mexico, D.F.
Metro: Salto del Agua

An international seafood restaurant in an elegant setting, Danubio has the air of a Maxim's of Paris, only with far more reasonable prices. This stalwart of the city center dining scene is equally popular with tourists as it is with business professionals and politicians. The main décor is the many framed autographs and personal messages from celebrity clients over the years, including former president Vicente Fox, author Carlos Fuentes, and my personal favorite, Gabriel García Márquez. It also has an old-fashioned, well-heeled charm car-

Restaurante Danubio

ried through by the formal and courteous staff. As for the menu, fish and shellfish are the stars. For a light meal or a heavy appetizer, try the excellent *sopa verde con mariscos* (green soup with seafood), a savory *perejil*-infused broth (the herb is similar to cilantro) brimming with chunks of haddock, shrimp, and clams. The grilled crayfish (*langostinos*), lobster thermidor, and fish dishes are all highly recommended. Open daily 1–10 PM. $–$$$.

EL CARDENAL

55-5521-3080, 5521-8815
Palma 23, Col. Centro, Mexico, D.F.
Metro: Zócalo

Long considered one of the best restaurants in the Centro, El Cardenal has maintained its quality and status over the years. The menu celebrates the full range of Mexican regional specialties and a blend of old and

Taco Corner

There are plenty of taquerías in the city center that offer cheap, tasty, and quick meals. Some are icons, others hidden treasures, and a few are probably best avoided. The ones below fall under the first two categories.

El Huequito

55-5518-3313

Ayuntamiento 21, Col. Centro, Mexico, D.F.

Metro: San Juan de Letrán

An institution, this little hole in the wall (literally "the little hole") has been around for 50 years. The proprietor takes a Soup Nazi approach to his work, but he slaps together a mean *taco al pastor* (marinated pork sliced off the spit), and for a few extra pesos, you can order a double portion of meat. Open Monday to Saturday 9:30 AM–10 PM. $.

Los Gueros

Lopez 93, Col. Centro, Mexico, D.F.

Metro: San Juan de Letrán

This tiny spot in a nondescript part of the city center is known for one thing, and that's the succulent *tacos de cabeza de res*, or tacos made from the meat from the head of the cow. Don't let the thought freak you out: they're delicious. Open Monday to Saturday 9 AM–9:30 PM. $.

Mi Taco Yucateco

55-5512-4965

Ayuntamiento and Dolores, Col. Centro, Mexico, D.F.

Metro: San Juan de Letrán

The specialty here is *cochinita pibil* (marinated slow-roasted pork, a Yucatán classic). Unlike the majority of taquerías in the city, these guys cook it the old-fashioned way: beneath the earth, the way it was traditionally roasted in a pit. The result keeps the crowds coming back for more. Open Monday to Saturday 1 PM–7 PM. $.

Salón Corona

55-5512-9007

Bolívar 22, Col. Centro, Mexico, D.F.

Metro: Allende

Many feel this place is a must-do while you're in the Centro. It combines the ambience and local color of a cantina with cheap and good beer on tap, and of course, delicious tacos, which come with a full range of fillings, including turkey, beef, nopales, *pastor*, and more. Don't forget to sample the pickled carrots. Open daily 9 AM–midnight. $–$$.

Si No Le Gusta Me Voy

Si No Le Gusta Me Voy

Corner of Lopez Street and Vizaínas, Col. Centro, Mexico, D.F.

Metro: Salto del Agua

I love this place for many reasons. The name, for one: "If you don't like it, I'm going." They mean it, too; if you don't like their food . . . but of course, you will. The steak and potato tacos are to die for, and so is the *longaniza* (sausage) and pork combos. Open Monday to Saturday 12–6 PM. $.

new. For recipes from the ancients, try the much-loved *gusanos de maguey* (cactus worms) wrapped in cheese, the *caldo Xóchitl* (a typical broth made with shredded chicken, rice, chiles, avocado, and tortilla strips), or *escamoles* (ant eggs). If they're in season, the *chiles en Nogada* (a Puebla specialty made with chiles stuffed with a mix of pork, beef, olive, almonds, and raisins) is a must-try. And the freshly grilled fish wrapped in chile adobo sauce is a terrific entry from Mexico's coast. A branch of the restaurant is located in the lobby of the Sheraton Centro Histórico. Open daily 8:30 AM–7 PM. $$–$$$.

HOSTERÍA SANTO DOMINGO
55-5526-5276
Belisario Dominguez 70, Col. Centro, Mexico, D.F.
Metro: Allende

In operation since 1860, Mexico City's oldest restaurant is housed in what was once part of the 16th-century Santo Domingo Convent. The décor and furnishings certainly are traditional, with colorful punched paper, historical photos, heavy doors, and a mural that shows the adjacent Plaza de Santo Domingo as it was in centuries past. But its reputation lies in its cuisine. It is rumored to have the best *chiles en nogada* in the city, and its mole poblano (chicken breast cooked in a traditional, chocolate-and-chile-based sauce) and *pechuga ranchera* (chicken breast cooked in a pasilla chile and cream sauce) is equally celebrated. The restaurant also has daily live music from 3 PM, featuring bass, violin, and piano. Open Monday to Saturday 9 AM–10:30 PM, Sunday 9 AM–9:30 PM. $–$$.

LA CASA DE LAS SIRENAS
55-5704-3345
República de Guatemala 32, Col. Centro, Mexico, D.F.
Metro: Zócalo

La Casa de las Sirenas (House of the Mermaids) offers a hard-to-beat combination of location, setting, ambience, and excellent cuisine. Occupying a three-story colonial mansion, the restaurant is divided into three distinct spaces: the ground-floor tequila saloon (which stocks over two hundred varieties of the spirit), a second-level bar and indoor dining hall, and an open terrace on the third floor overlooking the back of the Metropolitan Cathedral.

On a sunny day, this is one of the best places in the city center for a respite from active sight-seeing. In one corner is a tortilla stand where a smiling lady pounds out a constant supply of fresh tortillas. The mole is outstanding, as is the *molcajete*, a combination of meat, white cheese, and nopales served in a stone bowl for which the dish is named. For something a little different, the roast duck in tamarind sauce is succulent and flavorful. And if you want a lighter meal, the restaurant's signature salads (try the *ensalada hortaliza*, made with goat cheese, lettuce, spinach, avocado, and basil) and selection of hearty soups will do nicely. It's a personal favorite, and well worth the slightly higher prices. Open Monday to Thursday 1 PM–11 PM, Friday and Saturday 1 PM –2 AM. $–$$$.

LA FONDA DE DON CHON
55-5542-0873
Regina 160, Col. Centro, Mexico, D.F.
Metro: Merced

Want an authentic pre-Hispanic Mexican dining experience? Then head to La Fonda de Don Chon, the city's most well-known Aztec restaurant. For all its fame (or perhaps notoriety), it's an unpretentious place where you can dine on delicacies like *gusanos de maguey* (fried cactus worms), fried grasshopper, roast armadillo, and venison. It's been popular for generations with locals and tourists, celebrities, politicians, and even food channels . . . in other words, they've been doing this for a long time, and they've been doing it right. Open Monday to Saturday noon–6 PM. $–$$.

LA ÓPERA

55-5512-8959
Avenida Cinco de Mayo 10, Col. Centro,
Mexico, D.F.
Metro: Bellas Artes

A historic cantina, La Ópera was opened in 1876 by two French ladies. The interior is a rich throwback to another era, with deep booths, ornate wooden bar, gilded roof, and baroque accents. It's had its share of famous patrons; Zapata once dined here, and so did Porfirio Díaz; but it was Pancho Villa who left his mark on the place: you can still see the bullet hole fired from his gun on the ceiling. The bilingual menu is a mix of Spanish and Mexican cuisine: the former includes delicacies such as eel, tongue, brains, and bull testicles, among more well-known imports like Serrano ham. For Mexican food, try the snails with chipotle sauce (a house specialty), the avocado stuffed with shrimp, and the tasty *antojitos,* or finger foods. Trios and other live music are a common sight, and the stiff but professional service conforms to the old-fashioned appeal of the place. Open Monday to Saturday 1–11:30 PM, Sunday 1–5:30 PM. $–$$.

LOS GIRASOLES

55-5510-3281
www.restaurantelosgirasoles.com
Calle Tacuba 8, Col. Centro, Mexico, D.F.
Metro: Allende

A large, bright, and colorful restaurant overlooking Plaza Manuel Tolsá, Los Girasoles is a natural gathering spot for power lunches, but it should be on your list too, thanks to its flavorful cuisine, pleasant ambience, and innovative specials. The menu celebrates classic dishes from every region and throws in a few nouveau Mexican creations like duck tacos,

tamarind mole, and chicken breast stuffed with plantain and rice. Even the tortilla chips served tableside are a cut above the norm. Open Tuesday to Saturday 1 PM–midnight, Sunday and Monday 1–9 PM. $$–$$$.

LOS MERCADERES

55-5510-3687, 5510-2213
Avenida Cinco de Mayo 57, Col. Centro,
Mexico, D.F.
Metro: Allende

A modern Mexican bistro, Los Mercaderes is a stately fixture on Avenida Cinco de Mayo. The elegant décor, with soft classical music piped in, makes for an intimate, sophisticated space in which to sample the classically Mexican cuisine. Its gourmet breakfasts are a must to start your day if you're staying in the area. For lunch and dinner, the *sopa de médula* (marrow soup), a tomato-infused broth with *flor de calabaza* and nopales is a good introduction to the menu. They pride themselves on their filets, and the duck cooked in a pear chipotle sauce is terrific. Vegetarians should pounce on the *chile hojaldrado,* a house specialty of chile poblano stuffed with goat cheese and nuts. The peppercorn-crusted tuna steak adds a nice continental touch to the menu. Open Monday to Wednesday 8 AM–10 PM, Thursday to Saturday 8 AM–1 AM, Sunday 8 AM–8 PM.

MERCADO SAN JUAN ARCOS DE BELÉN

Corner of Arcos de Belén and Lopez
Metro: Salto del Agua

This long, squat orange building is a good distance from the Alameda Central, but it's home to a large indoor market that has a plethora of cheap eateries, offering everything from *pancita* (tripe) to mole to enchiladas and other staples of Mexican food. Just choose a stall, grab a stool, and either order in Spanish or point and smile. Open daily 7 AM–5 PM. $.

ATTRACTIONS, PARKS & RECREATION

ALAMEDA CENTRAL
Between Avenida Juárez and Avenida Hidalgo, off Paseo de la Reforma
Metro: Bellas Artes or Hidalgo

During the reign of Tenochtitlán, this broad open plaza hosted the *tianguis,* or traditional market. The Spanish converted it into a public square, making this beautiful park over 400 years old. It's seen its share of history. One end of the park, once known as El Quemadaro, was where infidels captured by the Spanish Inquisition were publicly burned at the stake.

Today, the Alameda is one of the most pleasant of Mexico City's parks, a refreshing green space in a densely packed urban center, with fountains, sculptures, and vibrant life. You'll almost always find a street performer (ranging from outlandish costumed "statues" to clowns to musicians), a children's puppet theater on some weekends, and vendors selling street food and knickknacks. Among the fountains and monuments, none is more impressive than the **Hemiciclo a Benito Juárez**, a wide semicircle of marble columns flanking a statue of the beloved Mexican leader. Also keep an eye out for the *policías charros,* the mounted police in sombrero and full cowboy regalia, who monitor the park.

The Alameda is bordered by the exquisite Palacio de Bellas Artes, and the Franz Mayer and Diego Rivera Mural museums, and is close to several other noteworthy places to visit. Free.

Policías charros *on patrol at the Alameda Central*

ANTIGUO COLEGIO DE SAN ILDEFONSO

55-5702-6378, 5795-5922
www.sanildefonso.org.mx
Justo Sierra 16, Col. Centro, Mexico, D.F.
Metro: Zócalo

One of the most important and historic centers of art and education in the country, the Old San Ildefonso School was where the Mexican muralist movement was born, and it is home to works by its most celebrated masters before they were famous. The school was founded in 1588 by the Jesuits, and flourished until the Jesuit order was banished from the new empire in 1767 by King Carlos III. Following the Mexican Revolution, José Vasconcelos, the public education minister under President Álvaro Obregón, began a project to educate the masses through free displays of visual art. Vasconcelos contracted a number of unknown artists to paint the Colegio, which was at the time the National Preparatory School. Among those who participated were Diego Rivera, Jean Charlot, Fernando Leal, Davíd Alfaro Siqueiros, and José Clemente Orozco, among others. They would become the founding fathers of the muralist movement, one of Mexico's most enduring and powerful artistic endeavors. Among their best work here are Rivera's remarkable *La Creación,* in the amphitheater; Orozco's *Cortés y la Malinche,* showing the conquistador and his consort naked, holding hands; and Charlot's stark depiction of the massacre in the Templo Mayor. Open Tuesday to Sunday 10–6. $.

BALLET FOLKLÓRICO

55-5512—2593, 5130-0900
www.bellasartes.gob.mx
Corner of Eje Central Lázaro Cárdenas and Avenida Juárez at the Palacio de Bellas Artes
Metro: Bellas Artes

The much-vaunted Folkloric Ballet is one of the city's most celebrated performing arts events. Not so much a ballet as a collage of regional folk dances from all over Mexico and from different eras, it is a spectacle of music, costumed pageantry, and skill. From Aztec ritual dances to mariachis, it is a fine production that also benefits from its majestic setting in the Palacio de Bellas Artes. Performances run Wednesday at 8:30 PM and Sunday at 8:30 and 9:30 PM. $$$–$$$$.

BICYCLE RENTAL

By the eastern side of Metropolitan Cathedral on the Zócalo
Metro: Zócalo

This small booth sponsored by the Ministry of the Environment offers inexpensive bicycle rentals, and bikes are a perfect way to get around the city center and accelerate your sight-seeing. The ministry suggests five routes to various sights, but you can easily map your own way around. As an added incentive, your first two hours are free. Open Monday to Saturday 9–4. $.

CASA DE LOS AZULEJOS

55-5512-9820
www.sanborns.com.mx
Avenida Maderos 4, Col. Centro, Mexico, D.F.
Metro: Bellas Artes

¡Lucha!

Mexico's *lucha libre* (literally "free fight"), or professional wrestling, is one of its most colorful sports and has an immensely popular following. The image of the masked and costumed Mexican wrestler is well known beyond Mexico, but here they are part of the social fabric. Famous *luchadores* are practically saints (one of the most famous is the Saint, or *el Santo*, who's son also got into the business under the catchy name *Hijo del Santo*, or Son of the Saint), and their masks are sold at stalls and shops around the country. It's a tremendous, campy spectacle, full of ridiculous theatrics, flying bodies, and bloodthirsty crowds. And it's all staged . . . right?

One of my friends in Mexico had briefly trained as a *luchador* before leaving the business.

Lucha libre

The aptly named House of Tiles is an architectural gem located on a prime corner of the city center. It was built in the 16th century and was later covered in azulejo blue Talavera tiles from Puebla. The legend behind the lovely façade dates back to the 18th century, when the house belonged to one Count of Orizaba. Allegedly the old count, no great believer in positive reinforcement, told his lazy son: "You will never go far in life nor will you ever build a house of tiles." After that somewhat cryptic condemnation, the son proved his father wrong by covering his house with the tiles you see today. The home was later turned into the exclusive Mexico City Jockey Club, and then in 1903, the Sanborn brothers opened a soda fountain and pharmacy here, in what would become a national chain. Inside is the trademark Sanborns multipurpose store, its most attractive restaurant, and a mural by José Clemente Orozco. Daily 7 AM–11 PM. Free.

Before watching my first *lucha libre* fight, I went with him and a few other friends to Sports Gym Villalobos, a famous gym for *luchadores* in the Centro Histórico. Here I saw the practice ring, the storied tradition of *lucha libre* all over the walls . . . these were *not* the potbellied, out-of-shape wrestlers Americans typically associate with *lucha libre* (as parodied by Jack Black in the film *Nacho Libre*). These guys were imposing specimens.

That night I attended my first wrestling match. While we were watching the display of brute pummeling combined with impressive aerial acrobatics, my friend the onetime *luchador* explained who was who, and what each was known for. He also told me how bruising and dangerous the sport really is, and after watching one wrestler carried away on a stretcher (fake or not, it looked bad!), I believed him.

One of the most fun parts of watching the sport live is the crowd. Fathers will urge their children to scream the most ill-wishing insults upon their heroes' enemies, and the cries for blood, death, and total annihilation are hysterical. Sure, it's choreographed. But it takes skill, and it's a ton of fun to watch . . . and that's what sport is all about.

There are two *lucha libre* arenas, and neither is in the best part of town. If you go, take a *sitio* taxi there and back. The venues themselves, however, are quite safe. Of the two, Arena México is the more famous and venerated *lucha* institution.

Arena Coliseo
55-5526-1687
www.cmll.com; www.ticketmaster.com.mx
República de Perú 77, Col. Centro, Mexico, D.F.
Metro: Garibaldi
Fights scheduled Tuesdays at 8 PM and Sundays at 5 PM.

Arena México
55-5588-0508
www.arenamexico.com.mx; www.ticketmaster.com.mx
Dr. Lavista 197, Col. Doctores, Mexico, D.F.
Metro: Cuauhtémoc
Fights typically scheduled Tuesdays at 7:30 PM and Fridays at 8:30 PM.

CATEDRAL METROPOLITANA (METROPOLITAN CATHEDRAL)
55-5521-2447, 5510-0440
At the Plaza de la Constitución (Zócalo)
Metro: Zócalo

The largest cathedral in the Americas is a monumental work of architecture and symbolism, and deserves some historical context. When the conquistadores conquered Tenochtitlán in 1521, they chose this site, near the adjacent Templo Mayor, for their first place of worship. A chapel was constructed in 1524 from the ruins of the Aztec temple, marking not only a symbolic but a physical transfer of spiritual power. But as the Spanish empire settled in, the governors of New Spain decided they wanted a more impressive

Catedral Metropolitana

religious monument, and plans for the cathedral began in the late 1500s. The prior chapel (the first built in the Americas) was taken down as the newer, grander replacement took shape, but the cathedral would be built in stages over the next two centuries. Even today it is rare to see it without a scaffolding, as restoration work is a never-ending effort. This is also due to the fact that, like other buildings in Mexico City that are built on its soft subsoil, the church has partially sunk into the ground.

Because of the time it took to build, the cathedral is a showcase for no less than five architectural styles that relate its evolution: the 17th-century detailed baroque principal façade of the main church and Churrigueresque façade of the adjoining Sagrario chapel; the 18th-century neoclassical bell towers and the 19th-century dome, which was the work of Manuel Tolsá; and the earlier Renaissance style of the other façades. The cathedral is based on the Gothic churches popular in Spain, the fifth school to round out the architectural mélange, which somehow come together nicely despite their contrasting philosophies.

If the exterior seems large, the interior is no less physically imposing: a cavernous hall arrayed in the shape of a cross, the cathedral is comprised of five naves, 14 chapels, a choir, and a sacristy. There are enough artistic and architectural gems inside to warrant a guided tour, but if you prefer to go your own way, take note especially of the towering, incredibly ornate baroque altarpiece in the central Altar of the Kings; two beautiful paintings by Juan Rodríguez, the Three Wise Men and the Assumption of the Virgin; the Capilla de San Felipe (Saint Phillip's Chapel), where lie the remains of Emperor Agustín de Iturbide; the baptistery and baroque hallway of the adjacent tabernacle; and the two 18th-century organs, among the largest in the Americas. Beneath is a massive crypt where Mexico City's former bishops lie entombed. Open daily 7–7. Free.

PALACIO DE BELLAS ARTES

55-5512–2593, 5130-0900
www.bellasartes.gob.mx
Corner of Eje Central Lázaro Cárdenas and Avenida Juárez
Metro: Bellas Artes

One of Mexico City's most beautiful and iconic buildings, the white-marble Palace of Fine Arts is a distinctive landmark. It was begun in 1904 by Italian architect Adamo Boari, who left the job unfinished in 1916 after numerous delays (not the smallest of which was the Mexican Revolution). A Mexican student of Boari's, Federico Mariscal, finally took over the project in 1932, completing it in 1934 and making it a unique architectural blend of art nouveau and art deco, adorned with Greco-Roman and Aztec motifs. Fronting a large open plaza, the building is a picturesque masterpiece made all the more dramatic by the open space in front, with its sculpted gardens and statues.

Within is a theater (home to the Folkloric Ballet and other events) with a stunning 22-ton Tiffany glass curtain depicting the Ixtaccíhuatl (the Sleeping Woman) and Popocatépetl (the Smoking Mountain) volcanoes, a museum of architecture, and impressive artwork by Rufino Tamayo, David Rivera, and José Clemente Orozco, among other masters. In particular, note Rivera's dramatic science-and-industry-themed El Hombre Contralor del Universo (Man, Controller of the Universe) on the third floor. This is a re-creation of a mural Rivera had made for Nelson Rockefeller, intended for the Rockefeller Center. Rivera had depicted several world leaders in the mural, including Vladimir Lenin. Rockefeller objected and, when Rivera refused to remove it, had the mural scraped off the wall. In this rendition, Rivera threw in Karl Marx and Friedrich Engels, and then got personal by adding in an unflattering John D. Rockefeller. There's a guided tour from Tuesday to Sunday at 1 pm. Free, $ for galleries, free on Sunday.

PLAZA DE LA CONSTITUCIÓN (THE ZÓCALO)
Bordered by Avenida Tacuba, 16 de Septiembre, Pino Suárez, and República de Brasil
Metro: Zócalo

The main attractions around the Plaza de la Constitución, or the Zócalo, merit their own listings, but I've included the huge plaza here as a destination of its own because, even if you don't walk into the immense Catedral Metropolitana on its north side, visit the Palacio Nacional on the east side, or head to the Templo Mayor on the northeast corner, I'd still ask you to come to this colossal plaza and take a long look around. This is the very heart of Mexico, and has been for almost 700 years. The Zócalo is the second-largest public plaza in the world (after Moscow's Red Square), and is all the more dramatic for its complete absence of greenery or adornment. Its sparseness makes a powerful statement, as does its single feature: the absolutely massive Mexican flag in its center.

However, this is hardly a tranquil environment. Traffic rages around the plaza, pickpockets are known to operate, vendors line up in front of the cathedral, and crowds gather on a daily basis. Political rallies and speeches are often held here. Also, you're likely to catch costumed Aztec dancers performing in the plaza on most days, but definitely on weekends and special occasions. Free.

PALACIO DE CORREOS
55-5510-2999
Corner of Eje Central Lázaro Cárdenas and Calle Tacuba
Metro: Bellas Artes

A post office isn't usually on a sight-seeing list, but this one probably outstrips your local branch with its unusual sand-colored stone façade and ornately detailed Gothic and Arabesque architecture. The interior is also worth a look, and contains a museum and postal library. Open Tuesday to Friday 9:30–5:30, Saturday and Sunday 9–3. Free.

PALACIO DE ITURBIDE
55-5225-0234
Avenida Madero, Col. Centro, Mexico, D.F.
Metro: Allende

Slow-moving Mexicans?
Visit the Zócalo on a sweltering summer's day, when there is just a mild breeze, and you might witness a most curious phenomenon: a cluster of Mexicans huddled around the flagpole, inching together in a seemingly random direction. This baffling sight was explained to me by a local guide: Because there is no tree in sight in the Zócalo, there is no shade. Resting laborers will flock to the only respite from the sun that can be found: the shadow of the huge flag. As the flag flutters and swings lazily on its pole, the Mexicans follow suit, keeping under its relatively cool protection.

The Palacio de Correos

The residence of Agustín de Iturbide when he was crowned emperor in 1822 is a prime example of the baroque style popular in the 18th century. It was built between 1780 and 1785, and was in its time the tallest building in the city. Now the interior hosts periodic art exhibits. Open Monday to Friday 9–2:30 and 4–8. Free.

PLAZA GARIBALDI
Eje Central Lázaro Cárdenas and Avenida República de Honduras
Metro: Garibaldi

Plaza Garibaldi is one of those places I wish I could be more excited about. Named after the Italian freedom fighter Giuseppe Garibaldi, this broad plaza surrounded by bars and restaurants is famed for its concentration of mariachis. On weekends, it is literally packed with a roving armada of the colorful folk singers; sounds like a blast, right? Unfortunately, it has also attracted a shadier element and is not considered safe at night unless you're in a group. I don't recall a single time when my friends in the city suggested or even seconded my vote to hang out in the plaza. While it can be a fun place to barhop, its combination of tourist-trap atmosphere (the mariachis charge a hefty fee per song) and unsavory characters especially in the streets around the plaza keep many locals away. Still, it remains a Mexico City institution. Free to visit, $–$$ for a song.

PALACIO NACIONAL
55-3688-1202
Eastern side of the Plaza de la Constitución
Metro: Zócalo

Mariachis at the Plaza Garibaldi Credit: Mexico Tourism Board

Overshadowed by the Metropolitan Cathedral, the National Palace is an impressive building in its own right, and one suffused with history and art. Made of a red stone called
tezontle and quarry, it is the official residence of Mexico's president. The 17th-century
building was built over an earlier palace that housed Hernán Cortés and, before him,
Montezuma. It was also the residence of the viceroys of New Spain.

Walk inside and, above the central door, note the Bell of Dolores, which was rung by
Miguel Hidalgo, the hero of the War of Independence, in 1810, as he declared Mexico's
independence. (The bell was rung in the town of Dolores in Guanajuato but brought to the
palace by Porfirio Díaz, who began the tradition of the *grito,* when the president rings the
bell each year on September 15 to a cheering mass of people in the Zócalo.) Be sure to visit
the Diego Rivera murals on the upper floors. Among the striking works are a series that
depict Mexico's history, from life in the Aztec world to the arrival of Cortés, to the revolution, to the American invasion in the 19th century. Open daily 9–5. Free.

PLAZA DE LA SANTA VERACRUZ
Across the Alameda Central on Avenida
Hidalgo
Metro: Bellas Artes

The Iglesia de San Juan de Dios

This tucked-away cobblestone plaza is
completely dwarfed by the neighboring
Alameda Central but contains a wealth of
religious and cultural sights. Adorned with
stone fountains, it is framed beautifully by
two small churches. The most dramatic of
these is the Iglesia de la Santa Veracruz,
which, thanks to Mexico's subsoil, is
slightly sunken into the ground. The tilted,
somber façade is a striking visual. The
church was founded on December 18,
1568, but was redone in the 18th century in
a baroque style. Ironically, it houses the
tomb of neoclassical master architect
Manuel Tolsá. Opposite Santa Veracruz
stands the brighter (and straighter) Iglesia
de San Juan de Dios, which has a unique
concave façade and geometric tilework.
Within you'll find a figure of Saint Anthony
of Padua, patron saint of matchmaking and
finding lost things. The small, intimate
space between the churches also houses
two museums: the outstanding Museo
Franz Mayer and Museo Nacional de la
Estampa. Churches open daily 10:30–1:30
and 4:30–6:30. Free.

SECRETARÍA DE EDUCACIÓN PÚBLICA

55-3601-1000
Calle Argentina 28, Col. Centro, Mexico, D.F.
Metro: Zócalo

The Ministry of Public Education may sound like an interminably dull destination to most tourists, but you'll be pleasantly surprised if you're a fan of the muralist movement. In a series of more than 120 panels spanning two blocks and three stories is an epic work by Diego Rivera depicting life in Mexico, from its festivals to its industries to its religious influences. Other murals found in the complex are by Davíd Alfaro Siqueiros, Jean Charlot, Amado de la Cueva, and other muralists. There is also a self-portrait of Rivera on the stairwell between the second and third floors. Monday to Friday 9–5. Free.

TEMPLO DE SAN FRANCISCO

Avenida Madero and Calle Gante
Metro: Bellas Artes

Walk down Avenida Madero from the Alameda to the Zócalo and you can't miss this impressive church. The first Franciscan convent in Mexico City, San Francisco was built over Emperor Montezuma II's zoo, of all things, and was founded by Cortés in 1524. It used to be much larger than the present church (a newer construction), whose ornate Churrigueresque façade dates from 1716. The large gilded altarpiece inside also dates from the 18th century. Open daily 7–8. Free.

PLAZA DE SANTO DOMINGO

Corner of Belisario Domínguez and República de Brasil
Metro: Zócalo

Located three blocks north of the Zócalo, this plaza is worth the walk for its place in the history of the city. Once the site of Cuauhtémoc's palace, it was the second most important square in the city center, and remains a beautiful open space bordered by historic architecture and monuments. The plaza was also the central seat of worship for the Dominican order, which is credited with bringing the Inquisition to Mexico; the **Templo de Santo Domingo**, with its baroque and neoclassical architecture, dominates the north end of the plaza. There is a plaque on the wall of the former convent marking the place that served as the *Quemadero,* where heretics were burned at the stake from 1596 to 1771.

To the right is the **Antiguo Palacio de la Inquisición**, which housed the dreaded tribunal of the Inquisition and which now, in a curious twist of fate, is a museum of Mexican medicine. On the south side of the plaza is the **Portales de los Evangeslistas,** under whose archways sit public clerks and scribes, ready to write and print love-letters, documents, and anything else you need. It is a practice that has been carried out here for over 100 years. Finally, in the center of the plaza stands a sculpture of Josefa Ortiz de Dominguez, a fervent supporter of Mexico's War of Independence.

TORRE LATINOAMERICANA

55-5518-7423
Corner of Eje Central Lázaro Cárdenas and Avenida Madero, Col. Centro, Mexico, D.F.
Metro: Bellas Artes

The tall, slender tower across from the Palacio de Bellas Artes has a viewing platform on its upper floors with sweeping vistas of the city on a clear day. It gets very crowded on weekends, but on weekdays the calmer environment will give you a better experience to soak in the sheer size and depth of the city. Open daily 9:30 AM–10:30 PM. $.

CULTURE

MUSEO DE ARTE POPULAR

55-5510-2201
www.map.df.gob.mx
Revillagigedo 11, Col. Centro, Mexico, D.F.
Metro: Juárez

Definitely on my do-not-miss list for anyone who takes an interest in Mexican art and folklore, this exceptional, wonderfully organized and presented museum is tucked away a block south of the Alameda and right behind the Sheraton. The three floors display popular and folk art from the 18th to the 21st centuries in an ultramodern setting that combines exhibits, video, and instruction.

The first floor showcases the essence of the country's art: pottery, painted clay, hats, textiles, handwoven baskets, and the like. The informative bilingual descriptions will tell you that a hallmark of Mexican art is the

The Torre Latinoamericana

participation of almost all members of the family in its creation. The second floor is devoted to art and the sacred. Here you'll find a colorful plethora of masks, icons, effigies, costumed skeletons, and *alebrijes*, which are fantastic combinations of real and mythical creatures. The museum offers many temporary exhibits and special events throughout the year, and their gift shop is an excellent source for arts and crafts. Open Tuesday to Sunday 10–6, Thursday until 9. $.

Note: Many museums in Mexico City charge extra for the use of cameras. Before you complain, consider that a great many museums don't let you take pictures at all, so a nominal fee for the privilege of snapping a shot isn't a bad deal.

The Museo de Arte Popular

MUSEO DEL TEMPLO MAYOR

55-5542-4943, 5542-4784
www.templomayor.inah.gob.mx
Seminario 8, Col. Centro, Mexico, D.F.
Metro: Zócalo

If you asked me to pick one single sight to visit in Mexico City above all others, I would point you toward the Templo Mayor for its place in history, its astounding museum, and its enduring symbol as the former might of the Aztec empire. Huey Teocalli, as the Aztecs called it, was the political, symbolic, and spiritual center of the Mexica empire. It was here that ritual sacrifices were made at the altars of the gods Tlaloc and Huitzilopochtli, which crowned the main pyramid (the latter had the slightly larger of the two shrines). Typical of Aztec construction, the temple was expanded 12 times over seven major phases, with sub-sequent layers covering earlier ones, beginning with the first humble temple in 1325, until it reached close to 200 feet in height at its peak in 1521. Around it was a vast complex of more than 70 buildings constituting a sacred square and including the most important institutions of the ancient capital.

When Cortés arrived, he and his conquistadores were stunned by the majesty and artistry of this mighty city. It was at the Templo Mayor where the ill-fated Montezuma greeted the conquistadors, and it was here where some of the bloodiest battles for domi-nation were waged. Cortés ordered the magnificent temple destroyed, and after the Spanish victory, it was left to the vanquished Aztecs to destroy their former city and use its remains to build the new one.

Today, a walkway takes you around the ruins before leading to the excellent museum. Of particular note are the seated figure of Chac-Mool, the messenger of Tlaloc, at the foot of his altar on the Templo Mayor; La Casa de las Águilas (House of the Eagles), one of the most important and aristocratic buildings in the sacred center; the temple of Quetzalcoatl; and the Tzompantli altar, with its 240 stone skulls arrayed in rows; and the Red Temple, known for its fine mural.

But this is only the first part of the Templo Mayor experience. After touring the ruins, enter the magnificent museum, which has an astounding collection of Aztec artifacts that best displays the beauty, complexity, spirituality, and creativity of the empire. The museum has eight halls and between six and seven thousand immaculately preserved or restored pieces. One of its most important is the massive stone disc depicting the dismembered body of Coyolxauhqui, the moon goddess, which was excavated in 1978 and spurred the major archaeological project that would uncover the forgotten treasures of the Templo Mayor. The stone relief relates the legend of Huitzilopochtli springing from his mother's womb in full armor and killing his sister, Coyolxauhqui. The war god cut off her limbs and threw her into the sky, where she became the moon.

The Templo Mayor is a place of incredible resonance, history, and symbolism, and is one of Mexico's most rewarding cultural highlights. Finally, if you speak Spanish, be sure to check out the Templo Mayor Web site, among the best online resources of any of Mexico's cultural attractions. Open daily 9–5. $, free on Sundays.

The Templo Mayor

MUSEO FRANZ MAYER

55-5518-2266
www.franzmayer.org.mx
Avenida Hidalgo 45, Col. Centro, Mexico, D.F.
Metro: Bellas Artes

On the north side of the Alameda in the Plaza de la Santa Vera Cruz lies this interesting museum located inside a 16th-century mansion that was once a hospital (an interesting side-note: in the 19th century, Emperor Maximilian turned it into a hospital for prostitutes). It houses an eclectic collection of art gathered over the years by German philanthropist Franz Mayer from Mexico, Europe, and Asia. Religious paintings from New Spain and portraits dominate the main gallery, which also includes a rare display of 15th- and 16th-century German paintings, 16th-century Flemish tapestries, and exquisite period furniture. Also of note are the reliefs in wood from the 16th to the 18th centuries, as well as the fabulous collection of Talavera pottery. Don't miss the two-story library, with its rich wood paneling and stock of over 14,000 books including 800 editions of *Don Quixote*, and the lovely, leafy courtyard at the back, where the café makes for a tranquil stop. Open Tuesday to Sunday 10–5. $, free on Tuesday.

MUSEO JOSÉ LUIS CUEVAS

55-5522-0156, 5542-6198
www.museojoseluiscuevas.com.mx
Academia 13, Col. Centro, Mexico, D.F.
Metro: Zócalo

A modern art museum housed in what was once a 16th-century convent makes for an interesting contrast, but it is here where the private collection of Mexican sculptor José Luis Cuevas is displayed. Cuevas amassed over 1,800 works from Mexico and around the world, including such masters as Davíd Alfaro Siqueiros, Picasso, Rembrandt, and of course, Cuevas himself. In fact, the most dramatic piece of art in the museum is his colossal sculpture in the main patio under the glass ceiling. *La Giganta* (The Giantess) is a woman from the front, but from behind is a man (actually a self-portrait of the sculptor). Open Tuesday to Sunday 10–6. $.

MUSEO MURAL DIEGO RIVERA

55-5512-0754
Across the Alameda Central on the corner of Balderas and Colón
Metro: Hidalgo

There aren't too many museums around that were built primarily for a single work, but Diego Rivera's staggering 1947 mural, *Sueño de Una Tarde Dominical en la Alameda Central* (Dream of a Sunday Afternoon in the Alameda Central), is worth such distinguished exclusivity. The mural was located in the Hotel del Prado, which was destroyed in the 1985 earthquake. Remarkably, the mural survived and was relocated here, where it stands dominating one wall in a room that offers two levels of viewing. True to its name, the colorful mural shows the park, but in typical Rivera fashion, it is crowded with a pantheon of notable characters from Mexican history and folklore, and equally populated with depictions of Mexico's religious, political, and social struggles. Among those portrayed are

Hernán Cortés, General Santa Anna, Benito Juárez, Emperor Maximilian, and Porfirio Díaz. Also depicted is Frida Kahlo with her arm around the shoulder of a self-portrait of Rivera as a boy. Open Tuesday to Sunday 10–6. $.

MUSEO NACIONAL DE ARTE

55-5130-3459, 5130-3460, 5130-3400
www.munal.com.mx
Calle Tacuba 8, Col. Centro, México City, D.F.

Section of Diego Rivera's Sueño de Una Tarde Dominical en la Alameda Central

The stately gray building on Tacuba Street dominating one end of Plaza Tolsá was once the Palacio de Communicaciones, but in 1982 was converted into the National Museum of Painting, and later the National Museum of Art. Directly in front of the museum is one of Manuel Tolsá's most famous works: *El Caballito,* a regal statue of King Carlos IV astride his horse. Within the spacious interior is a rich chronicle of five centuries of art in Mexico, from the early colonial period to contemporary masters like Diego Rivera, Frida Kahlo, and Rufino Tamayo. There are free guided tours every Tuesday and Sunday at noon and 2 PM. Open Tuesday to Sunday 10:30–5:30. $, free on Sundays.

MUSEO DE LA CIUDAD DE MEXICO

55-5522-9936
www.cultura.df.gob.mx
Pino Suárez 30, Col. Centro, Mexico, D.F.
Metro: Pino Suárez

Housed in a 16th-century former mansion, the museum of the city of Mexico has the daunting task of capturing the history of this ancient metropolis in a comparatively small (but beautiful) space. It does what it can, centering on maps, models, and a fine library. Perhaps its most intriguing feature lies outside: a great stone serpent head at the base of one corner taken from the ruins of Tenochtitlán. Open daily 10–6. $.

NIGHTLIFE

CENTRO CULTURAL DE ESPAÑA

55-5521-1925/1926
República de Guatemala 18, Col. Centro, Mexico, D.F.
Metro: Zócalo

The Spanish Cultural Center may not sound like a great place to hang out at night, but it is. By day, it's a beautiful building owned by the Spanish government showcasing temporary art exhibits. By night, on weekends, the rooftop café's tables are pushed to one side and it becomes a funky nightspot that draws a young crowd. The open-air dance floor under a clear domed ceiling is small but hopping, thanks to a DJ or live acts. Open Thursday to Saturday 10 PM—2 AM. $.

LA CASA DE LAS SIRENAS

55-5704-3345
República de Guatemala 2, Col. Centro, Mexico, D.F.
Metro: Zócalo

La Casa de las Sirenas has a wonderful tequila bar on the ground floor that stocks over two hundred varieties of the spirit. The service is excellent, the ambience more sophisticated than most *tequilerías,* and the location, right behind the cathedral, prime. Open Monday to Thursday 1 PM—11 AM, Friday and Saturday 1 PM—2 AM. $—$$$.

PASAGÜERO

55-5512-6624
Motolinía 33, Col. Centro, Mexico, D.F.
Metro: Bellas Artes

A young crowd, a hip minimalist environment, cheap beer, and a variety of music and entertainment are the calling cards of this trendy nightspot. From concerts to plays to movie nights, the vibe is ever changing. As for music, the choice ranges as DJs or live bands crank out everything from electronica to jazz. Open Thursday to Saturday 9 PM—2 AM. $.

PASAJE AMÉRICA

55-5521-4375
Avenida Cinco de Mayo 7, Col. Centro, Mexico, D.F.
Metro: Bellas Artes

The latest "in" nightspot in the very heart of the city center, Pasaje América is a funky, modern space that attracts excellent DJs and plays terrific dance music. If you want to party with the trendy crowd, this is a good place to start. And speaking of beginnings, start your night off with the namesake Pasaje América cocktail, made with Bacardi, pineapple juice, lemon juice, and coconut cream. Open Thursday to Saturday 11 PM—5 AM. $.

PLAZA GARIBALDI

Eje Central Lázaro Cárdenas and Avenida República de Honduras
Metro: Garibaldi

A favorite haunt for mariachis, tourists, and *rateros* (thieves), the plaza is also a popular nighttime destination thanks to its collection of bars. Some of these are better avoided, but these two are among the institutions that keep Garibaldi going after the sun goes down.

PULQUERÍA HERMOSA HORTENSIA
North side of the plaza

If you've never tried pulque, the liquor made from the sap of the maguey plant, this bare-bones, popular watering hole is the place to sample the strong, nutty-flavored liquor. The oldest *pulquería* in the city center even has a special pulque prayer scrawled on its wall. Open Tuesday to Saturday 10 AM–midnight. $.

TENAMPA
55-5526-6176
www.salontenampa.com
Plaza Garibaldi 12

The large paintings of mariachis on the walls, diner-style booths, and a mural celebrating Mexican cinema are the hallmarks of this legendary cantina, which has been in business since 1928. A large space with three different halls (one a private room), this is a nice place to come for a tequila, margarita, or beer, a few *antojitos,* and the songs of the mariachis. Open Sunday to Thursday until 3 AM, Saturday until 4 AM. No cover.

ZINCO JAZZ CLUB
55-5512-3369
www.zincojazz.com
Motolinía 20, Col. Centro, Mexico, D.F.
Metro: Bellas Artes

Located in what once was a bank vault is this ultracool jazz lounge. Modeled after old-fashioned underground clubs, Zinco attracts a bohemian crowd, which gathers to sip cosmos and martinis while listening to live jazz, R & B, blues, and funk. The menu is surprisingly good, ranging from ceviche to *arrachera* flank steak. Open Monday to Saturday 10 PM–3 AM. $–$$, depending on the act.

SHOPPING

ARTE MEXICANO
55-5518-0300
www.arte-mexicano.com.mx
Monte de Piedad 11, Col. Centro, Mexico, D.F.
Metro: Zócalo

You can't beat the location of this arts and crafts store, right on the Zócalo. For that privilege, you'll pay higher prices than in other places, but you'll also get good-quality products. Among the souvenirs and items you'll find here are jewelry, pottery, and other handicrafts. There's also an exhibition space and a restaurant here. Open Monday and Tuesday 8–5, Wednesday to Sunday 8–8. $–$$$$.

FONART

55-5521-0171
www.fonart.gob.mx
Avenida Juárez No. 89, Col. Centro, Mexico, D.F.
Metro: Hidalgo

One of the stores of the National Foundation for the Promotion of Handicrafts (the acronym in Spanish is FONART), this branch gives you three reasons to visit. First, it is conveniently located near the Alameda; second, there is no negotiation on prices (for those of you who hate haggling, this is a blessing); and third, it stocks a solid variety of arts and crafts from all over Mexico, including all the usual suspects (pottery, onyx figurines, textiles, and other typical items). The downside? You'll pay a premium for all the above. Open Monday to Saturday 10–7. $–$$$.

MERCADO DE ARTESANÍAS DE LA CIUDADELA

Avenida Balderas and E. Pugibet
Metro: Balderas

It's a bit of a walk from the Alameda, but La Ciudadela is colorful, fun to explore, and crammed with stalls selling everything from acoustic guitars to swizzle sticks. La Ciudadela is not the place to go for that exquisite piece of pottery, but you will find some nice pieces and a tremendous variety of inexpensive trinkets and kitschy souvenirs. One interesting specialty here is items made in Mexico City, a relative rarity in the souvenir trade. Be ready to bargain if you go. Open daily 10–6. $–$$$.

The Mercado de Artesanías La Ciudadela

MERCADO DE SAN JUAN

Corner of E. Pugibet and Buentono
Metro: San Juan de Letrán

A few highly uninteresting blocks south of the Alameda lies the San Juan Market, a large co-op of vendors. I found it disappointing and not worth going out of the way for. Unlike other markets, the vendors here were unusually aggressive (perhaps because it was a weekday and the market near deserted). English is widely spoken and there is plenty of variety, but the quality isn't consistently good and the place isn't all that interesting. Far more appealing was the nearby church and food market. Open Monday to Saturday 9–7, Sunday 9–4. $–$$$.

NACIONAL MONTE DE PIEDAD

55-5278-1800, 5278-1700
http://dns.montepiedad.com.mx
Monte de Piedad 7, Col. Centro, Mexico, D.F.
Metro: Zócalo

Am I really recommending you to a pawnshop in Mexico City? Yup. But this pawnshop, right across the street from the Catedral Metropolitana, has been helping the needy since 1775. Today, it caters to a more well-heeled crowd and specializes in secondhand jewelry, but you can also purchase art, antiques, and even cars (not the most practical souvenir). Open Monday to Friday 8:30–6, Saturday 8:30–3. $$$–$$$$.

SOMBREROS TARDAN

55-5512-3902/9162
www.tardan.com.mx
Plaza de la Constitución 7, Col. Centro, Mexico, D.F.
Metro: Zócalo

If you're looking for stylish headgear, Tardan is the place to be. From cowboy hats to fedoras, they have a huge selection, and they've been making them since 1847. Their *sombreros tejanos* are a favorite, classic style, but all their products are well made and elegant. If you're looking, they even carry graduation caps. Open Monday to Saturday 10–7. $$–$$$$.

TIENDA DEL MUSEO DE ARTE POPULAR

55-5510-2201, 5510-3133
www.map.df.gob.mx
Metro: Juárez
Revillagigedo 11, Col. Centro, Mexico, D.F.

I can make a strong case for doing your souvenir shopping at the excellent store in the lobby of the Museum of Popular Art. A new addition to the museum (it was opened in 2006), the store is not a for-profit outfit; it serves to continue the work of the museum. The items are diverse and of excellent quality, with a blend of traditional handicrafts and some interesting and unusual items. I also found the prices to be more reasonable than other, more prominent, arts and crafts stores. Open Tuesday to Sunday 10–5. $–$$$.

WEEKLY & ANNUAL EVENTS

FESTIVAL DE MEXICO EN EL CENTRO HISTÓRICO

March–April
55-5277-9697, 5277-9817, 2614-2241
http://festival.org.mx
Throughout the Centro Histórico
Metro: Zócalo

Celebrating its 25th year in 2009, the Festival de Mexico is an almost three-week-long extravaganza that brings hundreds of thousands of people to the city center. Spread over more than 60 locations, it features a variety of events ranging from performing arts to academic events. The 2009 edition included opera, dance, plays, and numerous musical acts, among other performances. $–$$$.

EL GRITO AND MEXICAN INDEPENDENCE DAY
At the Zócalo
September 15 and 16
Metro: Zócalo

To see a Mexican crowd like no other, head to the Zócalo on the night of September 15. Hundreds of thousands of people wearing the colors of the flag or traditional dress, packing flags, shaving cream, and an exuberant excess of national spirit, file into the plaza. At 11 PM on the 15th, the president appears on the balcony of the National Palace and gives the *grito* (shout), echoing but not quite repeating the words of Miguel Hidalgo, who kicked off the War of Independence. The shout is:
¡Viva México! (Long live Mexico!)
¡Viva los héroes de la patria! (Long live the heroes of the motherland!)
¡Viva la república! (Long live the republic!)
The jubilant horde below screams along and then fireworks erupt around the plaza. This is Mexico's most important national holiday, and no city celebrates with more passion and pomp than Mexico City. Free.

Noche de Alebrijes *display*

NOCHE DE ALEBRIJES
October/November
55-5510-2201
www.map.df.gob.mx
From the Zócalo to the Alameda via Cinco de Mayo and on down Paseo de la Reforma

This event has only been held since 2007, and the date isn't fixed, but it takes place toward the end of the year. Check the Web site of the Museo de Arte Popular, which produces this colorful procession of *alebrijes,* or half-animal, half-demonic whimsical creatures. Mounted on floats, they are paraded through the city center at midnight. It's a visual spectacle worth catching. Free.

DÍA DE LOS MUERTOS (DAY OF THE DEAD)
November 1 and 2
At the Zócalo
Metro: Zócalo

This two-day celebration in honor of the dead, which encompasses All Saints' Day and All Souls' Day, is my favorite in Mexico for its Tim Burton–esque gathering of skulls and elaborate altars to honor the deceased. There are many customs associated with the event, including providing food to the dead, ordering sugar skulls from local bakeries imprinted with the names of family members (alive and deceased), and parades of those iconic skeletal figurines and altars. One such parade can be seen at the Zócalo on November 2. Free.

DÍA DE LA REVOLUCIÓN (REVOLUTION DAY)
November 20
At the Zócalo
Metro: Zócalo

If Independence Day is the most revered national holiday, Revolution Day is probably the most political. Social events, civic ceremonies, rousing speeches, and parades mark the event. Free.

CHRISTMAS AND THREE KINGS DAY
December and January
Alameda Central
Metro: Bellas Artes or Hidalgo

During the Christmas season, the Alameda is beautifully adorned with Santa Claus displays, festive lights, and decorations. After the 25th, the focus changes to the Three Kings, who are generally more important than Santa throughout the Latin world. Free.

LA LAGUNILLA MARKET
Sundays
Corner of Rayón and Allende
Metro: Garibaldi

This massive flea market, held once a week on Sunday, is home to all manner of goods, from mariachi outfits to luggage to . . . well, just about anything else. The market has long been known for bargains; the tourist trade has driven costs up a bit, but not so much that you can't find a deal. Three basic rules to follow are: bargain aggressively; watch out for pickpockets; and don't wander east into the notorious neighborhood of Tepito. Open 10–7. $–$$$$.

SUNDAY CONCERTS
Sundays
At the Zócalo
Metro: Zócalo

If you want to catch a free show, join the crowds heading to the Zócalo in the afternoon. Every Sunday at 6 PM there is a free concert here.

CHAPULTEPEC AND POLANCO
You could think of Chapultepec and Polanco as the Central Park and Beverly Hills of Mexico. The analogy works on many levels. El Bosque de Chapultepec (the Chapultepec

Bosque Chapultepec

Forest) is not only the city's largest and greenest area and a popular gathering spot for families, but also home to world-class museums. Neighboring Polanco is Mexico City's ritziest neighborhood and its main destination for fine dining, exclusive shopping, and chic nightlife. With a contingent of high-end boutique and chain hotels, it's also a great place to stay, but the cultural offerings are slim.

These are pleasant, spruced-up parts of town that are among the safest places in the city. The calm, tree-lined streets of Polanco seem a world away from the chaotic bustle of the Centro Histórico. Even if you're not staying here, you should make at least one trip for its terrific restaurants. Spread over 540 acres, Chapultepec, which means "grasshopper hill" in Nahuatl, has a few must-visit cultural highlights, along with a zoo, amusement park, lakes, auditorium, theater district, castle, and a broad avenue dotted with beautiful sculptures. But there are no hotels of note in this neighborhood, and dining options are sparse. The park is so vast that it is divided into three sections, but it is the first section that will have the most value for tourists.

Chapultepec is located about 3 miles west of the Zócalo, a straight shot down Paseo de la Reforma if you're in a bus, taxi, or car. Once Reforma enters the park, it becomes a broad road with a tree-lined walkway in the middle dotted with sculptures and statues. Beyond is one of Mexico's wealthiest residential neighborhoods, Las Lomas. The metro stations that service Chapultepec and Polanco neighborhoods are Auditorio, Chapultepec, and Constituyentes for the park, and Polanco for its neighbor (however, many addresses in Polanco are a long walk from the metro station).

LODGING

CAMINO REAL POLANCO MÉXICO

55-5263-8888
www.caminoreal.com
Mariano Escobedo 700, Col. Anzures,
Mexico, D.F.
Metro: Chapultepec

Named for the Royal Road that connected
six missions in present-day California, the
Camino Real Polanco is a contemporary,
eye-catching property located on the border of the Chapultepec Park in Polanco.
True to the other properties managed by
this fine local chain, the hotel is a celebration of Mexican art and style, in this case
focusing on the modern. The Camino Real
presents a bold face to the visitor, with a
funky, swirling and sloshing fountain outside the ultramodern red, white, and yellow
building. The lobby is a sleek and stylish
multilevel space headlined by a Rufino
Tamayo mural titled *Man Facing Eternity*.

The rooms, from single-bedrooms to
the two-floor suites, are all spacious (with
ample closet space) and continue the
hotel's bright color palette and modern
décor. The public spaces include a large
open-air pool, the literally over-the-water
Blue Lounge, and the beautiful Moon
Lounge, which looks like it was imported
from Miami's South Beach. Interestingly,
the hotel's best restaurants are a departure
from its Mexican roots, but offer some
world-famous names: Le Cirque and the
China Grill. Finally, the hotel has ample
meeting space and business facilities, and
is a perennial favorite with business execu-
tives for its marriage of sophisticated
appeal, top-class amenities, and corporate-
account dining options. $$–$$$$.

CASA VIEJA

55-5282-0067
www.casavieja.com
Eugenio Sue 45, Col. Polanco, Mexico, D.F.
Metro: Polanco

Suite at Casa Vieja

This ultra-exclusive boutique hotel is indeed an "old house," located on a quiet, leafy street in Polanco, but the description is something of a simplification. A visit here is an immersion into Mexican art, folklore, and rustic luxury. The handsome, ivy-draped 19th-century mansion has just ten suites, each different and all named after a Mexican artist (except for "Lola," named for the founder of Casa Vieja). The rooms are all painted in bright colors, and come with plush beds and full kitchen with bar stool and counter. More than a hotel, it's a comfortable, refined living space that is personal, intimate, and purely Mexican. However, it is one of the pricier lodging options around, even in posh Polanco. $$$–$$$$.

FIESTA AMERICANA GRAND CHAPULTEPEC

55-2581-1500
www.fiestaamericana.com
Mariano Escobedo 756, Col. Anzures, Mexico, D.F.
Metro: Chapultepec

The flagship property of the Fiesta Americana chain, this tall glass and steel tower rises above Chapultepec Park, distinctive for its round turret and fantastic views of the forest and Chapultepec Castle. While it caters especially to business professionals, with extensive meeting, banquet, and business facilities, it's a top-class choice for any traveler. The hotel has a full-service spa and fitness center, and many of its 203 rooms have an exercise bike, a handy personal touch. Rooms and suites are comfortable and tastefully decorated, with plenty of space to spread out. If you can swing it, the Grand Club rooms offer panoramic views, access to a private lounge with complimentary daily American breakfast, nightly snacks and nonalcoholic drinks, and butler service. $$–$$$$.

HÁBITA HOTEL

55-5282-3100
www.hotelhabita.com
Presidente Masaryk 201, Col. Polanco, Mexico, D.F.
Metro: Polanco

One of the hippest and hottest hotels in Mexico City, the Hábita is minimalist chic, with design elements that are sure to please its equally hip clientele. The hotel is deceptively simple and luxurious. You could walk by without ever noticing it, and even the lobby is almost nonexistent, as the restaurant takes up most of the ground floor. The rooms are large and aesthetically bare, but the effect works with the hotel's theme. Of course, amenities like flat-screen TVs, DVD players, direct high-speed Internet dataports, low-to-the-ground beds with plush mattresses, and stylish bathrooms help. There are 36 rooms and suites in total, making this a small, intimate oasis of cool in the heart of Polanco. I also love the public spaces at the Hábita. The restaurant (named simple El Lobby) offers inventive contemporary Mexican cuisine. The rooftop has a small gym next to a secluded open-air Jacuzzi tub; a compact, artfully designed open-air heated pool along one edge, with comfy chaise lounges for sunbathers; and a cool lounge. From floor to ceiling, it's an ultramodern concept carried through with a creative use of space and plenty of style. $$–$$$$.

HOTEL NIKKO MÉXICO

55-5283-8700
www.hotelnikkomexico.com
Campos Elíseos 204, Col. Polanco, Mexico, D.F.
Metro: Auditorio

Housed in a tall tower with rounded corners that begins a small but exclusive "hotel row" in Polanco, the Nikko stays true to its Japanese roots with distinctly Asian accents, dark-wood furnishings, minimalist, contemporary touches, and the hotel's best restaurant, Benkay, a good place for classic Japanese food in a classic Japanese setting. Along with its neighbors, the Nikko is popular with business travelers and event planners, thanks to its large-capacity (745 rooms) 24-hour business center and meeting facilities. One of the hotel's strengths is its full-service fitness center, which includes a driving range, tennis courts, swimming pool, and gym. Given the price and the diversity of hotels in the D.F., the Nikko is a safe and reliable option. $$–$$$$.

JW MARRIOTT

55-5999-0000
Andres Bello 29, Col. Polanco, Mexico, D.F.
www.marriott.com
Metro: Auditorio

One of a cluster of four modern towers that straddles Polanco and Chapultepec, the JW Marriott has long enjoyed a stellar reputation, in great part because it strives to go beyond the typical hotel ambience. The lobby and rooms are a pleasant departure from chain-hotel uniformity, decorated in bright colors and full of local flavor. The hotel is architecturally unique as well, a tall building employing several geometric architectural styles that make it a distinctive landmark. Its lovely rooftop heated pool, well-equipped gym, and full-service spa round out the amenities for guests, and its business and meeting facilities make it a popular choice for business travelers. $$–$$$$.

PRESIDENTE INTERCONTINENTAL

55-5327-7700
www.intercontinental.com
Campos Elíseos 218, Col. Polanco, Mexico, D.F.
Metro: Auditorio

The large and impressive Presidente Intercontinental offers guests plenty in addition to lodging. The rooms are warm and relaxing, offering a workspace and great views of the park or the neighborhood (the suites are an opulent upgrade). One of the hotel's best assets is its dining: it boasts six completely different restaurants, including the Palm steakhouse and among the city's top choices for French and Chinese cuisine. The 24-hour fitness center was upgraded in 2005 and offers great views of the park in addition to a variety of equipment. Its 17 meeting rooms can accommodate over 1,500 people. And the large, split-level lobby is practically a destination unto itself, with a piano bar, a proper British tearoom, travel agent, tour company, ATM, florist, and newsstand, among other services. $$–$$$$.

W HOTEL MEXICO CITY

55-9138-1800
www.whotels.com/mexicocity
Campos Elíseos 252, Col. Polanco, Mexico, D.F.
Metro: Auditorio

The first and only (for now) W Hotel in Latin America, this branch of the ultrahip, ultrastylish chain has made its mark on the D.F. with its posh new digs alongside some of Polanco's most exclusive hotels. The 237-room hotel splurges on its guests as much as they need to splurge to afford a room here. The predominant colors are red, black, gray, and white, a sleek combination carried throughout the hotel. The rooms follow the latest contemporary fashion, with custom-built iPod docking stations, multijet showers (many with large soaking tubs), desk and work area, and in-room hammocks.

The W has two very happening bar/lounges, a nightclub on the terrace, a superb restaurant in Solea, and one of the best spas in Mexico City. It also places special emphasis on client service, following a philosophy of personal attention that the hotel calls "Whatever/Whenever." All in all, it's one of the most polished and trendy addresses in the city, and if you can afford the steep price, it's well worth it. $$$–$$$$.

DINING

ADONIS

55-5250-2064, 5531-6940
Homero 424, Col. Polanco, Mexico, D.F.
Metro: Polanco

A hidden local treat, Adonis is a splash of Arabia in Mexico. The elegant décor, with beautiful lamps and artwork, is Middle Eastern, and the menu predominantly Lebanese. It's an authentic and flavorful change from the norm, and you can probably dine on their fine mezes alone: try the stuffed grape leaves and hummus. If you want the full works, you can't go wrong with the grilled chicken or lamb *kafta,* and the *kibbe* (a kind of dumpling made with bulgur and stuffed with ground meat) are tasty. There is live piano music from 3 to 8 PM, but Thursday through Saturday night is the best time to come, when there is live belly dancing and an upstairs club after hours. Open Monday to Wednesday 1 PM–12 AM, Thursday to Saturday 1 PM–2 AM, Sunday 1–7 PM. $–$$.

EL BAJÍO

55-5281-8246/45
Alejandro Dumas 7, Col. Polanco, Mexico, D.F.
Metro: Auditorio

In an otherwise expensive and posh neighborhood, the colorful and homey El Bajío will take you back to the humble charm of Mexico. This is the Polanco offshoot of the original in the northern part of the city, where chef Carmen Ramirez, known as Titita, has achieved legendary fame. This branch is a clean and new space with an

Colorful basket arrangement at El Bajío

open kitchen, dominated by Mexican décor that includes a huge wall of handwoven baskets. The menu is Mexican home-cooking, with tacos, tostadas, gorditas, quesadillas, an excellent variety of soups, and other typical fare. For a truly homemade recipe, try the pork and *chicharrón* (fried pork skin) meatballs, or Titita's fine mole with chicken. Open Monday to Saturday 8 AM–11 PM, Sunday 9 AM–10 PM. $–$$.

COMO

55-5250-1596
www.restaurantcomo.com
Horacio 253, Col. Polanco, Mexico, D.F
Metro: Polanco

This cozy Italian-Argentine bistro is proof that you don't have to drop a suitcase full of

Taco Corner

While Polanco is known for its high-end gourmet restaurants, no neighborhood in Mexico comes without its taquerías, and Polanco is no exception.

El Fogoncito

Liebnitz 54, Col. Anzures, Mexico, D.F.

55-5531-6497

While this is a chain, it's much harder to find in the city than the more ubiquitous franchises, and in my opinion, it's the best of all the chains. The secret ingredient here is the Gouda cheese put in many of the tacos, and the *chicharrón de queso* (crispy-fried wafer-thin cheese slices) makes for a delicious appetizer. For your entrée, try the *barbacoa* with nopales and cheese, or the *taquitos dorados*, made with shredded chicken. This is also the most restaurant-like of the places on this list, a proper sit-down affair with plenty of ambience. $–$$. Open Sunday to Tuesday noon–2 AM, Wednesday noon–3 AM, Thursday to Saturday noon–5 AM.

El Rey Del Suadero

55-5545-0550, 5545-9374

Horacio 206, Col. Polanco, Mexico, D.F.

Metro: Polanco

When you see a line of people queuing up outside a nondescript joint late at night in ritzy Polanco, chances are the place will have good, cheap food. El Rey del Suadero (which translates to a tender cut of beef) doesn't disappoint. Steak is king here, and the three *arrachera* tacos with strips of juicy steak are heaven after a late night out. Open Monday to Wednesday 10 AM–2 AM, Thursday 10 AM–3 AM, and Friday and Saturday 10 AM–4 AM. $.

Taquería Los Parados

55-5281-2831

Newton 74, Col. Polanco, Mexico, D.F.

Metro: Polanco

As the sign proclaims, this place has been making tacos *al carbon* (grilled steak) since 1965, and even serves up rib-eye or T-bone tacos, in addition to a variety of other typical street-food fare. Try the *huaraches* (a long, flat tortilla with meat or vegetable toppings) and *gorditas* (tacos served with *pan arabe*, or pita bread). Open daily noon–1 AM. $.

El Turix

55-5280-6449

Emilio Castelar 212, Col. Polanco, Mexico, D.F.

Metro: Polanco

Turix means "dragonfly" in Nahuatl. But you won't eat insects here; instead, come for the outstanding *cochinita pibil* (slow-roasted marinated pork), which you can have on tacos, *panucho* (a crispy corn tortilla), or *torta* (sandwich). Open daily 11 AM–1 AM. $.

cash to enjoy a night out at a popular restaurant in Polanco. The Argentine side of the menu specializes in various cuts of beef, including *bife de chorizo* (rib eye), *vacío* (flank steak), and chorizo (sausage).

Among the Italian entrées are a great duck ravioli and a mix-and-match combination of pasta (fettuccine, linguini, gnocchi, and more) and sauce (chipotle, salmon, four-cheese, and a homemade

Neapolitana). After dinner, relax with a glass of wine from the well-stocked and reasonably priced cellar, and enjoy the bubbly ambience late into the night. Open daily 1 PM–2 AM. $$.

EL LOBBY

55-5282-3100
www.hotelhabita.com
Presidente Masaryk 201, Col. Polanco, Mexico, D.F.
Metro: Polanco

The rustic-chic restaurant in the lobby of the Hábita Hotel is simply called El Lobby, but the menu is anything but simple. The décor is highlighted by long mirrors and a central station where coffee, wine, cheeses, oysters and other *fruits de mer,* and charcuterie are served. The man who conceived the theme is Enrique Olivera, one of the most exciting chefs in Mexico, who is also owner and chef of nearby Pujol. At El Lobby, expect innovation: the chef plucks ideas from around the world but usually throws in a bit of Mexico: examples are the cream of mushroom with *epazote* (a local herb) and the succulent shrimp cooked in a garlic *mojo* with a cilantro risotto. For dessert, go for the pear tart with tequila ice cream. Open daily 7 AM–11 PM. $$–$$$.

LOS GIRASOLES

55-5282-3291
www.restaurantelosgirasoles.com
Presidente Masaryk 275, Upper Floor, Col. Polanco, Mexico, D.F.
Metro: Polanco

The second and newer branch of this popular local standby, Los Girasoles (the Sunflowers) specializes in *alta cocina mexicana,* or refined Mexican cuisine, but beyond the excellent food, there is much to love about this place. Many dishes on the bilingual menu carry the story of their origin, adding context and history. The décor in the Polanco branch is modern and sophisticated, with a high arc of a roof and a tall barfront. As for what to order, seafood lovers shouldn't miss the red snapper in a sweet and tangy *jamaica* (hibiscus) sauce; and the restaurant is particularly proud of what it calls Symphony in Mexican Pink, a chicken breast covered in walnut and chipotle pepper sauce. Open Monday 1–11 PM, Tuesday to Saturday 1 PM –12 AM, Sunday 1–7 PM. $$.

IZOTE

55-5280-1671/1265
Presidente Masaryk 513, Local 3, Col. Polanco, Mexico, D.F.
Metro: Polanco

Izote is one of the most acclaimed restaurants in the city, and at its helm is Patricia Quintana, one of the most acclaimed chefs in Mexico. She brings to the table a mix of passion, tremendous knowledge of her country's ancient culinary roots, and a personal philosophy about food centered on a deep respect for the soul of Mexican cooking. The two-page menu, plus added daily specials, is thoughtfully composed, and is worthy of your three-course attention. Start with the refreshing avocado tartare with cured salmon in a shallot and vanilla dressing, or with the tamale tasting plate, a perfect introduction to a Mexican staple. The four mini tamales are filled with cheese and *epazote, flor de calabaza* (squash blossom flower), *cuitlacoche* (corn fungus—much tastier than it sounds); and chicken and tomato.

To follow up, carnivores should give a long look to the mole *de Oaxaca* with duck, steamed lamb wrapped in plantain leaves with a trio of sauces, or rib-eye tacos. Seafood fans might prefer the shrimp in a *jamaica* mole. (I've also tried a divine, smoky, cocoa-crusted steak with a hibiscus mole on the specials menu, which I hope becomes a fixture.) Considering what you get, the prices are remarkably affordable. Open Monday to Saturday 1 PM–12 AM, Sunday 1–6 PM. $$–$$$.

JASO

55-5545-7476
www.jaso.com.mx
88 Newton, Col. Polanco, Mexico, D.F.

A sleek new bistro nestled into a quiet street in Polanco and barely visible from the road, Jaso is a culinary refuge well worth the pilgrimage for its innovative cuisine. The menu is eclectic, focusing on a rich balance of flavor. While it leaves Mexico behind, for the most part, it doesn't fail to impress. Dishes are prepared via *sous vide,* foams, and other cutting-edge techniques and include some brilliantly unorthodox flavor combinations by chef Jared and his wife, Sonia, who created Jaso. Examples? Try the *garra de león* ("lion's mane"), a dish of scallops arranged around a cauliflower puree; the chicken breast cooked in milk curd with a sweet pea ravioli, black truffle butter and Manchego cheese; or the cooked-to-perfection salmon in eel sauce and broccoli puree. Paired with over 520 labels of wine in the *cava,* an outstanding and knowledgeable staff, and a modern, chic décor, Jaso is a fierce newcomer to the fine dining scene. With the skills and ingredients on display so far, it's destined to be a fixture. Open Monday to Saturday 2–11 PM. $$$–$$$$.

PUERTO MADERO

55-5545-6098
Avenida Masaryk 110, Col. Polanco, Mexico, D.F.
Metro: Polanco

Among the many Argentine temples of meat in Mexico City, Puerto Madero is among the most distinguished. Located in a stately two-story space, the restaurant is usually filled with a well-dressed crowd that doesn't mind paying top dollar for excellent items from the grill (which you can walk over and check out), large sides (including an interesting take on french fries), and some tempting seafood items (try the salmon or the octopus). The service, setting, and décor confirms Puerto Madero as a fine old stalwart in Mexico's most upscale neighborhood. Open daily 1 PM–1 AM. $$$–$$$$.

PUJOL

55-5545-4111, 5545-3507
www.pujol.com.mx
Petrarca 254, Col. Polanco, Mexico, D.F.

A transcending experience, Pujol is the creation of chef Enrique Olivera—one of the boldest and most creative new chefs in the country today. The restaurant is an exercise in what is known as *cocina del autor,* or "author's cuisine," but as Enrique himself puts it, it's just the chef at play. Fortunately, his tools—the most modern techniques, organic ingredients from ancient to modern Mexico, and years of experience traveling around Mexico and learning its culinary contributions—are used to produce artistic and delicious creations. The food at Pujol takes what is known about Mexican cuisine and adds an element of whimsy and inspiration from its author. The menu keeps changing, according to season, ingredients, and the chef's design, which makes this one place where the tasting menu is almost a spur-of-the-moment culinary voyage.

I started mine with a delightfully out-of-the-box, creamy "cappuccino" of *flor de calabaza* (squash blossom) served in a clear mug with a coconut milk foam. From there I sampled crunchy *chapulines* (grasshoppers) fried in lemon, butter, and salt, and served with tortillas, guacamole, and radish, before moving on to a succulent local trout prepared with wild mushrooms, chile pasilla, and baby *elote* (corn) in a roasted onion sauce. I finished off with a deconstructed lime pie made with a meringue that took 24 hours to perfect and about five seconds to consume.

This is just an indication of the fusion of techniques, ingredients, and concepts that is the cuisine of Pujol. And then there's the wine cellar, selected with such a discerning eye it has garnered awards from *Wine Spectator* magazine for six years running. The expertly trained staff (they never need to write down your order) only complements one of the city's most irresistible dining destinations. Open Monday 1–6 PM, Tuesday to Saturday 1–11 PM. $$$–$$$$.

SOLEA

55-9138-1800
www.whotels.com/mexicocity
Campos Elíseos 252 at the W Mexico, Col. Polanco, Mexico, D.F.
Metro: Auditorio

Chef Eduardo Osuna has made sure that Solea is not just a sexy-looking restaurant in a sexy hotel. The cuisine here is nouveau Mexican delivered with considerable flair. Try the melon carpaccio, New York strip steak tacos, or duck three ways to get a sense of how this menu is composed. Seafood lovers will enjoy the steamed grouper, while anyone with an eye for dessert should go for the chocolate cake with a liquid chocolate center smothered in chile powder. Open Sunday to Tuesday 6:30 AM–12 AM, Wednesday to Saturday 6:30 AM–1 AM. $$$.

SPUNTINO

55-5281-1211
Virgilio 40, Col. Polanco, Mexico, D.F.
Metro: Auditorio

This popular Argentine bistro facing elegant Lincoln Park in Polanco is a lively and casual local hangout that seems to always draw a fun, hip crowd. Meat is king here, with a choice of grilled steaks, sausages, and chicken. There's not much fanfare to the food, but plenty of taste, and one great way to go about sampling a bit of everything is to order the *parrillada para compartir,* or shared mixed grill, which includes several cuts of beef, a perfectly grilled chicken, and roast veggies. It comes on a mini-grill that keeps the food hot while you work your way through it. Spuntino also has a decent selection of pastas and wood-burning brick-oven pizzas. Open Monday to Wednesday 9 AM–11:30 PM, Thursday to Saturday 9 AM–12:30 AM, Sunday 9 AM–8 PM. $$.

ZHEN SHANGHAI

55-5327-7756
www.intercontinental.com
Metro: Auditorio
Campos Elíseos 218 at the Presidente Intercontinental, Col. Polanco, Mexico, D.F.

After visiting the small and rather sad Chinatown in the Centro Histórico, I was, to say the least, pleasantly surprised by Zhen Shanghai. It was one of the best and most memorable meals I had in Mexico. The newest restaurant at the Intercontinental flawlessly executes flavorful and authentic Cantonese cuisine. The star of the menu is the Peking duck, which is served in two ways. It is prepared tableside (a chef was brought in from China to teach the staff exactly how to go about slicing the skin off), with the skin served in crepes and the meat presented in a lettuce wrap. Truly outstanding stuff. If you're not a duck fan, the plump jumbo shrimp with fresh vegetables is a fine choice.

But you'll really appreciate Zhen Shanghai when you know what has gone into it. Four different chefs, each with a different specialty, are in charge of their own stations: steam, wok, dim sum, and barbecue. The beautiful tea presentation, including a fine porcelain tea set, is imported from China (so are the teas), as is a special water purifier reserved just for tea. You can even find a selection of Chinese wines (the only place in Mexico to stock them) to go with your meal, part of an extensive *cava.* Add the sophisticated and tasteful Eastern décor, and you have one of the city's best restaurants. Open daily 1 PM–1 AM. $$$–$$$$.

ATTRACTIONS, PARKS & RECREATION

AWAY SPA

55-9138-1800
www.whotels.com/mexicocity
Campos Elíseos 252 at the W Mexico, Col. Polanco, Mexico, D.F.
Metro: Auditorio

The W certainly doesn't have the only spa in Mexico City, but it probably has the most posh one, and it's the only hotel in the city to boast a *temazcal,* or traditional sweat lodge, on the premises. A natural adobe dome in a chic, modern setting is a bit incongruous, but it's a great place to try an ancient ritual: you enter the *temazcal* with a shaman, who directs a meditation while pouring tea and herbs onto the heated stone center. In addition, the spa offers a wide range of facials, body and skin treatments, and massages, including many that are taken from pre-Hispanic tradition. After, relax in the pool or at the refreshing juice bar. $$$–$$$$.

Bosque Chapultepec, First Section

Bordering the Anillo Periférico, Avenida Constituyentes, Rubén Darío, and Mariano Escobedo
Metro: Chapultepec and Auditorio

The first section of Chapultepec Forest is closest to Mexico's main tourist sights, and contains the most recreational and cultural attractions. The five museums in this part of the park are covered below in the "Culture" section; in addition, you will find the following here:

MONUMENTO A LOS NIÑOS HÉROES

East of the Park at the foot of Chapultepec Castle
Metro: Chapultepec

This dramatic and somber monument to the *Niños Héroes* (Child Heroes) commemorates a pivotal moment in the Mexican-American War, when U.S. troops marched into Mexico City and engaged a battalion of Mexican soldiers at Chapultepec Castle. On September 13, 1847, when an American victory was all but assured, six young cadets aged 13 to 19 chose to give their lives to the republic rather than surrender. Their names were Juan de la Barrera, Juan Escutia, Francisco Márquez, Agustín Melgar, Fernando Montes de Oca, and

Temazcal *at Away Spa*

The Monumento a los Niños Héroes

Vicente Suárez. The last of them, Juan Escutia, is believed to have wrapped his body in a Mexican flag and thrown himself from the castle of Chapultepec to his death.

The act of courage is honored today with this memorial of six tall, white columns arrayed in a semicircle around a marble statue. In 1947, just before the 100th anniversary of the battle, President Harry Truman visited the monument and observed a moment of silence. When asked by reporters why he had stopped, the president replied: "Brave men don't belong to any one country. I respect bravery wherever I see it." Open 24/7. Free.

PARQUE ZOOLÓGICO DE CHAPULTEPEC (CHAPULTEPEC ZOO)

www.chapultepec.df.gob.mx
Metro: Auditorio
Located off Paseo de la Reforma and Calle Arquímides across from the Anthropology Museum

The Chapultepec Zoo boasts almost 2,000 animals representing over 200 species from around the world. It has been delighting locals since 1923, and is still a tremendously popular destination for *chilangos*. It's a large and well-maintained park, which can be seen on foot or aboard a small train. Next to the zoo is a botanical garden. A treat for the kids, it will also put a smile on your face since it won't cost you a penny to enter. The park is open Tuesday to Sunday 9–4:30. Free.

LAGO DE CHAPULTEPEC (CHAPULTEPEC LAKE)

Metro: Auditorio

A large, if somewhat greenish, body of water circling an island, the lake is frequently dotted with rowboats and paddleboats, available near the park entrance off Reforma. Open daily 9–5. $.

PASEO DE LA REFORMA

Metro: Auditorio

If you want to enjoy an afternoon stroll under a canopy of trees while admiring beautiful art, walk down the pedestrian median of the Paseo de la Reforma from the Auditorio station or the Museum of Anthropology toward the entrance of the park. Along the way you'll pass lovely statues and sculptures, along with the entrance to the lake, the zoo, the museum, and other attractions. Open 24/7. Free.

Bosque de Chapultepec, Second Section

West of the Anillo Periférico between Avenida Constituyentes and Paseo de la Reforma

The second part of the park is not as heavily trafficked as the first, and has plenty of secluded trails and areas accommodating strolling couples, families on a picnic, and anyone else who enjoys the outdoors. Attractions here include museums, restaurants, and Mexico City's first amusement park:

AUDITORIO NACIONAL

55-5280-9250, 55-5325-9000 (for tickets)
Paseo de la Reforma 50, Bosque de Chapultepec
Metro: Auditorio

Mexico City's main arena is a huge modern space that has played host to some of the biggest acts in the world. You can also catch live feeds here of performances of the New York Metropolitan Opera. Behind the massive auditorium is a small grouping of theaters showing a wide range of plays, all in Spanish, many of them quite good, and all inexpensive. Open Monday to Saturday 10–7, Sunday 11–6. $–$$$$, depending on performance.

Sculptures line the Paseo de la Reforma

LA FERIA, CHAPULTEPEC MÁGICO

55-5230-2121, 1-800-4624-246
www.feriachapultepec.com.mx
Metro: Constituyentes

This large and fully loaded amusement park has got it all: towering roller coasters (the newest of which is a three-loop thrill ride called, in English translation, Infinite Mountain), rides for all ages, a haunted house, go-karts, an arcade, and plenty of eateries, and it puts any park in the U.S. to shame, at least in terms of cost. If you and the family need a break from the cultural circuit, this is a fun diversion, but be warned that everything is in Spanish. Open Tuesday to Friday 10–6, Saturday 10–7, Sunday 10–8. $–$$.

PARQUE LINCOLN
Bordering Calles Emilio Castelar, Luis G. Urbina, Edgar Allan Poe, and Aristóteles in Polanco
Metro: Auditorio

My favorite small park in Mexico City is a long rectangle of greenery and art in a relaxed, restaurant-fronted section of Polanco. The sculptures here are especially beautiful, particularly an intertwined work titled (in English translation) *Shock of Conscience: Man and the Earth*. The park also has a wide, shallow pool and an aviary. Open 24/7. Free.

CULTURE

Bosque Chapultepec, First Section
Bordering the Anillo Periférico, Avenida Constituyentes, Rubén Darío, and Mariano Escobedo
Metro: Chapultepec, Auditorio, and Constituyentes

Chapultepec is home to some of the city's cultural treasures; the outstanding museum of anthropology, an 18th-century castle, and two art museums headline the list:

CASTILLO DE CHAPULTEPEC
55-50-61-9214, 5241-3100
www.castillodechapultepec.inah.gob.mx
Metro: Chapultepec

No visit to Chapultepec would be complete without a trip to Chapultepec Castle. At the crest of a hill, it is a scenic landmark that has, over time, woven itself into the history of the city. The original castle was built between 1785 and 1787 by the viceroy of New Spain. It was a military academy after the War of Independence, and the site of the infamous battle of 1847 during the Mexican-American War when the *Niños Héroes* fought to their death in defense of their country. When Maximilian became emperor, he and his wife, Carlota, made it their home, infusing it with a European identity it retains to this day. After Maximilian's ouster, it became the official residence of Mexican presidents until 1932. Finally, in 1939 it was converted into a museum by Lázaro Cárdenas.

To get to the castle, you can either enjoy the mildly strenuous uphill walk or, for a nominal fee, take a train to the gate. The castle is separated into two permanent exhibits. The former military school now houses the national history museum and contains a wealth of art, artifacts, and historical records dating from the 1500s and the clash of two civilizations. In particular, note the outstanding murals in this part of the museum. There is a room devoted to murals by Davíd Alfaro Siqueiros depicting, in vivid and stark colors, the violent transition from the Porfiriato to the revolution. Also, at the main entrance to the museum, look up for a moving mural of the last of the Niños Héroes falling to his death, wrapped in a flag.

The other part of the museum is the Alcázar, the palatial residence of Maximilian and

Sculpture in Parque Lincoln

Castillo de Chapultepec

Carlota, where opulent 19th-century furnishings can be viewed in different rooms, along with a terrific display of royal carriages. After, walk the grounds for spectacular views of Paseo de Reforma spread out before you, and take in the sculpted gardens around the castle. Open Tuesday to Sunday 9–5. $.

MUSEO DE ARTE MODERNO

55-5211-8331, 5211-8045
www.conaculta.gob.mx
Metro: Auditorio

Another fine museum in Chapultepec Park, the MAM has an expansive collection of contemporary Mexican art housed in a '60s style building. Here you'll find some outstanding work, especially from the postrevolutionary Mexican realist school, by the nation's most celebrated artists, including Diego Rivera, Davíd Alfaro Siqueiros (his *Devil in the Church* is a particularly evocative piece), José Clemente Orozco, and Rufino Tamayo. One of the museum's most famous pieces and an icon of Mexican art, *The Two Fridas* (a double-portrait of Frida Kahlo) has recently come home after a world tour. Don't forget to visit the sculpture garden outside. All descriptions are in English and Spanish. Open Tuesday to Sunday 10–5:30. $.

MUSEO DEL CARACOL

55-5061-9241
Metro: Chapultepec

On the way up to (or down from) Chapultepec Castle, the Spanish-only Museo del Caracol (Snail Museum) is a worthy stop for a visual chronicle of modern Mexican history. Named for the snail-shell shape of the building, the museum takes you on a winding tour of the country's struggle for freedom and independence in the 19th and 20th centuries through a series of dioramas. At the end of the museum you'll find, in a separate room, the Mexican Constitution. Open Tuesday to Sunday 9–4:15. $.

MUSEO NACIONAL DE ANTROPOLOGÍA

55-5553-6554/6253
www.mna.inah.gob.mx
Off Paseo de Reforma and Calzada Gandhi
Metro: Auditorio

I don't think I can say enough about Mexico City's National Museum of Anthropology. It's easily one of the best museums of its kind in the world, with a collection of pre-Hispanic art and artifacts so vast (more than 10,000 original pieces), well organized, and breathtaking that one visit alone will never be enough. Every time I have been here, I have seen something new and wondrous, from an intriguing trip into the Mayan underworld to exquisite remnants of the temples of Quetzalcoatl. It is such an extensive chronicle of indigenous history and society that you would do well to watch the introductory video in the main entrance, and then map out the rooms and cultures you want to focus on when you enter. Whichever you pick, you will see some of the best examples of pre-Columbian art in the world. The museum is bilingual, but I recommend investing in a headset to enjoy the experience in greater comfort.

The museum is also a great place to learn the difference between the cultures that made up Mesoamerica. From deities to farming practices, it does a stellar job of organizing, and celebrating, the complex history of Mesoamerica. Picking out a single piece of importance here is next to impossible, but do note the architectural marvel of the single massive pillar supporting a huge concrete overhang in the courtyard. Of all the museums in Mexico, this one should be at the top of your list. Open Tuesday to Sunday 9–7. $.

MUSEO RUFINO TAMAYO

55-5286-6519
www.museotamayo.org
Metro: Auditorio or Chapultepec

A beautiful work of modern architecture meant to house beautiful works of modern art, Museo Rufino Tamayo is a dramatic showpiece not only for the works of Rufino Tamayo, one of Mexico's most important artists, but also his eclectic collection of contemporary art, which includes Andy Warhol, Pablo Picasso, Fernando Botero, and Salvador Dalí. In addition to the permanent collection, the museum hosts interesting workshops and temporary expositions throughout the year, as well as jazz nights. Outside the museum are several sculptures and a beautiful modern garden with concrete flowerbeds crisscrossing a shallow pool. Open Tuesday to Sunday 10–6. $.

Bosque Chapultepec, Second Section

Bordering the Anillo Periférico, Avenida Constituyentes, Rubén Darío, and Mariano Escobedo
Metro: Chapultepec, Auditorio, and Constituyentes

Museo Rufino Tamayo

PAPALOTE MUSEO DEL NIÑO

55-5237-1881
www.papalote.org.mx
Metro: Constituyentes

This bright blue building houses a hands-on museum for kids that fully encourages poking, prodding, and playing with exhibits associated with science and the human body. It also boasts a state-of-the-art digital dome with which to view the universe and an IMAX theater. The museum is in Spanish. Open Tuesday, Wednesday, and Friday 9–6, Thursday 9–11, Saturday and Sunday 10–7. $.

SALA DE ARTE PÚBLICO SIQUEIROS

55-5203-5888
www.siqueiros.inba.gob.mx
Metro: Polanco

There is precious little of cultural significance to tourists in Polanco, so the former house of Davíd Alfaro Siqueiros, which he donated to the people of Mexico, is a welcome destination. Now a showcase for his work, the hall also organizes contemporary art exhibitions throughout the year. Open Tuesday to Sunday 10–6. $.

NIGHTLIFE

ÁREA

55-5282-3100
www.hotelhabita.com
Presidente Masaryk 201 at the Habita Hotel, Col. Polanco, Mexico, D.F.
Metro: Polanco

The rooftop bar at the Hábita is an open-air, late-night lounge that epitomizes the stylish minimalism of the hotel. The best seats in the house are the plush white sofas in front of the long coal-fed fireplace. The music is varied, the tapas-style menu surprisingly good, and the martinis the signature drink; sometimes movies and videos are played on a projection screen to add to the ambience. Open Thursday to Sunday until 2 AM, when the bar closes. No cover.

BAMBAATA

55-5531-5828
www.bambaata.com
Moliere 237, Col. Polanco, Mexico, D.F.
Metro: Polanco

Bambaata is a modern and sleek-looking hip-hop lounge. I particularly like the booths, which offer plenty of privacy, and the bright montage of a nighttime city skyline, along with the photo montage behind the bar, are nice touches. This is a place to relax, munch on tasty snacks and *antojitos*, and, on weekends, listen to live hip-hop bands. Open Monday to Saturday 6 PM–2 AM. No cover.

BAR FLY

55-5282-2906
Plaza Mazaryk, Presidente Masaryk 393, Col. Polanco, Mexico, D.F.

An injection of Havana in Polanco, Bar Fly draws a mixed crowd of well-to-do *chilangos* who come for the change of pace from the typical pub/lounge/club scene. The reason to be here is the excellent live bands, especially the house band, Son Acá, which plays a variety of Caribbean music. Spread over two floors, it's small but packed with people chilling out with mojitos and Latin finger foods (or, weirdly, sushi rolls), and listening to great music. Open Tuesday to Saturday from 10 PM. $–$$, depending on the band.

BUÁ

55-5282-0601
Juan Vazquez de Mella 481, Col. Polanco, Mexico, D.F.
Metro: Polanco

One of the most exclusive nocturnal addresses in Polanco, Buá caters to an elite crowd. It rewards them with a club experience that combines a sound and light spectacle with a combination of the latest English and Spanish hits and the requisite smattering of oldies. Plush lounge seating, an extensive drinks menu, and better-than-average finger foods courtesy of a nearby restaurant are among the perks. Try to go on Wednesday, when the club, along with Fashion TV, hosts a fashion show. It's among the more expensive options around, but you get what you pay for. $$

KARISMA
55-5280-1872
Campos Elíseos 219, Col. Polanco, Mexico, D.F.

A huge hit with tourists and international celebrities, thanks to its location across from the big luxury hotels in Polanco, Karisma is a visitor-friendly introduction to Mexican cantina culture. The drink-and-dine menu is multilingual and explores all of Mexico. While the interior is pleasant enough, opt for the outdoor seating, where you can people-watch and enjoy the atmosphere. Tequilas and beers are the most popular accompaniment to the local cuisine. Open daily 12 PM–2 AM. $$–$$$.

MOON BAR
55-5263-8887
www.caminoreal.com
Mariano Escobedo 700, Col. Anzures at the Camino Real Hotel, Mexico, D.F.
Metro: Chapultepec

A touch of Miami Beach in Mexico, the white-canopied outdoor cabanas equipped with waterbeds are the best seats in the house for late-night lounging. Soft lighting and the stars help set the tone at this sexy spot in the Camino Real Hotel, and the live DJ helps keep the party going. Open Wednesday to Saturday 9 PM–3 AM. No cover.

SKYYBAR
55-5545-0848
Presidente Masaryk 133, Col. Polanco, Mexico, D.F.
Metro: Polanco

This popular lounge and bar has five locations in Mexico City, and the one in Polanco attracts a yuppie crowd. Of course, a late-night sushi and carpaccio menu, wide selection of martinis, and a signature cosmopolitan drink tends to do that. The décor is focused more on style than on comfort, but the changing neon lights, long marble bar, and great music keeps the place crowded. Open Monday to Saturday 6 PM–3 AM. No cover.

SUITE VIP
55-5282-2514
Plaza Mazaryk, Presidente Masaryk 393, Col. Polanco, Mexico, D.F.
Metro: Polanco

One of the larger clubs in the neighborhood, Suite VIP is built to accommodate a crowd that loves to get on the dance floor. With Spanish and English pop, house, and hip-hop at full volume, expect to keep bumping with an active, young, and hip clientele until early morning. When you need a break, navigate to the long bar, order a sushi roll if you're in the mood, and enjoy a cocktail. Open until 4 AM or later on weekends. No cover.

SHOPPING

A word about the shops listed here: in Polanco, you'll find a vast range of American and international luxury-brand names, from Hugo Boss to Chopard, as well as more moderate labels like Puma, Lacoste, and Diesel. For the purposes of this book, I've stuck, for the most part, to Mexican designers and stores.

MARCARIO JIMÉNEZ

55-5281-7783
www.macariojimenez.com
Séneca 57, Col. Polanco, Mexico, D.F.

Jiménez was born in Guadalajara and trained in Milan, and his women's collections are graceful and feminine and incorporate a variety of themes and styles, from glam rock to punk. His men's line is sophisticated and sleek, and eminently wearable. Among his numerous awards and accolades, Jiménez was selected in 2006 by Aeromexico to design its new crew uniforms. Open Monday to Friday 10–7, Saturday 10–3. $$$–$$$$.

MARINGO

55-5281-5529
www.maringo.com.mx
Presidente Masaryk 264, Col. Polanco, Mexico, D.F.
Metro: Polanco

Catering to working women, Maringo offers a sophisticated look in well-tailored, elegant, and affordable clothing, especially business suits, and accessories. It's a popular local chain with stores around the country. Open daily 10–8:30. $$–$$$.

Pasaje Polanco

Pasaje Polanco

Presidente Masaryk 360, Col. Polanco, Mexico, D.F.
Metro: Polanco

A small and pleasant outdoor shopping center in the heart of Polanco, Pasaje Polanco has an eclectic mix of boutiques. Offering everything from adorable baby clothes to fancy pet accessories, this cute pedestrian arcade bordered by cafés and restaurants is worth a stroll and, at the least, some serious window-shopping. Here in brief are some of the boutiques you'll find:

COCO BELLO

55-5281-2923

An interesting store that stocks unique gift items, curios, and party accessories. Open daily 11:30–7. $–$$$.

HELGUERA

55-5282-1140

A nice selection of jewelry designed by Gustavo Helguera and featuring semiprecious stones. Open Monday to Saturday 11–3 and 4–8. $$–$$$$.

LA ESQUINA AZUL

55-5282-0937

Trendy and chic women's clothes focusing on a bright, fresh, and youthful style. Open Monday to Friday 11–1 and 4–7:30, Saturday until 7. $$–$$$.

LAS ARTESANALES

55-5280-9515

One of the few places in the area you can find quality arts and crafts, even though the prices are, naturally, higher than elsewhere in the city. Open Monday to Saturday 10–8, Sunday noon–8. $$–$$$$.

PARUOLO

55-5280-9179

A stylish line of Argentinean shoes for men and women. Open Monday to Saturday 11–7. $$$–$$$$.

PEPA POMBO

55-5280-1044
www.pepapombo.com

Plaza Mazaryk, Presidente Masaryk 393, Col. Polanco, Mexico, D.F.
An internationally known Colombian designer with stores in Colombia, Mexico, and the U.S., Pepa Pombo offers a look as fun and vivacious as her name. Her knitted tops, pants, and skirts are all handmade in Colombia and have a rich, detailed look and feel. Recommended for dynamic and out-of-the-box creations. Open daily 11–7. $$$–$$$$.

PINEDA COVALIN

55-5280-2179
www.pinedacovalin.com
Campos Elíseos 215, Col. Polanco, Mexico, D.F.
Metro: Auditorio

A Mexican high-fashion brand and brainchild of two contemporary designers, Pineda Covalin specializes in elegant shoes, bags, ties, and accessories. The products combine the beauty and culture of ancient and modern Mexico with expert craftsmanship and finishing. There are several stores around the world, including Miami and Arizona, and this branch is conveniently located across from the big luxury hotels in Polanco. Open Monday to Saturday 10–8, Sunday 10–2. $$$–$$$$.

PLAZA ANTARA
55-5280-1412
www.webantara.com
843 B Ejército Nacional, Col. Polanco, Mexico, D.F.
Metro: none nearby

If you visit only one shopping center in Mexico City, make it this one. You might not buy anything at Antara, the D.F.'s most exclusive mall, but you're sure to appreciate the architecture and design of the place, from its funky neon-lit entrance to the open-air center itself, with landscaped shrubs, zen-like niches, and plenty of fashionable boutiques. Among the names you'll recognize are Armani Exchange, Bebe, Kenneth Cole, and Zara. Stores open daily 11–8. $–$$$$.

TANE
55-5282-6200
www.tane.com.mx
Presidente Masaryk 430, Col. Polanco, Mexico, D.F.
Metro: Polanco

For fine (predominantly) silver and gold jewelry, Tane is among the most exclusive destinations in Mexico City. A local chain with branches all over Mexico and stores in Texas and Arizona, Tane has a distinguished name and reputation. The jewelry is artistic and understated but elegant, and the store also stocks beautiful silver objets d'art. Open Monday to Friday 10–7, Saturday 11–7. $$$–$$$$.

WEEKLY & ANNUAL EVENTS

CHARREADA
Throughout the year, usually on weekends
55-5277-8706/8710
www.nacionaldecharros.com
Av. Constituyentes 500 Puerta 4, 3a. Sección de Chapultepec, Mexico, D.F.
Metro: Constituyentes

The *charreada*, or rodeo, is a storied Mexican tradition. To check out Mexico's national sport in Mexico City, call or visit the Web site of the Asociación Nacional de Charros, which hosts *charreadas* throughout the year. The Mexican rodeo is a colorful display of skill. Riders dressed in traditional *charro*, or cowboy, clothing enter the arena to the accompaniment of mariachi bands, and undertake a series of challenges including riding and roping. A special event at any *charreada* is the *escaramuza* (skirmish), in which a team of women riders in traditional dress perform tricks and moves while riding sidesaddle. Events held throughout the year. Free or $, depending on event.

Escaramuza is a display of skill and grace Credit: Mexico Tourism Board

SWAN LAKE
Spring
Bosque de Chapultepec
55-5282-1964

A special performance in a lovely setting, Mexico's National Dance Company hosts an annual outdoor production of Tchaikovsky's *Swan Lake* at Chapultepec Park. The perform-ance takes place on the Lago Mayor, using the islands in the center of the lake as the stage. The timing of the performance varies each year, but is typically held between February and April. $$.

TIANGUIS DE POLANCO
Sunday
Between Calles Galileo and Aristóteles
It's not the biggest or the best weekly market in Mexico City, but the Tianguis at Polanco is another weekend gathering of vendors selling fresh produce, trinkets, knickknacks, and, especially, great street food. Open 9–6. $–$$.

CONDESA, ROMA, AND INSURGENTES SUR

The bohemian residential neighborhoods of Condesa and Roma present a different side of Mexico City. They are home to leafy avenues, plazas and parks, art deco architecture, pleasant cafés, hip restaurants, art galleries, and an eclectic mix of bars and clubs. Condesa used to be the "in" neighborhood in the city, before Mexico's elite moved on to other pastures, but it still retains its sense of former grandeur, and is still an expensive and sought-after part of the city to live in. Roma is similar in style but has a more blue-collar, under-developed character to it. It has lovely hidden pockets and promenades, but it also has areas that are best avoided at night. While these neighborhoods don't have the cultural richness of Chapultepec or the Centro Histórico, they are better known for their laid-back charm and hip social scene. Two outstanding boutique hotels have helped bring tourists here, but one of my favorite ways to spend a day in Condesa and Roma is to meander along its avenues, stroll around its parks, and enjoy a strong coffee at one of its fine cafes.

Dividing Condesa and Roma is Avenida Insurgentes, a long and broad avenue that is the longest in Mexico and believed to be the longest road in the world. From Condesa, Insurgentes Sur is a straight shot all the way down to the cobblestone neighborhood of San Ángel, the UNAM, and beyond. Because it quite literally cuts through such a huge part of the city, Insurgentes is home to hundreds of restaurants, businesses, and—most of all— traffic. In fact, it got so congested that a new public transportation system called the Metrobús was recently installed. The clean, efficient buses follow an exclusive lane in the

Colonia Roma

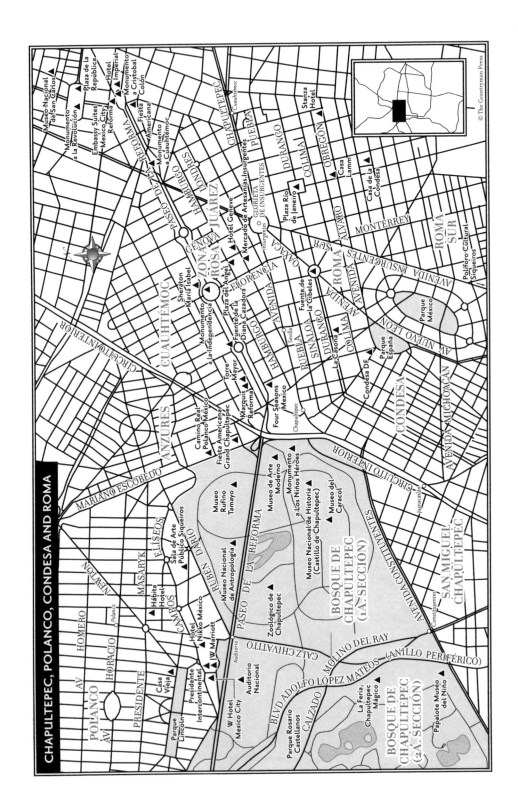

CHAPULTEPEC, POLANCO, CONDESA AND ROMA

middle of the road, with frequent platform-like stations along the way. They have replaced the careening *peseros,* at least on this road, which has helped circulation.

I once made the questionable decision of walking along Insurgentes Sur from Condesa to San Ángel. Four hours later, after crossing three nondescript neighborhoods—Nápoles, Del Valle, and Mixcoac—I had greatly enjoyed Davíd Alfaro Siqueiros's unusual Polyforum building; eaten a decent meal at La Fonda de Santa Clara; and for the most part regretted the interminable walk down the traffic-packed thoroughfare. I advise you to avoid my mistake and use Insurgentes primarily for what it is—a means to get from one place to the other.

LODGING

CASA DE LA CONDESA

55-5574-3186, 5584-3089
www.extendedstaymexico.com
Plaza Luis Cabrera 16, Col. Roma Sur,
Mexico, D.F.
Metro: Insurgentes

A bargain option for those who are staying in town for more than a few days, Casa de la Condesa provides furnished apartments with fully equipped kitchen, some with separate bedroom and living areas. Amenities include laundry service, daily housekeeping, and 24-hour concierge. The rooms are bright and functional, and while they're not the most fashionable, they're a great deal. $–$$.

CONDESA DF

55-5241-2600
www.condesadf.com
Avenida Veracruz 102, Col. Condesa,
Mexico, D.F.
Metro: Chapultepec

The Condesa DF is by far the hippest, hottest, and trendiest hotel in Condesa, and one of the most popular in Mexico City. From the exterior, you'd never know it. The vintage car parked outside the stately old mansion at the corner of a leafy park in a quiet cul-de-sac disguises the splashy modern interior. Then you walk in and notice the aquamarine-colored walls,

contemporary furnishings, and the fashion-forward clientele, and you realize why this place gets so much well-deserved hype. Set around a triangular atrium, the 40 rooms (16 of them suites with patios) aren't overly spacious, but they are stylish, with iPods, flat-screen TVs, plush beds, heavy wood screens, and contemporary furnishings.

The stylish Condesa DF fits in with the art deco style of the neighborhood

The hotel also has an excellent eclectic restaurant (with breakfast included), a relaxed rooftop bar, steam room, and hot tub. $$$–$$$$.

LA CASONA

55-5286-3001, 800-5CASONA
www.hotellacasona.com.mx
Durango 280, Col. Roma, Mexico, D.F.
Metro: Sevilla

If it's the boutique experience you're after, La Casona will delight you. This intimate hotel housed in a soft-pink 19th-century mansion exudes old-fashioned charm. Each of the 29 rooms is unique, tastefully decorated, and quite spacious. Many have warm floral patterns, and all have a writing desk in one corner, a welcome perk for a writer. The hotel has a meeting room, business center, and gym for business travelers, but it's the lovely rooms and the welcoming staff that make it stand out. $$–$$$.

STANZA HOTEL

55-5080-0900/0903
www.stanzahotel.com
Álvaro Obregón 13, Col. Roma, Mexico, D.F
Metro: Insurgentes

This large, clean, and well-appointed hotel amounts to a terrific bang for your buck. Recently updated and revamped, the Stanza has 130 large rooms that are basic but comfortable, all with cable TV, in-room safes, and free wireless Internet. The hotel also has room service, a small gym, and an even smaller business center, and at these prices, the add-ons are truly a bargain. $.

DINING

BISTROT 61

55-5219-3983
Álvaro Obregón 61, Col. Roma, Mexico, D.F
Metro: Insurgentes

A funky spot that looks like a college hangout, Bistrot 61 has the feel of a gathering place for struggling artists, intellectuals, and writers. The cheap prices, particularly a steal of a daily set menu, are reasons enough to come, but the food—classic Mexican all the way—doesn't disappoint, either. You'll find all the staples of Mexican cooking, from *chilaquiles* (fried corn tortillas covered in green or red sauce with a variety of toppings) to tacos to more-filling entrées. Open daily 8 AM–11 PM. $–$$.

CASA LAMM

55-5514-8501, 5514-8504
www.lamm.com.mx
Álvaro Obregón 99, Col. Roma, Mexico, D.F
Metro: Insurgentes

One of the most sophisticated and chic restaurants in Colonia Roma, the Casa Lamm Cultural Center's dining space, housed in a 1911 mansion, reflects the style and former grandeur of the neighborhood. In complete contrast to the turn-of-the-century opulence of the house itself, the restaurant is set off in a modern, high-ceilinged, open-air space with glass walls, on a wooden deck built over a shallow pool of water. The overall effect is quite incongruous from the rest of the mansion, but also quite pleasant. The menu is international, with Mexican flavor thrown in. For example, try the filet with *cuitlacoche,* cheese, *epazote, rajas poblanas,* and potatoes lyonnaise. I can also recommend the *esmedregal,* or cobia, bathed in an agave and lemon sauce on a bed of mashed potatoes, with a hint of chile and a side of Portobello mushrooms. Lamm stays open late into the night, and the bar makes excellent margaritas and martinis. Open Monday to Friday 8 AM–3 AM, Saturday 9 AM–3 AM, Sunday 9 AM–5 PM. $$–$$$.

CONTRAMAR

55-5514-3169, 5514-9217
Durango 200, Col. Roma, Mexico, D.F.
Metro: Sevilla

Casa Lamm

Contramar is an immensely popular neighborhood bistro that attracts fans from all over the city. The open kitchen, thatch roof, and handwoven basket lamps add to the informal, down-home vibe of the place, where seafood is the star. The restaurant keeps such limited hours that it's common to find lines waiting for a table and the chance to enjoy the excellent *pescado a la talla* (a delicious whole-grilled-fish dish), *mejillones al chipotle* (mussels in chipotle sauce) or fresh peel-and-eat shrimp. Open Monday to Friday 1:30–6:30 PM, Saturday and Sunday 1–6:30 PM. $$-$$$.

EL PATIO

55-5241-2600
Avenida Veracruz 102 at the Condesa DF,
Col. Condesa, Mexico, D.F.
www.condesadf.com

At the Condesa DF, everything is warm and sociable, and at its restaurant guests are invited to "Meet the Menu." Chances are, you'll be delighted to make El Patio's acquaintance. The food is a palate-pleasing blend of international flavors. The grilled scallops in a Thai basil curry, for example, are savory and aromatic. The Peking duck salad (no crepe) with mixed greens, orange, and baby lotus root, is an inventive twist to a Chinese classic. But my favorite dish was the melt-in-the-mouth black cod cooked in a tequila miso glaze. There's a wide variety of mixed drinks to consume before, during, or after your meal, including a basil julep, ginger cosmo, and a *horchata* martini. But save room for dessert, especially the chocolate fondant with caramel popcorn and vanilla ice cream. You can dine in the leafy open-air patio, which gets cast in a pinkish light at night, or opt for one of the rooms set off to the right, if you want a more intimate setting. Open Monday to Friday 7 AM–midnight, Saturday and Sunday 8 AM – 1 PM. $$$-$$$$.

FONDA GARUFA

55-5286-8295
www.garufa.com
Michoacán 93, Col. Condesa, Mexico, D.F.
Metro: Patriotismo

This is a quintessential Condesa eatery: casual, affordable, friendly, and with solid culinary chops. Salads, pastas, and grilled meats are the forte here; among the latter, you have a choice of Argentinean cuts, some with special sauces (try the filete Garufa, marinated in brandy and served with a red wine butter and fries); one of the few places where you'll find ostrich; as well as grilled salmon or cobia. Among the pastas, the salmon fettuccine is a good choice, as is the inaccurate but very tasty fettuccine *Hindú*, with chicken served over a cilantro, ginger, yogurt, onion, and chile sauce. For dessert,

try the *crepa de rompope*, a Mexican take on eggnog served in a crepe. Open Monday to Wednesday 8 AM–12 PM and 1 PM–12 AM; Thursday to Saturday 8 AM–12 PM and 1 PM–1 AM, and Sunday 8 AM–12 PM and 1–11 PM. $$.

FONDA DE SANTA CLARA

55-5663-0519
www.fondadesantaclara.com
Insurgentes Sur 1839, Col. Guadalupe Inn
Metro: Barranca del Muerto

Located along Avenida Insurgentes, la Fonda de Santa Clara is a reliable option for cuisine from Puebla. It also has a bright and homey ambience, with punched paper hanging in the air and a colored glass roof spilling warm hues of light around the dining hall. The traditional Poblano dishes include *chiles en nogada* (from July to

Taco Corner

El Califa

55-5271-7666/6285
Altata 22, Col. Condesa, Mexico, D.F.
It's not just the ludicrously long hours and home delivery that make this taquería popular; it's also a cut above most other joints, in both taste and price. One of its specialties is the *pollo al pastor*, a tasty chicken taco made with a marinade that is typically offered only with pork. Open daily noon to 5 AM. $.

El Greco

55-5553-5742
Michoacán 54, Col. Condesa, Mexico, D.F.
Metro: Chilpancingo
Tacos with *pan arabe*, or pita bread, are popular enough in the city, and they're the specialty at El Greco. The pork and steak tacos are also popular, and this place serves some of the best desserts you'll find at a taquería. Open Monday to Saturday 2–10 PM. $–$$.

El Güero

55-5286-4496
Amsterdam 135, Col. Condesa, Mexico, D.F.
Metro: Chilpancingo
Also known as Tacos Hola, the specialty at this tiny lunch-only joint is a bit off the taco chart: grilled liver with onions. The ready-made tacos *guisados* (with stewed meat) are excellent, and they come with rice, beans, and guacamole or cheese. Open Monday to Friday 9 AM–4 PM, Saturday 9 AM–2 PM. $.

September) and *mole poblano* (try the enchiladas with a trio of moles) are specialties, and the staff is very friendly. Open Monday to Saturday 7:30 AM –10 PM, Sunday 7:30 AM–7 PM. $$.

LA TECLA

55-5525-4920
Durango 186-A, Col. Roma, Mexico, D.F.
Metro: Insurgentes

One of Roma's best restaurants for *alta cocina Mexicana,* or refined Mexican cuisine, La Tecla is an absolute bargain for the quality and creativity of its food. It's an unpretentious spot with rustic décor, friendly service, and above all, great food. Start off your meal with a flavorful bowl of *flor de calabaza* (squash blossom) soup with *elote, rajas,* and mushrooms, or the breaded Brie with raspberry sauce and burnt chipotle. Then move on to the signature steak, with Roquefort and *cuitlacoche.* The *róbalo* (sea bass) with an *elote* tart in a poblano sauce is another terrific option. For dessert, a popular classic is the crepes with *cajeta* (caramel) and nuts. Open Monday to Saturday 1:30 PM–12 AM, Sunday 1:30–6 PM. $–$$.

LIGAYA

55-5286-6268/6380
www.ligaya.com.mx
Nuevo León 68, Col. Condesa, Mexico, D.F.
Metro: Chilpancingo

My favorite restaurant in the Condesa imparts a sense of homecoming . . . and I mean that literally. Housed in the former residence of owner Gonzalo Serrano, the restaurant retains the family home's charm and intimate atmosphere; it has purposely been left as it was to give the semblance of distinct rooms and environments (there's even a working doorbell outside), with a dedicated kids' room on weekends. At the same time, the décor is done in a chic style all its own. Grass carpeting in the main dining room, plenty of greenery and plants inside and out on the leafy terrace, and the frequent art expositions are part of its contemporary style.

All this good taste translates to the eclectic menu, which is defined by flavor rather than nationality but nonetheless has strong Mexican influences. My favorite appetizer is the simple, crunchy and tasty tostada with avocado and tuna, and among the entrées, the red snapper cooked in an orange butter sauce and chicken in black cherry sauce are creative and delicious. To finish off your meal, try the trademark Milky Way cake, a self-explanatory and decadent dessert. Ligaya has a well-deserved place among Condesa's best eateries, and there's a second branch now in Santa Fe. Open Tuesday to Saturday 2 PM–1 AM, Sunday 2–5:30 PM. $$–$$$.

THAI GARDENS

55-5256-0500/0505
www.thaigardensgroup.com
Tamaulipas 100, Col. Condesa, Mexico D.F.
Metro: Patriotismo

My favorite Thai restaurant in Mexico City offers excellent, authentic fare in a charming setting. The upstairs dining room has traditional low tables with a sunken floor for your legs and a leafy balcony. The tea menu alone is terrific, full of aromatic herbs and tropical fruit flavors. The bartender, Laura Laura Lopez, is a magician who can make you a custom cocktail to suit your personality. And as for the food, Madame Taz, one of the owners of this international mini-chain, is one of only ten chefs authorized to cook for the royal family of Thailand . . . need I say more? Open Monday and Tuesday 1–11, Wednesday 1–midnight, Thursday to Saturday 1–1, and Sunday 1–10. $$ - $$$.

ATTRACTIONS, PARKS & RECREATION

PARQUE ESPAÑA

Avenida Veracruz and Avenida Nuevo León, Col. Condesa, Mexico, D.F.
Metro: Chapultepec or Sevilla

The crescent-shaped Parque España is a verdant space with paved footpaths snaking
through it. The park's main monument is a modern sculpture of an open right hand dedicated to Lázaro Cárdenas. It is located two blocks west of the larger and more popular
Parque México. Open 24/7. Free.

PARQUE MÉXICO

Avenida México and Avenida Michoacán, Col. Condesa, Mexico, D.F.
Metro: Chilpancingo

An icon of Condesa, Parque México (whose official name is Parque San Martín), has a distinctive oval shape courtesy of its former days as a hippodrome. Today it's a leafy, sunlit
oasis where couples nestle on amusement-park-like stone benches with fake wood
canopies, and where families and joggers come out for a breath of fresh air. The park has
its share of art deco construction, including a funky clock tower, fountain, and amphi-

Fountain at Parque México

The Cibeles Fountain in Plaza Madrid

theater. Around the park you'll find buildings featuring the art deco architecture for which Condesa is famous. Open 24/7. Free.

PLAZA RÍO DE JANEIRO
Orizaba and Durango, Col. Roma, Mexico, D.F
Metro: Insurgentes

To get an introduction to and feel for Roma, get off at the Insurgentes metro stop and walk down Orizaba a few blocks to Plaza Río de Janeiro, distinguished by a completely incongruous gurgling fountain featuring a statue of David. Surrounding the plaza are some of the neighborhood's most distinctive buildings, including a redbrick house with "eyes" called the Edificio Río de Janeiro but more commonly known as la Casa de las Brujas (the House of the Witches). From here, you can direct your feet west, down Durango toward Plaza Madrid and the beautiful Cibeles Fountain, a copy of the one in front of the post office in Madrid, Spain; or you can continue walking down Orizaba (or one block parallel, on Córdoba) toward the heart of the neighborhood. Along the way, you'll see the cafés, restaurants, and art deco buildings that make this neighborhood such an attractive place to visit. Open 24/7. Free.

CULTURE

CASA LAMM

55-5514-8501, 5514-8504
www.casalamm.com.mx
Álvaro Obregón 99, Col. Roma, Mexico, D.F
Metro: Insurgentes

If for nothing else, visit the Casa Lamm just to peek inside the 1911 mansion, which is now home to a jewelry store, excellent bookstore, library, and art gallery. Casa Lamm also hosts numerous workshops and courses, but for the casual tourist, the house, books, and art are enough to make it an interesting destination. Open Tuesday to Sunday 10–6. Free.

POLÍFORO CULTURAL SIQUEIROS

55-5536-4520/4522
www.polyforumsiqueiros.com.mx
Insurgentes Sur 701, Col. Nápoles, Mexico, D.F.
Metro: San Pedro de los Piños

If there is one reason to visit Insurgentes Sur, make it the Polyforum, the unusual dodecagonal building built in the form of a diamond, covered inside and out with murals by Davíd Alfaro Siqueiros. The structure is itself an architectural jewel, but it's been called

The bold and dramatic Políforo Cultural Siqueiros

a diamond of Mexican culture for its dramatic artwork. The building's origins date to the 1960s, when one Don Manual Suárez commissioned a mural from Siqueiros with a theme taken from his experience in prison. Siqueiros began what would be his seminal work, which led to the design and creation of the Polyforum.

The exterior features 12 dramatic murals each representing a different theme, from mythology to Christ to the atom. The building faces a small garden featuring a wall on which are painted the fathers of the muralist movement. Inside, there is a café, small museum, theater, and the large hall that houses Siqueiros's *La Marcha de la Humanidad en la Tierra y hacia el Cosmos, Miseria y Ciencia* (The March of Humanity on Earth and toward the Cosmos, Misery and Science). It is the largest mural in the world, a wondrous but almost frightening and cultish depiction that reflected the artist's socialist views. The best time to visit the center is on weekends, when you can see a light show featuring a recording of Siqueiros talking about his work and his vision. Open daily 9–7. Museum is free, $ to see the hall and its mural.

NIGHTLIFE

BENGALA

55-5553-9219, 5211-4690
www.bengalabar.com
Sonora 34, Col. Roma, Mexico, D.F.

East meets West meets Mexico; that about sums up Bengala (Bengal), a stylish bar that is among Roma's most fashionable. Come here to relax and chill out amid Eastern-themed décor, with a plate of dumplings or wontons and a Bengala rum (rum with a dash of lemon and grenadine). There's a live DJ every night except Tuesday and Thursday, which is reserved for jazz. Open Tuesday to Saturday 8 PM–3 AM. No cover.

BAR IMPERIAL

55-5525-1115, 5208-0566
Álvaro Obregón 293, Col. Condesa, Mexico, D.F.
Metro: Sevilla
A newcomer to the hip Condesa bar and club scene, Bar Imperial is marvelously goth. From the floor-to-ceiling chandelier that hangs down from the second-floor VIP rooms to the red velvet lounge, it's got a great vibe. The crowd is more sexy-chic than black-lipstick, and the bar has great music, with live bands performing on the first-floor stage when a DJ is not in the house. Open Tuesday to Saturday 10 PM–4 AM. $.

CELTICS

55-5211-9081
http://celticspub.com
Tamaulipas 36, Col. Condesa, Mexico, D.F.
Metro: Chilpancingo

It's hard not to notice the large number of British and Irish pubs that have taken hold in the D.F. *Chilangos* love them, and Celtics, which stays packed late into the night, is no exception. It's got the pub atmosphere down pat, complete with the requisite Boston

Celtics jersey, dartboard, and even two stuffy armchairs by the fireplace. Drinks aren't cheap, but that never seems to stop the locals. There's another branch in Polanco. Open Monday to Saturday 1:30 PM –3:30 AM, Sunday 5 PM–3:30 AM. No cover.

CIBELES
55-5208-1456/2029
Plaza Villa de Madrid 17, Col. Roma, Mexico, D.F.
Metro: Insurgentes

This posh see-and-be-seen spot is richly decorated with plush, oversized chairs, leather daybeds and sofas, gilded mirrors, and dim lighting. Walk in and you'll feel as if you've been invited to the den of an eccentric rock star with retro tastes. The music is equally eclectic, a medley of world beats, jazz, and other sounds better suited to lounges than clubs. It's so popular that it fills up fast, but if you want to kick back with a glass of absinth, wine, or neat whiskey, and hang with Mexican celebs and elite, call ahead and reserve. Open Tuesday to Sunday 7 PM–close. No cover.

HOOKAH LOUNGE
55-5264-6275
www.hookahlounge.com.mx
Campeche 284, Col. Condesa, Mexico, D.F.
Metro: Chilpancingo

True to its name, the Hookah Lounge is an Arabesque nightspot where the draw is literally the *nargileh* (water pipe, or hookah). The best way to enjoy it is to snag a comfy booth under a hanging Turkish lamp and puff away at the flavored tobacco of your choice while you enjoy a signature cocktail and snack on the decent Middle Eastern menu. Open Monday to Saturday 1 PM–2 AM, Sunday 5–11 PM. $$.

LA PATA NEGRA
55-5211-5563/4678
www.patanegra.com.mx
Tamaulipas 30, Col. Condesa, Mexico, D.F.

A Condesa institution, La Pata Negra (the Black Foot) is a Spanish bar that has long attracted a sophisticated and well-heeled crowd intent on throwing back cocktails and feasting on the tasty and authentic tapas. Thanks to the clientele and a generally convivial atmosphere, it remains one of the most desirable nocturnal addresses in the neighborhood. The music switches up every day of the week, but Wednesday and Saturday nights are usually devoted to salsa. Open daily 1 PM–2 AM. No cover.

LA TERRAZA
55-5241-2600
Avenida Veracruz 102 at the Condesa DF, Col. Condesa, Mexico, D.F.
www.condesadf.com

A triangular-shaped rooftop sushi bar, "the Terrace" is a hip address on the lounge and bar map. It's got a relaxed vibe and is a great place to lounge on one of the giant round ottomans, order a "wokka" (a sake and vodka blend), and sample some of the most inventive sushi around. Open Sunday to Wednesday 7 PM—midnight and Thursday to Saturday 7 PM—2 AM. No cover.

LOVE
55-3096-5010
Medellín 35, Col. Roma, Mexico, D.F.
Metro: Sevilla or Insurgentes

A perennial favorite with the 20-something crowd, this overflowing club is hiply retro, from the massive disco ball to the music, a combination of '80s and '90s hits, electronica, and current pop and rock. It stays hot and happening thanks to its variety of fruity cocktails, devoted fan base, and unpretentious ambience. Plus, it stays open after much else in the neighborhood has closed. Open Wednesday to Saturday 10 PM—4 AM. $$ for men, free for women.

LUCILLE
55-5207-8441
Orizaba 99, Col. Roma, Mexico, D.F.
Metro: Insurgentes

Lucille is a laid-back pool hall with a great bar, lounge area, and cheap beers on tap, featuring a strong local brew called Cosaco. This is a fun neighborhood hangout made all the more likable for its gourmet pizzas, which feature interesting toppings like pear and goat cheese or avocado, tomato, and red onion. Open Thursday to Saturday 9 PM—2 AM. $-$$.

PM (POP MUZIK!)
Nuevo León 67, Col. Condesa, Mexico, D.F.
Metro: Chilpancingo

Never mind the cheesy name, this is a funky late-night spot with a dance floor that recalls John Travolta in his prime. The décor is retro with some modern touches, like the video wall behind the DJ. It's a large space with capacity for more than 200 people to bop to English pop and dance tunes. Open Thursday to Saturday 10 PM—3 AM. $$ (women)–$$$ (men).

SHOPPING

00: WARP
55-5211-7389
www.oowarp.com
Colima 220, Col. Roma, Mexico, D.F.
Metro: Sevilla

Looking for those hard-to-find retro Converse sneakers? Or those Adidas and Jeremy Scott originals? You'll find them at this tiny urban fashion outlet. The store has an excellent and rare collection of exclusive well-known brand-name items in addition to modern styles and a range of fun T-shirts. Open Monday to Thursday 12–8:30, Friday and Saturday 12–9, Sunday 1–8. $$-$$$$.

CHIC BY ACCIDENT

55-5514-5123
www.chicbyaccident.com
Colima 180, Col. Roma, Mexico, D.F.
Metro: Insurgentes

Visit this unique store for a few reasons. The name, for one. The furniture and home décor by designer Emmanuel Picault is a very unaccidentally chic and alluring mix of retro and modern. The artistic and inventive showroom-worthy pieces will have you calculating your weight allowance for transporting goods back across the border. Finally, check out Sexe by Accident, a collection of erotic furniture, art, accessories, and curios. If you're at all a fan of interior design, don't miss this boutique. Open Monday to Friday 10–8, Sunday 10–6. $$$–$$$$.

GALERÍAS INSURGENTES

55-5545-1000
www.galeriasinsurgentes.com.mx
Parroquía No.194, Col. Del Valle, Mexico, D.F.
Metro: Insurgentes Sur

One of the commercial highlights of Insurgentes Sur, this is a large shopping center, long and narrow and featuring French architectural accents. The shops are a mix of Mexican, American, and international labels. Open daily 11–8:30, Saturday until 9. $–$$$$.

MONSTER INSURGENTES

55-5514-2197
www.myspace.com/monsterinsurgentes
Insurgentes Sur 257-B, Col. Roma, Mexico, D.F.
Metro: Insurgentes

For a slice of the vibrant punk and rock culture in Mexico City, and its accompanying attire, head to Monster for T-shirts, apparel, and accessories, and to free your inner Marilyn Manson. Open daily 11:30–8. $–$$$.

NOT CLASSIC

55-5511-4622
www.notclassic.com
Tabasco 337 L-B, Col. Roma, Mexico, D.F.
Metro: Sevilla

Not Classic is kind of like Urban Outfitters only with local products. It carries a hodge-podge of everything from casual clothes to youthful art to esoteric items like funky laptop folios. Among the more interesting items are the gift sets, featuring age-appropriate (for 20- and 30-somethings) and sexual themes. The product names are in English, which is a plus for tourists. Open Monday to Friday 11–7, Saturday until 6. $–$$$.

TAROTS DEL MUNDO

55-1998-3301
www.tarotsdelmundo.com

Avenida Oaxaca 71, Col. Roma, Mexico, D.F.
Metro: Sevilla

Travelers with a psychic or spiritual bent will not want to miss this well-stocked shop (the name means "tarots of the world"). Inside is a remarkable selection of tarot card decks, some English, some Spanish, some vampiric—there's even a gummi bear tarot. The shop also carries books, incense, music, and medicine relating to the mystical world. Open Monday to Friday 11–8, Saturday and Sunday 11–6. $–$$$.

TREND
55-5574-4041
www.espaciocubo.com.mx
Popocatépetl 30, Col. Condesa, Mexico, D.F.
Metro: Sevilla

A small boutique that houses a collection by local label CUBO and other upcoming Mexican designers, Trend's fashions are modern, urban, and young. From flashy club wear to a line of sexy men's bathing suits, the focus is on style. Considering these are designer products, it's also affordable. Open Monday to Friday 11:30–7, Saturday 1:30–6:30. $$–$$$$.

WEEKLY & ANNUAL EVENTS

MERCADO
Weekends
Along Álvaro Obregón between Orizaba and Frontera
Metro: Insurgentes

Many neighborhoods in the D.F. are known for their weekend markets, but the Roma market is celebrated for its laid-back ambience. You can find a variety of goods here, from food to clothes to art, as you stroll along the pedestrian median on Álvaro Obregón and browse in relative peace. Open generally 10–6. $–$$$$.

PASEO DE LA REFORMA AND ZONA ROSA

Modeled after the Champs Élysées and built by Emperor Maximilian as part of his rampant Europeanization of the city, Paseo de la Reforma is the city's most regal road, cutting a broad swath through the city. Punctuated by some of Mexico City's most iconic statues, fountains, and monuments, Reforma is also home to the tallest building in Latin America, the soaring **Torre Mayor** (plans are under way to erect a new building that will surpass even this skyscraper); the stock exchange and other finance centers; and some of the city's top-class hotels and restaurants. Just off Reforma lie numerous embassies, the monolithic Monument to the Revolution, and the Zona Rosa neighborhood. The road links the Centro Histórico to Chapultepec, and then extends south until it reaches the modern neighborhood of Santa Fe.

As crowded with hotels as the avenue is, Reforma is experiencing a growth spurt with the addition of two prestigious hotels in 2009 and 2010. It is worth walking some portion of the road, if only to feel the constant throb of city life and take in the beautiful monuments. But the best way to navigate it is to hop on one of the innumerable *peseros* that run up and down the road every day.

Directly south of Reforma, between the Monumento de la Independencia and Monumento a Cuauhtémoc, is the Zona Rosa, or Pink Zone. A once-hip neighborhood, the Zona has seen better days but still offers some value to tourists. It has its worthy dining destinations, pedestrian-only streets, a fun market, and a well-known antiques district, and is a popular destination for gay locals and tourists, thanks to its hopping alternative nightlife. However, I can safely say that I found this neighborhood to be the most over-hyped in the city.

LODGING

EMBASSY SUITES MEXICO CITY–REFORMA
55-5061-3000
www.embassysuites.com
Paseo de la Reforma 69, Col. Tabacalera, Mexico, D.F.
Metro: Juárez or Revolución

The Embassy Suites Reforma

A relatively new addition to the Reforma hotel strip, the elegant glass tower of the Embassy Suites is an unmistakable landmark located off the Monumento a Cristobal Colón. The all-suite hotel is designed to offer comfort, luxury, and room to spread out. Each suite has smart, contemporary furnishings with a separate bedroom, 32" flat-screen TV, high-speed Internet access, Italian bed linens, and bathrooms outfitted with marble accents. Guests also receive a complimentary gourmet breakfast and manager's reception every evening. The hotel has a small but new gym, a cozy pool with attached whirlpool, ample business facilities, and even a Starbucks in the lobby. Its restaurant, Evita, has excellent Argintinean cuisine. $$–$$$.

FIESTA AMERICANA
55-5140-4100
www.fiestaamericana.com
Paseo de la Reforma 80, Col. Juárez, Mexico, D.F.
Metro: Juárez

This large and distinctive building facing the Monumento a Cristobal Colón is a basic business hotel. The more than 600 rooms and suites don't offer much in the way of luxury, but they are among the more affordable options on Reforma. The hotel has ample business facilities, including event space for up to 1,100 people. Its public spaces include the Lobby Bar, which has live music every night and a solid Mexican restaurant in Fonda de Santa Clara, which specializes in Poblano cuisine. $–$$.

FOUR SEASONS MEXICO

55-5230-1818
www.fourseasons.com
Paseo de la Reforma 500, Col. Juárez, Mexico, D.F.
Metro: Insurgentes

You don't need a guidebook to tell you that the Four Seasons is one of the most refined hotels in the city. Instead, I'll tell you about the little things that truly set this place apart. For one, there's its understated, almost hidden presence; the neoclassic European architecture was meant to blend in with the style and elegance of Reforma's original design. In fact, this building was built specifically to be a Four Seasons hotel in 1994. It's the only AAA Five Diamond–rated hotel in the city, and it's been given the distinction for 13 years running. Most of the tastefully decorated, spacious rooms face the handsome courtyard and have luxury amenities including LCD flat-screen TVs, bathrooms with bathtub and separate shower, and L'Occitane bath products. Another example of small extras: the in-room safe is designed to fit your laptop, and even has an outlet so you can charge your computer while it's locked away.

The hotel's courtyard restaurant, Reforma 500, is a popular power-lunch spot favored by politicians and the city's elite. The athletic club includes a full-service spa for guests only. (The Four Seasons Bangkok sent its massage therapists here for training in Thai massage.) And for the hotel's celebrity and VIP guests, there is a private elevator directly from the garage to the eighth floor, where the hotel's executive suites are located. For those who can afford it, the Presidential Suite has a royally furnished parlor that by itself is the size of three regular guestrooms. $$$$.

GRAN MELIÁ MEXICO REFORMA HOTEL

55-5128-5000
866-43MELIA (from the U.S.)
www.meliamexicoreforma.com
Paseo de la Reforma 1, Col. Cuauhtémoc, Mexico, D.F.
Metro: Hidalgo

Occupying a commanding spot just a block after Reforma leaves the Alameda Central, the AAA Four Diamond Meliá is a worthy branch of this Spanish deluxe hotel chain. An attractive pink and tinted-window building from the outside, its expansive lobby is set at the base of a soaring atrium. The hotel has close to 500 rooms furnished in a sophisticated European style, one of the better spas in the city, and a gym and indoor heated pool enclosed in a solarium. You'll have to pay for Wi-Fi access in the room, but it's free in the lobby. The Meliá's restaurants include L'Albufera, which serves excellent Spanish/Mediterranean cuisine, and Miró, which offers a terrific breakfast buffet with Mexican specialties. $$–$$$$.

HOTEL GENEVE

55-5080-0870
877-657-5799 (from the U.S)
www.hotelgeneve.com.mx
Londres 130, Col. Juárez, Mexico, D.F.
Metro: Insurgentes

Established in 1907, the venerable Geneve is an elegant, old-fashioned stalwart in the heart of the Zona Rosa. The façade and the lobby have the look of an old European luxury property, and the fabulous library, complete with rolling ladders, chandelier, and portraits, is my favorite spot in the place. Even the hotel's restaurant, a branch of the Sanborns chain, is an elegant place to dine. The 243 rooms aren't quite as glamorous, but they have detailed wood furniture from the same era and modern amenities that include wireless Internet, cable TV, in-room safe, and minibar. The Geneve has plenty of character and charm, at a great price. $$.

HOTEL IMPERIAL

55-5705-4911; 800-714-2909 (in Mexico)
www.hotelimperial.com.mx
Paseo de la Reforma 64, Col. Juárez,
Mexico, D.F.
Metro: Juárez or Hidalgo

Another example of a moderately priced hotel housed in an exceptional space, the triangular, gold-domed Hotel Imperial is a graceful turn-of-the-century building done in a classic French style. Don't expect the same panache from the rooms, which are decent but less exciting than the exterior and the polished lobby. $$–$$$.

MARQUIS REFORMA

55-5229-1200
www.marquisreforma.com
Paseo de la Reforma 465, Col. Cuauhtémoc.
Mexico, D.F.
Metro: Chapultepec

A distinct hotel done in art deco style, the pink, granite, and glass Marquis Reforma has long held a privileged reputation as a premier address for business and luxury travel. It is one of the pricier and more lavish options along Reforma. The lobby is dominated by an over-the-top, mirror-reflected statue of two Indians in mid-dance, but the richly appointed rooms have a more understated opulence and are quite comfortable. The large marble bathrooms are a treat, and living plants in the room are a welcome touch. There are a variety of suite options, with the two-floor presidential suite being the most sumptuous. The hotel has a full-service spa, a pool with a curved glass wall overlooking the city, and a large, sunlit, glass-domed gym—one of the nicer fitness centers you'll find. The business center on the mezzanine level is well staffed and well equipped, and the service at the Marquis in general is outstanding. $$$–$$$$.

SHERATON MARÍA ISABEL

55-5242-5555
www.sheratonmariaisabel.com
Paseo de la Reforma 325 Col. Cuauhtémoc,
Mexico, D.F.
Metro: Insurgentes

Inviting and spacious rooms with sink-into-sleep plush mattresses, one of the best places to see mariachis in the city, and prime location all combine to make the Sheraton María Isabel an excellent choice. The hotel sports a fully equipped business center, outdoor heated pool, small but well-stocked fitness center, and tennis courts. It has 24 meeting rooms designed to accommodate up to 1,500 people, headlined by a multitiered executive council room. But the best place to hang out at the Sheraton is without question the Jorongo Bar, which has a fantastic mariachi show every night. The staff is excellent and responsive, and the USA Times, a brief compilation of the world's newswires delivered daily to your door, is a unique and professional touch. $$–$$$.

DINING

EVITA

55-5061-3000
www.embassysuites.com
Paseo de la Reforma 69, Col. Tabacalera,
Mexico, D.F.
Metro: Juárez or Revolución

Evita's traditional Argentinian menu focuses on the parrillada, or grill. Start your meal with an empanada, or turnover, or provoleta (grilled provolone cheese) with onions and peppers. Then attack the savory, juicy steaks of various cuts, from the small *entraña* (skirt steak) to the massive *lomo Evita*, a tenderloin that tips the scales at over 2.5 pounds. If steak's not your thing, there's a selection of pastas, seafood dishes, salads, and oven-baked pizzas. The restaurant also has a well-stocked wine list. Open Monday to Saturday 12:30 PM–midnight, Sunday 12:30–10 PM. $$–$$$$.

FONDA EL REFUGIO

55-5525-8128, 5207-2732
www.fondaelrefugio.com.mx
Liverpool 166, Col. Juárez, Mexico, D.F.
Metro: Insurgentes

It's not often that a restaurant as hyped as this one lives up to its reputation, but Fonda el Refugio is a Zona Rosa institution for good reason. Set in a colonial house, it is a warm and friendly place especially favored by tourists thanks to the English-language menus and its dedication to traditional Mexican cuisine. The free guacamole and handmade tortillas are just the beginning of the goodies at the Fonda. From *gusanos de maguey* (cactus worms) served with handmade tortillas to *escamoles* (ant eggs; think of it as a different type of caviar), you'll find exotic Mexican delicacies as well as seasonal dishes like *chiles en nogada* and *romeritos* (an omelet made with the romerito herb and dried shrimp, a classic Christmas meal). Less adventurous palates will enjoy the moles, tacos, enchiladas, and other popular fare. Open daily 1–11 PM. $$.

Taco Corner

Tacuqui

Corner of Río Lerma and Río Elba, Col. Cuauhtémoc, Mexico, D.F.
Metro: Chapultepec

Right behind the Torre Mayor, this small joint offers charcoal-grilled (*al carbón*) chicken and steak tacos, served with nopales and onions, with an optional spicy chile sauce. Open Monday to Saturday 5 PM–11 PM. $.

Unnamed

Located on the island where Paseo de la Reforma meets Chapultepec Park, Col. Cuauhtémoc, Mexico, D.F.
Metro: Chapultepec

Nope, this stall with a blue awning doesn't have a name; no phone number, either; and to make it even harder to access, it's open only two days a week. But if you can make it out here, you'll be rewarded with excellent *barbacoa* (slow-cooked mutton) or *pancita* (sheep's stomach cooked with spices) tacos. Open Tuesday and Friday 6:30 AM–3 PM.

The no-name taqueria? Just call it good

World-class cuisine in an elegant setting are the hallmarks of Les Moustaches

LES MOUSTACHES

55-5533-3390, 5525-1265; 800-000-7824
www.lesmoustaches.com.mx
Río Sena 88, Col. Cuauhtémoc, Mexico, D.F.
Metro: Insurgentes

One of my favorite restaurants in the city, Les Moustaches offers an unparalleled combination of sophisticated French cuisine in an exceptional setting. The restaurant is housed in an elegant white mansion just off Reforma. Its two floors offer a variety of dining areas, from the chic, modern lower dining room beneath a lovely second-floor bay window, to the more refined chandelier-lit upper-level dining hall, with its statues, piano (the piano player plays solo during lunch and is accompanied by a violinist for dinner), and a private room.

Start your meal with a glass of Moët (no need to order by the bottle), and then dive into the terrific cuisine. You'll find a few Mexican twists to the predominantly French menu, such as the delicious abalone in a chipotle cream sauce. But purists will prefer the *escargot provençal*, foie gras, and French onion soup. For entrée, try the salt-crusted rack of lamb, sole Veronique (baked in Hollandaise sauce with skinned grapes), or duck in Dubonnet sauce. The tableside sautéed mangoes in amaretto, served in a glass with vanilla ice cream, is a flashy and tasty dessert, but I'd opt for one of their decadent soufflés (lemon, Grand Marnier, Midori, and cappuccino, are among the flavors). The service is swift, courteous, and professional, among the best I've found in the city (the champagne sorbet palate-cleanser is a refreshing extra touch). Open Tuesday to Saturday 1–11:30 PM, Sunday 1–6 PM. $$–$$$.

MERCADO INSURGENTES

Liverpool 167, Col. Juárez, Mexico, D.F.
Metro: Insurgentes

One end of this popular market is devoted to food stalls. You might even hear a mariachi playing in one corner as you dine on *tortas* (sandwiches), enchiladas, and other platters of typical Mexican fare. You can get a soup and entrée combo for a bargain (I recommend the fried liver and onion), and be on your way in no time. Outside the Londres Street entrance to the market is Jorge's stall, where a venerable lady makes a mean sandwich. Open Monday to Saturday 9:30 AM–7:30 PM, Sunday 9:30 AM–4 PM. $.

MESÓN PUERTO CHICO

55-5705-6414
José Maria Iglesias, Col. Tabacalera, Mexico, D.F.
Metro: Revolución

A pure Spanish *mesón* ("inn"), this restaurant, tucked away along an off-the-beaten-path road leading from the Monument to the Revolution, serves traditional Spanish cuisine in a lovely old house highlighted by landscape murals of the Spanish seaport Santander. This is the place to sample Old World classics like *morcilla de Burgos* (blood sausage), *pulpo a la Gallega* (boiled octopus with paprika, potato, salt, and olive oil), and *gambas al ajillo* (shrimp in garlic). Entrées include *callos a la Madrileña* (a savory tripe stew), a mouthwatering oxtail stew, and, on Thursdays, a terrific paella. Those who know Spanish food will recognize it's the real deal. Open Monday to Saturday 1–10:30 PM, Sunday 1–7:30 PM. $$–$$$.

TEZKA
55-9149-3000
www.tezka.com.mx
Amberes 78, Col. Juárez, Mexico, D.F.
Metro: Insurgentes

Founded in 1994 by famed chef Juan Mari Arzak (awarded Michelin's top three-star rating), Tezka celebrates the culinary traditions of Spain's Basque Country with outstanding creative and artistic cuisine that blends in a bit of Mexico. The menu changes frequently but always offers an inventive exploration for the palate. For example, the homemade duck ham salad combines deliciously cured slices of duck breast atop twin cakes of greens and sprouts. Then there's the architectural masterpiece of the *atún ajillo y sandía,* a filet of tuna molded into a tower, served with a square cake of what you'll swear is watermelon but is actually potato. As a final touch, the tower is filled with a delicious watermelon dressing. And finally, order the "chocolate hamburger," a deceptively simple-sounding dessert. There's a reason Tezka has won the AAA Four Diamond award seven years in a row. Open Monday to Friday 1–5 PM and 8–11 PM, Saturday 1–5 PM. $$$–$$$$.

ATTRACTIONS, PARKS & RECREATION

MONUMENTO A LA REVOLUCIÓN
Avenida de la República and La Fragua, Plaza de la República, Col. Tabacalera, Mexico, D.F.
Metro: Revolución
Ironically, the Monument to the Revolution was never meant to be a monument at all, but rather the Palacio Legislativo, housing the legislature of the now-reviled Porfiriato. Then the revolution happened, which ended Porifirio Díaz's long reign, and this colossal art deco dome was built over the spot to commemorate the bloody insurrection. It is a sober testament, with four mighty columns supporting a massive dome. Note the bas-reliefs on each corner, symbolizing independence, the reform, and agrarian and workers' laws. Within the monument lie urns containing the remains of key figures from the revolution: Francisco Madero, Venustiano Carranza, Plutarco Elías Calles, and Lázaro Cárdenas. Open 24/7. Free.

Culture

MUSEO SAN CARLOS

55-5566-8085, 55-5566-8342
www.mnsancarlos.com
Avenida Puente de Alvarado 50, Col. Tabacalera, Mexico, D.F.
Metro: Revolución

In an otherwise nondescript part of the city center, several blocks east of the Alameda Central, this beautiful neoclassic palatial mansion houses one of the most important and impressive collections of European art in Mexico. The building itself is worth the visit, with its impressive, pillared oval courtyard dotted with white marble sculptures (there's a bust here of Manuel Tolsá, the architect to whom the work is attributed). Within are extensive exhibits dating from various schools (Gothic, Renaissance, neoclassic, baroque, and Impressionist, among others) and dating from the 13th century. Among the masters on display here are Rubens, Tintorreto, Vernet, and Rodin. Open Wednesday to Monday 10–6. $, free on Sunday.

MUSEO DE LA REVOLUCIÓN

55-5566-1902, 5546-2115
www.cultura.df.gob.mx
Plaza de la República, Col. Tabacalera, Mexico, D.F.
Metro: Revolución

This Spanish-only museum, located at the foot of the Monument to the Revolution, chronicles over 80 years of history, focusing on the violent Mexican Revolution that took over a million lives and profoundly changed the course of Mexico's history. The museum is organized by historical stages, from the triumph of the liberals in the 1800s and the reign of Maximilian to the Porfiriato, and features exhibits devoted to different industries, the suffering of the labor class, and the role of women fighters in the war. The paintings by Davíd Alfaro Siqueiros and José Clemente Orozco at the end are digital copies. Open Tuesday to Sunday 9–5. $.

Nightlife

BAR JORONGO

55-5242-5555
www.sheratonmariaisabel.com
Paseo de la Reforma 325 at the Sheraton María Isabel Col. Cuauhtémoc, Mexico, D.F.

Quite possibly the best place to see mariachis in the city, Bar Jorongo lets you enjoy these ambassadors of Mexican music in the comfort, safety, and pleasant atmosphere of a posh bar and lounge. The outstanding mariachi band dominates a stage at one end, around which are organized plush leather seats around small tables. At the far end is the bar, which also has great views of the band. Sure, it's pricier than a trip to Plaza Garibaldi, but it's a great night out in style. Open Monday to Wednesday 7 PM–2:30 AM, Thursday to Saturday 8 PM–3 AM. $$.

The Monuments of Reforma

Paseo de la Reforma gets much of its grandeur from the monuments interspersed along its length from the Alameda to Chapultepec. These include:

Fuente de la Diana Cazadora—A beautiful, wide fountain topped with a nude Diana the Hunter in the act of pulling back her bow.

Monumento a la Independencia—Better known simply as *el Ángel* (the Angel), this tall column topped with a gold statue symbolizing Winged Victory is an iconic image of the city. The four seated statues at the column's base represent peace, war, law, and justice, while the white figures above it are heroes from the independence movement. The bronze, gold-coated angel currently atop the column is a replacement of the original, which was destroyed in the 1957 earthquake.

Monumento a Cuauhtémoc—Standing atop an ornate plinth and holding a spear is Cuauhtémoc, the last king of the Aztecs, honored here for defending his empire. The names of other kings and native motifs are inscribed on the pedestal.

Monumento a Cristobal Colón—Just a city block from Cuauhtémoc stands Christopher Columbus, the man who helped usher his downfall. At the base of his pedestal sit four friars.

El Caballito—Depending on your taste, you'll either love or hate this monument, located to one side of a rotary dominated by a large fountain. The name means "the little horse," but there's nothing little about this modern yellow sculpture, and some would say there's nothing too horse-like about it either.

El Ángel

The monolithic Monumento a la Revolución

IRISH WINDS PUB

55-5208-0929/0513
www.irishwindspub.com.mx
Río Tiber 71, Col. Cuauhtémoc, Mexico, D.F.
Metro: Insurgentes

A classic pub, Irish Winds has Celtic-themed décor; a kitchen serving shepherd's pie, corned beef, and other typical fare; more than 40 brands of domestic and imported beer; and a range of scotch and Irish whiskeys. Add great live rock music from Thursday to Saturday nights (with healthy participation from the crowd), and it's not surprising that this place stays packed. Open Tuesday and Wednesday 1 PM–midnight, Thursday to Sunday, 1 PM–3 AM. No cover.

LIPSTICK

55-5514-4920
Amberes 1, Col. Juárez, Mexico, D.F.
Metro: Insurgentes

A popular gay hotspot in the Zona that welcomes a mixed crowd, Lipstick has a minimalist, chic atmosphere, with a bar on the ground floor that includes a dance floor and DJ, and a pleasant terrace above for a more relaxed ambience. The house drink is the *moradito,* or vodka with grape juice, but that probably won't catch your eye as much as the drag queen hostess and the bartenders. Open Wednesday to Saturday 10 to late. $–$$.

LIVING

55-5286-0066
www.living.com.mx
Paseo de la Reforma 483, Col. Cuauhtémoc, Mexico, D.F.

Among the city's most celebrated gay clubs, Living is glamorous, outlandish, and full of pomp and overblown theatrics. Every weekend, a new themed show inaugurates a night of frenzied fun on the massive dance floor, which plays mostly trance, house, and electronica. Heterosexuals are welcome, and there's also a spot reserved for gay women. Note: at press time, Living was about to change location; check their Web site for further details. Open weekends 10–4. $$.

SHOPPING

BERSHKA

55-5207-1503
Calle Londres and Genova, Col. Juárez, Mexico, D.F.
Metro: Insurgentes

The sister store to Zara (they're owned by the same group), Bershka has a fresh look that caters to a younger crowd. The store in the Zona Rosa is one of many in Mexico, where it has caught on thanks to hip clothes at affordable prices. Open daily 9–8. $–$$$.

FONART

55-5328-5000
www.fonart.gob.mx
Paseo de la Reforma 116, Col. Juárez, Mexico, D.F.
Metro: Hidalgo

Another branch of the National Foundation for the Promotion of Handicrafts, FONART is a good place to find a solid variety of arts and crafts from all over the country, although the prices are slightly inflated. Open Monday to Saturday 10–7. $–$$$.

MERCADO INSURGENTES

Liverpool 167, Col. Juárez, Mexico, D.F.
Metro: Insurgentes

A cluster of stalls line the narrow alleys of this crafts market, where you'll find a large selection of silverware, pottery, textiles, trinkets, and other souvenirs. With more than 200 of them, it's something of a maze to navigate. Haggle like a pro if you're intent on buying something. Open Monday to Saturday 9:30–7:30, Sunday 9:30–4. $–$$$.

PLAZA DEL ÁNGEL

Between Hamburgo, Londres, and Florencia and Amberes
Metro: Insurgentes

This indoor plaza is really a series of hallways connecting high-end antiques shops. You'll find a mix of items here, including plenty of European and colonial arts and furniture, religious art, art galleries, and carpets. Some vendors flaunt museum-quality pieces, along with museum-quality attitudes. When I inquired about a lovely 18th-century writing desk, I was given its price ($20,000) with an air of dismissive finality that quickly sent me to another neighborhood. Store hours vary, generally 11–7. $$$–$$$$.

Plaza del Ángel

WEEKLY & ANNUAL EVENTS

ANTIQUES FLEA MARKET
Weekends
Between Hamburgo, Londres, and Florencia and Amberes at Plaza del Ángel
Metro: Insurgentes

The sedate and stiff antiques market at Plaza del Ángel takes on new life on the weekends, when vendors pour in to sell their wares in the public spaces between the established antiques shops. It's a good time to visit the plaza, as you'll have a chance to comparison shop and haggle. Generally open 10–5. $–$$$$.

CICLOTÓN
Sundays
Paseo de la Reforma

A family and environmental program organized by the government shuts down traffic on Reforma every Sunday, converting it into a promenade for bikers, joggers, and people out for a stroll. It's a great time to be out walking this emblematic road and checking out its many monuments. Sundays 7–2. Free.

COYOACÁN AND SAN ÁNGEL

Two picturesque neighborhoods well south of the city center, Coyoacán and San Ángel, have a character all their own. Their colonial-era architecture, cobblestone streets, romantic ambience, and legacy as an artists' haven have made them a much-loved part of the city, favored by both locals and tourists seeking a quieter, more relaxed change of pace. This is an old part of the city that, for the most part, has yet to undergo the urbanization you find everywhere else. Instead, it is an almost detached refuge, whose cultural gems (Diego Rivera and Frida Kahlo lived here; so did Leon Trotsky), sidewalk cafés, fine restaurants, and beautiful plazas will easily lure you. San Ángel, in particular, is also home to a thriving arts and crafts community, and the boutiques here are worth a visit. Just south of San Ángel is Barrio Loreto, which has a unique shopping center highlighted by a terrific museum. Note: at press time, the main plaza in Coyoacán was a dug-up mess due to a much-needed public works project. Many vendors and shopkeepers in and around the plaza were up in arms about the whole thing, but thankfully, the project was due to be completed by the time this book is released.

There are only two downsides about these neighborhoods: they aren't easily accessible by the metro, and there is a scarcity of hotels. Whichever stop you get off at (Coyoacán or Viveros for Coyoacán and M.A. Quevedo for San Ángel), be prepared to walk to get where you want to go. *Peseros* can get you closer, but you'll need to tell the driver where you're going. To make things easier on yourself, call a *sitio* taxi.

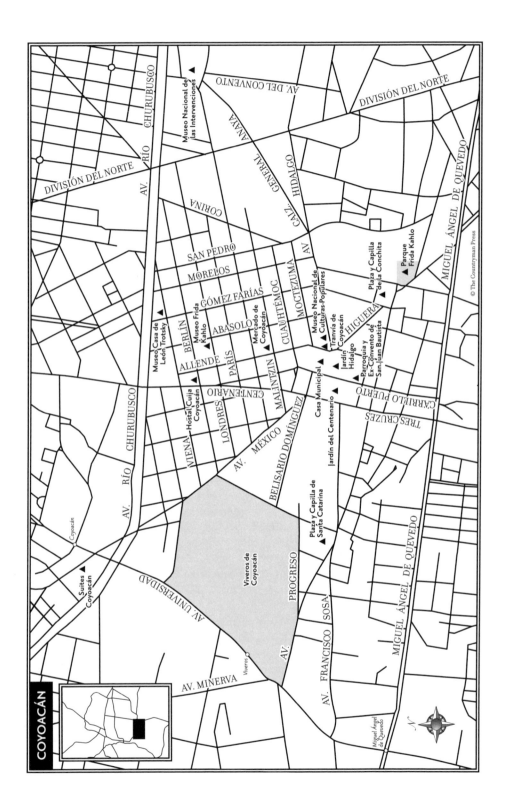

COYOACÁN

DIVISIÓN DEL NORTE
DIVISIÓN DEL NORTE

AV. DEL CONVENTO

RÍO CHURUBUSCO
ANAYA
CAIZ. HIDALGO
CALZ. GENERAL
CORINA

Museo Nacional de
las Intervenciones ▲

MIGUEL ÁNGEL DE QUEVEDO

© The Countryman Press

SAN PEDRO
MORELOS
GÓMEZ FARÍAS
ABASOLO
ALLENDE
BERLÍN
PARÍS
CENTENARIO
LONDRES
VIENA

AV. MOCTEZUMA
CUAUHTÉMOC
MALINTZIN

Museo Casa de
León Trotsky ▲

Museo Frida
Kahlo ▲

Mercado de
Coyoacán ▲

Museo Nacional de
Culturas Populares ▲

Tranvía de
Coyoacán ▲

Jardín
Hidalgo ▲

Parroquia y
Ex-Convento de
San Juan Bautista ▲

Plaza y Capilla
de la Conchita ▲

Parque
Frida Kahlo ▲

HIGUERA

Hostal Cuija
Coyoacán ▲

Casa Municipal ▲
Jardín del Centenario ▲

CARRILLO PUERTO

TRES CRUZES

AV. MÉXICO
BELISARIO DOMÍNGUEZ

AV. RÍO CHURUBUSCO

AV. UNIVERSIDAD

Coyoacán

Suites
Coyoacán ▲

Viveros de
Coyoacán

Plaza y Capilla de
Santa Catarina ▲

PROGRESO

AV. FRANCISCO SOSA

MIGUEL ÁNGEL DE QUEVEDO

AV. MINERVA
Viveros

AV.

Miguel Ángel
de Quevedo

N

Coyoacán Credit: Mexico City Tourism Board

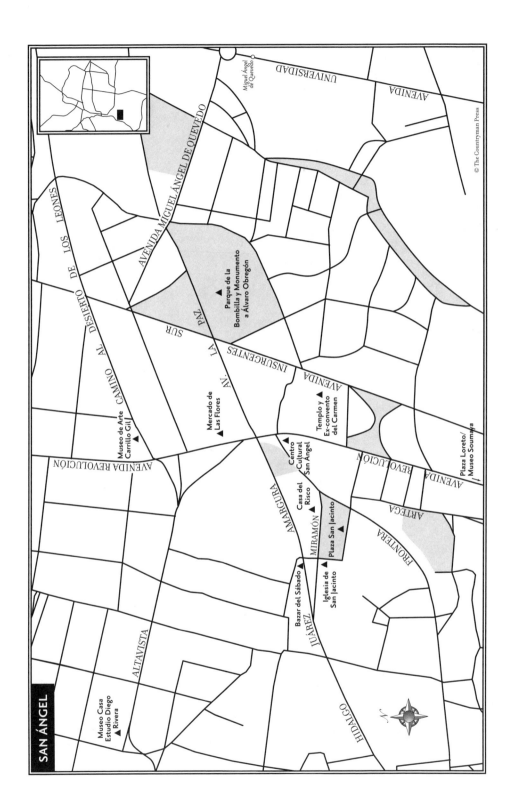

SAN ÁNGEL

Miguel Ángel de Quevedo

UNIVERSIDAD

AVENIDA

© The Countryman Press

AVENIDA MIGUEL ÁNGEL DE QUEVEDO

CAMINO AL DESIERTO DE LOS LEONES

AV. LA PAZ SUR

AVENIDA INSURGENTES

Parque de la Bombilla y Monumento a Álvaro Obregón

Museo de Arte Carrillo Gil

AVENIDA REVOLUCIÓN

Mercado de Las Flores

Templo y Ex-convento del Carmen

Centro Cultural San Ángel

AVENIDA REVOLUCIÓN

Plaza Loreto / Museo Soumaya

AMARGURA

Casa del Risco

MIRAMÓN

Plaza San Jacinto

ARTECA

FRONTERA

Bazar del Sábado

JUÁREZ

Iglesia de San Jacinto

ALTAVISTA

Museo Casa Estudio Diego Rivera

HIDALGO

N

LODGING

HOSTAL CUIJA COYOACÁN

55-5659-9310, 5539-5736
www.hostalcuijacoyoacan.com
Berlín 268, Col. del Carmen, Coyoacán,
Mexico, D.F.
Metro: Coyoacán

Given the dearth of hotels in the area, this
new hostel is a welcome option conveniently located right next to the Museo
Frida Kahlo. Basic, small, and clean, the
hostel has two private rooms, and shared
lodging sections with bunk beds for men
only, women only, and mixed groups.
There's also a laundry, communal dining
area, and garden. $.

SUITES COYOACÁN

55-5534-8353
www.suitescoyoacan.com
Avenida Coyoacán 1909, Col. Del Valle,
Mexico, D.F.
Metro: Coyoacán

Your best bet if you're determined to stay in
the area, this small, all-suite property has
modestly furnished but spacious rooms,
each with separate living and sleeping
areas, full kitchen, high-speed Internet
access, and cable TV. The hotel also offers
24-hour security, laundry and ironing services, a gym, and a small meeting room.
Considering the price and location, it's not
a bad deal at all. $$.

DINING

CAFÉ EL JAROCHO

55-5658-5029
Cuauhtémoc 134, Col. del Carmen,
Coyoacán, Mexico, D.F.
Metro: Viveros

Although it's not quite a dining destination,
I have to mention El Jarocho because to
exclude it from my review of Coyoacán

would be tantamount to sacrilege. This sto-
ried corner institution has no seating but is
the best place to get a strong cup of Mexican
coffee. Order an espresso or cappuccino
(you can also buy coffee by the half kilo or
kilo), and stand around with the rest of the
crowd who make routine pilgrimages to the
joint. Open daily 6 AM–2 AM. $.

CANTINA LA GUADALUPANA

55-5616-1253/1269
www.laguadalupanacantina.com
Avenida de la Paz 45, Col. San Ángel,
Mexico, D.F.
Metro: M.A. de Quevedo

This legendary cantina has a few locations
around the city, but the one in San Ángel is
my favorite for its prime location off Plaza
San Jacinto and authentic ambience. With
its decades-old tradition, it's a friendly
place for locals and tourists to enjoy the
typical cantina experience—order drinks,
which come with complimentary small
plates of food—or explore the extensive a la
carte menu. Open daily 1 PM–1 AM. $$.

CAPICUA

55-5616-5211, 5616-4600
www.capicua.com.mx
Avenida de la Paz 14, Col. San Ángel,
Mexico, D.F.
Metro: M.A. de Quevedo

There is a smaller branch of this tapas bar
and restaurant in Condesa, but I prefer the
leafy, airy space of the Capicua in San
Ángel, where the ambience, excellent cuisine, and superlative staff combine to make
for one of the best dining experiences in
the neighborhood. Capicua offers two
choices for visitors: you can sample from
the ample selection of tapas or choose one
or two as an appetizer and move on to the
main course. I chose the former and didn't
regret it. The tapas range from traditional
Spanish—Serrano ham (the true pork con-
noisseur will be delighted to learn that

Capicua has true Iberian ham, made from free-range, semi-wild, acorn-fed pigs), octopus a la Gallega, and *morcilla,* or blood sausage—to creative Mexican and fusion—such as *arrachera* steak with beans and chiles on toast, or the deliciously crisp and moist tuna tartar with avocado served on tostadas. For dessert, allow 25 minutes for the divine semisweet chocolate cake with banana ice cream, or enjoy the *tosta con chocolate,* a Mexican take on the chocolate-covered pretzel. Open Monday to Saturday 1 PM–1 AM, Sunday 1–6 PM. $$–$$$.

LOS DANZANTES

55-5658-6451
Plaza Jardín del Centenario 12, Col. Villa Coyoacán, Mexico, D.F.
Metro: Viveros

One of the champions of Mexican fusion cooking, Los Danzantes (the Dancers) was one of the first restaurants I was introduced to as an example of nouveau Mexican cuisine. The whimsical menu is an exploration of basic Mexican ingredients in an unusual but successful (often European-inspired) presentation. The restaurant is also known for its own bottled mezcal, the distilled spirit made from the agave plant. While the ambience inside the restaurant is nice, try to snag an outdoor table and watch the traffic flow by along the plaza. Open Sunday to Thursday noon–11 PM, weekends until 1 AM. $$–$$$.

FONDA EL MORRAL

55-5554-0298
Allende 2, Coyoacán, Mexico, D.F.
Metro: Viveros

Try and make it to the Fonda for breakfast, which is excellent and runs until 12:30 (a nice brunch option). You can choose from one of seven set menus, picking from such standbys as huevos rancheros, *huevos con chilaquiles,* and *huevos a la Mexicana.* The Fonda also offers a full range of Mexican specialties, including *pozole, cochinita pibil,*

enchiladas, and the like. Their handmade tortillas are very tasty. Open daily 7:30 AM–10 PM. $$.

FONDA SAN ÁNGEL

55-5550-1641
www.fondasanangel.com.mx
Plaza San Jacinto 3, Col. San Ángel, Mexico, D.F.
Metro: M.A. de Quevedo

In the very heart of San Ángel, this colorful institution has been consistently solid for 20 years. An extremely popular restaurant with tourists and locals, the Fonda combines a lovely colonial setting and bright décor with delicious Mexican cuisine. Try the *nopales* salad or share a few *antojitos* as an appetizer. For your entrée, the chiles rellenos (especially *cuitlacoche* and shrimp) are delicious. Meat is big on the menu, with a tender *arrachera,* an ample *tampiqueña* platter (steak served with grilled strips of poblano chile, beans, and slices of white cheese), and a mix-and-match option of steak with a variety of sauces. The pleasant outdoor seating under a large canopy is the best place to be, especially as the roving mariachi band can get a bit loud inside. Open Monday to Saturday 9 AM–midnight, Sunday 10 AM–9 PM. $$–$$$.

JARDÍN DEL PULPO

Malintzin 89 at Mercado Coyoacán
Metro: Viveros

I was going to mention Mercado Coyoacán in general for its cluster of *marisquerías,* or casual seafood eateries, located just a few blocks north of Coyoacán's central Plaza Hidalgo. But I had to give the colorful Jardín del Pulpo (Octopus Garden) its own place in the sun. So do hordes of other people who swarm here on weekends. From biting-fresh ceviches to whole roasted fish, the seafood here is simply prepared, tasty, and cheap. You can even get paella and fish and chips. Open daily until 6 PM. $–$$.

PAXIA

55-5550-8355
www.paxia.com.mx
Avenida de la Paz 47, Col. San Ángel,
Mexico, D.F.
Metro: M.A. de Quevedo

If it's not the best restaurant in San Ángel, it's certainly in the top three, and among the elite in the city. Paxia, which means "peace" in Nahuatl, is an example of Mexican cuisine at its most refined. Start your meal with a Paxia original, the *lotería* (lottery), which is a tasting menu of tequilas and mescals. It's the perfect introduction to Mexican liquor, and it's beautifully presented in a custom-crafted wooden setting.

The menu is pure Mexican, but in a nod to nouveau cuisine, Chef Daniel Ovadía adds an ever-changing selection of specials that reinterpret traditional recipes. Take his version of the classic *Budín Azteca,* a savory *mille feuille* tart with chicken, tortilla, butter, and mushroom. Chef Ovadía substitutes duck for chicken, black truffle for mushroom, and foie gras for butter, creating a sumptuous, decadent dish. His more traditional *cochinita pibil* is marinated for 18 hours before being slow-cooked to succulent perfection. Also, check out his rotating red, white, and green color-themed tasting menus, an inventive way to sample several dishes. You'll also find some unique moles here, including one made with seven fruits that lends a distinct flavor to the recipe. Sublime cuisine in an artful presentation makes Paxia a destination for gourmets and gourmands. It's pricey, but more than worth it. Open Monday to Thursday 1–11 PM, Friday and Saturday 1 PM–1 AM. $$–$$$$.

SAKS

55-5616-1601
www.saks.com.mx
Plaza San Jacinto 9, Col. San Ángel, Mexico, D.F.
Metro: M.A. de Quevedo

Saks is one of my favorite places in San Ángel, a beautifully converted mansion with outdoor seating, a pleasant staff, and an emphasis on healthy, flavorful food. Saks offers two great dining areas: the indoor courtyard or the outdoor, streetside tables. Either way, you'll have access to bands of mariachis who pass through periodically, keeping the atmosphere lively. But the food is what sets this chain (the original is in Insurgentes Sur) apart. Saks's mantra is *lo más natural,* or "the most natural," and the menu verifies it with fresh, organic foods prepared simply and with plenty of flavor. If you're on a diet, the *nopales*

Taco Corner

El Chupacabras

Churubusco and Coyoacán, Col. Coyoacán

A great name (*chupacabras,* literally "goat sucker," is a mythical beast) and the great taste of steak, cecina, and chorizo make this place a longtime hit. Throw in some nopales, fried onions, and beans, and you've got a small but delectable meal. Open Sunday to Thursday 7 AM–3 PM, weekends 24 hours. $.

Plaza Hidalgo

There are no set hours, but you can almost always find decent taquerías around Coyoacán's central plaza. Near the church, there is one in particular that sells excellent *tacos de cabeza* (meat from the goat's head). $.

asados, or grilled cactus leaves with white cheese, *epazote*, and grilled onions is healthy and delicious; the salads are also crunchy-fresh and satisfying. For more hearty appetites, try the Mediterranean-inspired tuna filet over hummus or the *huachinango al horno* (grilled red snapper) in a white wine sauce with black olives, spinach, and sun-dried tomato. Saks also has its share of traditional Mexican entrées. Open Tuesday to Saturday 7:30 AM–midnight, Sunday and Monday 7:30 AM–6 PM. $–$$.

LA TABERNA DEL LEÓN
55-5616-2110, 5616-3915
www.monicapatino.com.mx
Altamirano 46 at Plaza Loreto, Col. Tizapán de San Ángel, Mexico, D.F.
Metro: M.A. de Quevedo

Even if you hate shopping with a passion, there are two reasons to make the trek south from Plaza San Jacinto along Revolución to Plaza Loreto: Museo Soumaya and La Taberna del León, the wonderful restaurant of famed local chef Monica Patiño. Set in a warm and inviting colonial home, with rich wood décor and colorful murals, the restaurant focuses on cuisine that is rich without being pretentious, creative without being confusing. So an appetizer of grilled oysters with a not-too-strong chipotle sauce, or octopus salad with pickled nopales, is more about taste combinations than culinary invention. The sea bass in a three-chile sauce is one of the signature entrées, and the balsamic-and-honey-roasted duck is a sweet-and-sour treat. Open Monday to Saturday 2–10 PM, Sunday 2–6 PM. $$–$$$.

ATTRACTIONS, PARKS & RECREATION

MONUMENTO A ÁLVARO OBREGÓN
Insurgentes and Miguel Ángel de Quevedo, Col. San Ángel, Mexico, D.F.
Metro: Viveros

In a pleasant park known as the Jardín de la Bombilla, fronting a long shallow fountain, the stately monument to General Álvaro Obregón commemorates a key figure in the Mexican Revolution. Obregón rose from the ranks of the poor to become military commander and then president of Mexico in 1920. He fought alongside Francisco Madero and, after the latter was killed, with Pancho Villa and Venustiano Carranza against Victoriano Huerta. After Huerta was ousted, Carranza and Obregón found themselves pitted against former allies Pancho Villa and Emiliano Zapata. By the end of the struggle, Obregón stood alone as the leader of his country. After a brief hiatus following his first term in office, Obregón was reelected in 1928. In July of that year, he was seated at a café in San Ángel called La Bombilla when a man came up and shot him in the face. The monument is built over the spot where he died, and inside is a statue of Obregón (missing his right arm, which he lost during a battle with Pancho Villa in 1915). Open 24/7. Free.

PLAZA HIDALGO

Between Felipe Carrillo Puerto, Caballocalco, Belisario Dominguez, and Francisco Ortega, Coyoacán
Metro: Viveros

The heart of Coyoacán is this picturesque zócalo with a second, adjacent plaza called Jardín Centenario. This is a lovely area to visit, with its bubbling fountain of frolicking coyotes, a 19th-century kiosk, the colonial-era municipal hall (which used to be one of Hernán Cortés's palaces), and the 16th-century Templo de San Juan Bautista, a former Dominican convent, framing the square. Around the plaza, a network of streets wind through the neighborhood, whose tucked-away mansions and country homes include the former residence of la Malinche, the interpreter and consort of Cortés, on Higuera Street; the home (on Londres Street) and garden (on Higuera Street) of Frida Kahlo; and, farther out, the former home of Leon Trotsky. The plaza is usually a hub of activity, especially on weekends, when vendors of all kinds gather and people lounge about, enjoying the atmosphere. Open 24/7. Free.

PLAZA SAN JACINTO

Madero and Dr. Galvez, Col. San Ángel, Mexico, D.F.
Metro: M.A. de Quevedo

Smaller and more quaint than Plaza Hidalgo, Plaza San Jacinto is an oasis of colonial architecture, fine arts, crafts, and furniture shops, and a bustling Saturday market that is one of the best in Mexico City. With its boutiques and restaurants, it is also one of the more pleasant destinations for tourists to while away a few hours. Two buildings of note here are the San Ángel cultural center, which looms over one corner, and the church of San Jacinto. Open 24/7. Free.

TRANVÍA DE COYOACÁN

55-5659-7198, 5658-4027
www.tranviadecoyoacan.com.mx
Avenida Hidalgo in front of the Museo Nacional de Culturas Populares
Metro: Viveros

These bright, old-fashioned trolleys putter around the neighborhood, offering guided tours to the neighborhood's major sites and pointing out the homes where important people live or lived. While Coyoacán is best enjoyed on foot, this isn't a bad way to get around. Tours run from Monday to Friday 10–5, Weekends 11–6.

VIVEROS DE COYOACÁN

Just off the Viveros metro stop at Avenida Universidad
Metro: Viveros

One of the larger parks in this part of the city, Viveros is a verdant area with trails and footpaths for joggers and bikers. It's a nice place for a stroll, but nothing worth going out of the way for unless you're looking for a jogging track or the park's large flower market. Open daily 6–6. Free.

CULTURE

CENTRO CULTURAL ISIDRO FABELA (CASA DEL RISCO)
www.isidrofabela.com
55-5616-2711
Plaza de San Jacinto 5 and 15, Col. San Ángel, Mexico, D.F.
Metro: M.A. de Quevedo

This 17th-century house along the edge of Plaza San Jacinto contains a museum with a small collection of Mexican baroque religious art and furniture, and European paintings including portraits of Flemish, Dutch, British, and Spanish royals. But the most interesting fixture in the center is the monumental fountain—made out of plates, tiles, bowls and other ceramics from China, Europe, and Mexico (including Talavera), mirrors, and seashells—that dominates the main courtyard. The center also hosts frequent art expositions. Open Tuesday to Sunday 10–5. Free.

MUSEO CASA ESTUDIO DIEGO RIVERA Y FRIDA KAHLO
55-5550-1518/1189
Diego Rivera and Altavista, Col. San Ángel Inn, Mexico, D.F.
Metro: Barranca del Muerto

It's a bit out of the way (the best way to get here is to hop on a *pesero* from the metro station heading south on Revolución, get off at the intersection of Altavista, and take another *pesero* to the museum), but worth it for fans of Diego Rivera and Frida Kahlo. The two unusual modern buildings built by Juan O'Gorman were the studio and workshop of

Studio of Diego Rivera

Rivera, and where he lived with wife Frida from the early '30s until his death in 1957. The museum contains notable paintings by Rivera, including a beautiful portrait of his friend Dolores del Rio, which occupies a prominent place in his studio, and a collection of large papier-mâché folkloric figures (also check out the cool bathtub mural in the bathroom). Open Tuesday to Sunday 10–6. $, free on Sunday.

MUSEO DE ARTE CARRILLO GIL
55-5550-6260
www.museodeartecarrillogil.com
Revolución 1608, Col. San Ángel, Mexico, D.F.
Metro: Barranca del Muerto

Housed in a severe gray block of a building, the Museo de Arte Carrillo Gil is one of the best centers of modern art in the city. The almost 1,800 pieces, over 1,400 of which come from the private collection of its founder, include diverse artistic expressions, from painting to lithographs to video and photography. There are works here by Mexican icons Rivera, Orozco, and Siqueiros, as well as Picasso and Paul Klee, to name just a few international masters. Open Tuesday to Sunday 10–6. $, free on Sunday.

MUSEO DEL CARMEN
55-5616-2816, 5616-1177
http://museodeelcarmen.netfirms.com
Revolución 4 y 6, Col. San Ángel, Mexico, D.F.
Metro: M.A. de Quevedo

Housed in a former Carmelite convent, this museum is worth visiting both for its collection of colonial art and the structure that contains them. The predominantly 17th- and 18th-century religious art is impressive, as is one hall of indigenous folk art depicting various dances and costumes. You can visit the bare cells with their spartan furniture as you pass through the old convent. But whatever you do, don't leave without walking down into the crypt, where you'll see a room full of intact but desiccated mummies. These were exhumed in 1916, and are in amazing, if creepy, condition. Also don't miss the sacristy, with its elaborate gilded roof and beautiful relics. Open Tuesday to Sunday 10–4:45. $.

MUSEO FRIDA KAHLO
55-5554-5999
www.museofridakahlo.org
Londres 247, Col. El Carmen, Coyoacán, Mexico, D.F.
Metro: Coyoacán

One of Mexico's most internationally celebrated contemporary artists, Magdalena Carmen Frida Kahlo y Calderón leapt into the global consciousness after Salma Hayek further immortalized her in Hollywood. Even before then, her bright blue house in Coyoacán was one of the city's most visited cultural highlights. Kahlo's life was marred by physical and emotional pain, not least of which was the widespread belief (which lasts to this day) that she had little real talent and owed everything to her more renowned husband, Diego Rivera. Her work certainly reflects her emotions: dark, defiant, vibrant, and self-reflective. The house where she was born is a microcosm of her life: personal items, paintings, letters, and, of course, her work can be found here. I particularly liked the room of letters, which contained Diego and Frida's correspondence with each other and with friends and notable personalities of the day.

Two of the letters deserve special mention: one is from Nelson Rockefeller, objecting to Rivera's intention to include Lenin in a mural Rockefeller was commissioning, and the other is Rivera's response that he would prefer to destroy his work rather than omit the Communist leader. (The mural in question can be seen at the Palacio de Bellas Artes.) The museum gives you a sense of the social circles in which the pair traveled. Pablo Neruda, Georgia O'Keefe, Henry Ford, Gertrude Stein, Leon Trotsky (one of Kahlo's supposed lovers) . . . all were in some way connected to the artists. You'll see her artwork and that of her husband's, but the museum (which is bilingual) is more about the life and times of Frida Kahlo. Open Tuesday to Sunday 10–6. $.

MUSEO LEÓN TROTSKY

55-5658-8732
Rio Churubusco 410, Col. El Carmen, Coyoacán, Mexico, D.F.
Metro: Coyoacán

In the 1920s, two men fought for control of Russia in the wake of the October Revolution: Leon Trotsky and Josef Stalin. History, of course, tells us who won this battle. Trotsky was forced to leave his homeland (his third exile), and his flight from the anti-Bolshevik purge launched by Stalin took him around the world to Turkey, Norway, and finally, Mexico City. Along the way, Trotsky escaped an assassination attempt and lost his son, his daughter and son-in-law, and his first wife. So it is not so surprising that he turned his house into a small fortress, with watchtowers, steel doors, and round-the-clock guards. Unfortunately, the security measures failed; in 1940 he was murdered (stabbed with an ice pick) by a Stalinist agent named Ramon Mercader. The room where Trotsky died has been left intact, and the museum contains many of his personal effects. Open Tuesday to Sunday 10–5. $.

MUSEO NACIONAL DE LAS CULTURAS POPULARES

55-4155-0920
www.gob.mx/wb/SFP/SFP_Museo_Nacional_de_las_Culturas_Populares
Hidalgo 289, Col. del Carmen, Coyoacán, Mexico, D.F.
Metro: Viveros

The National Museum of Popular Cultures celebrates the incredible diversity of Mexico through a variety of temporary exhibitions and fairs. These are often quite good and worth visiting. There's a beautiful *árbol de la vida* (tree of life) in the entrance, notable for its size and detail, which symbolizes the mixing of the indigenous and Hispanic races. Open Tuesday to Thursday 10–6, Friday to Sunday 10–8.

MUSEO NACIONAL DE LAS INTERVENCIONES

55-5604-0981/3723
www.inah.gob.mx
20 de Agosto and General Anaya, Col. San Diego Churubusco, Mexico, D.F.
Metro: General Alaya

To truly appreciate the battered history of this country, you need only visit the Museum of

Interventions, which chronicles the invasions Mexico has suffered throughout its existence. Another way to look at it would be to say it is a historical tribute to the Mexicans' spirit and willingness to fight for their land. From independence to successive battles against the French, Spanish, and Americans, it is a record of over 100 years of war. It is only fitting that the museum is located in a 16th-century Franciscan convent that served as a military barracks in the 19th century and was the scene of an important battle with the Americans in 1847. The museum is far from the main attractions in Coyoacán but easily accessible from the metro. Open Tuesday to Sunday 9–6. $.

MUSEO SOUMAYA
55-5616-3731/3761
www.museosoumaya.com
Avenida Revolución and Río Magdalena at Plaza Loreto, Col. Tizapán de San Ángel, Mexico, D.F.
Metro: M.A. de Quevedo

A small museum with an astounding collection of European art, Museo Soumaya is a cultural treasure given to the people of Mexico by telecommunications mogul Carlos Slim's foundation. Among the masters visible here is a jaw-dropping number of sculptures by Rodin, works by Degas, Gauguin, Dalí, Renoir, Miró, and Matisse, as well as notable works by Mexican painter Rufino Tamayo. It may be a bit out of the way, but the Soumaya packs quite an artistic punch. Open Wednesday to Monday 10:30–6:30, Friday and Saturday until 8:30. Free, guided tours $.

NIGHTLIFE

CANTINA LA GUADALUPANA
55-5616-1253/1269
www.laguadalupanacantina.com
Avenida de la Paz 45, Col. San Ángel, Mexico, D.F.
Metro: M.A. de Quevedo

There's no better place in San Ángel to spend a typically Mexican night throwing back tequilas and mezcales with the locals. Your drinks come with complimentary bites to eat, ensuring your stomach can handle just one more. . . . Open daily 1 PM–1 AM. $$.

CAPICUA
55-5616-5211, 5616-4600
www.capicua.com.mx
Avenida de la Paz 14, Col. San Ángel, Mexico, D.F.
Metro: M.A. de Quevedo

A fine restaurant during the day, the atmosphere at Capicua gradually morphs into a lounge after 8 PM. There are a few reasons to recommend it for a casual night out: the long bar in the front and comfy seating makes for a relaxed environment; the flavored martinis are made with real fruit; and then there's Capicua's specialty, the sangria. There are no less than eight varieties here. Three are reds (mixed with port, bourbon, and, of all things, chai); two are rosé (a version with cassis, and, the *cubana,* made with white rum and Midori); and three are white (hibiscus, mint, and violet). Open Monday to Saturday 1 PM–1 AM, Sunday 1–6 PM. No cover.

CLÁSICO

55-5550-7750
San Jerónimo 26, Col. San Ángel, Mexico, D.F.
Metro: M.A. de Quevedo

A retro 1980s club that will take you back to your Boy George years, Clásico lives up to its name. The interior is plush and sophisticated, and the great music ranges from the '70s to the '90s, including Spanish and English hits. The dance floor, with its Disco Fever neon-colored panels, is the club's best feature. No cover. Open Thursday to Saturday from 10 PM–2 AM.

CLICK

55-5616-0742
Altamirano 46 at Plaza Loreto Col. Tizapán San Ángel, Mexico, D.F.
Metro: M.A. de Quevedo

A chic space in the Plaza Loreto shopping center, Click is one of the few large clubs in its neighborhood. It's dimly lit, with small tables clustered around a stage, a large dance floor, and huge media screens, and its entrance is located in the basement garage, giving it a sense of exclusivity. Thursdays are themed nights, with contests and special promotions. Open Thursday to Saturday 10 PM–4 AM. $$ men, women free.

EL HIJO DEL CUERVO

55-5658-7824
Jardín Centenario 17, Col. Coyoacán, Mexico, D.F.
Metro: Viveros

A rustic and bohemian bar that's long been popular for its unpretentious ambience, El Hijo is a frequent gathering spot for a diverse crowd. The best nights to come are Tuesday, when there is a live jazz band, and Thursday, when there's a rock cover-band. If you can, snag a seat outside on the terrace. Open Monday to Wednesday 5 PM–11 PM, Thursday to Sunday 1 PM–1 AM. No cover.

MAMÁ RUMBA

55-5550-2959
Altamirano 46 at Plaza Loreto Col. Tizapán San Ángel, Mexico, D.F.
Metro: M.A. de Quevedo

A large and well-known Cuban dance hall, this is the newer branch of the one in Colonia Roma. While this one has a capacity of 450 people, it still gets packed (much like its sister), to the point where you'll be bumping elbows on the dance floor and won't find a table unless you reserve ahead of time. The live bands are terrific, and unlike the Roma branch, you can actually get into this one. Open Wednesday to Saturday 9 PM–3 AM. $–$$, depending on band.

SHOPPING

ALTAVISTA 147
www.altavista147.com.mx
Altavista 147, Colonia San Ángel Inn, Mexico, D.F.
Metro: Barranca del Muerto

As it's located right next to the Museo Estudio Diego Rivera, you might want to duck into this über-exclusive mall after the museum for a little power shopping (or power window-shopping, depending on your budget). The boutiques here include Hugo Boss, Carolina Herrera, Louis Vuitton, and, for beautiful but pricey Mexican silver and gold jewelry, Tane. Open daily 11–8. $–$$$$.

AYLLU
55-5616-4204
www.ayllumex.com
Frontera 4, Local E, Col. San Ángel, Mexico, D.F.
Metro: M.A. de Quevedo

A small boutique, Ayllu sells men's and women's clothing made of natural cloth with no artificial chemicals or colors. The men's shirts, primarily in white and off-white, are comfortable and well tailored. The store name comes from a Quechua word that means "community." Open Monday to Saturday 10–7, Sunday 11–6. $$–$$$.

MANDALA
55-5550-2131
Plaza San Jacinto 20B, Col. San Ángel, Mexico, D.F.
Metro: M.A. de Quevedo

This small store on Plaza San Jacinto stocks a line of well-made traditional clothing as well as artifacts. The colorful embroidered shirts in particular are worth the reasonable prices. Open Tuesday–Sunday 11–7. $–$$.

MERCADO DE FLORES
Avenida Revolución between La Paz and Altavista, Col. San Ángel, Mexico, D.F.
Metro: M.A. de Quevedo

I haven't tested the theory, but I hear that there is at least one stall here selling flowers at any time of day. But to see the flower market in full bloom, go during regular business hours. The aroma and bright colors alone are worth a stroll past. Hours vary, but stalls are usually open Monday to Saturday 10–7, Sunday 11–5. $–$$$.

PLAZA LORETO
55-566-3731
www.plazaloreto.com.mx
Avenida Revolución and Río Magdalena at Plaza Loreto, Col. Tizapán San Ángel, Mexico, D.F.
Metro: M.A. de Quevedo

The Mercado de Flores

A small shopping mall set in a refurbished mill and former paper factory, Plaza Loreto is architecturally more interesting, and more historic, than your typical shopping center. Most of the stores here are local brands, and it is also home to the excellent Soumaya museum, a very good restaurant in La Taberna del León, and a kids' entertainment zone that includes an animal petting station. Store hours vary. $–$$$$.

TOCA MADERA
55-5616-4748
Plaza San Jacinto 15, Colonia San Ángel, Mexico, D.F.
Metro: M.A. de Quevedo

One of the nicer furniture and crafts shops in the area, Toca Madera is set in a beautiful space on the corner of the Plaza. The items here are contemporary but explore styles from all over Mexico, and are notable for their fine quality. In addition to large pieces for the home, you can pick up a lovely, well-made souvenir. Open Monday to Friday 10–6, Saturday 10–7, Sunday 11–5. $$–$$$$.

WEEKLY & ANNUAL EVENTS

BAZAR SÁBADO
Saturdays
Plaza San Jacinto 11, Col. San Ángel, Mexico, D.F.
Metro: M.A. de Quevedo

In my opinion the best arts and crafts market in the city, the Saturday Bazaar always attracts hordes of locals and tourists, thanks to its tremendous variety of ceramics, clothing, curios, jewelry, leather goods, and decorative items. It's not the place to bargain for a discount, but it's definitely worth a visit. There's also a pleasant restaurant in the central courtyard of the bazaar. The market has informally spread beyond its enclosed borders to the rest of the plaza, where artists display their works and vendors set up shop, often selling kitschier items than what you'll find inside. Open Saturday 10–7. $–$$$$.

MERCADO DE ARTESANÍAS DE COYOACÁN
Weekends
Felipe Carillo Puerto 25, Col. Coyoacán, Mexico, D.F.
Metro: Viveros

Adjacent to the Jardín Centenario is this sprawling market that isn't quite as sophisticated in clientele or wares as the famed Bazar Sábado, but certainly cheaper and a more typical market experience. There's a great variety of handicrafts sold here, from ceramics to onyx figurines to traditional clothes. Open weekends 11–7. $–$$$.

SANTA FE

If you're a business traveler, you might be heading to Santa Fe, a relatively new business district located in the western part of the city. Far from the Centro Histórico, Santa Fe is accessible by Paseo de la Reforma and Constituyentes (the cheapest and best way to get here is to take a bus straight down Paseo de la Reforma, although it's a long ride). The area is still dealing with some major issues, most notably the lack of public transportation (traffic during rush hour is a nightmare, and there is no metro anywhere near it) and the questionable move on the part of the government to develop the area without taking care of basic infrastructure (water is trucked in daily).

Santa Fe is a showcase for cutting-edge architecture

Nevertheless, Santa Fe is worth mentioning for its incredible architecture: it's as if Mexico's most forward-thinking architects were given carte blanche to build whatever their creativity inspired. The result is a futuristic minimetropolis worthy of Japanese anime montages. With marvelously unusual buildings with marvelously appropriate nicknames (like the Torre Pantalón, or Trouser Tower, and La Lavendería, the Washing Machine), it is a modern architectural playground. There is precious little here of cultural value, but thanks to its businesses and nearby college campus, Santa Fe has some fine restaurants and hotels, a decent nightlife, and the largest mall in the country. An interesting note about the lodging: bucking the common trend, hotels in Santa Fe are crowded during the week but empty out on weekends, when businesses are closed. That being the case, steep discounts are offered for weekend stays.

LODGING

FIESTA AMERICANA AND FIESTA INN SANTA FE

55-1105-5000
www.fiestaamericana.com
Calle 3 no. 55, Col. Lomas de Santa Fe, Mexico, D.F.

Hands down Santa Fe's most beautiful and dramatic hotel, at least architecturally, the Fiesta Americana and the adjacent Fiesta Inn together form a P shape that are among the district's most unique structures. The former is the more luxurious hotel, while the lattercaters to business travelers. The Fiesta Americana has large, comfortable rooms done in a modern style to complement the rest of the building, with excellent facilities, dining, and even a hip late-night lounge. Guests of the Fiesta Inn next door pay less but have access to its ritzier neighbor. With 14 meeting rooms and a 24-hour business center, it's obviously a great business hotel, but the shuttle service to the Centro Histórico should appeal to leisure tourists as well. $–$$$$.

NH SANTA FE

55-9177-7380
www.nh-hotels.com
San Juan Salvador Agraz 44, Col. Santa Fe, Mexico, D.F.

A sleek glass tower, the NH Santa Fe is all about clean lines, modern architecture, and minimalist style. The rooms are pleasant and contemporary, and the hotel boasts not

The Torre Pantalón

one but two terrific restaurants. Its gym, with views of the district, is small but has everything you need. $$–$$$.

SHERATON SUITES SANTA FE

55-5258-8500
www.sheraton.com/suitessantafe
Guillermo Gonzalez Camarena 200, Col. Lomas de Santa Fe, Mexico, D.F.

An all-suite hotel located across from the unusual Lavandería building, the Sheraton has well-appointed rooms, many with nice touches (flat-screen TVs, marble bathrooms) and all with kitchenettes equipped with microwave and refrigerator. The hotel's gym, with steam bath and outdoor jogging track, is one of the larger and better ones in the neighborhood. A full range of business and meeting facilities is also on offer here. $$$.

DINING

PAXIA

55-2591-0429
www.paxia.com.mx
San Juan Salvador Agraz 44 at the NH Hotel,
Col. Lomas de Santa Fe, Mexico, D.F.

Located just off the NH's main entrance,
Paxia has carved out an elegantly rustic
space for itself. From the custom-made
service for the tequila and mezcal samplers,
to the combination of traditional Mexican
gastronomy and Chef Daniel Ovadía's
whimsical creations, this is one place that
pulls out all the culinary stops. He's called it
"comfort food reloaded," and it's a good way
to put it. How else would you describe a
chicken quesadilla served with a black mole
in a sugar-crusted martini glass, made for
dipping and eating? Or the *molcajete* with
carnitas made with shredded octopus
instead of the traditional shredded pork?
It's an experience to dine here, and one that
I recommend heartily. Open Monday to
Thursday 1–11 PM, Friday and Saturday
1 PM–1 AM. $$–$$$$.

ROSATO

55-1105-5000
Calle 3 no. 55 at the Fiesta Americana, Col.
Lomas de Santa Fe, Mexico, D.F.

A pleasant café in the secluded lower level
of the hotel, Rosato is a mix of Italian and
Mexican cuisine. The menu ranges from
pizza and sandwiches to fusion dishes exe-
cuted with refinement and taste. All the
bread is made in-house, always a reliable
indicator of quality, and is served with one
of four flavored butters. Try the crispy and
delicious *flor de calabaza* appetizer, stuffed
with eggplant mousse and black truffle. The
tuna tartar with couscous and yogurt is also
a delicate and tasty dish. For an entrée, the
gnocchi with mascarpone cream, nuts, and
a hint of honey is excellent. Open daily
7 AM–11 PM. $$–$$$.

NIGHTLIFE

ABSINTH BAR

55-5292-0631
Mario Pani 6, Col. Lomas de Santa Fe, Mexico, D.F.

One of my favorite bars in Mexico City, Absinth celebrates the revival of a drink that was
banned in the U.S. and still remains largely prohibited, even as it enjoys a resurgence in
Europe. It's now among the most popular drinks in Mexico City, and at this two-level bar,
you can see what you've been missing. The place has a sophisticated, retro underground
feel to it, helped by the 1920s photos, Parisian ceiling lamps, old-fashioned booths, and
Toulouse-Lautrec posters. A staircase takes you to the second floor, which has a dance
floor and a secluded area showing erotic movies. The drink of choice is the *ada verde*, or
"green fairy," which comes with a whole ritual that involves sugar being set on fire. Before
you leave, don't miss the very cool Alice-in-Wonderland-themed bathrooms. Open
Monday to Wednesday 11 AM–midnight, Thursday to Saturday 11 AM–4 AM. No cover.

BLACK DOG

55-5148-2525
Vasco de Quiroga 3900, Col. Lomas de Santa Fe, Mexico, D.F.

A classic Irish pub, Black Dog looks like it came straight from the U.K, with comfy arm-chairs around a fireplace, a large bar area with plenty of seating, and even a kids' menu. You can sit in the terrace or inside, and enjoy a Guinness or a whiskey with an authentic Irish menu to complement it. Friday and Saturday usually features live acts. Open Monday to Saturday 2 PM–3 AM. No cover.

SHOPPING

CENTRO COMERCIAL SANTA FE

55-3003-4330
www.centrosantafe.com.mx

Vasco de Quiroga 3800, Col. Lomas de Santa Fe, Mexico, D.F.
The largest shopping mall in Mexico, Centro Comercial Santa Fe has over 300 shops, a golf range, plenty of restaurants, and four department stores, including a Saks Fifth Avenue. The mall has a mix of local and international brands. Open daily 11–8, Saturday until 9. $–$$$$.

BETWEEN AND BEYOND THE NEIGHBORHOODS

While each of the above neighborhoods offers a rich and diverse experience for the tourist, there are plenty of other attractions around the city that deserve mention for their religious, cultural, or even commercial value. In one way or another, they add to Mexico's local flavor. I've grouped what I feel are the most important and interesting ones below.

Around the Centro Histórico

CENTRO ARTESANAL BUENAVISTA
Aldama 187, Col. Buena Vista, Mexico, D.F.
Metro: Buenavista

Located behind the Buena Vista suburban train station, this massive arts and crafts market, housed in a huge warehouse, sells a fantastic variety of merchandise ranging from furniture to clothes to artifacts. While it isn't as accessible as La Ciudadela or Mercado San Juan in the Centro Histórico, I find the products are as good or better, and the prices are very reasonable. The best day to come is Saturday, when you can combine it with a trip to the Tianguis Cultural El Chopo, listed below. Open daily 9–6. $–$$$$.

MERCADO LA MERCED
Between Santa Escuela, General Anaya, Rosario, and Cerrada del Rosario, Col. Merced Balbuena, Mexico, D.F.
Metro: La Merced

From piñatas to produce, toys to tarot card readings, and spoons to shrines, you'll find it all at La Merced, the city's biggest market. Located southeast of the Zócalo and accessible directly from the La Merced metro, the market is a fascinating and entertaining jumble. Spread out over several blocks, it is divided by category, and spending an hour or two exploring its accumulated wares can be quite fun. And if you're in the market for chiles, welcome: they have them in abundance. Open daily 7–6. $–$$$.

PLAZA DE LAS TRES CULTURAS AND TLATELOLCO

55-5583-0295
Eje Central Lázaro Cárdenas and Avenida Ricardo Flores Magón, Col. Nonoalco-Tlatelolco, Mexico, D.F.
Metro: Tlatelolco

This plaza, a good distance from the Alameda Central and Zócalo but worth the decent walk from the metro, is quintessentially Mexican. It is named for the three cultures represented in this single space: the Aztec ruins of Tlatelolco, the 16th-century Ex-Convento de Santiago Tlatelolco, and the more contemporary office building and residential complex. Tlatelolco was a twin city to Tenochtitlán and in its heyday boasted a massive, vibrant market that was at its time a wondrous sight, according to the conquistadores. It was also here that the final and decisive battle for the New World was fought, when, on August 13, 1521, the Aztecs led by Cuauhtémoc were defeated by the Spanish. Thousands of Aztec warriors were slain in the last resistance to the conquistadores, and a plaque in the plaza commemorates the date as "Neither triumph nor defeat, but the painful birth of the mixed-race nation that is Mexico today."

The ruins of Tlatelolco dominate the plaza and are well organized for visitors, with raised walkways and bilingual plaques describing the temples and structures. Of particular interest is the Templo Calendário, decorated with niches symbolizing the days according to the Mexica calendar; the unusual circular temple to Ehécatl-Quetzalcoatl, where 41 human burials (believed to be part of a petition for rainfall during the drought of 1450–55) were excavated in 1987; and the Templo Mayor, or main temple, which, like Tenochtitlán, boasted two altars to Huitzilopochtli and Tláloc. Open daily 8–6. Free.

The ruins of Tlatelolco at the Plaza de las Tres Culturas

TIANGUIS CULTURAL EL CHOPO

Calle Aldama, Col. Buena Vista, Mexico, D.F.
Metro: Buenavista

For a heavy infusion of punk and goth, visit the tremendously fun el Chopo market on Saturdays. Located on Aldama Street, just behind the Buena Vista train station (from the metro, just follow the black-clad, cloaked, and mohawk-sporting crowds), this quiet neighborhood transforms once a week into a market that's Mexico's version of Carnaby Street. El Chopo sells all kinds of punk, goth, and rock items, from clothes that would make Tim Burton proud to leather-studded gimp masks to all manner of accessories. It is especially known for its bootlegged, rare, and out-of-print cassettes, CDs, and LPs. While most of the stuff is pirated, you can find some rare items. I've heard that Sinead O'Connor once visited the market, saw one of her albums, and bought it back from the seller. El Chopo also brings together interesting live acts (I remember one rather odd group of Mexican visigoths blowing on bagpipes). Open Saturdays 10–5. $–$$$.

North of the Centro Histórico

BASÍLICA DE GUADALUPE

55-5577-6022
www.virgendeguadalupe.org.mx
Plaza de las Américas 1, Col. Villa de Guadalupe, Mexico, D.F.
Metro: La Villa-Basílica

The monumental Basílica de Guadalupe is the holiest shrine in Mexico and the second-most visited Catholic church in the world after St. Peter's in the Vatican. But the numbers alone don't tell its story. This is the epicenter of the Catholic faith in Mexico; it was here that the image of the *Virgen de Guadalupe,* the most precious and revered symbol of faith in the country, was first seen in the 16th century by a humble indigenous man named Juan

The Basílica de Guadalupe Credit: Mexico Tourism Board

The Legend of *la Morenita*

The story of *la Morenita*, or the Dark-Skinned One, as the Virgin of Guadalupe is known, begins in 1531 and intertwines Catholic and Aztec spirituality. A native peasant named Juan Diego was visiting the hill of Tepeyec when the Virgin Mary appeared to him in the form of a young mestizo woman cloaked in a blue mantle.

On her instruction, Diego traveled to Mexico City, where he shared his vision with Juan de Zumárraga, the bishop-elect of Mexico City. Zumárraga refused to believe him. Twice, Diego was rebuffed, and twice sent back by the Virgin. Zumárraga then demanded proof of the miracle. On Diego's third visit to Tepeyec, the Virgin told him to gather flowers from the surrounding hillside and present them to the bishop. The devout Diego did so, wrapping the flowers in his cloak. He returned to Zumárraga, and when he opened his cloak the flowers fell to the floor, and both men saw the Virgin's image emblazoned on the cloth. The bishop took this as a sign and ordered the construction of a church at the spot where the miracle occurred.

Juan Diego's cloak hangs in the basilica dedicated to *la Morenita*. And as a happy postscript to the story, Diego himself was canonized in 2002: he's the first Mexican to achieve sainthood.

Diego. *La Virgen* is omnipresent in modern Mexico, and it was from here that her message spread.

Today, the site of the miracle is a large complex made up of several structures. The old basilica (itself the second one built here; the first is located up the hill), which has a notable tilt and has been the source of near-continuous restoration for years, has only recently been opened to the public. Inside is a religious-art museum. However, it is literally overshadowed by the massive newer one next to it. This modern circular construction, inaugurated in 1976 to handle the enormous masses of pilgrims who flocked to the site, was designed to resemble a pilgrim's tent, or the Virgin's cloak. It can hold up to 10,000 people, with the atrium capable of holding 50,000. It also houses, ensconced behind the altar, safely protected behind a sheet of bulletproof glass, the most sacred religious artifact in all of Mexico: the image of the Virgin imprinted on the cloak of Juan Diego in 1531. Visitors can take a short conveyor-belt ride behind the altar to view the image. Outside, you can also visit the small chapel to the side of the older basilica and check out the modern bell tower.

On December 12, Mexico celebrates the *Día de Nuestra Señora de Guadalupe*, or Day of Our Lady of Guadalupe. On this day, commemorating the day Juan Diego saw the vision of the Virgin, the plaza comes alive with the press of millions of worshippers; it's an almost unreal sight. Open daily 6–9. Free, $ for the museum.

South of the Centro Histórico

CUICUILCO

55-5606-9758, 7150-0403
Insurgentes Sur and Anillo Periférico Sur
Metro: None (From Universidad, take a *pesero* marked "Cuicuilco")

The ruins at Cuicuilco are a fair trek from the city center, but are significant for their unique structure. Unlike other pyramids, Cuicuilco's main temple has a circular shape. The

The ruins of Cuicuilco

large, grass-covered mound is pretty much all that is left from a thriving ancient city of 20,000 inhabitants—one of the first urban communities to settle in the Valley of Mexico—on the southern shores of Lake Texcoco. Cuicuilco flourished between 600 B.C. and A.D. 200. The city was centered on a large ceremonial center dedicated to Heuhueteotl, the god of fire. It was abandoned after the eruption of the nearby Xitle volcano, which covered the city in lava. Much of the lava has been removed, leaving the main sites visible to tourists. Nearby, check out the small museum, which has an artist's depiction of how Cuicuilco may once have looked. Open Monday to Saturday 9–5. $.

MUSEO DIEGO RIVERA ANAHUACALLI

55-5617-4310
www.anahuacallimuseo.org
Museo 150, Col. San Pablo Tepetlapa, Coyoacán, Mexico, D.F.
Metro: Tasqueña to Xotepingo (light rail)

The Anahuacalli is one of the more interesting structures in the city to house a museum. Built by Diego Rivera (with the help, after his death, of his longtime friend Dolores Olmedo), it was intended to be a city of the arts modeled after a pre-Hispanic *teocalli*, or temple. Built out of volcanic rock, it certainly looks like a temple, and it contains part of Rivera's astounding collection of over 56,000 pieces of Mesoamerican art. Open Tuesday to Sunday 10–2 and 3–5. All visits are guided. $ (entrance fee includes a visit to the Frida Kahlo museum).

SIX FLAGS MÉXICO

55-5339-3600

www.sixflags.com.mx

Carretera Picacho Ajusco 1500, Col. Tlalpan, Mexico, D.F.

Metro: Tasqueña, M.A. Quevedo, Copilco, or Universidad (transfer to bus)

I'm guessing you didn't come to Mexico City to ride on roller coasters. But if I'm wrong, or if the kids need a treat after one too many murals or ruins, Six Flags has the best collection of rides in the country. In addition to the fastest wooden roller coaster (in Mexico they're called *montañas rusas,* or Russian mountains) in Latin America, it's got the terrific Batman ride, and plenty of family and kids' rides. Hours and days open vary, generally 10–8. $$$.

UNIVERSIDAD NACIONAL AUTÓNOMA DE MEXICO (UNAM)

www.unam.edu.mx

55-5622-8222

Ciudad Universitaria, beginning from Insurgentes Sur and Universidad

Metro: Universidad

Founded in 1551 by King Phillip II of Spain, Mexico's National Autonomous University is the oldest in the Americas. It was housed in the city center until the 1950s, when it was moved south to a rugged part of town called *el Pedregal,* or the Rocky Land. Here, the massive complex of the Ciudad Universitaria, or University City, was established. UNAM is more than the educational heart of Mexico; it's also a cultural treasure, designated a UNESCO World Heritage Site in 2007 for its impressive architecture and stunning murals. Amid vast green spaces (a tribute to the open spaces of ancient Mexico), University City is divided into three zones:

1. The **Olympic Stadium,** designed to resemble the volcanic cones typical of the surrounding topography, is a colossal structure that can seat up to 80,000 people; a Diego Rivera mosaic can be seen above the main entrance. This is the place to come for incredibly raucous soccer games, which are watched with gladiator-competition-like excitement from the sport's rabid fans.

2. The **Sports Field** is a huge area comprising various courts, pitches, and tracks. The handball courts, modeled after the ball courts of the ancients, are among the most ingenious architectural creations in the campus.

3. The **School Zone,** which is divided into five main faculties; this is the main part of the campus, where the university's half million or so students study. Here are also some of its most spectacular buildings and murals, including:

   Central Library—UNAM's most iconic building; the library's four sides are covered by a Juan O'Gorman mosaic.

   Rectoría—The university's administrative building has unusual 3-D murals by Davíd Alfaro Siqueiros jutting out from its walls.

   Sala Nezahualcóyotl—This impressive theater hosts concerts throughout the year.

   Museo Universitario Arte Contemporáneo—UNAM's newest museum houses a collection of contemporary art in a dramatic new building in the university's cultural center.

The Central Library at UNAM

Located nearby is the surprisingly good **Café Azul y Oro,** a great place for a lunch break.

Espacio Escultórico—This student hangout is a rather incongruous assortment of sculptures bordered by a long, low wall of volcanic rock.

UNAM is located south of San Ángel. The easiest way to reach it is by Metrobús straight down Insurgentes Sur. You can also take the No. 3 metro to the last stop, Universidad, and from here hop on one of the many shuttles that take you directly into the campus.

Xochimilco

Xochimilco, which means "the place of the flower beds" in Nahuatl, is a borough of Mexico City located far to the south, where a wonder of ancient technology and ingenuity can transport you back in time to the era of the Aztecs. This area, designated a UNESCO World Heritage Site, is famed for its network of canals that wind through floating artificial islands called *chinampas.* These were creative solutions devised by a migrant tribe called the Xochimilcas, who lived here between the 10th and 14th centuries. The *chinampas* were constructions of reed, soil, and wood that helped the Natives farm the earth of Lake Xochimilco. The project was so successful that, before long, a vast network of islands covered the lake, forming canals between them. It is through these canals that you can journey today. They are the last remnants of what the lakeside towns of ancient Mexico once looked like. The canals are the highlight at Xochimilco, but there are a few other sites worth visiting here as well.

GETTING THERE

The most direct way to get here is by taxi. If you're driving, hop on the Anillo Periférico highway to Prolongación División del Norte, which will take you into the city center and the piers. However, public transportation is by far the cheapest and often quickest option. Take the metro line 2 to Tasqueña, and then board the *tren lígero* (light rail) to Xochimilco.

ATTRACTIONS, PARKS & RECREATION

THE CANALS OF XOCHIMILCO
55-5676-8879, 5673-7890
Embarcadero ("Pier") Fernando Celada, Avenida Guadalupe I. Ramírez, Xochimilco
Metro: Xochimilco (light rail)

I've heard the floating islands of Xochimilco often referred to as the Venice of Mexico. Insofar as you get to climb aboard a boat and be punted along canals, I agree. But I still find the comparison inaccurate. That's no knock on Venice; it's a beautiful city. Xochimilco, on the other hand, is a marvel of ancient engineering and a living chronicle of pre-Hispanic life.

It's also tremendous fun to board one of the brightly colored boats, or *trajineras* (you can join as part of a group or reserve one just for yourself), and let the boatmen shunt you around. As you enjoy the ride and the greenery around you, other boats will pull up alongside with vendors selling delicious food (enchiladas, moles, and other standard fare) and with mariachi bands ready to play for a nominal tip. To really enjoy the tranquility of your surroundings, go during the week. Open daily, generally between 9–8. $$.

CONVENTO DE SAN BERNARDINO DE SIENA
Pino and Miguel Hidalgo, Xochimilco
Metro: Xochimilco (light rail)

A few blocks east of the Embarcadero Fernando Celada is this large and sober-looking Franciscan convent. Founded in 1535, it is famed for its retablos, or altarpieces, which are

A trajinera floats along the canals of Xochimilco Credit: Mexico Tourism Board

over 400 years old and include notable pre-Hispanic designs. The last Indian governor of Xochimilco, Apoxquiyohuatzin, is buried here. Open daily 10–1 and 4–8. Free.

PARQUE ECOLÓGICO DE XOCHIMILCO

55-5673-8061, 5673-7890
Periférico Oriente 1, Col. Ciénaga Grande, Xochimilco
Metro: Xochimilco (light rail)

You'll need a taxi to get to this vast ecological park, which includes a botanical garden and one massive flower-and-plant market. Similar to the canals, it is a land of artificial lakes, but more unknown and less commercial. It's a tranquil, remote oasis where you can walk, bike (available for rent at the park), ride the train, or, on weekends, travel by *trajinera*. Open Tuesday to Sunday, 10–4 in winter, 9–6 in winter. $.

CULTURE

MUSEO DOLORES OLMEDO PATIÑO

55-5555-0891
www.museodoloresolmedo.org.mx
México 5843, Col. La Noria, Xochimilco
Metro: Tasqueña to La Noria (light rail)

A relatively new museum (it opened in 1994), this lovely hacienda, and the vast collection inside it, belonged to Dolores Olmedo, a longtime friend of Diego Rivera's. It houses a large number of Diego and Frida's works but is also home to a huge pre-Hispanic art collection as well as a section devoted to folkloric arts and crafts. The café on the veranda is a serene spot to take a break. Open Tuesday to Sunday 10–6. $.

5

EXCURSIONS IN AND AROUND MEXICO CITY

Within the borders of Mexico City are enough cultural, historical, and commercial destinations to occupy a visitor for several journeys . . . and that's not even taking into consideration what lies just beyond the city limits. Within the Federal District and the state of México are awe-inspiring pre-Hispanic ruins, silver cities, and eco-retreats. This chapter is dedicated to helping you get the most out of your visit to the city, as well as highlighting the best excursions within and around the D.F.

MEXICO CITY ITINERARIES

First-time visitors to Mexico City have a dizzying range of options for what to see and do, and prioritizing your time can be a daunting exercise. The following three-day and week-long itineraries should help you organize your time.

Three Days in Mexico City

Day 1

Your first full day in the city should be devoted to the Centro Histórico:

Start in the **Zócalo**, where you can visit three of the city's most important attractions: the **Catedral Metropolitana, Palacio Nacional,** and **Templo Mayor.** These sites will easily occupy you up to lunch (and even that's ambitious). Head to Calle República de Guatemala, just behind the cathedral, where you can enjoy a fine Mexican meal on the terrace at **La Casa de las Sirenas.** Afterward, walk another block away from the Zócalo to Justo Sierra Street. Turn right here to reach the **Antiguo Colegio de San Ildefonso,** worth a look for its tremendous murals.

Retrace your steps to República de Guatemala, turn right and walk west. The road becomes Calle Tacuba, which is lined with colonial-era buildings. Tacuba will lead to the Alameda Central and the gorgeous **Palacio de Bellas Artes.** From here, enjoy the leafy respite of the Alameda. On its south side, pay a visit to the **Hemiciclo a Benito Juárez** monument as you walk across to the **Museo Mural Diego Rivera.** Spend the rest of the afternoon at the **Museo de Arte Popular,** located on Calle Revillagigedo behind the Sheraton. You won't find a more thorough and well-presented overview of Mexican folk art and culture anywhere in the country, and its museum shop is an excellent source of quality souvenirs.

After a full day of cultural highlights, freshen up at your hotel before enjoying a reward-

Santa Prisca Church in Taxco

ing meal. One recommendation is to head to Paseo de Reforma and **Les Moustaches** for an elegant French dinner. If you want to stick to Mexican cuisine, try **La Fonda el Refugio** in the Zona Rosa. Either option gives you the chance to see Reforma's monuments lit up at night. After dinner, it's mariachi time. **Plaza Garibaldi** is a taxi ride away, but I recommend the short walk along Reforma toward the **Monumento a la Independencia**. At the corner is the Sheraton María Isabel and **Bar Jorongo**, a terrific place for mariachi. Your other choice for nightlife is the **Ballet Folklórico** at the Palacio de Bellas Artes.

Day 2
Reserve this day for Chapultepec and Polanco:

Head first to the Bosque de Chapultepec and spend the day at the **Castillo de Chapultepec** and **Museo Nacional de Antropología,** with a visit to the **Monumento a los Niños Héroes** after the castle.

I'd be remiss if I didn't advocate at least one taquería while you're in the city; so after the museum, take a *sitio* cab to **El Fogoncito** on Calle Leibnitz, just outside the park in Polanco. From here, ask the restaurant to call you another taxi and head to Masayrk Avenue, the main shopping district in Polanco. Browse to your heart's content and relax at one of its fine cafés until dinner. My vote for an outstanding meal is **Pujol,** for nouveau Mexican, and **Izote,** for a blend of classic and new. If you want something more moderate and classically Mexican, **El Bajío** will serve just as well. For a taste of Mexico's posh nightlife scene, head to one of the clubs or lounges listed in the "Nightlife" section under Polanco in Chapter 4.

Hemiciclo a Benito Juárez

Day 3

Coyoacán and San Ángel round out your three-day itinerary:

Begin in Coyoacán, where you can spend the morning wandering its plazas and streets and visiting the **Museo Frida Kahlo** and **Museo Leon Trotsky.** Try to time this trip for a Saturday, and take a taxi to San Ángel's Plaza Jacinto and the **Bazar Sábado,** where you'll find excellent arts and crafts.

Have lunch at **Saks,** or for a break from classic Mexican, at **Capicua.** Then explore this lovely neighborhood, check out the mummies at the **Museo del Carmen,** and if you're a Diego and Frida fan, visit the **Museo Casa Estudio Diego Rivera y Frida Kahlo.**

For dinner, you can't beat **Paxia.** At night, **Mamá Rumba** has Cuban music and dance, and **Clásico** has a great retro '80s ambience.

A Week in Mexico City

Day 1

Take time to explore the **Zócalo:**

Begin with a hearty breakfast at **Los Mercaderes,** and then follow the morning Day 1 itinerary outlined above (you might want to rent a bike at the government-sponsored stand near the Catedral Metropolitana). After lunch, walk the streets of Tacuba, Madero, and 5 de Mayo. Visit the **Secretaría de Educación Pública,** the **Templo de San Francisco,** and stop for a coffee break at **Casa de los Azulejos.** You can walk to **Plaza Santo Domingo** or take the subway to Tlatelolco and from there walk to the **Plaza de las Tres Culturas.** To make full use of this day, dine in the city center (two recommendations are **Danubio** for superb seafood and **La Ópera** for its ambience and history). From here, you can hit **Plaza Garibaldi** for a night of kitschy mariachi fun, or check out one of the hotspots in the Centro, like **Zinco Jazz Club** or **Pasaje América.**

Day 2

Devote this day to the Alameda Central.

There are four sites in and around the square worth visiting: the **Palacio de Bellas Artes** on its eastern corner; the **Plaza de la Santa Veracruz** and **Franz Mayer Museum** on its northern side; the **Hemiciclo a Benito Juárez;** and the **Museo Mural Diego Rivera** to the west. Also allocate plenty of time for the **Museo de Arte Popular,** located on Calle Revillagigedo behind the Sheraton. If it's a clear day, head to the top of the **Torre Latinoamerica,** just across from the Palacio de Bellas Artes, for panoramic city views. Have lunch at **Los Girasoles** on Calle Tacuba or **El Cardenal** at the Sheraton, and reserve some time to souvenir shop at **La Ciudadela (Mercado de Artesanías de la Ciudadela)** arts and crafts market or **FONART.** At night, you can follow the 3-day itinerary for Day 1, ending at **Bar Jorongo** or the **Ballet Folklórico.**

Day 3

Follow the three-day itinerary for Day 2, covering Chapultepec and Polanco.

Day 4

Take a journey into the past with a trip to the breathtaking ruins of **Teotihuacán.** Many tour companies combine this excursion with a visit to the **Basílica de Guadalupe,** a convenient way to see two of the country's most significant sites. For dinner, my recommendation is to

Templo de San Francisco

return to Polanco and try one of the excellent options listed in the "Dining" section under Polanco in Chapter 4.

Day 5

Take a trip to the bohemian neighborhoods of Condesa and Roma. While there are cultural highlights like **Casa Lamm,** this day is more about strolling through parks, leafy avenues, and pleasant cafés, followed by lunch at Casa Lamm or **Contramar.** Or take an organized tour, like Journeys Beyond the Surface, listed below. At night, dine at **Ligaya** in Condesa and then either stick around for the hopping neighborhood nightlife, or book yourself a seat at the arena for some *lucha libre.*

Day 6

Follow the three-day itinerary for Day 3, covering Coyoacán and San Ángel.

Day 7

Visit the timeless floating gardens of **Xochimilco,** where a boatsman will punt you through canals made by pre-Hispanic engineers. Lunch and live music are provided boatside. While you're here, spend some time at the **Museo Dolores Olmedo,** a beautiful sanctuary of art, and the 16th-century convent in the town center.

TOURS AND TOUR GUIDES

A word about tours in Mexico: the vast majority of them will require patience. Patience, that is, to travel to a prearranged gift shop on the way to your destination, where you will likely sit through a lecture on tequila production, silversmithing, or any number of other trades, and then be given the "opportunity" to buy one of the shop's products. Many customers will hate the hour or more spent on this distraction, along with being forced to eat at designated, prearranged restaurants when they arrive at their destination.

But if you want to take a tour from Mexico City, these are necessary evils you'll have to endure. The good news is that, while the stores that fall on these routes are usually pricier than what you'll find in local markets and shops, they generally carry good-quality merchandise. Also, the instructional element of the stop can be pretty interesting (on one tour I learned about the many ways the indigenous tribes used the maguey plant). And finally, you are never *required* to make a purchase, and if you make it clear you're not interested, you'll be left alone. Of course, tours within the city (like the Turibus; see listing below) don't have these side-trips.

Much more important to your satisfaction is the quality of the tour itself; whether the guide knows what he or she is talking about; whether he or she speaks passable English; and whether the tour itself is comfortable. There is no end of tour companies in Mexico, but I've listed these for their reliable service or their niche, themed excursions.

CITY DISCOVERY

419-244-6440
www.city-discovery.com/mexico
Departs from select hotels in the city

A U.S.-based agency with a variety of affordable tour packages within and around Mexico City. $$–$$$$.

GAY MEXICO CITY TOURS

602-265-3486
http://gaymexicocitytours.com
6035 N 7th Street, Phoenix, AZ 85014
Departs from Phoenix, AZ

Robert Bitto will be your guide, from the U.S. through Mexico City, on a weeklong cultural tour tailored for the gay community. His tours are centered on gay-friendly areas of the city, but also include excursions around and beyond the D.F. Tours are planned well in advance, are limited to 12 people per tour, and are only held a few times a year, so if you're interested, book early. $$$$.

JOURNEYS BEYOND THE SURFACE

59-5922-0205, 55-1497-9610
www.travelmexicocity.com.mx
Fraccionamiento Sarabia 112, Col. San Juanito Texcoco, Mexico
Tours and meeting points arranged beforehand

Mojdeh Hojjati offers a departure from the typical tour. She tailors cultural and educational immersions into the city, showing visitors sides of Mexico City that they wouldn't normally see. You'll get to meet social activists, community leaders, historians, artists, and a variety of other people who are part of the fabric of the D.F. For those who don't speak Spanish, she is on hand to translate for you. If you're looking for a cultural experience that takes you from the confines of a tour bus and puts you on the ground, let Mojdeh help you discover what's beneath the surface of Mexico City. $$$-$$$$.

MEXICO SOUL AND ESSENCE

55-5564-8457
www.mexicosoulandessence.com
Amsterdam 269 Piso 8, Colonia Condesa, Mexico, D.F.

This niche company specializes in culinary tours in and around Mexico City, focusing on the many food-themed festivals that take place throughout the year in different communities. It also offers cultural and walking tours. $$$-$$$$.

OLYMPUS TOURS

55-5684-8921
www.olympus-tours.com
Departs from select hotels in the city

Olympus offers a variety of tours, including Mexico City and special events (ballet, bullfighting, and more), as well as nearby sites and towns including Teotihuacán, Cuernavaca, and Taxco, and multiday excursions. The guides are knowledgeable and friendly. $$-$$$$.

TURIBUS

55-5563-6693, 55-5598-6309
www.turibus.com.mx
Board at designated stops, including the Zócalo and the Alameda Central in front of the Hemiciclo a Benito Juárez Turibus runs an almost three-hour route to the major sites in

In the Inner City with Mojdeh and Luis

For most *chilangos*, the neighborhoods of Tepito and La Romita are best avoided at any hour of the day. For Mojdeh Hojjati, they're two pockets of the city she knows inside and out. On a personalized walking tour, she introduced me to these neighborhoods.

Tepito is among the most infamous neighborhoods in Mexico City. It is known as a thieves' colony, a criminal quarter, a haven for drug dealers and gangs. Its patron saint is *la Santa Muerte* (Saint Death), the saint of lost causes, who even has her official church here. And Tepito is the center of *fayuca* traffic. *Fayuca* is the name given to contraband goods smuggled in from the U.S., and in Tepito it has created a market where you can buy just about anything. It was *fayuca*, according to community leader Luis Arévalo, which changed the social dynamic of Tepito more than anything else. Before that, this was a community of people who made and fixed things: cobblers, electricians, skilled laborers who could take appliances apart and put them back together.

But the neighborhood is also known for one other thing: its fighters. Since the 1950s, Tepito has produced a string of fine boxers, most recently Luis Villanueva Paramo, better known as Kid Azteca, and Marco Antonio Barrera. But I didn't meet any boxers; I didn't go for the thriving flea market. No, I went to see a children's puppet theater in an inner city compound that I would never walk into on my own. I went with Arévalo, who is intent on reenergizing and renewing his community. And watching kids pour in from the projects to delight in this simple spectacle in the heart of Tepito was one of the most moving experiences I had in Mexico City. Arévalo has also helped organize a **Martes de Arte** (Tuesdays with Art) weekly gathering where you can hear music, check out what vendors are selling, and meet some of the friendliest people you'll find in the city.

Mojdeh also took me to La Romita, a hidden corner of Roma Norte of similarly ill fame. Another hive of thieves with a history of violence, it was also a picturesque section of town with a quaint plaza, small church, and colorful murals. In one afternoon, she showed me saw a Mexico City that was unfamiliar, gritty, fascinating, and beautiful.

Children's puppet show in Tepito

Chapultepec, the Centro Histórico, Condesa, and Roma. It's your classic open-roofed dou-ble-decker bus tour. The bright red buses are a good option for those who want to take it all in before deciding where to focus their time. You can get on and off at any stop throughout the day with your ticket. They recently added a new southern route which covers Coyoacán and San Ángel. Tours run 9–9 daily. $$.

WAYAK

55-5518-1726
800-823-2410
www.hostelcatedral.com

Departs from the Hostel Catedral, with pickup options at some other hotels and hostels
A terrific budget option, the tours arranged by the Hostel Catedral through Wayak range from Teotihuacán to Puebla to a night of *lucha libre* wrestling. Free walking tours of the city are also conducted Monday to Friday at 10. $$.

TEOTIHUACÁN

The ancient city of Teotihuacán is one of the most spectacular ruins in all of Mexico, a UNESCO World Heritage Site, and deservedly the most visited day-trip destination outside Mexico City. Teotihuacán, which means "place where gods were born," was the heart of a mighty empire built by a remarkably advanced civilization that vanished into history as mysteriously as it appeared. Who the Teotihuacanos were and where they came from remains a mystery. But what they left behind was indelible evidence of their onetime glory.

While the area was first populated in around 500 B.C., it is only around 100 B.C. that Teotihuacán began to take shape. It became a major center of commerce and trade, as well as a religious and spiritual capital, and its influence spread throughout Mexico. In addition to their skill as builders and craftsmen, the Teotihuacanos were proficient in astrology and science. By A.D. 600, the city had grown to be the sixth-largest in the world. Just 150 years later, it was abandoned. Many believe its downfall was due to a combination of overpopu-lation, a growing lack of resources and water, destruction from within, and invasion from without.

It was the Aztecs, who arrived on the scene 500 years later, who gave the city and its principal structures their name. Like them, we remain in awe of Teotihuacán.

Getting There

Almost every tour operator conducts tours to Teotihuacán; tours can be arranged from your hotel or by contacting the tour company directly. These are typically full-day tours com-bined with another attraction like the Basílica de Guadalupe. You can also organize a pri-vate tour through your hotel or the Sectur (Ministry of Tourism; 800-008-9090). If you're driving, your quickest route is to take Insurgentes Norte to the Autopista México-Pachuca (Highway 85D, a toll road) out of the city. Buses leave frequently from Mexico City's Terminal Central del Norte for the site (look for the AUTOBUSES SAHAGUN sign). Make sure you get on the bus marked LOS PIRÁMIDES and ask the driver when the last bus returns to the city (usually 6 PM).

THE RUINS OF TEOTIHUACÁN

59-4956-0276, 59-4956-0052

The ancient city of Teotihuacán is remarkable for the size of its monuments (which altogether cover roughly 12 square miles) and its neat geometric layout. When you visit, be sure to take comfortable shoes, a hat, sunblock, sunglasses, and plenty of water (although this is available on-site). You should also be prepared for a hike up the steep steps of the main pyramids; and finally, expect to be blown away. Here are the main points of interest at the ruins:

Visitors Center

Your first stop should be the Visitors Center, located at the southwest entrance to the ruins. Here you'll find an excellent museum that will give you a great visual overview of the city, a restaurant, and restrooms.

La Ciudadela

Directly across from the Visitors Center is la Ciudadela (the Citadel), a massive walled square that houses the Templo de Quetzalcoatl, or Temple of the Feathered Serpent. This is the most beautiful, though not nearly the largest, of Teotihuacán's structures. It is famed for the ornate carvings of stone serpent heads and bas-reliefs of Tlaloc, the rain god, that jut out along one side (the sculptures along the other three sides were destroyed long ago). The detailed work, and the large number of human remains found buried here by archaeologists, attests to the temple's importance as a ceremonial center.

The ruins of Teotihuacán Credit: Mexico Tourism Board

Calzada de los Muertos

The broad road stretching from the northern to southern ends of the city is called the Avenue of the Dead, something of a misnomer by the Aztecs. As you walk along this road, with the Temple of the Sun looming on the right and the Temple of the Moon in the distance, you'll pass several smaller structures believed to be residences and other temples.

Pirámide del Sol

The Pyramid of the Sun is an awe-inspiring structure that dominates the landscape of Teotihuacán. Believed to be the third-largest pyramid in the world, it is over 700 feet wide and more than 200 feet high. During the era of the Teotihuacanos, there was a temple atop the pyramid, and it was painted red. A climb up to its peak is highly recommended, and although the more than 250 steps are quite steep, the view from the top is worth it. For a slightly surreal experience, visit on the days of the winter and summer solstices, when pilgrims dressed in white scale the pyramid and stretch their arms out to receive its heightened spiritual energies.

Pirámide del la Luna

At the north end of the Avenue of the Dead, occupying one side of a plaza, stands the Pyramid of the Moon. The second-largest pyramid in the city, it is still worth the climb up for its incredible view of the Calzada de los Muertos stretched out before you. In the plaza around the pyramid are several other important buildings, including the brightly colored Palace of Quetzalpapalotl (Quetzal-Butterfly), a mythical bird-butterfly hybrid that's painted on the walls, and the Palace of the Jaguars, where you can see a mural of jaguars.

TAXCO

The famed silver city of Mexico, Taxco—full name Taxco de Alarcón—is a quaint town with a (literally) treasured legacy. The city was originally named Tlacho, or "place of the ball courts," by the Aztecs, and it paid tribute to the Aztec empire. Cortés discovered Taxco shortly after his conquest of Tenochtitlán, and it quickly became renowned for its silver. In the 1700s José de la Borda, a Spaniard of French descent, discovered a rich vein of silver and gave Taxco a second silver boom, further cementing its status as the silver capital. Borda became one of the richest men in New Spain. He in turn gave back to the town, establishing the beautiful Santa Prisca Church, which is one of Taxco's colonial treasures. The act spawned a popular saying: "Dios a darle a Borda, y Borda a darle a Dios" (God giveth to Borda, and Borda giveth to God).

By the 20th century, many of Taxco's silver mines had been exhausted. An American named William Spratling breezed into town and, upon seeing the quality of the local craftsmanship, opened a workshop here. He did astoundingly well, and inspired a second boom in Taxco that continues today.

A visit to Taxco is not just about browsing its famed silver boutiques. This is a picturesque city nestled against a hill, with winding cobblestone streets, distinctive architecture, and a rustic, old-fashioned charm.

Getting There

Taxco is about 110 miles southwest of Mexico City in the state of Guerrero. By car, take the Anillo Periférico to the Autopista México-Cuernavaca (Highway 95D). You can choose the toll road (quicker) or the free road; continue past Cuernavaca and stay on 95D. The drive

The quaint hillside city of Taxco

should take between three and four hours. To get to Taxco by bus, head to the Central Del Sur terminal. Buses depart frequently and take around three hours. There are two bus stations in Taxco, both a short taxi or *combi* (VW minibus) ride from the center of town. Also, check the weather before you go: when it rains in Taxco, it pours.

ATTRACTIONS, PARKS & RECREATION

CASA BORDA
762-622-6617
Plaza Borda 1, Taxco

Across from Santa Prisca in the main plaza, the 18th-century home built by Borda is now the Guerrero State Cultural Center. There are frequent events here, as well as some old classrooms and exhibit halls. It's nothing too exciting, but an interesting piece of history in the *zócalo,* and a good place to find out what's going on around town. Open Tuesday to Sunday 10–5. Free.

CASA HUMBOLDT Y MUSEO VIRREINAL DE TAXCO
762-622-5501
Juan Ruiz de Alarcón 12, Taxco

An 18th-century home named for one of its more famous guests—German explorer and man of science Baron Alexander von Humboldt—the museum has little to do with the German and plenty to do with 18th-century Taxco. The collection of artifacts here, including items belonging to Borda and relics from nearby Santa Prisca, are as interesting as the house itself, a winding, rickety structure that's fun to wander through. There's a small arched terrace that offers lovely views of the hillside. Open Tuesday to Saturday 10–6, Sunday 10–4. $.

IGLESIA SANTA PRISCA Y SAN SEBASTIÁN
762-622-0184
Plaza Borda, Taxco

No offense to silver, but this is Taxco's crown jewel, at least from an architectural point of view. The ornately baroque Santa Prisca, completed in 1758, was paid for by José de la Borda in return for the millions the town gave him in silver. It's safe to say he spared no expense. The elaborate pink façade shows sculptures of Santa Prisca (a Roman Christian condemned to death and thrown to the lions in the Coliseum) and Saint Sebastian (pierced by arrows for converting prisoners to Christianity) framing a relief of Christ being baptized in the River Jordan. Inside, the goldleaf work of the soaring altars is outstanding.

Taxco's Pozole

If you want to try a typical Guerrero dish famous in Taxco, head for the nearest *pozolería,* which serves, or course, *pozole.* This is a hearty stew made with hominy, meat (almost always pork), chile, lime juice, avocado, and other ingredients. The most central place to get it is the **Pozolería Tía Calla** in Plaza Borda (722-622-5602).

Everything here was made in Mexico with the exception of the organ, which was brought from Spain and transported to Taxco by mule.

In particular, note the paintings by Miguel Cabrera, one of Mexico's most celebrated colonial painters. There are two for which Santa Prisca is especially famous: a portrait of Jesus crucified with his arms in a Y shape, rather than the traditional stance, and an extremely controversial painting of a pregnant Virgin Mary. (Cabrera was jailed by the Vatican for his work.) Behind the sacristy is another gallery of Cabrera's that includes a self-portrait and portraits of José de la Borda and his son Manuel, who was the church's first priest. Open daily 10–8. Free.

MUSEO GUILLERMO SPRATLING
762-622-1660
Porfirio A. Delgado 1, Taxco

Surprisingly not a museum about Taxco's silver industry, the Museo Guillermo Spratling, named after the American William Spratling, is primarily a fine display of pre-Hispanic art that was given by its namesake. Open Tuesday to Saturday 9–5, Sunday 9–3. $.

TOURISM OFFICE
762-622-2274
Avenida de los Plateros 1, Taxco
Open Monday to Friday 9–3:30, Saturday 9–1.

SHOPPING

I'd be remiss if I didn't mention the silver shops that Taxco is so famous for. They are all over town, selling a variety of products that range in quality and price. To make sure you're buying the real deal, look for the "0.925" stamp that indicates authenticity. Below are just a few that carry excellent quality.

ANGEL ORTIZ 0.925
762-622-3858
Plazuela de los Gallos 5

Representing new blood in a centuries-old industry, Angel Ortiz brings a fresh style to Taxco's silver retailers. Ortiz's designs are bold and exciting, and different from what the majority of his competitors are doing. $$–$$$$.

LEDESMA PLATEROS
762-622-1983
Local No. 32, Level 1, Centro Joyero, Plazuela de Bernal #10, Taxco

Located just behind the *zócalo*, Ledesma carries on a 50-year-old tradition of fine quality silver in creative designs. The store owners are amiable and friendly, and specialize in jewelry, tableware, and home décor. $$–$$$$.

ALLERES DE LOS BALLESTEROS

762-622-1076
www.ballesteros.net
Avenida de los Plateros 68, Taxco

One of the most high-end silver retailers in Taxco (they have stores in Mexico City as well), Ballesteros has been around since 1937. Expect to find very good quality and workmanship. $$–$$$$.

WEEKLY & ANNUAL EVENTS

FERIA NACIONAL DE PLATA

Last week in November
The National Silver Fair brings together hundreds of artists who compete for the distinction of top silversmith. Free.

SEMANA SANTA

Easter Week
The holy week of Easter is celebrated annually with one of the most dramatic processions in the country. On the Thursday before Easter, the *Procesión de los Penitentes* (Procession of the Penitents) makes its slow way from the Ex-Convento San Miguel to Santa Prisca. Many participants carry heavy statues of saints, but bringing up the rear is an awesome sight: a column of self-flagellating penitents dressed in black or bare-chested, chained, many bearing wooden crosses. The procession is carried out, and witnessed, in pin-drop silence. On Saturday, a second procession reenacts the three times Jesus fell while carrying the cross. Free.

TULA

The legendary Toltec capital of Tula (originally Tollán) was founded around the 10th century by a high priest of the cult of Quetzalcoatl (according to legend, Quetzalcoatl himself). While it would never reach the height of Teotihuacán (and is not nearly as popular a site today as the great city), Tula was still the major capital of its era, boasting roughly 50,000 inhabitants at its zenith. It was an advanced society that knew how to build dams and canals, and spawned great artisans who worked especially with obsidian. The Toltecs also played a critical role in the development of central Mexico. Many believe they were the first truly militaristic society, one that used its armies to subjugate nearby tribes. In this sense, the Toltecs were the forerunners of the Aztecs.

Tula suffered a similar fate to Teotihuacán, in that it experienced a rather sudden and very final demise. However, its reign was much shorter. Evidence points to a great fire and destruction of the city in the 12th century, and it was eventually sacked by rival tribes.

Getting There

Tula is located about 50 miles north of Mexico City in the state of Hidalgo. By car, take the Circuito Interior to Avenida Ejército Nacional Mexicano, which becomes Boulevard Manuel Avila Camacho. This road turns into the Autopista México-Querétaro (Highway 57D). Continue on this road until you come to México 126, which takes you into town. Follow the signs for LAS RUINAS (the Ruins) to get to Tula. By bus, head to the Terminal del

Norte and catch an Ovnibus, run by **Autotransportes Valle de Mezquital** (55-5567-6791, www.gvm.com.mx). These are comfortable coaches that make trips every half hour from 6:20 AM—9:15 PM daily.

ATTRACTIONS, PARKS & RECREATION

THE RUINS OF TULA

773-732-0705
Carretera Tula-Tlahuelilpán

Today, Tula comprises a cluster of restored and reconstructed temples, buildings, ball courts, and four mighty statues that have made the ruins famous: *los Atlantes,* or the Atlanteans. Still, as you walk along a cactus-lined boulevard to the main plaza, you can almost imagine the metropolis that once stood here, a city of plazas and pyramids, canals and bridges, and beautiful sculptures. The site is open Monday to Sunday 9—5.

Jorge R. Acosta Museum

This small museum at the entrance to the site does a good job explaining the history of Tula and depicting how it must have looked in its heyday. The museum has a minor collection of artifacts from the site, as well as books and leaflets about the Toltecs. You can hire a guide here to take you around.

The Atlanteans at Tula

El Coatepantli

A protected "wall of snakes," *el Coatepantli* is one of the most intricate carvings to be found at Tula. It was the prototype of the designs found in Aztec cities later on. The reliefs show numerous animals and human skeletons being devoured by giant rattlesnakes.

Juego de Pelota (Ball Court) 1

One of two ball courts to be excavated in Tula, this one still has traces of the original carving in the southwest corner. Archaeologists found the remains of a warrior dressed in garments symbolic of Tlaloc, the rain god, at this site.

Pirámide B

Pyramid B, as it's labeled on the map of the site, is also known as the Pyramid of the Morning Star, and it is the most famous of all of Tula's monuments. Not a large pyramid, it is adorned with carvings of eagles, jaguars, coyotes, and pumas but is far more known for the four massive, solemn warrior statues standing sentry on its peak. The Atlanteans, or *Atlantes*, measure

La Plaza del Taco

If you want to eat in downtown Tula before you head back to Mexico City, look no farther than the Plaza del Taco, on the corner of Cinco de Mayo and Colegio Militar, across from the bus depot. This collection of taquerías has typical Mexican street food, from tacos to hot dogs (not the hot dog you're used to) to simple platters. Pick the stall that looks good to you, sit on the picnic-style table, and order away.

about 16 feet in height, were used to hold up the roof of a sacred temple that once stood here, and were not visible to the public. They are majestic sights, but unfortunately, three of the four are replicas; the originals were taken down due to overexposure to the elements. From the top of this pyramid you'll have a great view of the adjacent ruin, notable for its ordered rows of broken columns, called the Burnt Palace, which was damaged by invading tribes (probably the Aztecs).

Pirámide C

While its neighbor gets all the attention, Pyramid C is believed to be the most important religious structure in Tula. It was constructed in similar fashion to the great pyramids of Teotihuacán, showing the linkage between the two societies.

Juego de Pelota 2

This ball court is very similar in design to the one in Chichén Itzá. The platform in front of the court was known as the Tzompantli. It was here where the skulls of the decapitated were placed.

CATEDRAL DE SAN JOSÉ
Zaragoza Street, Tula

This fortress-like cathedral in Tula's *zócalo* is worth a visit if you're in town. Built between 1543 and 1554 by the Franciscans, it is a classic example of Renaissance architecture and the meshing of religion and invasion in the New World. Inside, note the unusual, colorful triptych, which shows Christ in distinctly Tulan surroundings, with none other than Quetzalcoatl next to him.

VALLE DE BRAVO

One of Mexico City's premier weekend getaways, Valle de Bravo combines the serene beauty of a manmade lake, the redolence of surrounding pine forests, a rainbow of flowers, and the quaint scenery of a 16th-century village with cobblestone streets and whitewashed houses with red-tiled roofs. It's the perfect haven for the tourist who loves to be outdoors. Nestled around the shores of Lake Avándaro, Valle offers plenty of water sports; the forests are popular hiking destinations; and even the air contributes, with thermal conditions making for ideal hang gliding and parasailing. This isn't the place to be for ancient ruins or impressive remnants of a colonial past. Instead, people come here to hike, bike, sail, glide, and relax. It's also home to one of the most impressive spa hotels you'll find in Mexico, as well as the scene of a spectacular natural wonder: the migration of the monarch butterflies.

Parasailing in Valle de Bravo Credit: Mexico Tourism Board

Getting There

Valle de Bravo is located just over 90 miles west of Mexico City. By car, take Paseo de Reforma to the Carretera Federal México-Toluca (Highway 15D). Once you get to Toluca, Highway 15D turns into Paseo Tollocan. Stay on the road until you come to Highway 134. Turn left and follow 134 to Carretera Toluca-Valle de Bravo. Turn right here and follow the road to Valle. Buses leave from Mexico City's **Terminal Poniente** every 20 minutes for Valle. The one-way trip takes about three hours. Because of the distances, it's best to spend a night here unless you've just come for the butterflies. There are actually two neighboring towns located along the lake: Valle de Bravo and Avándaro. For the purposes of this book, I've focused on the former. Finally, note that because Valle is overwhelmingly a weekend destination, many restaurants and business are closed from Monday to Thursday.

Useful Numbers and Information	
Tourism Office	726-269-6200 Corner of Porfirio Díaz and Zaragoza
Bus Terminal	726-262-0213
Sitio Taxi	726-262-1312
Red Cross	726-262-0391
Fire Department	726-262-2727
Hospital	726-262-1646/1349
Police	726-262-0360/4498/0219
Online Resource	www.todovalle.net

LODGING

EL SANTUARIO

55-5281-4090 (from Mexico City)
726-262-9100
www.elsantuario.com
Carretera a Colorines Km. 4.5, San Gaspar del Lago, Valle de Bravo

In my opinion, there is nothing like El Santuario in Valle, and indeed in most of Mexico. This eco-resort and spa hotel is a complete escape from the city (*any* city), and offers an experience of total pampering and relaxation. A spectacular circular hotel cut into the hillside, El Santuario offers gorgeous views of the lake and the whitewashed houses nestled against the hill on the far shore. The rooms are rustically elegant and environmentally friendly: there is no air-conditioning, but the far wall is all windowed, and a glass sliding door lets in the mountain breeze. The rooms are furnished in a rich, polished wood, and are quite spacious, with a separate desk and seating area, large bathrooms, and the pièce de résistance: facing the outdoors is an in-room heated sauna pool, with an infinity edge that will make you feel as if you're floating above the lake. If you do nothing more than check in for the weekend, enjoy the terrific restaurant and fantastic spa services, and soak in your spa pool, you've had an amazing time. At least, I did.

El Santuario's spa is the largest in Latin America, and features over 160 treatments. (Your stay includes a complimentary oxygen treatment to get things going.) It also has a *temazcal* with adjacent pool for a refreshing dip after a shamanic session. And the staff is part of the experience: adorned in long robes and extremely courteous, they enhance the natural energy of the place

El Santuario

with their service. This is a wonderful hotel, an amazing value, and on its own worth the trip to Valle. $$–$$$.

MESÓN DEL VIENTO

726-262-0048
www.mesondelviento.com
5 de Mayo 11, Col. Santa María, Valle de Bravo

A pleasant, modern boutique hotel in the center of town, el Mesón del Viento (House of the Wind) has minimalist, tastefully furnished rooms with bleached wood accents, a very good restaurant, open-air pool in the courtyard, and a pleasant host. The hotel is affiliated with Fly Mexico, which conducts hang gliding and paragliding tours in the area, and offers package deals. A minimum of two to three nights is required, depending on when you go. $$–$$$.

RODAVENTO

55-5292-5032 (from Mexico City)
726-251-4182/83/84/85
www.rodavento.com
Km. 3.5, Valle de Bravo Los Saucos

Located away from the town, Rodavento redefines the all-in-one experience. Here you get a beautifully appointed suite in an architecturally stunning hotel, combined with a host of activities ranging from hiking and kayaking to rappelling and parasailing. Rodavento also has a beautiful restaurant and excellent spa services. It is tailored for longer stays (five to seven days), but will sometimes accept short-term guests. $$$$.

DINING

EL CALLEJÓN DEL ARCO

Corner of Independencia and Juárez
This narrow, cobblestone street that meanders away from the plaza is legendary with the locals for its collection of food stalls. It's known around here as the *callejón del ham-*
bre (hunger street) and its specialty is the *taco de barbacoa*. Open daily 2 PM–late. $.

LOS CHURROS DEL VALLE

726-262-1477
Vergel 104, Valle de Bravo

This simple, homey place is more than a *churrería*, although the churros (available only on the weekends) are great. It's the quintessential neighborhood eatery in Valle, where children's drawings line the walls and the simple but flavorful meals are prepared with organic vegetables grown on owner Sergio Reyes's farm. If it's available, try his *torta azteca*, a Mexican version of chicken potpie. The help-yourself fresh salad bar is a nice bonus. Open Monday to Thursday 1–5:30 PM, Friday to Sunday 1–11 PM or midnight. $.

LA MICHOACANA

726-262-4082
Calle de la Cruz 10, Valle de Bravo

Among the best traditional Mexican restaurants in Valle, La Michoacana (not the ice cream shop by the same name in the main plaza) offers good value for the money and a cozy environment. Try the signature trout or any of the regional specialties, like *cecina* or mole. Open daily 8:30 AM–11 PM. $$.

LOS VELEROS

726-262-0370
Salitre 104, Valle de Bravo

More than one person told me this was the best restaurant in town, and it's hard to argue. Located in a restored colonial house, the elegant ambience meshes nicely with the refined cuisine. Seafood is the specialty here, from the trout in black butter to sea bass casserole. But you can also pick from typical Mexican specialties such as *escamoles* (ant eggs), or go for selections from the French side of the menu. Open Friday to Sunday 1 PM–midnight. $$.

ATTRACTIONS, PARKS & RECREATION

Biking
Mountain biking is tremendously popular at Valle, and several shops offer rentals, routes, and tours.

CICLO VALLE
722-138-0161
Av. Toluca 107, Valle de Bravo

CLETAS VALLE
726-262-02191
16 de Septiembre, Valle de Bravo

PABLO'S BIKES
726-262-3730
Joaquin Arcadia Pagaza 402, Valle de Bravo

Hang Gliding and Parasailing
The thermals around Lake Avándaro are ideal for sports in the air, and loads of *chilangos* come here each week to glide or sail with the currents. These outfits offer tandem flights for beginners, instruction, and other services.

ALAS DEL HOMBRE
726-262-6382
www.alas.com.mx
Plaza Valle Locales 22 and 26, Valle de Bravo

FLY MEXICO
512-467-2529 and 800-861-7198 (U.S.)
726-262-0579 (in Mexico)
5710 Fairlane Drive, Austin, TX 78757
A U.S.-based business that offers hang gliding and parasailing out of Valle.

Water Sports
Sailing, motorboats, and skiing are popular at Valle, although most boats around the lake are privately owned.

ESCUELA DE SKI (SKI SCHOOL)
726-262-1485
Marina Nacional 115, Valle de Bravo
Offers courses and sessions in waterskiing.

OUTWARD BOUND
726-262-6031
http://www.obmexico.org
Base Camp, Valle De Bravo
Offers courses in sailing as well as other activities.

LOS PERICOS
726-262-0558
Embarcadero Municipal (Municipal Dock)
Valle's first floating restaurant also rents motorboats by the hour.

WEEKLY & ANNUAL EVENTS

BUTTERFLY WATCHING
November to March
The annual migration of millions of monarch butterflies from North America to central Mexico is one of the wonders of nature, and a rare and incredible spectacle for those visiting Valle de Bravo during the winter months. There's a protected reserve just north of Valle where you can see the forest canopy literally carpeted with the butterflies, and walking among them is a magical experience. When you visit Valle during this season, you'll find scores of eager naturalists and nature lovers on their way to the site. There are guides on horseback located at the village of Los Saucos, near the reserve, who are ready to take you to see the incredible, shimmering sight. You can also arrange for a guide from the tourism office in Valle. To see these delicate creatures cover every inch of the trees like so many falling leaves is an amazing and rare treat. $$ for guides, but worth it.

6

PUEBLA

Pride of the Conquistadores

Legend has it that Puebla was built by angels. There are certainly enough churches to give credence to the myth. But the truth is that the Spanish built this beautiful city from the ground up, rather than swallowing an existing indigenous town. Mexico's fourth-largest city is one of its most picturesque. It was truly the pride of the conquistadores, and it remains a place with its own unique artistic legacy, stunning architecture, a rich and refined culinary tradition, and special historic significance.

What Puebla lacks, relative to other destinations in Mexico, is a major pre-Hispanic monument. Fortunately, nearby Cholula boasts—believe it or not—the remnants of what was once believed to be the largest pyramid in the world. Surrounding the two cities is a network of quaint towns that gives this part of central Mexico a colloquial magic worthy of Don Quixote.

Fort Loreto was the site of the infamous battle on Cinco de Mayo

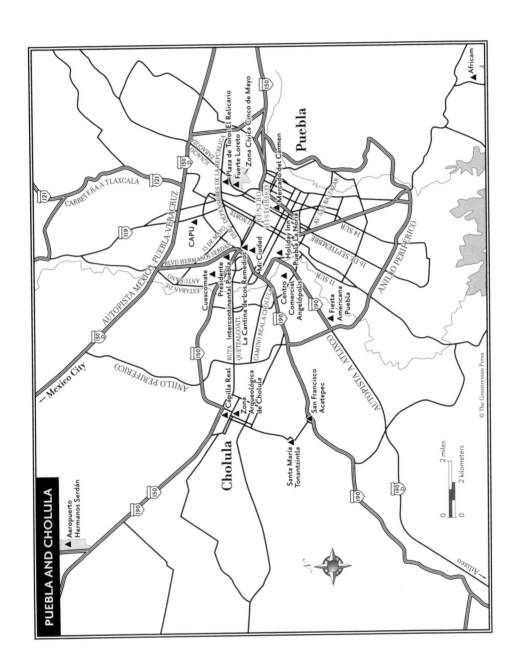

PUEBLA AND CHOLULA

Puebla

Cholula

Africam

Aeropuerto Hermanos Serdán

Mexico City

CARRETERA A TLAXCALA

AUTOPISTA MEXICO-PUEBLA-VERACRUZ

ANILLO PERIFERICO

AUTOPISTA A ATLIXCO

ANILLO PERIFÉRICO

El Relicario
Plaza de Toros
Fuerte Loreto
Zona Cívica Cinco de Mayo
Mercado del Carmen
CENTRO HISTÓRICO
IGNACIO ZARAGOZA
AV. DEFENSORES DE LA REPÚBLICA
II NORTE
15 DE MAYO
AV. SAN BALTAZAR
Holiday Inn
Puebla La Noria
16 DE SEPTIEMBRE
II SUR
14 SUR
CAPU
Mi Ciudad
Centro Comercial Angelópolis
Fiesta Americana Puebla
Cuexcomate
BLVD HERMANOS SERDÁN
ESTABAN DE ANTUÑANO
RUTA QUETZALCOATL
Presidente Intercontinental Puebla
La Cantina de los Remedios
CAMINO REAL A CHOLULA
Capilla Real
Zona Arqueológica de Cholula
San Francisco Acatepec
Santa María Tonantzintla

© The Countryman Press

2 miles
2 kilometers
0
0

Atlixco

Poblanos are justly proud of their home. Mole comes from here. So does Mexico's famed Talavera pottery. And Cinco de Mayo. Puebla's myriad church bells ring out a haunting melody. Its women have a reputation for their good looks. It offers the mesmerizing vista of snow-capped volcanoes. And it has one of the most amazing, and unexpected, wildlife parks you'll ever see. All in all, it is a place of remarkable beauty, culture, and tradition.

Getting There

By Car

Hop on Highway 150 from Mexico City, heading east. To get to Highway 150, you have a few options. An easy way from Polanco, Insurgentes, and Colonia Roma is to take Avenida Chapultepec to Calzado Ignacio Zaragoza, which will lead you to the highway. Another option is to take a central road like Avenida Cuauhtémoc, Insurgentes Sur, or Lázaro Cárdenas to Viaducto Presidente Miguel Alemán. Head east on the Viaducto and follow the signs to Puebla. You have a choice of the *cuota* (toll) or free road. Both are well paved, but the latter has more curves, some of them quite stomach-flipping at high speeds; the toll road is considered safer and faster.

By Bus

Bus travel to Puebla is easy and efficient. Buses depart every half hour from Mexico City's TAPO, Terminal del Norte, and Tasqueña stations, as well as Benito Juárez International Airport. You can get coach and first-class service to the **Central de Autobuses de Puebla** station, known as CAPU (222-224-6210, www.capu.com.mx). Bus lines that travel here include:

ADO
222-230-4000 (Puebla)
55-5133-2424 (Mexico City)
800-702-8000 (Toll-free in Mexico)
Boulevard H 5 de Mayo Norte No. 4222, Col. Las Cuartillas, Puebla

Estrella Roja (Red Star)
222-273-8300(Puebla)
55-5130-1800(Mexico City)
800-712-2284 (Toll-free in Mexico)
www.estrellaroja.com.mx
CAPU Station, Boulevard Norte 4222, Col. Las Cuartillas

UNO
222-230-4000 (Puebla)
55-5133-2424 (Mexico City)
800-702-8000 (Toll-free in Mexico)
www.uno.com.mx
Boulevard H 5 de Mayo Norte # 4222, Col. Las Cuartillas

Iglesia de la Compañía

By Air

Aeropuerto Internacional de Puebla
222-774-2804, 227-102-5066
www.aeropuertopuebla.com
Km. 91.5, Carretera Federal México-Puebla
The small Puebla airport services mostly regional airlines, but also Aeroméxico and
Continental Airlines.

GETTING AROUND

The Historic Center of Puebla is best experienced on foot. If the majority of your time will
be spent here, you won't need to worry about renting a car, and you'll need taxis only for
longer trips. However, there is plenty to see outside the city center. If you want to visit
Cholula and Atlixco (both highly recommended), you can travel by bus, taxi, or rent a car.

Taxis

At the CAPU bus terminal and at several points in the city, you'll find authorized taxi
kiosks offering rides at flat rates to specific destinations. Pay the attendant at the kiosk for
your ticket, and pay the driver nothing but the (optional, and always appreciated) tip. If
you can, avoid hailing a taxi on the street, but if you have to, make sure it's clearly labeled
and negotiate the fare before you set off. If it sounds too high, it probably is. You can have
your hotel arrange a taxi for you, or you can call directly. If you plan to do a lot of sight-seeing, you might want to talk to your driver about booking the taxi for the day. This can work

Useful Numbers and Information	
Area Code in Puebla	222
Any emergency	066
Ambulance	222-235-8631
Red Cross	222-234-0000/9939/9940, 213-7703/04
State Police	222-232-3154/2222
Police	222-243-1022/1104/7224
Hospitals	
University Hospital	222-229-5500, ext. 6127/6000
UPAEP Hospital	222-229-8100/02/03
Hospital Ángeles	222-303-6600
Tourist Information	5 Oriente Street 3, Centro Histórico, Puebla
	222-777-1519/20, 800-326-8656
Tow trucks/road service	222-234-4378, 222-288-8800/01/02/03/04
National Emergency & Tourist Info	800-987-8284
Online Resources	www.sectur.pue.gob.mx
	www.todopuebla.com
	www.vivecholula.gob.mx (for Cholula)

out to the same price as a car rental, and the convenience of having a chauffeur who knows where he's going can't be beat. Radio Taxi numbers in Puebla are 222-243-7055; 222-243-7212; 222-240-6299; 222-240-6369; and 222-237-7777.

Bus

Public buses here are convenient, numerous, and quite cheap. From Puebla's CAPU bus terminal, you can catch frequent and very inexpensive service to Cholula and Atlixco.

Car Rental

The following agencies are located in Puebla:

Avis (three locations)
222-249-6199
Blvd. Atlyxcayotl, Km. 5 Expressway at the Fiesta Americana Hotel, Puebla
Open Monday to Friday 9–7, Weekends 9–4.
222-249-6199
Blvd. Hermanos Serdán 104, Local 5, Puebla
Open Monday to Friday 8–7, Weekends 9–2.
222-298-9769
Puebla Airport, Carretera Federal Mexico, Puebla Km 91.5 Huejotzingo, Puebla
Open Monday to Friday 8–4.

Europcar (three locations)
222-224-2418
Blvd. Hermanos Serdán 796, Col. San Rafael Oriente, Puebla
Open daily 8–9.
555-207-5572
Circuito Juan Pablo II 3107, Col. Las Animas at the Puebla Hotel Angelopolis
Open daily 8–5.
222-224-2418
Puebla Airport, Carretera Federal Mexico, Puebla Km 91.5 Huejotzingo, Puebla
Open 24/7.

Hertz (two locations)
227-102-5050
Puebla Airport, Carretera Federal Mexico, Puebla Km 91.5 Huejotzingo, Puebla
Open daily 8:30–7:30.
222-249-0049
Boulevard Atlixco 307, Col. La Paz
Open daily 8:30–7:30.

A Brief History

After Cortés took Tenochtitlán, the Spanish set about colonizing their New World with vigor. They had two of the most important pieces to the new realm secured: a rich port in Veracruz and a new capital in what would become Mexico City. These cities became a vital trade route for the empire, and Puebla, nestled in a valley halfway between the two, was established as a resting stop along the way.

La Puebla de los Ángeles, or Puebla of the Angels, was the first city in New Spain that was not built upon the ruins of a conquered settlement. It was laid out according to an organized grid pattern, unlike the urban chaos of Mexico City. Puebla also grew quickly, thanks to its convenient location and the Spanish practice of encomienda, which gave the conquistadores generous land grants and allowed them to enslave the surrounding Native population to work the land. The system came with one important caveat: the beneficiaries needed to do their part to promote the growth of the Roman Catholic faith. Thus, as Puebla and nearby Cholula flourished, so did their religious institutions, and the sister cities gained fame for Puebla's magnificent cathedral and their many churches.

Puebla was also known for its fine arts and crafts. Its Talavera pottery became an example of excellence in Mexican craftsmanship, with workshops still following the centuries-old techniques today. The city was a showcase of baroque architecture, borrowing elements of Moorish design much like Spanish cities in the mother country.

While Puebla was not a focal point of the Mexican War of Independence, it was a hotbed of political unrest for much of the 1800s. On May 5, 1862, it became the site of one of the most symbolic battles in Mexican history, when a disciplined French army, marching toward Mexico City, was defeated by Mexican troops loyal to Benito Juárez. The battle took place at Forts Loreto and Guadalupe, and the Mexican troops were under the command of General Ignacio Zaragoza Seguín. Another soldier who distinguished himself in the fighting was one Porfirio Díaz.

Outnumbered and poorly equipped, the Mexicans pulled off a huge military upset, and Cinco de Mayo has gone down in Mexican lore as one of the greatest moral victories in the country's history. I say moral because the triumph at Puebla didn't last long. After the setback, the French returned, steamrolled the resistance, and marched into Mexico City, where they promptly made Archduke Maximilian emperor of Mexico. After Díaz took over, Puebla flourished under the Porfiriato, but discontent continued to bubble around the nation. When the Mexican Revolution was declared, one of its first skirmishes was in Puebla, at the house of the Serdán family, now a must-see museum.

In the 20th century, immigrants from Europe flocked to the city, especially Italians and Germans. The town also evolved from its agricultural roots to become an industrialized city that produces cotton and textiles in addition to pottery, and is home to a Volkswagen factory that not only manufactures the Beetle taxis you see buzzing around Mexico City, but cars that are distributed all over the continent.

CENTRO HISTÓRICO

Puebla's Centro Histórico, or Historic Center, was declared a Cultural Heritage Site by UNESCO in 1987 thanks to its magnificent Catedral de Puebla (Puebla Cathedral), stunning architecture, tree-lined plazas, and distinctive churches. The city has a modern side, but it is the city center—the cultural, historic, and artistic heart of the state of Puebla—that will captivate you.

As with most Mexican towns, you'll begin at the *zócalo,* a beautiful and wide plaza bordered by the cathedral, the municipal palace, fountains, shops, and hotels. The Historic Center also has a number of small museums, as well as pockets, corners, niches, and streets devoted to candy makers, woodworkers, and artists. It is replete with magnificent

CENTRO HISTÓRICO

14 ORIENTE
16 ORIENTE
12 ORIENTE
10 ORIENTE
8 ORIENTE
6 ORIENTE
2 ORIENTE
3 ORIENTE

14 NORTE
14 ORIENTE
18
16
14 NORTE
12 NORTE
12 NORTE

Mercado Gastronómico

14 SUR
12 SUR
10 SUR

Casa Reyna

10 NORTE
Iglesia de San Francisco
La Purificadora
Centro Comercial San Francisco

8 NORTE
BLVD. HÉROES DEL 5 DE MAYO

BLVD. HÉROES DEL 5 DE MAYO

8 SUR

AV. JUAN DE PALAFOX Y MENDOZA

18 ORIENTE
6 NORTE

Teatro Principal
Barrio del Artista
Museo Casa de Alfeñique
Mercado de Artesanías "El Parián"
Casona de la China Poblana
Ekos
Iglesia de la Compañía
9 SUR
Mesón Sacristía Compañía
Plazuela de los Sapos
9 ORIENTE
11 ORIENTE

18 ORIENTE
4 NORTE

Casa de los Hermanos Serdán
Museo Universitario (Casa de los Muñecos)
Hotel del Portal
El Ranchito
5 ORIENTE
Exconvento de San Juan (Biblioteca de Palafox)
7 ORIENTE
Museo Amparo
4 SUR

2 NORTE

18 ORIENTE
16 ORIENTE
14 ORIENTE
12 ORIENTE
10 ORIENTE
8 ORIENTE
6 ORIENTE
4 ORIENTE
Holiday Inn Centro Histórico Puebla
Zócalo
3 ORIENTE
Catedral
Mesón de Capuchinas
2 SUR
16 DE SEPTIEMBRE

5 DE MAYO
Iglesia de Santo Domingo de Guzmán (Capilla del Rosario)
Palacio del Ayuntamiento
Hotel Royalty
Antojitos Acapulco
Tourist Information Center
El Mural de Los Poblanos
Camino Real Puebla

Exconvento de Santa Mónica
Exconvento de Santa Rosa
3 NORTE
5 NORTE
Hotel Provincia Express
Museo Bello y Gonzalez
Fonda de Santa Clara
3 SUR

18 PONIENTE
16 PONIENTE
14 PONIENTE
12 PONIENTE
10 PONIENTE
8 PONIENTE
6 PONIENTE
4 PONIENTE
2 PONIENTE
AV. REFORMA
Aristos Hotel Puebla
NH Puebla
5 SUR
9 PONIENTE
11 PONIENTE

7 NORTE
3 PONIENTE
5 PONIENTE
7 PONIENTE
7 SUR

6 NORTE
9 SUR 6

11 NORTE
11 SUR
Museo Nacional del Ferrocarril
Paseo Bravo
13 NORTE
13 SUR

© The Countryman Press

architecture, from the neoclassic municipal palace, to houses decorated with azulejo tiles, to intricate and elaborate 18th-century baroque facades. And it is home to some of Puebla's best dining and lodging options, including many luxurious boutique hotels.

WHAT TO EAT: PUEBLA SPECIALTIES AND THEIR LEGENDS

To say that Puebla is known for its food is an understatement. Some of Mexico's most famous dishes originated here. The food that has made the city famous is intertwined with its history and culture, and many specialties have accompanying legends.

The first and most iconic dish is the world-famous **mole poblano,** a rich sauce made with chocolate, chiles, seeds and/or nuts, and a variety of other ingredients, based on the recipe. Mole poblano is typically served with chicken and enchiladas, but it is also eaten with pork and other dishes. But mole is actually used to describe any kind of sauce that is characterized by the way it's made (*moler* means "to grind" in Spanish). In addition to the poblano variety, there are other moles, like mole *de pipián,* made with pumpkin seeds. This mole can be either a red (mole *rojo*), or green (mole *verde*) sauce.

Mole is sacred in Puebla. It was invented by an order of Dominican nuns belonging to Santa Rosa de Lima Monastery. The story goes that, in 1697 or '98, the bishop of Puebla heard that the viceroy of New Spain was paying the town a visit, and he asked the nuns to prepare something special. One Sor Andrea de la Asunción had the bright idea of grinding chiles with a pestle, and adding sesame seeds, almonds, peanuts, chocolate, cinnamon, anise, sugar, clove, flour tortilla, and garlic. The sisters were so entranced with her work that one of them broke her vow of silence, exclaiming "¡Hermana, que bien mole!" or "Sister, how well do you grind!" (It sounds better in Spanish). Thus originated the mole poblano. The viceroy was so impressed with the dish that, as a gift, he had the nuns' kitchen tiled with beautiful Talavera tiles. Tourists can visit the kitchen today.

Mole is a Puebla classic Source: Mexico Tourism Board

Puebla's second-most-celebrated delicacy is *chiles en nogada,* a classic seasonal dish that is an unusual blend of sweet and savory. The recipe is made with poblano chiles stuffed with *picadillo* (a mixture of minced meat—typically beef and pork—fruits, and spices), drenched in a walnut-based cream sauce and drizzled with pomegranate seeds. The green chile, red pomegranate, and white sauce represent the flag of Mexico, and the dish is associated with Mexican independence.

According to Poblano lore, it was made for General Agustín de Iturbide, the victorious commander of the Mexican War of Independence, who became Mexico's first

Centro Histórico Walking Tours

To experience all there is to see and do in Puebla's Centro Histórico will take you more than one day. That being the case, I've put together the following two walking tours that cover what I feel are its best sights. Of course, there is also plenty to see and do beyond the Historic Center.

Tour One

Begin at the **zócalo** and walk to the **Catedral de Puebla.** After touring the cathedral, cross 5 Oriente Street to the **Biblioteca Palafox;** this site should only take you about 15 minutes to tour but is worth the visit (Note: booklovers will be tempted to spend 10 hours here).

Walk back across the *zócalo* and cross Avenida Juan de Palafox y Mendoza to reach the **Palacio Municipal.** Much of this building is closed to tourists, but you can walk inside and admire the architecture, and wander around the pleasant, vibrant plaza. If you're here on Sunday, you're likely to find a street fair in the square.

The neoclassic Palacio Municipal

emperor. In 1821, after signing the Treaty of Cordoba, which gave Mexico its independence, the general was on his way from Veracruz to Mexico City when he stopped at Puebla. The town held a feast in his honor, and once again, they called upon nuns (Augustine nuns, this time) to prepare the feast. The sisters came up with *chiles en nogada,* which has since become a national favorite eaten mostly during the months of August and September, when pomegranates are in season. There are restaurants that offer the dish year-round.

Across the street from the municipal palace on Calle 2 is the **Casa de los Muñecos,** which is, frankly, a rather weird museum, but one that has a terrific collection of Renaissance art.

If you want to break for lunch, a good, cheap, and fast option is right in front of you at **El Ranchito,** in the lobby of the Hotel el Portal at the corner of the *zócalo.* A pricier but excellent alternative is the **Mesón de la China Poblana** just down the road.

Continue east on Avenida Juan de Palafox y Mendoza to the corner of Calle 4 Sur and the **Iglesia de La Compañia,** the final resting place of *la China Poblana* (more on her later).

Walk one block south on Calle 4 to Calle 5 Oriente. On the left you'll see the **Plazuela de los Sapos,** a haven for antiques shops and home to an almost 200-year-old Sunday market. Stop at the corner of 5 Oriente and 6 Sur at a hole-in-the-wall institution called **La Pasita,** where you can try the signature, potent raisin liquor.

Walk to 7 Oriente and turn right, heading west, to 2 Sur. On your left will be the outstanding **Museo Amparo.** Give yourself at least two hours to enjoy the best of Puebla's museums.

Tour Two

Beginning again at the *zócalo,* walk north on Avenida 5 de Mayo, a pedestrian-only street lined with shops. After three blocks you'll come to 4 Poniente Street and the **Iglesia de Santo Domingo de Guzmán,** with its stunning **Capilla del Rosario** (Chapel of the Rosary).

After, walk north to the next block, Calle 6, and turn right. You're now on Calle Santa Clara, named after the convent of Santa Clara, and today known for the many candy shops that sell Puebla's distinctive sweets. Stop in at **La Central** and try one or two.

Continue east down 6 Oriente to the Casa de Aquiles Serdán (House of Aquiles Serdán), one of my favorite cultural stops in the city. After, you can briefly visit the **Iglesia de San Cristóbal** just around the corner on 6 Oriente and 4 Norte.

Continue on 6 Oriente and turn right on 6 Norte heading south. At the corner of 6 Norte and 4 Oriente, take in the ornate facade of the **Casa de Alfeñique.**

Turn left on 4 Oriente, and you'll find yourself between the crafts market **Mercado El Parián** and the **Barrio del Artista,** a neighborhood of artist studios and workshops. Browse at your leisure.

After, head north again. On the corner of 6 Oriente and 6 Norte is the **Teatro Principal.** Turn right on 8 Oriente and walk across the busy Boulevard Heroes del 5 de Mayo. You'll come to the modern convention center, and just beyond on a pedestrian walkway, a well-deserved and fabulous lunch at **La Purificadora.**

From the hotel, you'll need to get to 14 Oriente, which is just north of La Purificadora. It's a little confusing, but you'll be able to see the towers of your next destination: the **Iglesia de San Francisco.**

If you have the time and energy, make a final stop at the **Mercado Gastronómico,** at the corner of 14 Oriente and 12 Norte, where you can find all kinds of spices, foods, and stalls selling delicious local specialties.

While these are Puebla's culinary superstars, they are also just the tip of the iceberg. *Chalupas, molotes,* and *cemitas*—all popular street foods—hail from this city, as do chiles rellenos (stuffed poblano pepper) and other specialties. And finally, Puebla has its own brand of candies. To be honest, they're not really my thing, as they tend to be extremely saccharine, but they comprise mostly jellied fruits and nut-based sweets. One candy in particular has a unique story behind it. One day a girl from the Santa Clara convent decided to play a prank on one of the nuns who had left an empty pot simmering on the fire. She threw in sweet potato and sugar, figuring the resulting paste would be revolting, but when the nun returned and tasted it, she found the concoction delicious. The confection came to be known as *camotes*.

WHAT TO BUY: PUEBLA HANDICRAFTS

Puebla's most beautiful export is its unparalleled Talavera pottery, known worldwide for its quality craftsmanship. During the reign of the Spanish, Puebla was the chief ceramics producer in New Spain. There are cheap knockoffs to be found all over Mexico (and all over Puebla, for that matter), and for some tourists, the difference isn't enough to warrant forking over the additional pesos. But I firmly believe that those who can should seek out the real deal; it isn't exorbitant, and the artwork and tradition behind the finished product makes it an exceptional and authentic souvenir. To find out what makes Talavera so special, I went to the Santa Catarina workshop in nearby Cholula. A family-run operation, Santa Catarina is one of only a handful of certified Talavera producers in the state. Here's what I learned about the art of Talavera:

- Talavera is named for the Spanish town of Talavera de la Reina, and the practices originating there in the 16th century are followed to this day.

- *Talavera* is not a reference to the design of the piece, but rather to the process.

- Puebla is the only state in which the product is crafted completely by hand.

- Talavera uses a blend of two different kinds of clay native to the region; after mixing, it is set aside to absorb humidity to make it more malleable.

- The prepared clay is pressed by foot, molded into cubes, covered in plastic, and stored. When it's time to make a piece, the plastic is removed and the clay is kneaded repeatedly.

Talavera pottery crafted at the Santa Catarina workshop

It is then molded on the potter's wheel; after the piece is formed, it is left to dry for up to 12 weeks, then fired in a kiln at up to 1000°C—the orange-colored product that emerges is called *jahuete*.

- A design is stenciled onto the *jahuete* using templates that incorporate indigenous, Spanish, Far Eastern, and Moorish patterns and motifs.

- The piece is painted using natural dyes. Puebla's Talavera is known mostly for its azulejo-blue designs, but typical pieces are also made using cobalt and light blue, yellow, green, orange, and black.

- After the piece has been painted, it goes into the kiln again. They say Talave "sings"—this is because, as the piece is left to cool after it has been fired, it tin
- At any of these stages, irreparable imperfections and cracks can occur.

So how do you know you're buying the real deal? Every authentic piece of Puebla Talavera is marked with the signature of the producer and the DO, or *denominación de origen*.

Beyond Talavera, you'll find excellent ironworks, carved onyx, and embroidered textiles in Puebla. One indigenous tradition that has survived is amate paper, a coffee-colored, organic paper made from the bark of the amate tree, in which pre-Hispanic designs are cut out.

LODGING

ARISTOS HOTEL PUEBLA

800-901-0200 (toll free in Mexico)
www.aristoshotels.com
Avenida Reforma 533, Col. Centro
Histórico, Puebla

The Aristos in Puebla is located in a land-mark building in the Historic Center. Among its strengths are the friendly and helpful staff, and amenities that include a small, covered heated swimming pool; gym; central air-conditioning in the rooms; and a pleasant lobby with a piano lounge. Its rooms are spacious but gloomy, as are the hallways leading to them. Faded carpeting, bare furnishings, and small TVs (albeit with satellite channels) don't help, but its rea-sonable prices will attract those on a budget. $.

CAMINO REAL PUEBLA

222-229-0909
www.caminoreal.com/puebla
7 Poniente 105, Col. Centro Histórico,
Puebla

A colonial treasure in the heart of the city center, the Camino Real was once a 16th-century convent. The hotel, immaculately restored, takes the best of the original struc-ture and design of the period—wide patios and cloisters, colonial architecture and fur-nishings—and adds touches of modern ele-gance and comfort. Bathed in a rustic yellow hue, the rooms have marvelous antique wooden beds, original frescoes, wood-beam ceilings, and chandelier lighting, which art-fully convey a sense of New Spain luxury. Adding to its sense of history is the legend of the convent's founding: according to lore, a priest named Leonardo Ruiz de la Peña was caught in a storm and dragged into a rushing river by his horse. At the point of drowning, the priest prayed to the Virgin of the Immaculate Conception for help, promising to build a convent in her name if she would save him. She did, and he did, and you might want to throw up a prayer of thanks, too, after settling in. $$–$$$.

CASA REYNA

222-232-2109
www.casareyna.com
Privada Dos Oriente 1007, Col. Centro
Histórico, Puebla

Located on what was historically "the other side" (as in, the wrong side of the tracks) of Puebla, Casa Reyna has certainly helped dispel the inglorious past and usher in a more luxurious present. This hotel com-bines three 16th-century houses in a beau-tifully executed merging of the old (exposed redbrick archways) and the new (flat-screen TVs, clean, minimalist design). Its 10 suites are uniquely designed, with furni-ture that was custom-built for the hotel. The pieces are for sale, and they're worth the price. The hotel has Talavera décor throughout, from the spindles on the stairs, to the bathrooms, which all have Talavera sinks, to the crockery in the restaurant.

ra de la Reyna, one
kshops to be
cate of authenticity.

___ ___ ___A POBLANA
222-242-5336; 800-727-5775
www.casonadelachinapoblana.com
Corner of 4 Norte and Avenida Juan de
Palafox y Mendoza, Col. Centro Histórico,
Puebla

One of Puebla's boutique hotel gems, the
Casona de la China Poblana balances local
history and elegance. A 17th-century colonial mansion in the heart of Puebla, this
place is likely to take your breath away, with
its warm red walls and white-bordered
arches; open-air courtyard restaurant;
tastefully appointed lounging spaces; and
second-floor, plant-lined balcony with its

A suite at the Casona de la China Poblana

spectacular view of the Iglesia de la
Compañia. The hotel also has a very cool
bar in El Aposentillo.

But the 10 rooms, all uniquely designed,
are what make La Casona really stand out:
immaculate and romantic, they are as beautiful and welcoming as the rest of the hotel.
As for the hotel's name, in the courtyard
you'll find a statue of a dark-skinned
woman: this is *la China Poblana.* Legend has
it that she was an Arab (alternate accounts
say Indian) princess named Mirra who was
captured as a girl, sold into slavery, and
brought to Puebla in the 17th century. Mirra
came to be much loved and respected for
her spirituality and nobility. She spent the
remainder of her life in Puebla, dying in
the very house that now carries her name,
and her story. $$$–$$$$.

FIESTA AMERICANA PUEBLA
222-225-9300
www.fiestaamericana.com
Blvd. Atlixcayótl Km. 5, Fraccionamiento La
Vista, Puebla

Located in the newer part of the city, this
branch of the reliable Fiesta Americana is
ideal for the business traveler, thanks to its
business center, proximity to Puebla's
industrial heart, and access to the La Vista
Country Club golf course. Its reasonable
rates and location near the city's largest and
finest shopping center also make it appeal-
ing to families. The rooms are large and
comfortably furnished. All have views of
the golf course and/or the large, amorphous
outdoor pool. If you can, go for the two-
room, 1.5-bath junior suites. The hotel lies
between the historic center and Cholula.
$$–$$$.

HACIENDA SAN PEDRO COXTOCAN
222-199-7469, 199-5593
www.haciendasanpedrocoxtocan.com
Km. 78 Carretera Federal a México, Puebla

Living room fit for an hacendado *at San Pedro Coxtocan*

If you want an enriching lodging (and dining) experience quite removed from the norm, take a look at Hacienda San Pedro Coxtocan, a restored 16th-century hacienda steeped in history and romance. During the 19th century, a British couple named Harry and Rosalie Evans bought this former wheat plantation and moved in, on the cusp of the Mexican Revolution. When the rebellion broke out, the couple left Mexico, but Harry returned in 1917. He found the hacienda in the clutches of the revolutionaries, who killed him shortly after his arrival. When Rosalie learned of his fate, the heartbroken widow also returned to their home and defended it against repeated raids until she, too, was killed in 1924.

In more modern times, the hacienda gained renown for its stables and became quite the equestrian retreat. Among the distinguished guests who came to ride here were former presidents Ronald Reagan and George H. W. Bush. Today, the ranch has been converted into a beautifully rustic hotel, with only 11 rooms and acres of space to explore and enjoy. The rooms are spacious and retain the charm and ambience of the past, while offering comfortable beds, including a lovely sleigh bed in the huge master bedroom. The hotel has a fabulous living room, a long, high-ceilinged affair with candelabra, massive stone fireplace, and wooden furniture typical of its colonial roots.

All meals are freshly prepared and served at the formal dining table, where you'll feel like a Mexican landlord as you dine on the excellent farm-fresh cooking of the hotel's chef (all meals are included in the stay). After, make sure to visit the classic example of a typical Poblano-tiled kitchen.

Other fun niches in the place are the serene grounds, the library and game room, which includes a billiard table, and the cellar bar, a true bodega where you can retire for a nightcap after dinner. Removed from the city, the hacienda is a quiet retreat where you can lounge in a leather sofa with a book, visit the 16th-century chapel where Rosalie used to pray, or sink into a Jacuzzi tub, close your eyes, and listen to nothing. $$–$$$.

HOLIDAY INN CENTRO HISTÓRICO PUEBLA

222-246-0555, 223-6600
www.holidayinn.com
2 Oriente 211, Col. Centro Histórico, Puebla

This Holiday Inn is special. The landmark historic building was once the Palacio San Leonardo, the 19th-century home of one of the city's wealthiest families. Decorated in the French art nouveau style, the hotel has retained the opulence of the former residence, especially in the lobby, which boasts a magnificent stained-glass dome, an impressive chandelier, and a carpeted grand staircase. The lobby bar has original 19th-century illustrations, and the grand dining room could be straight out of a small Parisian palace. The sit-down reception is another touch of throwback elegance, as is the silver-tray room service. The hotel has had the same owner for 50 years, and he used to live here, so the standards have been consistent for decades.

The rooms don't reflect the same grandeur (the hotel would be far more expensive if they did), but they are clean and cozy, with polished wood floors, minimal décor, and—again, an old-fashioned touch—doorbells instead of knockers. For added peace and quiet, stay on the top floor, which doesn't allow kids. The outdoor pool has views of nearby churches, and the terrace is the best place to have your breakfast. $–$$$.

HOLIDAY INN PUEBLA LA NORIA

222-211-9000
www.holidayinn.com/pueblanoria
Circuito Juan Pablo II 1936, Col. Exhacienda La Noria, Puebla

A completely different entity from the Holiday Inn Centro Histórico, this branch, located just off the Mexico City–Puebla highway, is an affordable choice catering especially to business travelers. It's close to the sprawling Angelópolis shopping center, and a few minutes by car from the city center. A tall building, the Holiday Inn has great views both of the city and the surrounding volcanoes. The rooms are basic and come equipped with desks, TV, coffeepot, and free high-speed wireless Internet access. There's also a fitness center and pool on premises, and the lobby lounge often features live acts on weekend nights. $–$$.

HOTEL DEL PORTAL

800-087-0107
www.hoteldelportal.com
Juan de Palafox y Mendoza 205, Col. Centro Histórico, Puebla

The Hotel del Portal offers a number of benefits for the price. At the top of the list is its unbeatable location right on the zócalo, with a view that's best enjoyed from the hotel's wraparound balcony. Then there's the lobby restaurant, El Ranchito, which serves up tasty local fare at reasonable prices. There's also an incongruous Irish-pub-themed room in the lobby that's used for private meetings and groups. You won't fall in love with the rooms, which hark back to colonial days in their ascetic décor (white walls featuring prominent wrought-iron crosses), but the bright and leafy interior, coupled with the old-fashioned reception desk, lend the place a quaint, if faded, charm. There's also wireless Internet throughout and a business center. Finally, you'll love the hotel's bargain rates. $.

HOTEL PROVINCIA EXPRESS

222-246-3557, 246-3642
Avenida Reforma 141, Col. Centro
Histórico, Puebla

Not only is this one of the most inexpensive lodging options in the city center, it's also got plenty of character. Start with the mosaic work on the building's façade. The 37 rooms may be rather monastic, but the interior has vaulted ceilings, plenty of original décor, and a dark, gothic charm to it. Don't get me wrong; this isn't a luxury property. But as far as budget accommodations go, you get quite a lot of the flavor of colonial Puebla here. And it comes with free parking, cable TV, and laundry service. $.

HOTEL ROYALTY

222-242-4740
www.hotelr.com
Portal Hidalgo 8, Col. Centro Histórico, Puebla

Celebrating its 60th anniversary in 2008, the Hotel Royalty offers excellent location on the *zócalo* and reasonable prices. Its 45 rooms are frugal, but they are carpeted, clean, and come with basic amenities (TV, phone, room service, and laundry service). You can upgrade to a suite with a balcony overlooking the plaza for not much more in price. The hotel's lobby restaurant has typical Poblano cuisine with pleasant outdoor seating. $.

MESÓN DE CAPUCHINAS

222-232 8088
www.mexicoboutiquehotels.com/capuchinas/index.shtml
9 Oriente 16, Col. Centro Histórico, Puebla

A sister of the nearby **Mesón de la Sacristía Compañía,** this small hotel is in some ways its opposite. While its partner is lavishly decorated and stuffed with antique furnishings, this place is an exercise in elegant restraint. In contrast to the bright colors of its sister, Mesón de Capuchinas keeps to a muted, warm palette. But in other ways, it is very much the same. The rooms are comfortable and spacious, with gorgeous beds (many of them wrought-iron four-poster affairs) dominating a cozy living space. The antique furnishings are of the best quality. And the restaurant is excellent, complemented by fine cooking classes, an add-on feature for guests and visitors. With eight rooms in all, it's so private and tranquil that you'll feel like you've been invited to enjoy a friend's lovely home. The plate of cookies and sweets placed outside your door every day makes a stay here that much more special. $$.

MESÓN DE LA SACRISTÍA COMPAÑÍA

222-232-4513
www.mesones-sacristia.com
6 Sur 304, Callejón de los Sapos, Col. Centro Histórico, Puebla

Welcome to what I feel is the most whimsical hotel in Puebla, the Mesón de la Sacristía Compañía. Maybe it's the bright blue and pink paint. Or the dizzying collection of superb antiques and Talavera pieces that make this place feel like a gallery as much as a boutique hotel. Or the eight unique, ample, elaborately decorated rooms, which certainly aren't your typical accommodations. In fact, if more than one room is available, check out a few to see which one most appeals to you. Complementing the beautiful antiques is the artfully prepared cuisine. Mesón de la Sacristía Compañía is so renowned for its Poblano cuisine that it offers cooking classes—one of many reasons people choose to stay here. Add first-class service to the menu, and you have a hotel that is luxuriously homey . . . in a whimsical sort of way. $$.

NH PUEBLA

222-309-1919; 800-903-3300
www.nh-hotels.com
Avenida 5 Sur 105, Col. Centro Histórico,
Puebla

Housed in a building that not too long ago
was a bus terminal, the NH has made an
adept transition to its present incarnation
as a hotel. From the exterior blue paint to
the sleek, modern rooms, this is a distinctive property that's a bargain for the value.
Once you walk in, you'll forget all about its
public transportation past. The interior is
done in black, red, and white, and the
rooms have minimalist, dark wood décor.
Located in the Historic Center a few blocks
from the *zócalo,* it's convenient both for
tourists and business travelers, thanks to
two meeting rooms, a fitness center, and a
business center. It also caters to handi-
capped tourists. One of the hotel's nicest
additions is its rooftop open-air pool,
which is small but offers fine views of one
of the city's churches and, on a clear day,
the majestic volcano in the distance.
$–$$$.

PRESIDENTE INTERCONTINENTAL PUEBLA

222-213-7070, 800-9097-1005
www.ichotelsgroup.com
Avenida Hermanos Serdán 141, Col.
Amor, Puebla

This new, elegant property sits between
Puebla's Historic Center (2 miles away)
and Cholula (3 miles away). While its
location means lots of taxi rides for guests
who stay here, the Presidente compen-
sates with comfortable, modern rooms,
an impressive lobby with a lovely glass-
domed ceiling, and terrific service.
Sculptures and Talavera ceramics abound
in the public areas of the hotel, and the
pool in the courtyard is large and inviting.
Some rooms offer beautiful views of the
Popocatépetl and Ixtaccíhuatl volcanoes.

The hotel has a full spa and fitness center
open 24/7, and two restaurants. $$–$$$.

LA PURIFICADORA

222-309-1920
www.lapurificadora.com
Callejón de la Norte 802, Paseo San
Francisco, Barrio el Alto, Puebla

La Purificadora is my favorite hotel in
Puebla, and among my favorites in Mexico,
for a few reasons. For one, it is architec-
turally unique, a blend of minimalism, dra-
matic effect, rustic antiquity, and modern
chic. From the crumbling, exposed walls
left over from colonial times, the M. C.
Escher–like broad stairway, and the bare
coal fire-pits in the open-air lobby to the
modern, creatively designed rooms, the
hotel presents a delightful contrast. Even

Lobby, Hotel La Purificadora

the colors reflect the dichotomy: earth tones and pure white mixed with plush purple couches. At night, candles and fires fill the hotel, furthering the commingling of old and new.

The rooms maximize the given space and include flat-screen TVs, iPod stereos, sink-into-sleep beds, and contemporary décor. One of the coolest spots in Puebla is the upstairs bar and pool area. The pool, an open-air zero-level affair with a glass wall, offers swimmers spectacular views of the nearby Iglesia de San Francisco, while onlookers get great views of the swimmers. And the restaurant is one of the most innovative in the city, a must-visit if you're looking for creative Mexican cuisine.

La Purificadora is a gem, and a hidden one at that. You'll find no prominent signs above the door, and the hotel is tucked in a corner of town that is removed from the tourist bustle but still within the historic city-center limits. $$–$$$.

DINING

ANTOJITOS ACAPULCO
222-246-5628
Avenida 5 Poniente, Col. Centro Histórico, Puebla

This tiny stall has been here since 1962, and I can only hope it's here for another 40-plus years. The freshly prepared street food is delicious, and the garrulous woman serving it up makes for added entertainment. The menu is limited to *pelonas* (fried buns with beef and lettuce), *molotes* (fried, folded tortillas), tacos, flautas, and tostadas. As for the filling, try *picadillo* (a spicy ground mix) of beef or chicken, *tinga* (spicy shredded pork), cheese, *huitlacoche* (corn fungus), brain, and potato. Open daily 9:30 AM–11 PM. $.

CASA REYNA
222-232-2109
www.casareyna.com
Privada Dos Oriente 1007, Col. Centro Histórico, Puebla

The restaurant of the beautiful Casa Reyna hotel carries through the hotel's Talavera theme with colorful crockery handmade in the Talavera de la Reyna workshop. The menu is a collection of family recipes and includes all the Puebla favorites: *tinga, mole, pipián verde*. And chalupas *poblanas*—a great starter of small, round corn tortillas served up with shredded meat, onion, and salsa. If you're confused about which mole or *pipián* to order, go for the *plato de degustación de moles,* a sampler of four house mole recipes that includes the rare mole *blanco,* or white mole, made with *piñon* (pine nut) and pulque. The dish is available on its own, but I appreciated the sampler; as it turned out, I preferred the mole poblano and the *pipián verde* to the white mole. Open daily 9 AM–6 PM. $$.

Degustación de moles, *Casa Reyna*

CEMITAS LAS POBLANITAS

At the Mercado del Carmen, 21 Oriente
between Dos Sur and Cuatro Sur

People come to this traditional market
mainly for two reasons: to shop for mole
ingredients and other foods, and to queue
up to feast on a *cemita*—an absolutely colossal sandwich, freshly made in assembly-line
fashion. The fluffy sesame-seed buns are
crammed with avocado, breaded pork, white
cheese, ham, and chiles (there's a vegetarian
option as well). This is a bright, large stall
with a seating area, where, for less than $5,
you'll have probably the most enjoyable, not
to mention most filling, street food in the
city (between 200 and 300 *cemitas* are
served up every day). If you're feeling
adventurous, wash it down with a freshly
made *agua fresca,* or fruit juice (I say adventurous because you might regret it later).
Open daily 10 AM–5:30 PM. $.

EL MURAL DE LOS POBLANOS

222-242-0503, 242-6696
www.elmuraldelospoblanos.com
16 de Septiembre 506, Col. Centro
Histórico, Puebla

El Mural combines some of the best things
in Mexico: mural art linked to the town's
roots, outstanding cuisine, and genial hospitality. The restaurant is located in an elegant
18th-century house, and its name comes
from a full-length mural along one wall that
depicts some of the city's most important
citizens, including war hero Ignacio
Zaragoza, Carmen Serdán Alatriste, symbol
of the revolution, and *la China Poblana.*

The menu is a mix of Mexican and
Spanish, both of the classic variety. The latter includes *paella valenciana, callos a la
Madrilène* (tripe stew cooked with tomato,
bacon, chorizo, and ham), and *cabrito al
horno* (roast baby lamb). But I came for the
local specialties, and these didn't disappoint. I highly recommend starting with the
El Mural salad, made with jicama, apple,

pear, orange, carrot, lettuce, peanuts,
raisins, and pumpkin seeds. After, move on
to the mole poblano. Chef Gabriela Guzmán
Espinosa came out to share her mole recipe
with me, and the eight-hour process she
goes through to perfect it. When I tried her
creation, I found it lived up to the hype. Her
mole is also sold as a paste or sauce. For
variety, try the chicken enchiladas with
three different moles.

El Mural also has seasonal specialties; in
October and November the chef makes a mole
with goats specially prepared for the dish. In
August and September, *chiles en nogada* are
served. And in September, you can try a
regional delicacy: caterpillar and guacamole
tacos. For dessert, if you're a chocolate lover
you don't want to miss the *regalo Quetzalcoatl*
(Quetzalcoatl's gift). Open Monday to Saturday
1–11 PM, Sunday 1–6 PM. $–$$.

EL RANCHITO

222-891-8052
Avenida Juan de Palafox y Mendoza 205 in
the Hotel del Portal, Col. Centro Histórico,
Puebla

There are three branches of this restaurant
in Puebla, but this one is the most central,
located on the corner of the *zócalo*. Of
course, mole features prominently on the
menu, and includes scrambled eggs with
mole in the morning, chalupas with mole for
lunch, and the traditional mole with
chicken. I was also thrilled to find that El
Ranchito was one of the few places around
that serves the prized *chiles en nogada* all year
long. Non-Poblano Mexican specialties here
include *pozole* (a stew made with hominy,
pork, and beans) and *cecina* (a thin, cured,
salty cut of beef). I would also recommend
the *chocolate de metate,* a huge ceramic bowl
of hot chocolate made with chocolate ground
by hand, with no sugar added. The restaurant has a bargain buffet lunch, but I'd stick
to the a la carte menu, which is still a great
deal. Open Monday to Saturday 7 AM–11 PM,
Sunday 7 AM–9 PM. $–$$.

EKOS

222-242-5336; 800-727-5775
www.casonadelachinapoblana.com
At the Casona de la China Poblana, corner
of 4 Norte and Avenida Juan de Palafox y
Mendoza, Col. Centro Histórico, Puebla

The menu changes every month at Ekos, the
courtyard restaurant of the Casona de la
China Poblana hotel, but the food is always
an inventive international fusion.
Examples? The *rollo de pollo,* which is
chicken in a mole poblano sauce with
amaretto, wrapped in a roll with chile, *elote,*
and *flor de calabaza.* Or oven-roasted duck
in port sauce with fresh figs. You get the
idea: creative, sophisticated cuisine,
accompanied by more than 50 types of Old
World and New World wines. It also helps to
dine in the pleasant ambience of the boutique hotel, under the benevolent ceramic
gaze of *la China Poblana,* whose statue
resides in the main dining space. Open
daily 7 AM–11 PM. $$–$$$$.

FONDA DE SANTA CLARA

222-242-26593
www.fondadesantaclara.com
Poniente 307, Col. Centro Histórico, Puebla

A true *fonda,* or tavern, this has been a local
favorite since it opened in 1965. The
Talavera tiles, bright blue-and-white walls,
and convivial atmosphere make it feel like
the Mexican equivalent of your neighbor-
hood pub. It's known as much for its mole
(detecting a theme here?) as for other typical
Poblano dishes. One of the Fonda's special-
ties is *gusanos de maguey,* or cactus worms,
which are served crispy-fried to a golden
brown with a bitter mole sauce and tortillas.
In truth, it was crunchy and not at all worm-
like, but much more to my taste was the
standard mole poblano over chicken. Open
daily 8 AM–10 PM except May 1. $–$$.

LA CANTINA DE LOS REMEDIOS

222-249-0843
www.lacantinadelosremedios.com.mx
Avenida Juárez 2504, Col. La Paz, Puebla

Cantina de Los Remedios

The ambience here says it all: colorful, loud, and boisterous. Movie posters line the walls and ceiling, banners and local signs are plastered all over, and there's a painting of a chicken in a bikini. I'm not sure what that means, but it's part of the mojo that makes this the most popular cantina in Puebla. The menu has Mexican and international dishes, and is perhaps best known for its *molcajetes*—made with rib eye, shrimp, or skirt steak—and grilled meats. Beyond the food, the large margaritas, live mariachis, and fun vibe keep the place hopping. Open Monday to Saturday 1:30 PM–1:30 AM. $$.

LA PURIFICADORA

222-309-1920
www.lapurificadora.com
At La Purificadora Hotel, Callejón de la Norte 802, Paseo San Francisco, Barrio el Alto, Puebla

A local resident told me he didn't like the food at La Purificadora, and while I heartily disagreed with him, I can see why. This is not your typical Poblano restaurant, nor does it aspire to be. The food here is a modern (and delicious) interpretation of Mexican dishes. How do they reinterpret the classics? Take the *pipián verde* mole, which is served with a chicken osso buco, certainly a first in my travels. Or try La Purificadora's version of street-food-staple *tacos al pastor* (pork tacos), made with Kurobuta pork chops, pineapple, and guajillo pepper chutney. But my favorite dish was the succulent duck breast served in orange sauce with grilled oranges and jalapeño peppers. For an appetizer, the delicious asadero cheese cassoulete with sun-dried tomato and a shot of cold avocado shake is a must if you love cheese. Also, try to be here for the pull-out-all-the-stops Sunday brunch, one of the best I

Mi Ciudad interior

had in Mexico. Open Monday to Thursday 7 AM–11 PM, Friday and Saturday 7 AM– midnight, Sunday 7 AM–5 PM. $$–$$$.

MI CIUDAD

222-231-5326
Avenida Juárez 2507, Col. La Paz, Puebla

One of the most charismatic and colorful restaurants in the city, Mi Ciudad is a Poblano institution. The interior, done in a warm rustic orange color, has two lovely murals. One runs the length of the wall and depicts the domes of Puebla's iconic churches; the other shows a downtown Puebla street at night. As for the menu, specialties here include the classic mole poblano and *pipián verde,* and *chiles en nogada* from July to August. The *molcajete azteca de arrachera,* with strips of juicy steak, avocado, nopales, onions, and white cheese, is also delicious. The restaurant has frequent *ferias,* or fairs, dedicated to particular dishes or regions. Finally, there's an in-house *panadería,* or bakery, that makes fresh tortillas and bread. Along with the food, come for the live trios performing at night. Open Monday to Thursday 1 PM–12 AM, Friday and Saturday 1 PM–12:45 AM, and Sunday 1–7 PM. $–$$.

RESTAURANTE LA COMPAÑÍA

222-232-4513
www.mesones-sacristia.com
6 Sur 304, Callejón de los Sapos, Col. Centro Histórico, Puebla

Any place that is renowned for its cooking classes has a reliably excellent restaurant. And Mesón de la Sacristía Compañía has both. Start with the chalupas, which locals insist (not entirely without reason) is a must if you're visiting Puebla, or the *queso fundido* (a cheese fondue served with flour tortillas). Then move on to either the outstanding mole poblano (there is a mole sampling plate if you want to try different varieties), or the mole Sacristía, which is made with smoked chipotle. Another dish worth trying is the *enchiladas pobres,* a dish of chicken enchiladas served in a red sauce with aged cheese and avocado that hails from this traditionally impoverished neighborhood. You have a choice of dining in the art-infused courtyard of the hotel, the Talavera dining room, or the piano dining room. Guitarists or guitar trios perform at night. $$–$$$.

ATTRACTIONS, PARKS & RECREATION

AFRICAM

222-281-7000
www.africamsafari.com.mx
Km. 16.5, Carr. Cap. Carlos Camacho, Puebla
Puebla reservation office: 222-279-6332; 41 Pte. 2120-K Col. La Noria, Puebla

For me, Africam is the most unexpected and amazing surprise Puebla has to offer, a safari park to rival anything short of a trip to the Serengeti. It was opened by Captain Carlos Camacho in 1972, who wanted to share the beauty of Africa with Mexico. Interestingly, he found in his chosen location a topography and climate similar to that of central Africa, where most of the original 1,200 animals came from.

The park has grown exponentially since those days, and now occupies almost 500 acres, employs a staff of over 300, and houses more than 2,000 animals representing more than 250 species from around the world. A visit to the park is easily an all-day affair. If you want to start with the best the park has to offer, take your car, or the Africam bus, into the safari

Yes, it's a real white tiger, and yes, it can be found in Mexico's Africam Safari Park

park. You'll forget you're in the Americas when you see the expanse of Africa-like plains stretching before you, and it is literally breathtaking to drive within a few feet of free-roaming giraffe, buffalo, and deer, or enclosed rhinos, elephants, and other animals. You'll see lions in the distance, but nothing will compare to the separate, secure tiger enclosure. When one of the park's white tigers came within a foot of my car (car windows obviously must remain raised at all times), I snapped a photo that nobody, to this day, believes is real.

After the safari, explore the rest of the park. There are daily bird shows, a more traditional zoo-like Adventure Zone, butterfly garden, and the park's newest attraction, the Kangaroo area, which brings you within a handshake of wallabies and kangaroos. The park is easily accessible by car, taxi (about $12 each way), or by bus from Puebla's CAPU terminal. It's a complete departure from Puebla's colonial treasures, but it is no less inspiring and magical a place, and well worth the visit, especially considering the bargain price of admission. Open daily 10–5. $$.

BARRIO DEL ARTISTA
Begins at 6 Oriente with 6 Norte

The Artists' Quarter is a little niche bordering the bustling El Parián artisans market. Once home to fabric spinners, it has been revamped into an artist colony that doubles as an open-air gallery. It's quite pleasant to walk down the pedestrian-only street and browse through the collections (for sale, of course) mounted on easels outside each studio, and sometimes watch a resident artist at work. If you need a respite, stop at the Café del Artista and sit outside to people-watch. At one end is a picturesque plaza with a baroque stone fountain and a beautiful white sculpture of three Native figures. Studios are generally open daily 10–8. Free.

BIBLIOTECA PALAFOXIANA
222-777-2580, 242-8073
5 Oriente Avenue between 16 de Septiembre and 2 Sur on the second floor of the Colegio de San Juan, Col. Centro Histórico, Puebla

The oldest public library in the Americas, the Palafox Library is a unique treasure. Founded in 1646 by Bishop Juan de Palafox y Mendoza, this richly appointed room houses about 43,000 volumes, including 6,000 manuscripts that were at one point considered the most complete collection of printed texts in Spanish America. Among the rare works here are nine *incunables* (books printed between 1455 and 1500 in medieval type, at the dawn of the printing era), and seven books printed on the first Mexican presses (between 1539 and 1600). The handsome hall, with its baroque touches and wood paneling, is quite impressive, with an *atril*, or lectern, that revolves to allow scholars to consult several books at once. This is one of the oldest and most important centers of literature in Latin America, unequaled in scope and history. Open Monday to Friday 10–5, Weekends 10–6. $.

LA CATEDRAL DE PUEBLA
Corner of Avenida 3 Oriente and 16 de Septiembre

The most important and cherished landmark in the city, the Cathedral of Puebla, dedicated to the Immaculate Conception, deserves its fame. Designed by Francisco Becerra and Juan de Cigorondo, the massive cathedral was begun in 1575 and was completed in two phases, when the original plan—modeled after the cathedral in Valladolid, Spain—had to be reworked. It was consecrated in 1649, under the auspices of Bishop Juan de Palafox y Mendoza, the ninth bishop of Puebla. An austere and imposing structure, the cathedral was designed similar to the one in Mexico City, in the Herrerian style. Its two towers (one representing the Old Testament, the other the New) are the tallest in Mexico at over 200 feet in length.

The main façade is done in a Renaissance style with a few baroque touches. The large studded double-doors, flanked by white marble statues of Saint Peter and Saint Paul, form the main entrance. Once inside, you'll be struck by the cathedral's dimensions: the cavernous vaulted nave, the massive central dome, and the beautiful main altar. Also note that by day it is lit completely by natural light furnished by its 128 windows.

La Catedral de Puebla Source: Mexico City Tourism Board

The Cathedral of Puebla has many points of interest, and guides (in English and Spanish) are available if you're interested in a tour. It has 14 chapels, three organs (the smallest of which is also the most ancient), three pulpits (all in onyx), a beautiful choir fashioned in the Moorish style, and outstanding baroque artwork, with paintings by notable masters Miguel Cabrera (considered the greatest painter of New Spain) and Juan Martinez Montañez. Particularly impressive is the main altar, which was designed by Manuel Tolsá, with a magnificent bronze sculpture of the Immaculate Conception as its centerpiece. Between 16 columns of onyx, you'll find sculptures of the fathers of the Catholic Church. The chapel that's most often open is also the most popular, La Capilla de la Virgen de Gaudalupe, where you'll find the tomb of Puebla's first archbishop. Finally, note the statue of the *Virgen de la Defensa,* surrounded by six columns of onyx. She is the patron saint of Puebla.

Before you leave, ask one of the staff about the church bell in the tower (the second tower has no bell). Legend has it that the 8.5-ton bell was so heavy that angels had to lift it up and put it into place. There's a tower tour every day at 11, or you might even be able to negotiate a guided trip up to see the bell, which will also reward you with spectacular views of the city as well as the tiled dome of the church. Open 10:30–12:30 and 4:15–6 daily. Free.

The Churches of Puebla

Visiting every one of Puebla's churches (*iglesia* or *templo* in Spanish) would be a laborious exercise that may have you churched out before long. Instead, I'm listing the most interesting and beautiful of the city's religious institutions here. (I'm not including two former convents that are now museums—you'll find those in the "Culture" section below.) The Cathedral of Puebla, of course, stands apart as a must-see icon of the city. All churches in Puebla are generally open from 10–12:30 and 4:30–6 daily.

CONVENT OF SANTA CATALINA

3 Norte Street 201

The oldest convent in Puebla is also the first established by the Dominican order in all of New Spain. Its exact date of construction is unknown, but the convent was finished in 1750. Beyond its minimalist façade are some beautiful baroque altarpieces and a neoclassic main altar.

IGLESIA DE LA COMPAÑIA

Avenida Juan de Palafox y Mendoza 403

This large 18th-century church was built by the Jesuits and is a departure from the dour church interiors you'll often find in Puebla. Easily identified by its elegant white bell tower, it's also distinguished for housing, briefly, the tomb of *la China Poblana,* the Arab (or Indian) princess who was brought to Puebla as a slave and subsequently converted to Catholicism before living out her days in pious virtue. A plaque on the wall behind the main altar serves as a memorial of her burial. There is another, somewhat bizarre, record near the church doorway, marking the execution of a man who arrived in Mexico from Spain claiming to be a papal emissary. Apparently, the bishops of Mexico and Puebla bought his story for a while, but when they found out he was conning them, they executed

Iglesia de la Compañia

him and hung his head above the door to this *iglesia*. I challenge you to find two more contrasting inscriptions in a single church.

IGLESIA DE SAN FRANCISCO
Corner of 14 Oriente and 5 de Mayo

This 16th-century church, founded by the Franciscans, is a striking example of baroque art. Its redbrick and gray stone façade (built in the 18th century) fronted by Talavera reliefs and yellow painted bell towers with only the left tower completed—and that too left an unpainted dark gray—makes for an unusual color contrast. To the right of the church is the pilgrim's portal and the Chapel of the Third Order, now converted into a school. The side door here is the oldest in Puebla. The church's full name is **Templo Conventual de las Cinco Llagas de San Francisco,** a reference to the five wounds of Saint Francis of Assisi. Inside is a huge painting of the genealogy of the Franciscan order, as well as a chapel containing a sculpture of the Conquering Virgin, brought by Cortés to Mexico.

IGLESIA DE SANTO DOMINGO (CAPILLA DEL ROSARIO)
Corner of 5 de Mayo and 4 Poniente

The Church of Santo Domingo was built between 1571 and 1611, except for the left tower, which took another two centuries to complete. It was originally part of a Dominican monastery, and its gray exterior is appropriately somber. Inside, however, is another story, with gilded stucco touches and baroque altars. But the crowning glory of this church is the unequaled Chapel of the Rosary, considered one of the most significant achievements of Mexican baroque art in the country. Constructed in 1690, the chapel, an incredibly ornate, gaudy structure done in onyx, stucco laminated in 22-karat gold, and Talavera wainscoting, was in its time one of the greatest baroque artworks of New Spain and remains a dazzling tribute to this school.

COOKING CLASSES

222-232-4513
www.mesones-sacristia.com
6 Sur 304, Callejón de los Sapos, Col. Centro Histórico, Puebla

The cooking classes offered at the Mesón de la Sacristía Compañía are more than just a workshop on how to make Poblano specialties. My class began with an excursion to the nearby Mercado del Carmen, which was in itself a rewarding experience. Here we found an astounding variety of chiles (Mexican cuisine makes use of about 145 types of chile, but traditional mole poblano uses ancho, mulatto, and pasilla chiles), vegetables, fruit, herbs, and other produce, all spotlessly arranged and fresh. When we had collected our ingredients, we returned to the hotel, donned our apron and chef's hats (which you get to keep), and set to work on our goal, the hotel's mole recipe. I won't give away all the secrets, but I will share that the making of mole involves three primary types of cooking: boiling, roasting, and frying. I also learned along the way that true Mexican guacamole is made only with avocado, chile serrano, onion, cilantro, and lemon. Of course, we got to eat the finished product.

The cooking classes are offered in one, three, or five-day increments, or as a full-week workshop. With an average of five new recipes per day taught by a truly expert (and bilingual) staff, you can imagine how your culinary repertoire can expand. It's a fun and authentic way to take a little bit of Puebla back home with you. $$$–$$$$.

CUEXCOMATE

Corner of 3 Poniente and 4 Norte, Col. La Libertad, Puebla.

Volcanoes don't typically provoke exclamations of "Aww, how cute!" from onlookers. But Cuexcomate, considered the shortest volcano in the world, is an exception. The name means "mud pot" in Nahuatl. Standing at just 43 feet, with a diameter of 75 feet, it's an apt term. Cuexcomate was formed in the 11th century from an eruption of the nearby (and far bigger) Popocatépetl volcano. Now inactive, the volcano is open to visitors, who can descend a winding metal stairway into the crater. You won't find too much down there, but for bragging rights ("In Puebla, I walked into a volcano!"), it doesn't exact a strenuous price.

Ecotourism and Volcano Trekking

Puebla's outstanding natural surroundings lend themselves to ecotourism, with the magnificent neighboring volcanoes leading the way. Towering above the cities of Puebla and Cholula like a South American Mount Fuji is **Popocatépetl** ("Smoking Mountain" in Nahuatl), affectionately known as el Popo. The most beloved and nearest of the snow-capped volcanoes, it's visually dramatic . . . but also currently active, making trekking excursions to its peak all but impossible. In fact, it's one of the most active volcanoes in the country.

Then there's **la Malinche**, named by the Spanish in honor of the woman who helped the conquistadores in their quest across Mexico. The volcano straddles the states of Tlaxcala

Cuexomate, the world's smallest volcano

and Puebla. At about 14,000 feet above sea level, it's the fifth-highest peak in Puebla. The farthest of the big three is **Ixtaccíhuatl,** or Sleeping Woman (some say White Woman), the third-highest mountain in Mexico. While there's nothing stopping you from braving these slopes on your own, I recommend that you take advantage of one of the many ecotourism companies operating in and around Puebla if you want to tackle them. You can check with the main tourism office in Puebla for guides and general information (222-777-1519, 800-326-8656), or try one of these recommended outfits:

ECO TOURS PUEBLA

222-477-9255
www.descubrepuebla.com
Segunda Cerrada de la 25 Pte., Col. Volcanes, Puebla

Founded in 1998, this group offers a host of aerial, on-the-ground, and underground adventure tours. In addition to mountain treks, the company organizes scuba, caving, canyoning, rafting, parachuting, mountain biking, and horse-riding tours. $$$–$$$$.

SELVA AZUL

222-237-4887
Avenida 41 Poniente 2120–D, Col. Ex-hacienda La Noria. C.P. 72410. Puebla

From trekking up volcanoes (when they aren't smoking), to mountain biking across the vast natural expanse of the country, to rafting on La Antigua River, Selva Azul (which means "blue jungle") offers a slew of outdoor activities. $$$–$$$$.

PALACIO MUNICIPAL
222-777-1519, 777-1520; 800-326-8656 (for tour information)
Portal Hidalgo 14, Col. Centro Histórico, Puebla

Dominating one side of the *zócalo*, Puebla's City Hall is an elegant neoclassic structure done in the French style that was popular at the turn of the century in the era of the Porfiriato. While the current façade dates from 1906, this site has served as the seat of government for four centuries. The original town hall was erected in 1531 but was subsequently renovated, demolished, and rebuilt over the years. For most visitors, the only accessible parts of the Palacio are the double-arched courtyard and the marble stairway. A guided tour arranged through the tourism office will gain you access to the meeting room, where hang two royal certificates that give Puebla its title and its coat of arms. Open daily 9–8. Free for public access, $$ for tour.

PUEBLA TRANVÍA (TROLLEY)
222-273-8300, 213-9923
At the Zócalo

If you want something quainter than the modern double-decker tour buses offered by Turibus, you can opt for the shorter routes on the Puebla Trolley. There are two different routes, one that covers the city during the time of New Spain, and one focusing on Puebla in the 19th century. It is not as comprehensive an experience as the Turibus, but not a bad way to get around the city center. The colonial tour runs daily 10–6 every hour, and the 19th-century tour runs daily at 11:30, 1:30, and 3:30. $.

TEATRO PRINCIPAL
222-232-6085
Corner of 6 Norte and 8 Oriente, Col. Centro Histórico, Puebla

I wouldn't put Puebla's historic theater at the top of your to-do list, but if you're here during visiting hours, you should duck inside and check it out. Inaugurated in 1760, it's one of the oldest theaters in the Americas still in use today, and its interior retains the grandness of the days of the Spanish viceroys. I'd recommend watching a performance (in Spanish) here as well. Open daily 10–5, unless there is a function. $.

The Legend of Popocatépetl and Ixtaccíhuatl
According to Aztec mythology, Ixtaccíhuatl was a princess who fell in love with Popocatépetl, a brave warrior. The princess's father, a mighty ruler, knew of their love and, seeking to thwart it, challenged Popocatépetl to wage war against the tribe's enemy. The king vowed that if he returned victorious, the warrior would be bequeathed to his lover. While he was away, one of Popocatépetl's rivals sent a false message back to Ixtaccíhuatl that he had been killed in battle. Upon hearing the news, the princess died of grief. Popocatépetl returned in triumph, only to learn of his lover's fate. Heartbroken, the warrior carried her body to the mountains, where he built a funeral pyre for them and died next to his beloved. The gods, moved by their fate, turned them into mountains so they could forever remain together. To this day, Popocatépetl watches over his princess while she sleeps.

TURIBUS
222-226-7289, 225-9025
www.turibus.com.mx
5 Oriente Street 3, Centro Histórico, Puebla

The Turibus's red double-decker buses are a good way to gain an introduction to the city if you're on a tight schedule or want to soak it all in before deciding where to spend your time. If you elect the enclosed first floor, you obviously won't see nearly as much as on the open-air second level. The bus runs a continuous circuit of 14 stops, covering the major sights and putting you within walking distance of most of what the city has to offer, with insightful commentary thrown in. You can hop on and off all day with your purchase, and you can buy tickets on board. From the *zócalo,* the most central place to pick one up is outside the city's main tourism office (5 Oriente Street 3). Service runs every 40 minutes, daily 10–7:30 during low season, daily 10–9 during high season. $.

CULTURE

CASA DE ALFEÑIQUE
222-232-0458
Corner of 4 Oriente and 6 Norte Street, Col. Centro Histórico, Puebla

Alfeñique is the name of a white sugary candy made in Puebla, and once you see the ornate façade of this building—one of the most distinctive landmarks in the city—you'll see where it gets its name. Intricately detailed, the red-and-white building seems to be literally dripping with the white ornamentation. Indeed, its unique and picturesque exterior is more memorable than the state museum inside, which houses Indian codexes dating from the 16th century, numerous colonial artifacts, and, best of all, a collection of antique dresses and clothing featuring those worn by *la China Poblana.* Open Tuesday to Sunday 10–4:30. $.

CASA DE AQUILES SERDÁN
222-242-1076
6 Oriente Street 206, Col. Centro Histórico, Puebla

Bullet holes pockmark the wall of the house of Aquiles Serdán, now the Museo Regional de la Revolución Mexicana (Regional Museum of the Mexican Revolution). Along with the forts of the battle of Puebla, this site is the most important symbol and chronicle of Mexican heroism in the city. The Serdán family—two brothers and two sisters—were revolutionaries who opposed the despotic Porfiriato government. On November 18, 1910, government troops ambushed the family, opening fire on their home and killing the brothers. The sisters were jailed but escaped. Inside, don't miss the stark black-and-white mural depicting the brothers' fight against the government, the main hall that shows photos of the family and the mirror strewn with bullet holes, and the trapdoor under which the family tried to hide. You can even see the autopsy report on Aquiles, newspaper articles about the event, and photographs of the dead bodies. One room is devoted to the women who fought for Mexico, with vintage black-and-white photos headlined by Carmen Serdán Alatriste, the sister who escaped to become a Daughter of the Revolution. All descriptions are in Spanish. Open Tuesday to Sunday 10–5. $.

CASA DE LOS MUÑECOS

Corner of 2 Norte and Avenida Palafox, Col. Centro Histórico, Puebla

The 18th-century House of the Dolls is named for the tiled human figurines adorning its redbrick and tiled façade. There are many stories about the origin of the figures, but the most popular is that they are caricatures of the town council. The building now houses the Museum of the Autonomous University of Puebla, which has an unusual combination of exhibits. On the first floor there's a bizarre nod to anthropology and taxidermy, with several stuffed animals, shrunken human heads, and skeletons (including two mammoth bones). This is followed by an interesting collection of scientific, musical, and mechanical instruments and tools dating from the 17th to the 19th centuries. But most of the museum is devoted to an impressive compilation of colonial baroque and Renaissance art dating from the 16th century onward. One of the most impressive works here is *El Apostolado,* a set of 15 paintings by Juan Tinoco of the 12 apostles, Saint Paul, Jesus, and Mary. Open Tuesday to Sunday 10–4. $.

EX-CONVENTO DE SANTA MÓNICA

222-232-0178
18 Poniente Avenue 103, Col. Centro Histórico, Puebla

The 17th-century Convent of Santa Mónica is now Puebla's Museum of Religious Art, an appropriate home for a building with an interesting religious history. The Catholic nuns who once lived here were forced into hiding by the Laws of Reforma decreed by Benito Juárez in 1867, which called for the secularization of all religious orders. They lived underground for 70 years before they were discovered in 1935, operating in secret defiance of the order. Today the museum houses artifacts from other nearby convents, as well as colonial art and sculptures. It's a kick just to walk through its cramped halls and hidden passages. Note the secret window, which the nuns used to observe Mass in the adjoining church. Open Tuesday to Sunday 10–4:30. $.

Casa de los Muñecos has one of the most distinctive facades in Puebla

EX-CONVENTO DE SANTA ROSA

222-232-7792
3 Norte Street 1203, Col. Centro Histórico, Puebla

This former convent turned museum has something no other museum in the world can boast: the kitchen where mole poblano was born. For this reason alone, it's worth the visit to see the rustic, handmade earthenware cauldrons and the extensive azulejo Talavera tiling that was the gift of the viceroy for whom the dish was made. Beyond the kitchen, there's the museum's large and impressive collection of high-quality arts and crafts dating from the 16th to the 20th centuries. From 400-year-old Talavera to a massive earthenware cauldron (a "rice Jacuzzi") to ornate colonial furniture, the museum is quite diverse. You can also see a cell that's been re-created to depict the lives of the nuns who lived here. A strictly penitent order, the nuns were vegetarian and even eschewed chocolate (imagine the temptation they felt as they created the chocolatey mole). They never left these grounds, even to attend church, and were buried here. Open Tuesday to Sunday 10–4:30. $.

FUERTE LORETO

222-235-2661

www.inah.gob.mx

Ejercito de Oriente Ave., Centro Civico 5 de Mayo, Col. de Los Fuertes, Puebla

Want to know more about Cinco de Mayo? The Loreto Fort, also known as the Museo de la No Intervención (Museum of Non-Intervention), is where it all began. The fort was built in 1821 by the Spanish and became the focal point of the battle of Puebla in 1862, when 2,000 troops under General Ignacio Zaragoza defended the city against an army of 6,000 French soldiers. Outnumbered and outmatched by a superior force, the Mexicans still defeated the invaders. It would prove to be a short-lived victory, but the battle became a national symbol of the valor of the underdog Mexicans.

While there were a few heroes of note (among them Porfirio Díaz), no star shone brighter than that of Zaragoza, who urged his men on with stirring speeches ("Today you fight for a sacred objective . . . you fight for the mother country") and even visited the wounded French troops following their victory. He died four months after the battle on September 8, ill and in high delirium, and was said to have muttered, "Don't touch my soldiers, do what you will with me" in his last moments. Three days later, Benito Juárez decreed that Puebla de los Ángeles would henceforth be known as Heroica Puebla de Zaragoza (Zaragoza's Heroic Puebla). The name still stands.

Today, the fort houses a collection of artifacts from the battle, including flags, weapons, and uniforms. There are also several murals and paintings, including a series chronicling the ill-fated reign of Emperor Maximilian, and a beautiful ceiling mural depicting an eagle devouring a snake (the symbol of Mexico). The fort is part of a Civic Center that includes another fort (Fuerte de Guadalupe), which has been pretty much razed to the ground; a planetarium; two museums; and some beautiful monuments to Mexico's heroes. But the Loreto Fort is the highlight. Open Tuesday to Sunday 10–5. $.

MUSEO AMPARO

222-229-3850

www.museoamparo.com

2 Sur Street 708, Col. Centro Histórico, Puebla

Puebla's best museum has an incredible collection of pre-Hispanic as well as colonial art and artifacts. The museum, itself a beautiful modern facility, was named after the wife of the proprietor, and a portrait of her—done by Diego Rivera—hangs in the lobby. There's an even more beautiful Rivera work nearby: a mural of Puebla, featuring angels, volcanoes, the pyramid of Cholula, and the indigenous touches characteristic of Rivera's work. The pre-Hispanic section contains over 2,000 pieces ranging from all over Mexico and dating from A.D. 2500 to the 16th century. It is considered one of the most important and comprehensive collections in the country. The second floor focuses on the colonial era. The museum is very well organized and has bilingual descriptions. You can also get an audio tour or a guided tour for a nominal fee. Open daily except Tuesday, 10–6. $.

MUSEO BELLO Y GONZÁLEZ

222-232-9475
3 Poniente Street 302, Col. Centro Histórico, Puebla

José Luis Bello was a businessman of considerable means. But it was his son, Mariano, who is credited with the expansive collection of art that is now the Bello y González Museum. Inside this grand home you'll find diverse art, antiques, and furniture from all over the world, dating back to the 17th century. If that doesn't intrigue you, then go for the impressive Talavera room. A guided tour is included in the cost of the ticket. Open Tuesday to Sunday 10-5. $.

MUSEO NACIONAL DEL FERROCARRIL

222-246-1074/246-0395
11 Norte Street 1005 at Avenida 12 Poniente

Located in a former train depot, the National Railroad Museum is a departure from the norm as far as museums go in Puebla. Inside the large, open space are several now-defunct trains, from old-fashioned steam engines to Pullman coaches. There are 50 cars, cabooses, and engines for you to explore, and you can walk inside and capture the feel of the glory days of railroad travel. Some cars are also exhibits depicting the history of the Mexican railways since 1837 and showing picturesque railroad landscapes. Open Tuesday to Sunday 10–5. Free.

NIGHTLIFE

Nightlife in Puebla is quite transient. When I went to what I was assured had been for the past few years the hottest club in town, I found it had just closed. Many clubs and bars have a short shelf life, so if you find these listings outdated, ask around for the new "in" place to be. Better yet, head to nearby Cholula, which has a far better nightlife thanks to its college crowds.

LA CANTINA DE LOS REMEDIOS

222-249-0843
Avenida Juárez 2504, Col. La Paz, Puebla

One of the most popular watering holes in Puebla, la Cantina attracts people with its colorful décor, vibrant atmosphere, massive margaritas, and plenty of added incentives, like games, two-for-one happy hours, and live music. The cantina draws long lines on weekend nights, so plan to wait or come early. Open Monday to Saturday 1:30 PM–1:30 AM. $$.

EL APOSENTILLO

222-242-5336; 800-727-5775 (in Mexico)
www.casonadelachinapoblana.com

Corner of 4 Norte and Avenida Juan de Palafox y Mendoza at the Casona de la China Poblana, Col. Centro Histórico, Puebla

This cool gothic bar, which is designed like a grotto, is a great option to start off your night. The place has the underground feel of a speakeasy, and you can sit at the onyx bar or a table and order from an extensive wine menu or sample a cocktail before the late-night fun begins. Open Monday to Saturday 8 AM–10:30 PM, Sunday 8 AM–6 PM. $$.

EL BREVE ESPACIO
222-246-2693
www.elbreve-espacio.com
7 Norte Street 8, Col. Centro Histórico, Puebla

My favorite café in Puebla doubles as a suave, sophisticated nighttime haven for those who aren't crazy about the club scene. The café has a piano, and hosts numerous live acts ranging from jazz to classical to Cuban *trova*. It's a wonderful place to enjoy great music in an intimate setting, especially with owner Carlos González Orduña ready to mingle and chat with you. Open Monday to Saturday 6 PM–2 AM. $.

GAROTO'S DISCO
222-242-4232
www.garotosdisco.com
22 Oriente 602, Col. Barrio de Xanenetla, Puebla

Puebla's hottest gay club, Garoto's is located just off Cinco de Mayo Boulevard on Oriente Street. Now celebrating its tenth year, it has a loyal clientele, great music with a resident DJ, and creative drinks. Open from 9 PM onwards. $, no cover on Saturdays.

PLAZA DE SANTA INÉS
11 Poniente Street and 3 Sur, Col. Centro Histórico, Puebla

If you want to hear the mariachis strumming their jovial music after nightfall, head to one of the sidewalk cafés lining this plaza. After 6 PM, you'll find them strolling among the crowds, taking requests and accepting tips.

Plazuela de los Sapos
5 Oriente and 6 Sur, Col. Centro Los Sapos, Puebla

This plaza is home to antiques and furniture shops and has a bustling weekly market, but at night, its ambience changes as a cluster of bars open their doors. Live music and mariachis emanate from within, and the plaza becomes a laid-back hangout. Here are a few bars to be found in and around the plaza:

LA BÓVEDA
222-246-2555
6 Sur Street 503, Col. Los Sapos, Puebla

You can hear the music blaring from well outside this casual hole-in-the-wall. There's a small dance floor inside the somewhat cramped space, and the bar serves food until closing. Open daily 10 PM–3 AM. $.

FRANCOS BULE-BAR

222-232-3409

5 Oriente 402, Col. Los Sapos, Puebla

Located off the main plaza, this is a funky café during the day that keeps the upstairs bar open late. It's a comfy spot that has a mix of lounge and bar seating, a dance floor, and live DJ. Open Wednesday to Sunday 7 AM—3 AM. $—$$.

LA PASITA

222-232-4422

5 Oriente 602, Col. Los Sapos, Puebla

I'm cheating a bit here, because this diminutive bar is open only during the day, but it's worth the pit stop for its signature drink, *pasita*, a raisin-based liqueur. The place is small of space but big on personality: its owner is alternately a charming host or a cranky old curmudgeon, depending on his mood. If you're a single girl (or if you lie and tell him you are), you'll be given a cute little card with a poem. And if you can drink 100 shots of *pasita*, you'll get 100,000 pesos and a coffin. No one's done it yet, and an article on the wall tells of a man whose ambitious attempt landed him in the hospital. Behind the simple counter, the bar is a clutter of figurines, bottles, and curios. For a few pesos, you'll get your shot of *pasita*, which comes in different flavor combinations, along with a wedge of cheese. Bite the cheese before downing the potent shot, and don't take the 100-shot challenge. Open daily except Tuesday, 12:30 PM—5:30 PM. $.

LA FUGA DE DON PORFIRIO (DON PORFIRIO'S FLIGHT)

Avenida Juan de Palafox y Mendoza 414, Col. Centro Histórico, Puebla

This tiny bar is deserving of a quick stop or a game of chess with one of the local denizens, if only for its place in Puebla's history. On September 20, 1865, Porfirio Díaz, who was imprisoned by the French, escaped their clutches. According to the bar's owner, it was at this very spot where Díaz's friends were waiting with horses to whisk him away. Sometimes there is live music, and there's even a chance of some amateur palmistry, but above all, there's a quaint charm about the place. Plus, drinks are reasonably cheap. Open Monday to Saturday 6—10 PM, Sunday 1—9 PM. $.

Shopping

LA CENTRAL

222-232-5484

6 Oriente and 4 Norte 407, Col. Centro Histórico, Puebla

The candy shops on Puebla's famous Calle de Santa Clara (6 Oriente Street) continue a sacred tradition. The nuns of the Santa Clara convent were famous for their candies, and their secrets have been passed down to a cluster of shops along this road. Of these, perhaps none is as renowned as la Central. For over 50 years, this shop has carried on a family trade spanning generations. Here you can buy *camotes* (a sugary confection made with cooked sweet potato), *alfeñiques* (a white pastry made with almond), crystallized fruit jellies, and a host of other sweets. La Central is considered one of the best because they make all their products. Open 9—8 daily. $—$$.

CENTRO COMERCIAL ANGELÓPOLIS

www.centrocomercialangelopolis.com

222-303-0300, 303-0340

Boulevard del Niño Poblano 2510, off the Puebla-Atlixco highway, Col. Angelópolis, Puebla

There are two sides to Puebla: the old city and the new. In the latter, a dominant feature is Puebla's biggest mall, the Centro Comercial Angelópolis. This large shopping center is a typical mall in layout, basic services and shops. Department stores (mostly Mexican, but there is a Sears) and a great variety of local and international shops are located here, along with a food court and a cinema. Do you need to make it part of your trip? I'd focus on other areas. Stores open daily 11–8, restaurants noon to midnight. $–$$$$.

INSTITUTO DE ARTESANÍAS E INDUSTRIAS POPULARES (IAIP)

222-246-4526

Avenida Juan de Palafox y Mendoza 607, Col. Centro Histórico, Puebla

The nice thing about the small number of stores making up the Institute of Crafts and Popular Industries is that you can find a variety of good-quality local products here. You may pay a slight markup, and prices are fixed, but you're contributing to an organized effort to promote Native arts and crafts in the region. At the Puebla branch you'll find Talavera and clay ceramics, onyx and marble works, amate paper products, pewter, wood-works, and textiles and clothing. Open daily 10–6. $–$$$.

MERCADO DE ARTESANÍAS EL PARIÁN

2 Oriente and 6 Norte, Col. Centro Histórico, Puebla

This popular crafts market (the word *parián* comes from the Philippine word for "market") is located in a cobblestoned, Talavera-tiled town square built in 1801 and used by traders and merchants. Not much has changed; nowadays the plaza is home to myriad booths and vendors selling all manner of local (and some not local) products, including Talavera ceramics, onyx, embroidered textiles, and clothes. You'll also find arts and crafts made of glass, clay, and straw, among other materials. It's fun to browse and pick up an affordable souvenir (don't be afraid to haggle), but be warned: much of the Talavera pieces aren't the real deal. Open daily 10–7:30 $–$$$.

PLAZUELA DE LOS SAPOS

5 Oriente and 6 Sur, Col. Centro Los Sapos, Puebla

The Plazuela de los Sapos (Courtyard of the Toads), along with the Callejón de los Sapos that leads to it, is a great place to browse through antiques and furniture makers' shops. On Sundays there's a bustling flea market where you can find a few treasures and some decent bargains in antiques and rustic furniture. It's become a favorite local weekend hangout, and it has quite a legacy. A market has been held here since 1816. Hours vary, but the market is usually open from 10–7. $–$$$$.

Talavera

Again, not all pieces labeled Talavera are the real deal, and the easy way to ensure you're getting what you want is to head to one of the Talavera workshops in and around the city. These ones are all reliable and carry the prized DO, or *denominación de origen* branding on each piece, proving its authenticity. There are others of equal reputation in Cholula.

Mercado El Parián

TALAVERA ARMANDO

222-232-4702
http://talaverarmando.com
Mercado El Parián Local 34, 4 Oriente 8, Col. Centro Histórico, Puebla
6 Norte Street 408, Col. Centro Histórico, Puebla (Workshop)

Armando has thousands of pieces on display at various locations in the city, but I mention the first location because it is one place in the El Parián crafts market where you're sure to find authentic Talavera pieces. The other location listed offers guided tours of the Talavera process. Open daily 10–7:30. $–$$$$.

TALAVERA DE LA LUZ

222-246-1215
www.talaveradelaluz.com
Avenida Juan de Palafox y Mendoza 1413, Col. Centro Histórico, Puebla

A lovely variety of platters, bowls, pitchers, urns, murals, and tilework are the predominant pieces here. Another interesting item is the collection of ancient maps decorated with Talavera tiling. Open Monday to Friday 9–2:30 and 5–6:30, Saturday 9–noon. $–$$$$.

TALAVERA DE LA REYNA

222-229-3853
www.talaveradelareyna.com.mx
2 Sur 708 at the Museo Amparo, Col. Centro Histórico, Puebla

The main store and workshop of this Talavera producer is in Cholula, but there's a branch at the Amparo museum. Particularly fine specimens include the exquisite crockery, which can also be found at the Casa Reyna Hotel. Open Monday to Friday 9–6, Saturday 9–2. $–$$$$.

TALAVERA URIARTE
222-232-1598
www.uriartetalavera.com
4 Poniente Street 911

The oldest and most well known of Puebla's Talavera workshops, Uriarte was founded in 1824. You can tour the workshop, and there's a handsome showroom filled with pieces ranging from affordable keepsakes to priceless heirlooms. A branch store is in the Holiday Inn Centro Histórico. Open Monday to Friday 9–6, Saturday 10–5, Sunday 11–4. $–$$$$.

TIENDA ARTESANAL
222-240-5446, 222-240-5338
14 Poniente 305 at the Ex-Convento de
Santa Rosa, Col. Centro Histórico, Puebla

Talavera Uriarte

The shop inside the Ex-Convento de Santa Rosa is part of the National Commission for the Development of Indigenous Towns. It stocks embroidered clothing and textiles that made exclusively by local indigenous women, who set the prices for each item. Open daily 10–5. $–$$.

TIERRA VERDE
222-242-4026
5 Oriente Street 605, Col. Los Sapos,
Puebla

This little shop (the name means "green earth") has a very cool collection of colorful T-shirts, many with Mexican motifs such as famous wrestlers, personalities (Pancho Villa is a favorite), and sayings. You'll also find several gift items particular to *lucha libre* wrestlers, including dolls, masks, pillows and cushions, and funky knickknacks that make for an out-of-the-box souvenir. Open daily 10–8. $–$$.

WEEKLY & ANNUAL EVENTS

BULLFIGHTING
November to December and April through May
222-236-1868
Plaza de Toros El Relicario, Ejército de Oriente, Zona Cívica Cinco de Mayo

Honestly, it's not my thing, and I end up rooting for the bull, but even I can appreciate the strutting, macho pageantry of the matador. $$.

CINCO DE MAYO
May 5
222-235-2661
Ejercito de Oriente Ave. at Fuerte Loreto, Centro Civico 5 de Mayo, Col. de Los Fuertes, Puebla

While people north of the border (and in other parts of Mexico) may reach for the nearest Corona, in Puebla it's a very different celebration on May 5. Commemorating the greatest military victory in the town's history is no small thing, and the city honors the day with a military and school parade that culminates in Fort Loreto. Free.

FERIA DE CHILES EN NOGADA
August
Various parts of the city

The month of August is a statewide homage to *chiles en nogada,* the Poblano dish that has become a holiday culinary classic. Because this is the season for one of its key ingredients—pomegranate—restaurants around the city will offer the dish. $–$$.

FERIA DE PUEBLA
End of April to end of May
222-236-2049
Parque Ecológico, Col. Azcarate, Puebla

The Puebla Festival is the biggest annual cultural celebration in the city. It's a monthlong event stuffed with all things Poblano and Mexican and includes, among other things, singing and music festivals, rodeos, several live acts, bullfighting, arts and crafts booths, and a raffle. Free.

FERIA DE TURISMO DE NATURALEZA
Third week of June
At the *zócalo,* Col. Centro Histórico, Puebla

The year 2008 marked the first Ecotourism Festival in Puebla. The annual event includes arts and crafts, regional food stalls, and an emphasis on the diverse natural excursions Puebla has to offer. In addition, visitors can enjoy activities like tyroleans, wall climbing, and exhibits on indigenous medicines and herbal remedies. Free.

FESTIVAL DEL MOLE POBLANO
June
Various locations around the city

Not to be outdone by *chiles en nogada,* Puebla's other national dish—the mole poblano—gets to bask in its own month as well. Every June, restaurants vie for the town's best recipe, offering their own version of the classic dish. Picking from among them is no easy task, but it's a great time to come to the city and be gladly swallowed up by the mole mania. $–$$.

RODEOS
Sundays
222-283-6308
Carretera Tehuacán, Pte. 1032

Horses and rodeos are called *charreadas* in Puebla and are held in a *lienzo charro.* If you want to see this popular local Mexican sport (Zapata was quite a horseman and *charreada* fan), there's one held on most Sundays. $$.

CHOLULA

Puebla and Cholula go hand in hand. Visiting one without the other would be a bit like visiting Rome and skipping the Vatican. The analogy is especially appropriate when you consider the astounding number and variety of churches in the small town, which has earned Cholula the moniker the Sacred City. There is a popular local legend that there are 365 churches in the town, one for every day of the year. In fact, there are roughly 40 (the count varies depending on how you define the city limits), which still makes Cholula the city with the highest concentration of churches in Mexico. (There is another variation of the legend, promulgated by stubbornly proud Cholulans, that there are 365 church *domes* in the town . . . I'm not buying it.)

While you can easily make a day trip to Cholula, it deserves more than a few hours or even a day. You might consider staying here, thanks to some excellent boutique hotels, a roaring nightlife, and one of the most ingenious commercial centers you'll

Santuario de la Virgen de los Remedios, Cholula

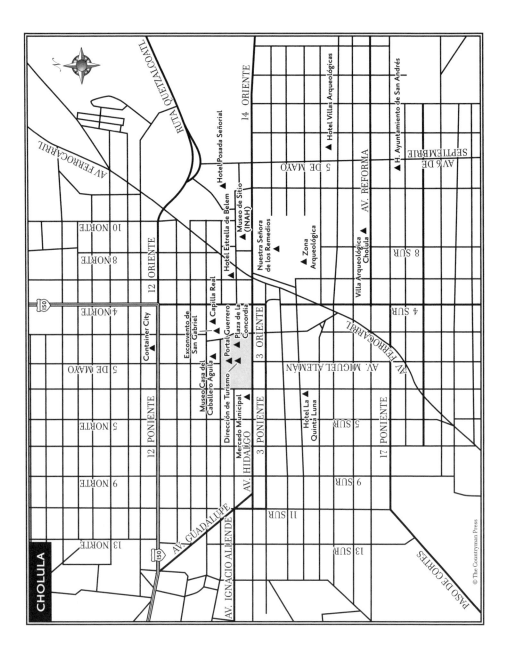

find. Cholula presents a quintessentially Mexican mix of tradition and modernity, indigenous and Catholic heritage. The latter is especially prevalent, as Cholula's most dramatic and breathtaking structure is a colonial church perched atop the ruins of what, at its base, was once the largest pyramid in the world.

It is also a little-known fact that Cholula is the oldest inhabited city in Mexico, and according to at least one historian, the oldest city in the Americas. There have been people living here for almost 2,500 years, and it was a major capital during Mexico's pre-classic period. It certainly blew away the conquistadores; Hernán Cortés called it "the most beautiful city outside of Spain." In fact, Cortés took in the might of Cholula and realized that it would be no easy task to defeat the Indians. So he tricked them, using la Malinche, his translator and mistress, to convey a false message that he was leaving, and in 1519, slaughtered them by the thousands.

The surprise assault on and massacre of Cholula was brutal enough to rival anything the conquistadores did elsewhere in the country, but it served two strategic purposes. For one, it caught the population of a major tribal power center by complete surprise and subjugated them almost immediately; and two, it served notice that the conquistadores were in the New World to rule.

Getting There and Getting Around

Cholula is easily reached by car or taxi from Puebla. Simply take Forjadores Boulevard in Puebla, which becomes Federal Highway 190 Puebla-Cholula; this takes you directly to the city. Cholula is only about 8 miles away, making for a quick ride, and taxis run the route all the time. You can also take a bus from Puebla's CAPU bus station to the city.

As for getting around, this city is also best experienced on foot. Cholula is actually comprised of two towns: San Andrés Cholula and San Pedro Cholula. Like Puebla, both have a *zócalo,* but the historic city center is built around the one in San Pedro, which is also called the **Plaza de la Concordia.** From here you can visit many of Cholula's historic monuments. The pyramid, Cholula's most impressive and fascinating landmark, straddles both towns, while San Andrés is home to the Universidad de las Américas, the university that gives the town its vibrant nightlife.

LODGING

ESTRELLA DE BELEM

222-261-1925
www.estrelladebelem.com.mx
2 Oriente 410, Centro Histórico, Cholula

Estrella de Belem (Star of Bethlehem) is a cute bed and breakfast offering six rooms in the heart of the historic center of Cholula. Set in a 19th-century house, each room is named after a Spanish painter, has classical music piped in, tiled floors, and rustic wood furnishing that is homey and simple rather than ostentatious. The two-floor junior suite, which shows the exposed original walls and has a sofabed on the second floor, is my favorite, but the hydro-massage tub and working fireplace in the ample master suite has a lot to recommend it as well. All rooms have flat-screen TVs, a nice modern touch to contrast the Renaissance art (copies of works by the painter the room is named after) and candelabras of another era. The hotel's pleasing white, red, and blue hues, grassy courtyard, and small rooftop terrace with garden and pool are further reasons to feel at home here. Rooftop spa services are also available, and the gourmet breakfast in the period dining hall is a great way to start your day. $$–$$$.

HOTEL REAL DE NATURALES

222-247-6070
www.hotelrealdenaturales.com/
6 Oriente 7, Centro Histórico, Cholula

A terrific budget option in the heart of the city near the Capilla Real O De Naturales

Estrella de Belem

church (hence the name), Hotel Real de Naturales is also one of the larger hotels in town, with 45 rooms, a restaurant, meeting space, a small gym, and rooftop pool. The rooms are simple but spacious, with tiled floors and basic furnishings, and surround a pleasant courtyard with a stone fountain, garden, and the red-hued arched colonnade typical of a cloister. $.

LA QUINTA LUNA

222-247-8915
www.laquintaluna.com
3 Sur 702, Centro Histórico, Cholula

The best hotel in Cholula is a labor of love, a quiet and serene sanctuary, and an elegant boutique property where you'll be made to feel like a guest in a friend's country home. Located only three blocks from the main *zócalo,* the home dates back to 1680 and belonged to Don Juan de León y Mendoza, who was a rare mix: a noble who claimed Native descent. The building was

left in a crumbling state for many years, until the Cárdenas González de Cossío family took it over and remodeled it. There is a photo album in the lovely library of the hotel that details how the place looked when the family first started work, and throughout its transformation into a beautiful boutique hotel.

Their efforts, vision, and imagination have paid off wonderfully. La Quinta Luna is a blend of old and new—exposed beams and archways and restored doors from the original construction mingling with contemporary art (all by local painters) and furniture. There are only seven rooms, located around a leafy courtyard, each different but all with supremely comfortable beds, modern décor, and large, well-appointed bathrooms. The hotel's restaurant is one of the best in Cholula, and the small rooms, coupled with the graciousness of the hosts (the family still calls the hotel home), give it a wonderful sense of intimacy. The second-floor terrace has gorgeous views of the city, church, and volcano. Extra touches that make this place special are the in-room spa services (hot-stone massages, chocolate mud baths, aromatherapy, and more) and the classical music concerts held monthly (sometimes at night, accompanied by a choir). This is an elegant and welcoming hotel that makes staying in Cholula an easy choice. $$–$$$.

DINING

KARMA BAGELS

222-296-9399

14 Poniente 109-B, San Andrés Cholula

Forget your typical cookie-cutter coffee chain; I'll take Karma Bagels over any of them. This funky, low-key hangout is the place to go to relax and chill out during the day or at night. Karma specializes in over-stuffed bagel sandwiches that even a former New Yorker can appreciate, with fillings such as smoked chicken with cheese and chimichurri sauce, a four-cheese-plus-cream-cheese concoction, and tasty vegetarian options. Enormous, mouthwatering salads are among the fare here, as are wine and fresh fruit juices. There's a pool table, Internet access, and a stage for the frequent live events. The major drawback to this place is that you might end up spending all day here. Open daily 11–11. $.

LA PÉRGOLA

222-247-0849

2 Oriente 403, San Pedro Cholula

A late-night eatery, La Pérgola is tucked away on a side street and barely visible unless you're looking for it. It has a cool charm greatly amplified by the mural of Jack Kerouac dominating one wall and the jute lamps. Inside the cozy two-floor dining room you can order very good thin-crust pizzas, sandwiches, bagels, and other light fare. Open Tuesday to Saturday 8 PM–2 AM. $.

LA QUINTA LUNA

222-247-8915

www.laquintaluna.com

3 Sur 702, Centro Histórico, Cholula

The city's best hotel also wins my vote for best restaurant. More a bistro than the typical Mexican eateries found in Cholula, La Quinta Luna's menu follows the seasons, but combines classic Mexican fare with international flair. Sticking with the theme of the hotel, the restaurant is cozy and intimate, its small dining room softly illuminating the few tables. Examples of its refined cuisine are the green salad with pear, strawberry, and Brie, chicken breast stuffed with *huitlacoche* in a white wine sauce, and tequila-flavored shrimp, a personal favorite. Open daily 8:30 AM–1 PM and 1:30–9:30 PM. $$.

LOS TULIPANES

222-247-1707

Portal Guerrero 13, Centro Histórico, Cholula

Centrally located right on the main plaza, Los Tulipanes has a tasty but very meat-centric menu. The highlights are the *crema de calabaza,* a pumpkin potage, the sizable *arrachera* steak, and the *cecina cholulera,* a large strip of thinly sliced beef served with guacamole, strips of chile, beans, and wedges of white cheese. If you need a full meal during your day of sight-seeing, head here. Open daily 8 AM–9 PM. $–$$.

RESTAURANTE COCOYOTLA

222-247-0151

Avenida Hidalgo 301, Centro Histórico, Cholula

A laid-back, friendly, and family-oriented place, Restaurante Cocoyotla is the place to go for large portions of typical regional cuisine. Start with a hearty soup like *sopa de medula* (marrow), *crema Cholula (flor de calabaza,* ham, and mushroom), or *consome Atlixco* (chicken, *flor de calabaza,* and cheese). Then proceed to the specialty: filets prepared in a variety of sauces (mushroom, mustard, pepper, and garlic are among the choices). The *cecina* (a thin, succulent, and salty cut of beef) for four is a good family meal, while the more adventurous may consider the *criadillas al ajillo* (bull testicles in garlic sauce). Open Monday and Tuesday 9 AM–6 PM, Wednesday to Sunday 9 AM–8 PM. $–$$.

ATTRACTIONS, PARKS & RECREATION

The Churches of Cholula

If you thought covering all the churches in Puebla was a tall order, prepare for the dizzying challenge of canvassing Cholula. The ones on this list capture what I feel are the most interesting and picturesque of the town's 40-odd churches. There's an interesting historical backdrop to the architecture here: when the style of the times dictated a change from the ornate baroque school to the more severe neoclassic, indigenous laborers were charged with executing the new designs. However, they didn't know how to do it, and they didn't know how to work with marble, which was imported for the churches. As a result, they made many churches in a bare, austere manner with very little Mexican influence. On the other hand, the remaining baroque churches boast an explosion of indigenous design and craftsmanship. Churches in Cholula are generally open from 10–12:30 and 4:30–6 daily.

CONVENTO DE SAN GABRIEL

2 Sur Street and Morelos Avenue, Centro Histórico, Cholula

The oldest church in Cholula, the Convento de San Gabriel was built between 1549 and 1552, on top of a pyramid dedicated to Quetzalcoatl (you can still see the pyramid floor inside.) The convent, located on the *zócalo,* is actually a cluster of several buildings that dominates one side of the square. The San Gabriel Church is a beautiful example of neoclassic architecture, gold and white with a gilded ribbed vault ceiling and a main altar with a depiction of God watching his son die. To the left is the baroque **Capilla de La Tercera Orden** (Chapel of the Third Order), which has a 16th-century baptismal font, and beyond that is the **Capilla Real o de Naturales.** The Royal Chapel or Chapel of the Natives was reserved for the indigenous population, and it's unusual among Mexico's religious structures. Modeled after a mosque, it features a remarkable 7 naves and 49 cupolas in one cavernous hall.

PARROQUÍA SAN PEDRO

4 Poniente and 5 de Mayo at Plaza de la Concordia

Founded by the prolific Bishop Juan de Palafox y Mendoza in 1640, the San Pedro Parish Church occupies another corner of the *zócalo,* facing San Gabriel. Its baroque tower is the highest in Cholula and its Churrigueresque cupola dates from the 18th century. The church is also notable for its dramatic painting of the Archangel Michael in full armor.

San Francisco Acatepec

SAN FRANCISCO ACATEPEC
Along Route 190, about 3 miles south of Cholula

San Francisco Acatepec is a brilliantly ornate masterpiece of the indigenous baroque style. The façade is a priceless work of redbrick and Talavera, and its red, blue, yellow, and white colors gleam especially after a rainfall. The interior is opulent and intricately carved, with heavy use of gold plating. Note the indigenous sun on the ceiling and the four mirrors, one on each wall, representing science, morality, history, and nature.

SANTA MARÍA TONANTZINTLA
Along Route 190 and the Puebla-Atlixco highway, 2.5 miles south of Cholula

A mile or so before San Francisco Acatepec lies Santa María Tonantzintla, one of the most interesting churches in Mexico. Compared to the interior, the colorful redbrick and tiled façade is almost dull. (Note the rather dark-skinned religious figurines.) Inside, you'll be greeted to a dizzying display of popular baroque Mexican architecture. It's as if those responsible for the design wanted to leave no corner of the church dome untouched, and the resulting ornamentation is either in overwhelmingly bad taste (if you're a purist), or a wonderful example of the blend of indigenous and religious art. Stucco figurines, pagan symbols, and golden decoration of fruits, flowers, children, birds, and saints give the church a distinctly whimsical and childlike charm. Of course, it's tremendously popular with children, but even adults will enjoy craning their necks in every direction to admire this most Mexican of churches.

Detail interior embellishment, Santa María Tonantzintla

SANTUARIO DE LA VIRGEN DE LOS REMEDIOS
Atop the Pyramid of Cholula

The most eye-catching and probably most photographed sight in Cholula is the church perched atop what looks like a great hill. The elegant spires and azulejo Talavera dome of the Santuario de la Virgen de los Remedios (Sanctuary of the Virgin of the Remedies) can be seen from afar, and on a clear day, has the magnificent Popocatépetl volcano as its backdrop. The original building was built in 1594, but successive earthquakes destroyed it, and the current church dates from 1874. It's not the most interesting of Cholula's churches, but the climb up is worth it for the breathtaking views.

THE GREAT PYRAMID TLACHIHUALTÉPETL
222-247-9081
Calzada San Andrés and 6 Norte Street

At a casual glance, you won't even see Cholula's most amazing sight; all you'll notice is a church built on a hill. No wonder the people who built this pyramid called it Tlachihual-tépetl, or "Handmade Hill." Move closer and you'll start to see the characteristic stepped slope of a colossal pyramid that is, at its base, over 1,300 feet wide per side and over 200 feet high.

To put those numbers in perspective, the Cholula pyramid was larger than the Pyramid of the Sun in Teotihuacán as well as that of Cheops in Egypt. In the typical style of Mesoamerica, it was constructed in different phases, with the Indians simply building over the previous version. Cholula's pyramid was completed in seven such phases, the first dating back to 500 B.C. and spanning until the 8th century, after which it was mysteriously abandoned. By the time the Spaniards came, the pyramid was already largely covered over by earth and grass, and the conquistadores built the Santuario de la Virgen de los Remedios church at its peak.

You might want to visit the pyramid's Museo de **Sitio** (see entry under "Culture") before you head to the site (included in the price), and I highly recommend hiring a guide at the museum entrance for a proper tour (a few dollars more). Once you enter, you'll realize this is one pyramid that you can actually walk *through*. Catacombs dug into the structure take you deep into its heart, with passages disappearing off where archaeologists excavated in 1931. The tunnels are at times both narrow and short, but once you emerge you'll find yourself in an open complex of excavated buildings comprising what had to have been a truly awesome structure at its zenith. The most important structures are clearly labeled in English and Spanish. Open Tuesday to Sunday 8–5. $.

Great Pyramid Tlachihualtépetl

TRANVÍA TURISTÍCO (TROLLEY)

222-261 2393
www.vivecholula.gob.mx
Tourist Information Booth at Avenida Hidalgo and Avenida Miguel Alemán, Cholula

Launched just as this book was being completed, the Tranvía is an old-fashioned mini double-decker that will take you to the main sights in and around the city. There is also a weekend night trolley tour, which recounts legends and myths as it putters around the old city. Tours leave daily every hour and a half from 10 AM–5 PM, with the nocturnal tours running Saturday and Sunday 6:30 PM and 8 PM. $.

CULTURE

CASA DEL CABALLERO ÁGUILA

222-261-2393
4 Oriente Street 1, Centro Histórico, Cholula

A 16th-century mansion on the corner of the *zócalo,* the House of the Warrior Eagle gets its name from the two reliefs that flank its entrance. It is one of the oldest civilian constructions in the city, with its lower floor dating back to the 1500s. Within are 2,000-plus artifacts from pre-Hispanic and colonial times. Open Thursday to Tuesday 9 AM–3 PM. $.

MUSEO DEL SITIO

222-247-9081
Calzada San Andrés and 6 Norte Street

Across from the northern entrance to the pyramid is the *sitio,* or site, museum that pertains to the structure. Two exhibits of note here are replicas of early murals found at the pyramid. The mural of the *chapulines,* or grasshoppers, shows a distinctly human depiction of the insects; the original, located in the western end of the pyramid, dates from the 2nd century and has not, as yet, been completely excavated. The other mural, a huge work spanning over 160 feet in length, is called *The Drinkers,* and shows Indians enjoying their pulque. The original is covered for protection at the site. The museum also has a model of the pyramid showing its various sections. Open Tuesday to Sunday 8 AM–5 PM. $.

NIGHTLIFE

BAR ANÓNIMO

222-261-6938
www.seranonimo.com
14 Oriente 1001, San Andrés Cholula

Bar Anónimo is the kind of place you can visit on a weekly basis and never get bored. The combination of lounge, full-service kitchen, comfy theater-style seating around a stage that shows movies when a band isn't playing, outdoor terrace, and unique circular building covered in graffiti all combine to make this a bar unlike any other. Its varied ambiences, diverse music (anywhere from acid jazz to dance), range of events and special nights, and excellent local and international acts also make it a perennial favorite nighttime hangout.

Order a martini Anónimo (vodka, cranberry juice, and Red Bull), and pick your atmosphere. Open Tuesday to Sunday 6 PM–2 AM. $–$$, depending on event.

BAR REFORMA

222-247-0149
4 Sur and Avenida Morelos, San Pedro Cholula

There's a saying around here that goes: "If you come to Cholula and don't come to Bar Reforma, you haven't come to Cholula." It's a fitting tribute to the oldest cantina in the city and one of its most colorful. The neon green sign above the saloon-like double-doors serve as a siren call to just about every Cholulan, who pack in the small bar to sample its best-known product: the homemade sangria, a family recipe of owner Antonio Arroyo Mijailidis (his granddad founded the place). Beware, this is strong stuff: I'm told that, by the second one you can no longer lie, and by the third you're in trouble. However, the first is what Antonio calls "45 pesos of complete happiness." Plenty of other drinks are served here as well, along with tacos and bagels from outside. The flowers hanging from the ceiling and the wall showing pictures of all the churches in the area (it's the only place to see all of them together) are the main décor. Come for the ambience, the conversation at the bar with the charismatic owner, and the 45 pesos of happiness. Open 6 PM–1 AM. $.

BOMBAY BAR

14 Oriente 606, San Andrés Cholula

Among the incredibly diverse array of bars and lounges on 14 Oriente Street is Bombay, a so-funky-it's-almost-weird little spot that's a mix of chintz, retro furniture, and Asian and eastern accents. Come for its flavorful martinis (chocolate, white chocolate, and the Bombay—vodka, Bombay Sapphire gin, and dry gin—are among the most popular), mojitos, caipirinhas, and absinthe shots. Tuesday night is when the bar is at its busiest and best. Open Monday to Saturday 1 PM–midnight except Tuesday, open until 1 AM. $.

EL TIGRE

222-261-7759
14 Oriente 611, San Andrés Cholula

A very popular club with the collegiate crowd, El Tigre (the Tiger) celebrated five thumping years in 2008; not a bad record for a disco. Inside is an almost temple-like environment with multiple columns around the dance floor and the dim lighting associated with loud music, alcohol, and late nights. Check for the frequent events, including Tuesday nights, which are called Foreigners' Tuesday. Open Monday to Saturday 10 PM–4 AM. $$.

JAZZATLÁN

222-304-2643
Avenida Morelos 419, Centro Histórico, Cholula

There's usually a live act playing at this hip and mellow spot near the *zócalo* and far from the madding club crowds. These guys are serious about their jazz, so much so that the menus are LP-shaped, the staff quite knowledgeable, and no talking is allowed while the band is playing. However, eating a few tapas or a slice of pizza, and drinking a cocktail (try the Coltrane Martini, which has ginger, vermouth, and apple liqueur) while you enjoy live jazz certainly is. No cover.

PULKATA
14 Oriente and 6 Norte, San Andrés Cholula

A little bit of David Lynch mixed with local tradition, Pulkata serves up pulque, the liquor made from the sap of the maguey plant. The place is a corner of a very unique person's imagination: shades of deep red, completely goth (there's a creepy puppet in one corner), coffee table made out of a TV, a disco *Virgin de Guadalupe* . . . it's a bit surreal. And how they squeeze in a live band into the cramped space is again a mystery, but it all gives Pulkata a unique and well defined place on the Cholula bar and club strip. Open Monday to Saturday 6 PM–1 AM. $.

Container City: Shopping, Nightlife, and Dining in an Itty-Bitty Commercial Space
It's not a pyramid or a church, but Container City is a must-visit destination for its sheer ingenuity. The name is self-explanatory: a tiny community of brightly painted cargo containers housing everything from restaurants and shops to a Mini showroom. Opened in January 2008, the concept is executed with so much style and creative use of space that, instead of feeling cramped and squashed, it's funkier than any mall and intriguing enough to warrant several hours of exploration. Here's some of what you'll find in Container City (located at 12 Oriente and 2 Norte in San Andrés Cholula):

Alejandra de Coss
222-261-7911
A fashion designer with a fresh look and enough talent to be selected by *Elle* magazine for her dresses, Alejandra de Coss has a small boutique here in the City. The container itself is quite artistic, painted white with elegant floral designs and a large window giving it the illusion of space. In addition to clothes, the store has a small stock of handbags and funky modern accessories. Open Monday to Saturday 10 AM–8 PM, Sunday 11 AM–6 PM. $$–$$$.

Container City

Araña Mambo
This health-focused lunch spot has a range of omelets, quesadillas, and sandwiches, all made with fresh local ingredients, but the specialty here is the burritos. These are massive and come with *arrachera* (steak), steak tips, *picadillo* (a spicy ground beef mix), chicken, ham, or mushrooms. Also served here are delicious natural juices and shakes,

PULQUE PARA 2

www.myspace.com/pulqueparados

8 Norte and 6 Oriente, San Andrés Cholula

Another *pulquería* of notable fame in Cholula, Pulque Para 2 (Pulque for 2) isn't quite as out-there as its offshoot, Pulkata. It's been serving pulque for years to a varied crowd, from college students to town governors. You can order yours neat or flavored (orange, grapes, and other fruits), or even with red wine. There's live music nightly, and a small space to dance. Open Monday to Saturday 6 PM–1 AM. $.

especially from the *remedios chinos* (Chinese remedies) menu, which offers up fruity combinations to combat sunburn (melon and orange), blocked nose (carrot and lemon), diabetes (strawberry and lemon), and other ailments. Sunday brunch is a lively affair with a DJ and a buffet menu. Open Monday to Wednesday 9 AM–8 PM, Thursday to Saturday 9 AM–1 AM, Sunday 9 AM–5 PM. $.

Bar Fónica

Think a cargo container is too small for a bar and disco? So did these guys, who decided to weld three containers together to make the largest space in Container City. The end product is Bar Fónica, a cool space with a white-lit bar, room enough for a decent crowd to dance or chill out in the outdoor lounge area, and enough pull to bring together notable local and international DJs. The sound quality is surprisingly good for a container. It also has an extensive specialty drink menu, made by a bartender who is from the Tom-Cruise-in-*Cocktail* mold. Try the Martini Fónica (vodka, your choice of fresh mango, tamarind or passion fruit juice, and a touch of natural sherry, all served up with a chile). Open Monday to Saturday 8 PM–3 PM. Free, $ cover if there is an international guest DJ.

Beat Box

www.labeatbox.com

Looking for a custom-designed vintage bicycle? How about a Planet of the Apes figurine? You'll find these esoteric, hard-to-find curios, along with urban art, exclusive items from popular labels (there's a skull-shaped Adidas slipper that I've never seen before), posters, and clothes at this one-of-a-kind store that is perfectly suited to a place like Container City. Open daily 10 AM–9 PM. $$–$$$$.

Bianco Fashion Room

222-261-7993

A showroom of clothes, gifts, and accessories by Poblano designers, Bianco focuses on a younger audience. From jeans to club wear to costume jewelry, you'll find it here, and since there is only one piece of every article in stock, there's an element of the unique thrown in. Open Monday to Saturday 10 AM–8 PM. $$–$$$.

Mandala Tea House

An Asian-themed teahouse, Mandala has about 50 different teas from Japan, China, India, Africa, and the rest of the world. And by the way, they sew their own tea bags. If you want something with a bit more kick, try the tea with vodka. The cute and cool café also has flavored hookah (banana, cherry, mint, melon, chocolate, and peach are among the choices). Open Monday to Wednesday 1 PM–midnight, Thursday to Saturday 1 PM–1 AM. $.

SHOPPING

Talavera

Like Puebla, Cholula has an ancient tradition of craftsmanship and its share of high-quality Talavera workshops. The ones listed here all carry the DO, or *denominación de origen* branding, certifying its authenticity and adherence to the traditional process.

TALAVERA DE LA REYNA

222-225-4058
www.talaveradelareyna.com.mx
Camino a la Carcaña 2413, Recta a Cholula, Cholula

The workshop of Talavera de la Reyna, which supplies the beautiful pieces found in the Casa de la Reyna hotel and restaurant, is located here, and tours are offered if you want to see how the process works. The shop has earned a reputation for innovation and use of contemporary designs in Talavera. Open Monday to Friday 9–6:30, Saturday 9–1. $–$$$$.

TALAVERA DE LAS AMÉRICAS

Shop
222-261-0367
4 Sur and Avenida Morelos, San Pedro Cholula
Workshop
222-247-1765
7 Poniente 510, San Pedro Cholula

The shop and gallery of Talavera de las Américas is in a separate location from its workshop, but both are in Cholula. The shop has the advantage of excellent location right next to the great pyramid. They stock a wide range of traditional Talavera ceramics, such as jugs, platters, tea sets, vases, and azulejo pieces. $–$$$$.

TALAVERA SANTA CATARINA

222-247-6614
www.talaverastacatarina.com
Prol. 14 Oriente 1402, San Andrés Cholula

Located between Cholula's city center and Puebla, this is another place where you can tour the workshop and see how Talavera is made. A relative newcomer, it has been chosen by museums and private collectors to reproduce valuable pieces. The shop has some exceptional items, with over 500 designs of the distinctive azulejo-blue Talavera alone, sculptures and tiled artwork, in addition to more typical items. $–$$$$.

WEEKLY & ANNUAL EVENTS

CARNAVAL DE HUEJOTZINGO

Saturday before Ash Wednesday
Huejotzingo

Just over 8 miles northwest of Cholula along the highway to Mexico City, the small town of

Huejotzingo is known primarily for two things: a 16th-century monastery dedicated to the Archangel Michael, and its famed carnival. Its full pageantry, fireworks, live music, and, above all, elaborate costumes make it one of the most colorful and popular in all of Mexico. The carnival has been held here since 1869, and is definitely worth the side-trip from Puebla or Cholula.

FERIA DE LA VIRGEN DE LOS REMEDIOS
First two weeks of September
Throughout Cholula

There are many small festivals in Cholula, but the Feria de San Pedro is the big annual religious fair, which is known for the *bajada de la Virgen* (descent of the Virgin). This is when the *Virgen de los Remedios* is taken down from her home in the Santuario de los Remedios church atop the pyramid, and is paraded through each of Cholula's neighborhoods.

MERCADO DE TRUEQUE
September 8
At the **zócalo**

To really see a market as it functioned in ancient times, check out the Mercado de Trueque, held on September 8. *Trueque* means "barter," and that's what this market is all about. Vendors of all kinds flock here, trading arts and crafts, ceramics, food, clothing, and various other items.

VANILOQUIO
Last weekend of November
Throughout Cholula

A beautiful and haunting tradition, the Vaniloquio in Cholula is marked by all of the city's churches ringing their bells in a musical carol attended by tens of thousands of people. Considering the number and proximity of the city's churches, you can imagine how magical this event is.

RITUAL A QUETZALCOATL
March

The annual festival to Quetzalcoatl, the most important and venerated deity of pre-Columbian Cholulans, is held at the Plaza of the Altars in the Great Pyramid during the time of the first equinox. The event begins in the evening, at 7 PM, with ritual offerings, dances, Native music, and poetry. It's a deeply symbolic and extremely popular event that draws large crowds each year.

ATLIXCO

There are many side-trips from Puebla that will enable you to explore different sides of Mexico, but there is something special about Atlixco. Maybe it's the stunning sight, on a clear day, of the town nestled against the base of a small hill with snowcapped El Popo towering above it; maybe it's the beautiful churches and former convents; or perhaps it's the

View of Atlixco and nursery

perfect year-round weather that has made Atlixco home to numerous plant and flower nurseries; whatever the reason, there is an aura about this small, charming town that engages the imagination of those who visit . . . at least, it did for me.

Getting There and Getting Around

Atlixco is about 16 miles from Cholula and roughly 22 miles from Puebla. To get here by car, simply hop onto the Puebla-Atlixco highway (Route 190D). You can also take a bus, which is frequent and extremely cheap, from Puebla's CAPU bus station. The bus drops you just two streets from the main plaza. As for getting around, Atlixco is small enough to cover on foot, with a taxi ride or two.

LODGING

ANTIGUA ALQUERÍA DE CARRIÓN
244-761-8080
www.antiguaalqueria.com
Nicolás Bravo 2, Atlixco

Ordinarily, I would say that a day trip is plenty of time to enjoy Atlixco, but if there is one reason to extend your stay, it's this beautiful boutique hotel. A 360-year-old house, it's located on an old cobblestone street and has beautifully captured its past. Brickwork floors and exposed brick walls in the rooms, orthodox owl-eye windows from the colonial days, wrought-iron and wooden furnishings, and plaster motifs mix with modern comforts and elegance in each of its 16 rooms. All its bath products are made by an indigenous community. The hotel's public spaces include a pleasant courtyard with a pool and green patio, a small massage room, and meeting space. And because it's in Atlixco, you'll pay a lot less for the luxuries of a high-end boutique hotel than you would in Puebla or Mexico City. It's hard to imagine that this place was once used as a butcher's shop, and before that, a jail. $–$$.

DINING

CHARLIE PACAYA'S
244-443-2315
Libramiento Izucar de Matamoros Km. 29 104, Col. Lomas de Tejaluca, Atlixco

Located on the road from Puebla to Atlixco, Charlie Pacaya's is a taxi ride from the center of the city, but it's worth it for the great food, friendly ambience, and panoramic views of the town and the volcano. The menu is El Salvadorian, and the highlight is the filets, which can be ordered tartar or with lemon, Roquefort, or Parmesan cheeses. You can also order flavorful pasta, salad, and seafood dishes, and the homemade bread is an excellent start to the meal. The open grounds outside include a children's playground, plant nursery, and garden, and the place has truly breathtaking views of the town, with El Popo as backdrop. Open daily 11 AM–8 PM. $–$$.

ITALIAN COFFEE COMPANY
244-445-0022
www.italiancoffee.com
Avenida Hidalgo 5-E, Plaza Colón, Atlixco

Don't let the name fool you. The Italian Coffee Company is a local chain; in fact, it originated in Puebla and is especially ubiquitous in the state. The one in Atlixco's central plaza is designed like a Moorish pavilion, with green and yellow stained glass and tiles. Sit outside on the terrace and enjoy a sandwich, panini, or croissant along with a cappuccino and biscotti. Open Monday to Friday 8 AM–10 PM, Saturday and Sunday 9 AM–10 PM. $.

MERCADO BENITO JUÁREZ
Avenida de Independencia between 3
Poniente and 5 Poniente

This is a large, typical market, but you want
to come here for what makes it famous: its
cecina. There are several stalls offering
their version of this thinly sliced, cured
meat, and the ladies serving them up will
engage in friendly banter, competition,
flirting . . . whatever it takes to lure you to
their particular place of business. Order by
weight or by plate, or browse around for
other delights such as *pozole,* moles, and
enchiladas. I make it a point to grab a meal
at markets, especially in small towns, and
this one does not disappoint. Open daily
8 AM–8 PM. $.

*Vendor at Mercado Benito Juárez displays her
cecina*

ATTRACTIONS, PARKS & RECREATION

PALACIO MUNICIPAL (TOURISM OFFICE)
244-445-1956
www.atlixco.gob.mx
Plaza de Armas 1, Atlixco

The municipal palace, located right on the central plaza, now houses Atlixco's tourism
office, a good place to start your tour of the town. The small office has a useful interactive
kiosk that will give you a thorough overview of what there is to see and do, and the excellent
staff will provide you with maps, information, and guides if needed. Open daily 8–8. Free.

PARQUE COLÓN
Plaza Colón, Atlixco

The central plaza in Atlixco is a beautiful open space, framed by the façade of the Palacio
Municipal and the Natividad Parish Church. Landscaped trees and shrubs, sculptures, and
tiled benches now occupy what was once the site of the ancient Indian *tianguis,* or market.
There are still plenty of food vendors, in addition to the Italian Coffee Company, around
the park and the plaza, along with cafés beneath the arcade along its western side. Free.

The Churches of Atlixco
Within a ten-block radius, Atlixco boasts no less than five former convents, representing
the Carmelites, Franciscans, Clarisas, Augustinian, and Mercedes orders. The Carmelites
and the Franciscans were the first to arrive, both during the 1500s. In the 17th century,
religious architecture flourished in the city, developing its own baroque stucco style that

infused its churches and convents with local artistry. Churches are generally open daily from 10 AM–12:30 and 4:30 PM–6 PM.

CAPILLA DE LA TERCERA ORDEN
16 de Septiembre between 5 Norte and 7 Norte

The Chapel of the Third Order, located two blocks from the main plaza, is representative of the baroque style that flourished in Atlixco in the 1800s. The front façade has floral motifs, pillars flanked by mermaids, and other elaborate details.

EX-CONVENTO DE SANTA MARÍA
At the base of San Miguel Hill, Atlixco

Follow Avenida Hidalgo uphill and you can't miss this large, ancient, rose-colored church, also known as the **Ex-Convento de San Francisco.** The convent's most interesting treasure is a *teocalli* that was once used for sacrifices to Quetzalcoatl before it was converted into a baptismal pool: the city's first Natives were baptized here. You'll also find frescoes showing traces of Spanish and indigenous styles.

EX-CONVENTO DEL CARMEN
Nicolás Bravo and 2 Sur, Atlixco

Beyond the yellow façade above the door, little now remains of this former Carmelite convent, which was built between 1600 and 1620. What can be seen is a bare cloister, the ruins of the cells, and an orange grove. One hall houses a small museum of indigenous artifacts, evidence of the role Atlixco once served as a midway stop on the road to Teotihuacán. Museum open daily 9 AM–6 PM. Free.

IGLESIA DE LA MERCED
3 Norte between 4 and 6 Poniente Streets

No chapel in Atlixco can approach the intricate beauty and painted baroque stucco of the blue-and-gold arched front-piece of la Merced. Much of the 17th-century convent is largely gone, but the church still stands. The ornate façade dates from the 18th century, and features decorative columns flanking a Moorish arch, floral and leaf patterns, and at the top, a statue of Saint Joseph with Baby Jesus.

IGLESIA DE SAN AGUSTÍN
Independencia Street and 3 Poniente

This church, built between 1589 and 1593, is noted for its fine white stucco work, which covers the bell tower and surrounds the doorways, and ornate baroque interior. Note the grouping of dark-haired cherubs circling the elaborate dome.

PARROQUÍA SANTA MARÍA DE LA NATIVIDAD
Plaza Colón, Atlixco

The large Parish Church of Saint Mary of the Nativity dominates one corner of Atlixco's central plaza. The neoclassic structure is the best-preserved church in the city. Note the elegant bell tower and the papal seal on the façade.

TEMPLO Y HOSPITAL SAN JUAN DE DIOS
11 Sur and 3 Poniente, Atlixco

This former church is now a working hospital but can still be seen during visiting hours. There is a pleasant cloister with a stone fountain, but you should contact the tourism office to organize a tour of the hospital's most fascinating exhibit: a gallery of paintings from the 14th to the 18th centuries that hang in a second-floor hall that was once used to house the dead. Most of these works were made by anonymous artists, but they collectively form a treasure trove of religious art that is almost a total secret. Visiting hours of the hospital are 9 AM–8 PM daily.

WEEKLY & ANNUAL EVENTS

HUEY ATLIXCÁYOTL
Last Sunday in September
San Miguel Hill, Atlixco

This annual festival is a mix of indigenous cultures representing the 11 ethnic communities of Puebla celebrating their heritage through dance. Attired in Native costumes, Otomí, Mixtec, Totonaca, Nahuac, and other tribes from surrounding towns participate in the colorful display of music and movement that has become one of the most important festivals of its kind in this part of Mexico.

7

Cuernavaca

Mexico City's Weekend Getaway

The City of Eternal Spring; that's Cuernavaca's moniker, and it's an appropriate one. Its lovely climate, bountiful flora, and plethora of spas are a prescription for rejuvenation and relaxation. It's the perfect complement to Mexico City's urban dynamic sprawl and Puebla's colonial charm. And yet, as I made my way around Mexico and told people I met about the book I was writing, many were naturally curious to know which areas would be included. When I revealed that one of the three principal destinations in the guide was Cuernavaca, the capital of the state of Morelos, my friends would automatically shake their heads and tell me I was barking up the wrong tree. There's nothing in Cuernavaca, they would say, pointing me toward Oaxaca or Guanajuato instead.

Scene from Diego Rivera's History of Cuernavaca and Morelos, Conquest and Revolution

For most *chilangos*, Cuernavaca is merely a weekend getaway, a chance to enjoy near-perfect year-round climate, refreshing waters, and luxurious spas. In fact, I often heard that the best way to visit the city was to befriend a rich family with a summer home here. People went with friends, relaxed in the family pool, and maybe went clubbing at night. Then they came back to the D.F.

Because of what I'd heard, by the time I got to my destination I was afraid I'd made an error and that one-third of my guide would have to be rewritten. I needn't have worried. Cuernavaca is more than just its spas and flowers; it's also the principal city in a state with fascinating historical adventures, natural wonders, and hidden surprises. The more I explored Morelos, the more it amazed me and the more I felt I had stumbled upon something special. By the end of my time in Cuernavaca, I was convinced I'd found the perfect destination for my guide. Let's see if you agree.

Getting There

From Mexico City, the best and easiest way to get to Cuernavaca is by bus. However, while I strongly oppose renting a car in Mexico City, it might be a good idea to rent one for your journey to Cuernavaca. While you're in the city, taxis and buses will serve you well, but a rental car opens up the rest of the state and its wonderful excursions. Unless you've hired a guide, a car can be your passport to Morelos.

By Car

From Mexico City, take the Autopista México-Cuernavaca (Highway 95-D). You can reach this road via Avenida Insurgentes and Calzado Tlalpan, or via the Periférico that loops around the D.F. Head south on the Periférico to the Insurgentes exit, which will take you to the highway. You can either take the Cuernavaca *cuota* (toll) or Cuernavaca *libre* (free) route. Both roads are well maintained and take you directly to your destination. Cuernavaca lies about 55 miles south of Mexico City. As you near the city, you'll likely see people on the road selling bushels of fresh roses and other flowers. These are incredibly cheap (Cuernavaca exports roses to the U.S.).

By Bus

You can catch a bus to Cuernavaca directly from Mexico City's airport or from one of the city's main bus terminals. The Terminal Central Del Sur Bus Terminal at Tasqueña is the busiest port for Mexico-Cuernavaca service, and you'll easily find a seat here. The one-way trip takes roughly one hour.

Useful Numbers and Information	
Area Code in Cuernavaca	777
Any emergency	066
Red Cross	777-315-3505
Metropolitan Police	777-311-2448
Fire Department	777-319-3866
Hospitals	
County Hospital	777-311-2209/10/50/37
Children's Hospital	777-101-0250
Tourist Information	777-314-3920/800-987-8224
Ministry of Tourism	777-314-3872
Emergency Highway Road Service	777-312-8050/312-8078
National Emergency & Tourist Info	800-987-8284
Useful Local Web Sites	www.clickoncuernavaca.com
	www.morelostravel.com
	www.icuernavaca.com

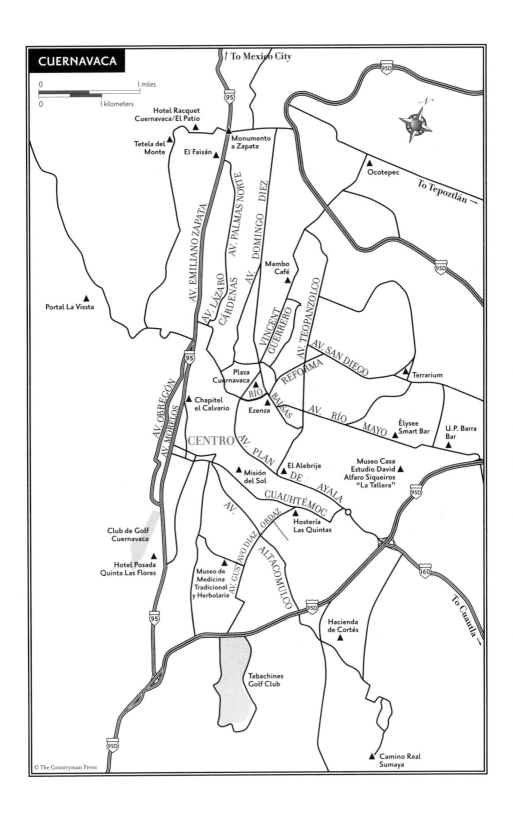

Estrella de Oro

777-312 3055 (Cuernavaca)

800-9000, ext. 105 (toll-free in Morelos)

55-5549-8520 (Mexico City)

www.autobus.com.mx

Avenida Morelos Sur 812, Col. Las Palmas, Cuernavaca

Pullman de Morelos

55-5549-3505 (Mexico City Terminal Central Del Sur Bus Terminal)

55-5786-9358 (Mexico City International Airport)

777-312-6063 (Cuernavaca Center Terminal)

777-312-9472 (Cuernavaca Casino de La Selva Terminal)

www.pullman.com.mx

The premier bus service to Cuernavaca, Pullman has two bus terminals in Cuernavaca: the Terminal Cuernavaca Centro on 12 Abasolo Street is just a few blocks away from the heart of downtown. The Terminal Casino de la Selva is farther away, on 102 Plan de Ayala Avenue, near the railroad station.

By Air
General Mariano Matamoros Airport

777-385-03-89

This small airport services national flights only. From Mexico City the distance is too short to warrant air travel, but if you're coming from other parts of the country, Avolar and Via Aerobus are the principal carriers that fly here.

Getting Around

Whether you're in a rental car or taxi, you're almost sure to end up stuck in traffic at least once. The city simply wasn't built to accommodate its population, and the resulting jams can be frustrating; if you're on the central Avenida Morelos on a weekend night, trying to travel the last five blocks to your destination, you'll hate your rental car with a passion. Fortunately, the city center is easily accessible to pedestrians; the majority of Cuernavaca's attractions are located within a few blocks of each other, and the city has some pleasant nooks and niches to explore on foot. There is also a *Tren Turístico* (Tourist Train) that loops around all the major attractions.

Taxis

Taxis are not metered here, so you should always ask the price of the trip before you hop in. Don't be afraid to haggle, and speaking Spanish will help you tremendously. The best way to travel by taxi is to have your hotel arrange one for you; some hotels have fixed taxi rates. A recommended service is **Citlali Radio Taxi** (777-311-3776/317-7525).

Bus

Not the most luxurious way to travel, the local buses are convenient, clearly labeled, and quite cheap.

Car Rental

The following agencies are located in or around Cuernavaca, and some offer drop-off and pickup service.

Europcar

There are three branches of this auto-rental chain in Cuernavaca, which offers decent rates:

Cuernavaca Airport
777-318-4329
Open 24 hours a day

Cuernavaca Centro
88 Morelos Sur Avenue
777-318-4329

At the Hotel Hacienda de Cortes
Plaza Kennedy 90
777-318-4329

Security Car Rental

866-500-8525 (U.S.)
777-311-3515 (Mexico)
800-730-1000 (toll-free in Mexico)
www.securitycarrental.com
Avenida Emiliano Zapata 611, Col. Tlaltenango, Cuernavaca, Morelos

A BRIEF HISTORY

Cuernavaca has been Mexico City's resort refuge since pre-Hispanic times. Its original inhabitants were the Tlahuicas, who settled here in the 10th century. When the Aztecs came, the area became more populated and served as a resort getaway for the nobility. In fact, the great Montezuma's mother was from this area.

Cortés himself saw the benefits of the climate and beautiful geography. He built his palace here, changed the name of the city from Cuaunáhuac, which meant "among the trees," to Cuernavaca, and made it his home base in Mexico; not surprising, since Spain had given him ownership of a huge area that included the entire present-day state. Cortés wanted a house of worship close to his residence, and in 1529 began the construction of the impressive Catedral de Cuernavaca. The palace and the cathedral are the two principal tourist sites in the city today.

The conquistador wasn't the only one to warm to Cuernavaca. In the 16th and 17th centuries, great haciendas were built by wealthy landowners. Over the next two hundred years, the hacendados would rule this land and grow rich off its soil. Their vast, luxurious estates and subjugation of the local townsfolk would incur the wrath of one Emiliano Zapata during the Mexican Revolution.

When the Austrian archduke Maxmilian became emperor of Mexico in 1864, he and his wife, Carlota, made frequent trips to Cuernavaca, and built a summer home here. In 1869, after Maximilian was ousted, Benito Juárez formalized the state of Morelos—named after José María Morelos, the hero of the War of Independence—and made Cuernavaca its

Cortés called this place home

capital. By the close of the 19th century, Morelos was a place of enormous social inequality. The elite lived in unparalleled luxury. Each hacienda was a self-sustaining unit with its own store, church, and security. Thirst for expansion led the hacendados to encroach on small villages and swallow up land and families with impunity. The stolen land attracted the ire of Zapata, who fought against the landowners, raided the haciendas, and led his army against the aristocracy. Many of the haciendas still stand as luxury hotels, and are well worth the visit for a glimpse into Mexico's past.

Following the revolution and the land reforms championed by Lázaro Cárdenas, the days of the hacendados came to an end in Cuernavaca and Morelos. In addition to its reputation as an ecotourism and spa resort, the city became known as the center of Spanish-language studies in Mexico. But Cuernavaca remained small for most of the 20th century, until the 1985 earthquake in Mexico City led to a population explosion.

LIFESTYLES OF THE RICH AND MEXICAN

Despite attracting an increasing number of foreign and local tourists, Cuernavaca remains principally a weekend getaway for Mexicans. Around the city center are lovely homes tucked away on quiet streets, many of which are empty from Monday to Thursday. Life here is governed so much by the weekend influx that some businesses (especially nightclubs) only open on weekends.

If you do visit Cuernavaca during the week, you'll enjoy a sense of quiet peace that disappears once the hordes from the D.F. arrive. Starting on Thursday, the Cuernavaca vibe starts to change. Restaurants get crowded, city streets get congested, and the press of people makes for a livelier scene overall. On the other hand, midweek is the time to hunt for bargains, with many hotels offering steep discounts to draw in the non-weekend tourist.

This is not the cheapest city in Mexico. The number and quality of its spas alone point to the type of tourists Cuernavaca welcomes. Many of its restaurants and hotels cater to a well-to-do crowd, although there are good deals and budget options to be found. Historically, the city has attracted a select minority of international elite. John Wayne was a fan; Woolworth heiress Barbara Hutton built a home here; the exiled shah of Iran was a guest, as was French superstar Brigitte Bardot.

The good news is that the clientele also helps make Cuernavaca a clean and safe destination. You'll consistently find foreigners here thanks to its spas, which attract people from all over the world (one spa was a favorite haunt of Tibetan monks), and Spanish-language schools. The educational niche has helped drive the youth movement in the city; its diverse nightlife will attest to that.

To be fair to my friends in Mexico City who warned me against making Cuernavaca a prominent part of this book, you really only need a few days to comfortably explore its major sites and attractions. But when you make Cuernavaca your base from which to explore the rest of Morelos, you'll find that nearly everything you want to see is at most two hours away by car.

Cuernavaca is a green and lush place. Its colonial charm, highlighted by 16th-century architecture and narrow, cobblestone streets, is complemented by its natural beauty—undulating hills and a mountainous horizon capped by two volcanoes: Ixtaccíhuatl (the Sleeping Woman) and Popocatépetl (the Smoking Mountain). Not surprisingly, it's a popular ecotourism destination, whether you like hiking, mountain climbing, bathing in sulfuric waters, or soaking in mineral springs.

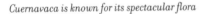

Cuernavaca is known for its spectacular flora

CUERNAVACA CITY CENTER

Las Mañanitas
ARISTA
La Casa Azul
Hotel Royal
La India Bonita
MORROW
Trattoria Marco Polo
Jardín Borda
HIDALGO
Catedral
Museo Brady
Hotel Casa Colonial
GUTENBERG
Palacio de Cortés
Casa Hidalgo
Gaia
Juárez 4
SALAZAR
CUAUHTÉMOC
LAS CASAS
ABASOLO
GUERRERO
AV. MORELOS
MATAMOROS
ALVARO OBREGÓN
AV. ADOLFO LÓPEZ MATEOS
AV. ADOLFO LÓPEZ MATEOS
PLAN DE AYALA
ATLACOMULCO
HUMBOLDT
NETZAHUALCOYOTL
GALEANA
JUÁREZ
BLVD.

© The Countryman Press

The Colonial City Center

Cuernavaca does not have the colonial beauty of Puebla, but it's got a pleasant historic center that will be your first stop in the city. This is where Cortés made his home, where Emperor Maximilian visited on his retreats away from the capital, and where other prominent residents have left their mark.

Cuernavaca's downtown revolves around the central *zócalo,* which is comprised of two plazas: the **Alameda** and the **Plaza de Armas.** This is the heart of the city, especially on weekends, when live music can be heard at the Alameda's Victorian gazebo (designed by none other than Gustave Eiffel, architect of the Eiffel Tower). At night, mariachis for hire patrol the plaza, available to play a tune or even hop in with their customers, travel to a party, and play for guests.

The dominant structure here is Cortés's Palace, now the **Museo de Cuauhnáhuac.** From here, a few blocks up Hidalgo Street on the corner of Hidalgo and Morelos, is the massive 16th-century Franciscan **Catedral de Cuernavaca,** the fortress-cathedral built at Cortés's request. Across from the cathedral is the **Jardín Borda,** a quiet, leafy sanctuary built in the

1700s. Nearby on Netzahualcoyotl Street is the **Museo Casa Robert Brady**, the museum and former home of one of Cuernavaca's more colorful citizens. These major landmarks make up the majority of the tourist sights in the city center.

North of the city center are the **Iglesia de Tlatenango** (Church of Tlatenango), the first chapel built in the Americas, and the **Iglesia de los Reyes** (Church of the Kings), a 16th-century church now famous for its sculptured walls designed by John Spencer, uncle of Diana Spencer, the Princess of Wales. To the south is the **Jardín Etnobotánico y Museo de Medicina Tradicional y Herbolaria**, an impressive botanical garden and herbolarium.

HACIENDAS AND SPA RESORTS

Cuernavaca has a variety of hotels, but there are two categories of lodging that are a destination unto themselves, offering a blend of dining, culture, and activities. The first is one of the hidden treasures of this area: the restored haciendas of the colonial Spanish elite who ruled this part of Mexico for hundreds of years, before Zapata and the Mexican Revolution brought them down. A stay in one of these grand estates is something special, both intrinsically Mexican and removed from modern-day Mexico.

The second option is the spa resort. While many hotels offer spa services, the resorts stand out for their focus on physical and spiritual relaxation. Lodging and dining here are part of the treatment, and the overall effect might just transport you from being a tourist visiting a new destination to a traveler discovering an oasis for the mind and body.

The resorts and haciendas listed here are not just limited to Cuernavaca, but can be found throughout the state of Morelos (at most an hour away from the city center). Even if you decide not to stay here, I recommend a visit for a meal, a treatment, or other service. Call ahead to see which places welcome the casual visitor and which require a booking or purchase.

Haciendas

HACIENDA COCOYOC

735-356-2211, 356-1211; 800-504-6239
www.cocoyoc.com.mx
Carretera Federal Cuernavaca Km 32.5, Cocoyoc 62736

Hacienda Cocoyoc (a Nahuatl term meaning "place of coyotes") is vast enough to require a map. With its 300 rooms, the hotel boasts four restaurants, three pools, a nine-hole golf course, and all kinds of amenities on its 22 acres. These include a disco and three bars, game room, gym, and horseback riding. For the romantically inclined there are horse-and-carriage rides available as well. And spa-lovers will flock to the **Spa Cocoyoc**, which is in a separate part of the estate and offers a full menu of services at reasonable prices.

Encompassing all of these facilities are the pristine grounds of the hotel. The aqueduct, with its gurgling, stepped fountain, is a beautiful visual centerpiece for the main lawn, and the large pool built under the redbrick skeleton of a former structure is very inviting. Throughout the hacienda are fountains, lush vegetation, and remnants of the original building. You can also visit a 16th-century chapel and monastery on the premises.

Of the hotel's restaurants, I give the nod to **La Chispa**, which offers an open-air dining area and terrific local cuisine. Among the menu's best items are the cuts of meat, highlighted by the *cecina,* a Morelos specialty of succulent, thinly sliced cured beef. The fish is

The pool at Hacienda Cocoyoc

also superb; try the *pescado totomoxtle,* a steamed fish in an adobo sauce, or the sea bass with citrus and pistachios. For all its recommendations, I found the rooms at Cocoyoc a bit bare and the bathrooms rather antiquated. (The upgrade to one of the 24 suites with private pools is money well spent.) Even with this shortcoming, however, Hacienda Cocoyoc is a remarkably affordable option for the experience it offers. $$-$$$$.

HACIENDA SAN ANTONIO EL PUENTE

777-365-6325/26/18
www.hotelhaciendasanantonioelpuente.com
Reforma No. 2 Fraccionamiento Real Del Puente, Xochitepec

Twenty minutes from downtown Cuernavaca, Hacienda San Antonio is one of the smaller haciendas, with only 50 rooms and a more modern feel than others on this list. The newer rooms are especially nice, with dark polished furniture and ample space, and elevator access, a rarity for haciendas. The hotel offers poolside spa services, a library, original chapel, Internet access in common areas (the thick stone walls of these haciendas are not conducive to modern technology), and a game room. The main pool is located under the framework of an old building, and a dip under its naked beams and exposed-brick pillars is a treat. Its **El Ingenio** restaurant is open to the outdoors, providing a pleasant ambience in which to try the traditional *cecina* or branch out into a menu of fusion cuisine. Two good options for the latter are the curried grilled chicken breast with a yogurt and green-apple sauce, and the fettuccine with tequila-glazed shrimp in a cheese sauce.

The hotel also has its share of legends. Zapata was attacked here. Many have reported seeing the ghost of a little girl wandering around the premises. You can see where the sugar trains used to come in. And one secluded section of the property has chipped-away mosaics and views of the 16th-century Real del Puente Bridge. $$-$$$$.

HACIENDA SAN GABRIEL DE LAS PALMAS

751-348-0636; 800-504-0736
www.hacienda-sangabriel.com.mx
Km 41. 8 Carretera Federal Cuernavaca, Chilpancingo, Amacuzac

I'll start with a negative here by saying the service at San Gabriel wasn't the best (although I was here during midweek, so that may account for some of the lethargy). However, if you can deal with a less-than-enthusiastic reception, this is a grand old estate founded by (who else?) Hernán Cortés in 1529. There's a wonderful authenticity to the place. The long, low, barrel-shaped ceilings are typical of colonial architecture. One can imagine the wealthy landlords seated in the leather-backed chairs at the long wooden dining table, or walking down the cobbled paths to the natural outdoor pool (there is a more modern pool near the restaurant); or even resting by the long, shallow fountain so reminiscent of the Alhambra in Spain. The stables are still in use, and the vine-draped walls and clusters of palm and amate trees add to the rustic beauty.

The rooms keep to the colonial style and are decorated to reflect their former luxury (think four-poster beds and antique furnishings). My favorite is the Alameda suite, which has a private grotto-like pool that alone is worth the price. The hacienda has the full-

Hacienda San Gabriel de Las Palmas

service **Amate Spa,** which has a *temazcal* (a pre-Hispanic sweat lodge), and it also boasts a unique jewelry shop that uses chemically treated leaves to create dramatic, unforgettable pieces. The restaurant, **El Amate,** serves up gourmet food; go for the tamales *de vagre* (tamales made from spiced catfish) or the duck breast with hibiscus sauce. Like many restaurants, San Gabriel also has its own special *cecina.* $$$-$$$$.

HACIENDA VISTA HERMOSA

734-345-5361
www.haciendavistahermosa.com.mx
Km. 7, Carretera Alpuyeca-Tequesquitengo, San José Vista Hermosa, Puente de Ixtla

You can feel and see history at this 16th-century estate, in the single, now defunct *chacuaco,* or smokestack, of its sugar days; the bare and in some cases broken walls of the original estate; and the starkly elegant redbrick archways that cross the pool amid lion-shaped fountains. It's a place that demands exploration.

Walk along the tall, palm-lined main path and see the signature *almenas,* or battle-ments, running the length of the walls. Then visit the chapel (most hacendados had private chapels on the premises), which can still be used for private functions. From here, check out the farm and the stables, which lead to an old rodeo. For a bit of fun, you can even take the dark and creepy tunnel through the dungeons to the restaurant and bar.

The hacienda offers plenty of activities, including mini golf, bowling, horseback riding, tennis, and a game room. Finally, there's the **Los Arcos** restaurant, framed under the stark stone outline of one of the buildings. The *cecina,* a house specialty, is a bit tangier than others I've tried. Another solid option is the *pollo trigarante* (chicken stuffed with cream cheese, spinach, and carrots and bathed in a red poblano sauce). The rooms continue the feel of living history, and the best ones come with a private pool. $$-$$$$.

HOTEL HACIENDA CORTÉS

777-315-8844; 800-220-7697
www.hotelhaciendacortes.com
Plaza Kennedy 90, Col. Atlamulco, Jiutepec

The closest of the Haciendas to Cuernavaca, this property was founded by, you guessed it, Cortés in 1643. The estate's many gardens, the well-preserved restoration of its early architecture, and more than comfortable rooms mark it as one of the best around. Its pool is an architectural treat, punctuated by dramatic columns and set in a secluded part of the property. Walk around the impeccable grounds and you'll see the remnants of an old aque-duct, plaques describing the history of the place, and beautiful sculptures dotted among the trees and the hacienda's principal gardens. But it's the rooms that are a clear cut above many of its competitors. Ample space, wrought-iron furnishings, and exposed brick walls make for sumptuous lodgings reminiscent of the old days. The hotel's restaurant, **La Casona,** located in the high-ceilinged main building of the hacienda, offers excellent food. $$$-$$$$.

Spa Resorts

HOSTAL DE LA LUZ

739-395-3374; 800-552-3550
www.hostaldelaluz.com
Carrretera Federal Tepoztlán, Amatlán Km. 4, Morelos

When the Dalai Lama himself assigns a destination the designation "place of peace," you know they're doing something right. And they're doing lots of things right at Hostal de La Luz. Set on a hillside with dramatic views of the rugged mountains (framed beautifully on the terrace by a sculpture of the Indian goddess Shiva), this is a retreat in the truest sense.

Hostal de la Luz is the combined product of people, nature, and science. The natural element comes from its clean air, panoramic vistas, and soil rich in ferrite, a mineral believed to enhance one's mental capacities. The resort, made of clay and adobe, blends perfectly into its environment. Each room is unique, cozy, minimalist in décor, and notable for its lack of technology. There are no TVs, no air-conditioners, and your cell phone will not work here. The resort is for adults over age 18 only, to ensure a quiet, meditative environment at all times.

The treatments and holistic services offered here come from around the world; *temazcal*, ashram, and even pyramid coexist with no bias and no religious slant. The focus is on total relaxation, and everything is designed according to feng shui principles. Three shamans are available to guide you through the various techniques and offerings, which run the gamut from an array of massages to a complete immersion in the self.

The spiritual energy of this place is backed by hard science. The herbs and plants used for medicinal purposes are all grown on the premises, and the treatments offered have been researched by neuroscientists, who come here to study. And finallly, the **Shambala Restaurant** serves hearty, healthy, and tasty meals. $$-$$$.

Hostal de la Luz

HOSTERÍA LAS QUINTAS

777-318-6301, 362-3949
www.hlasquintas.com
Boulevard Díaz Ordaz 9, Col. Cantarranas, Cuernavaca

There's much to recommend Hostería Las Quintas. The botanical gardens and lawns, with their myriad onyx sculptures, herbs, trees, and bursting flowers are a good start. The rooms range from comfortably modest to wonderfully romantic affairs with fireplaces and private Jacuzzis. The restaurant, **Verde Fino**, is excellent and offers a can't-go-wrong Sunday buffet. And, of course, there is the spa.

The Hostería offers a wide variety of massages and aesthetic services. It places an emphasis on fitness, offering classes in tai chi, tae-box, yoga, and aquarobics, among other activities. Beyond this is the traditional *temazcal,* where a shaman will guide you within the small, dome-shaped structure, pour hot water over a mix of herbs and rocks, and chant as you meditate and let the steam envelop your body. Two other specialties are the *janzu* and *flotarios*: both involve meditating while floating in the water (the latter in an enclosed space, the former in the open). $$-$$$$.

HOTEL VILLA BEJAR & SPA

734-347-0620
http://spa.villabejar.com.mx
Blvd. Lomas Tropicales S/N Esp. Lomas Tropicales, Tequesquitengo

Located on the shores of Lake Tequesquitengo, Hotel Villa Bejar is tremendously popular for its full-service spa and its relaxed ambience. In addition to the spa, the hotel has boat rides, personal watercraft, and waterskiing. Add yoga, mini golf, pottery classes, a full-service gym, and guided trips to Xochicalco and Tepoztlán, and it becomes clear why people flock here. The 45 rooms are a bit sparse, but the Moorish accents are attractive distinguishing features; it also helps that all the rooms overlook the lake. The gardens and pool are worth some of your time between spa treatments and aquatic excursions, and there is even a small sandy beach, a rarity in Morelos. Plus, Villa Bejar has something no other spa resort does: a ferryboat floating bar and disco (free for guests) that putters out to the middle of the lake on weekends, where a live band and a night of dancing on the lake await you. $$-$$$$.

MISIÓN DEL SOL

777-321-0999
www.misiondelsol.com
Avenida General Diego Díaz González 31, Col. Parres, Cuernavaca

Rivaled only by the Hostal de la Luz for the crown of best spa retreat in the state of Morelos, Misión del Sol (Mission of the Sun) is an experience that begins before you even check in. You park outside and have the option of walking up the steep hill or being shuttled in a golf cart to the reception. From here, you get a view of a large property dedicated to wellness and holistic healing. The buildings are all painted in muted earth colors, and the gardens and foliage are tended with precise care. Gravel paths take you around the property, past waterways, tennis courts, and the visually dramatic pool, with its steps painted in the colors of the sun.

Each room is unique and ranges from a standard double to a private villa that can accommodate six people. All the structures are made principally from adobe and wood, and follow feng shui principles. Two added touches are the open-sky showers and the beds, which come equipped with a magnetic system under the mattress to enhance comfort and relaxation.

You can tell that people are serious about their visit to the Misión del Sol. It's an adults-only destination. Classes, workshops, group meditations, and a general aura of inner reflection abound. The spa has more than 50 treatments and therapies designed to detox, reinvigorate, and rejuvenate. And the restaurant, **El Sol**, places a huge emphasis on nutrition (without sacrificing taste). It all makes for one of the most exclusive properties in this part of Mexico. $$$-$$$$.

PORTAL LA VISSTA

777-102-1861, 372-1865, 372-1875, 313-7005
www.portallavista.com
Chalma Sur No. 122 Col. Lomas de Atzingo, Cuernavaca

Set on a bluff with dramatic vistas that justify its title, Portal la Vissta is more than just a room with a view, although, wow, that view when the sun sets or when you're lounging by the open-air pool is something. Its 22 rustic suites are very cozy. The spa includes a *temazcal* and a *teizcalli* (in which you float in cool water and meditate after the heat of the steaming *temazcal*), and a meditation room. This place also has something the others don't: a pre- and post-surgical program revolving around plastic and aesthetic surgery. And their restaurant, **Spirale**, offers a fusion of local and international flavors. The hotel welcomes adults aged 16 and over only. $$-$$$.

LODGING

ARISTOS MIRADOR CUERNAVACA

800-901-0200
www.aristoshotels.com/
Nardo 202 Col. Rancho Cortés, Cuernavaca

Set far away from the city center and perched atop a steep hill, the Aristos Mirador has its plus points and its negatives. The former includes the beautiful views of the city, spacious rooms, and the large, inviting pool. Among the negatives are the dated décor, so-so service, and the remoteness of the place (continuous taxi rides from downtown Cuernavaca will lighten your wallet in a hurry). Still, this is one of the more affordable hotels in an exclusive suburb of the city. $-$$.

CAMINO REAL SUMIYA

777-329-9888
www.caminoreal.com
Interior Fraccionamiento Sumiya S/N, Col. José Parres, Morelos

Eschewing the Mexican colonial theme, the Camino Real Sumiya went Zen, opting for a Japanese-inspired hotel in harmony with Cuernavaca's vaunted reputation for rest and relaxation. It works beautifully, but it wasn't all their idea. The hotel was once the estate of Barbara Hutton Woolworth, who hired Japanese architects to build her home in Cuernavaca in the 1950s. The Camino Real merely took over where she left off. Sumiya means "place of peace, tranquility, and long life," and they tried hard to achieve all three. The pagodas, traditional Japanese gardens, and Asian accents throughout practically guarantee a peaceful environment. The rooms, which are characteristically minimalist, are certainly tranquil. And as for long life, ask about the magnetism and the energies to be found on the premises. It's a bit removed from the city center, but all told, the Sumiya makes for a picturesque, but not cheap, anomaly in Cuernavaca. $$$.

LA CASA AZUL

777-314-2141
www.hotelcasaazul.com.mx
Calle Mariano Arista, No. 17, Cuernavaca

La Casa Azul

In my opinion the most artistically beautiful and elegant hotel in the city, this boutique property is a lovely tribute to Mexican culture. The hotel itself has a spacious, clean ambience, its white walls, wide arches, and central fountain reminiscent of southern Spain. The deep blue pool, tucked against one side of the building, is visually stunning. And the open spaces invite guests to linger outdoors with a drink or a book.

But the rooms are what make La Casa Azul (the Blue House) stand out. Each is uniquely decorated according to a region in Mexico. Every piece of furniture was custom-ordered for the hotel, and the quality of the décor is unparalleled. From the colonial-era-inspired Guanajuato Room to the Mayan-themed Chiapas Room, each is meticulously assembled to reflect Mexico's rich and diverse culture. I particularly love the way the TV is usually masked behind some lovely piece of furniture, like a secret nod to the modern world. Add the pleasant open-air restaurant and La Casa Azul is a secluded treasure in the heart of the city. $$-$$$.

HOTEL CASA COLONIAL

777-312-7033
www.casacolonial.com
73 Netzahualcoyotl Street, Col. Centro, Cuernavaca

True to its name, this hotel feels like a colonial home. Set in an 18th-century building, it's one of the best values around thanks to its exceptional staff (some of the most amiable people I met in Cuernavaca); central location, steps from the *zócalo*; lovely layout (a central pool, 18 rooms spread throughout the house, and pleasant garden); and cozy, intimate rooms. Some have working fireplaces and all have polished wood furnishings and tiled floors. Perhaps because of its welcoming charm, the guests I met here were equally friendly. While there is no restaurant on the premises, the hotel's owners also own nearby **Casa Hidalgo,** one of the better restaurants in town. $$-$$$.

HOTEL POSADA QUINTA LAS FLORES

777-314-1244, 312-5769
www.quintalasflores.com
Tlaquepaque 1, Col. Las Palmas, Cuernavaca

Quinta las Flores is a great bargain for what you get: manicured lawns and colorful gardens, a heated pool, and spacious rooms furnished comfortably if not lavishly. If you can, go for the rooms with mini-balcony overlooking the gardens. Located on the southern end of the city, it's a cheap cab ride to the main attractions. The hotel also has a restaurant and a cute *palapa*, or thatched-roof bar. $$.

HOTEL RACQUET CUERNAVACA

777-1010-350; 800-002-5425
www.hotelescalinda.org.mx/cuernavaca/
Avenida Francisco Villa 100, Fraccion-amiento Rancho Cortés, Cuernavaca

Removed from the city center, this sprawling hotel offers more than just a pleasant retreat. Set amid manicured grounds are 38 comfortable rooms, 13 well-appointed suites, and one spoil-me-rotten presidential suite. The hotel's very good restaurant is slightly marred by the unflattering dolphin fountain in the otherwise lovely central courtyard, but that shouldn't stop you from booking a table here or lounging around in the evening.

This is a tranquil refuge that exemplifies what Cuernavaca is all about, but it is also one of the best-equipped hotels in town. The emphasis is on family and fun: the large swimming pool has a children's area, there are ample gardens and a children's playground, nine tennis courts (four lit at night), a game room, gym, mini golf, and even a small soccer court. The hotel also has three meeting spaces, including the impressive hall of flags. The spa, **Spaciel**, is modest in comparison to others in the city but is well equipped and has a focus on holistic treatment and spiritual as well as physical wellbeing.

Finally, there are the special historical

Courtyard at Hotel Racquet Cuernavaca

touches: the antique car parked outside the hotel lends a nostalgic air, and Cortés's shield adorning the front gate grounds this place in the past: this was once Cortés's ranch grounds and held his stables. The shah of Iran came here after his exile; so did Josephine Baker, John Wayne, and Diego Rivera. It's not cheap, but if you're looking for a bargain, check out the hotel's midweek rates, which are a steal. $$-$$$$.

HOTEL ROYAL
777-318-6480, 314-4018
www.hoteles-royal.com
Matamoros 11, Col. Centro, Cuernavaca

A great option for the backpacker and the budget traveler, Hotel Royal offers very basic accommodations at true bargain prices. This is more motel than hotel, but it's clean, well run, and is right in downtown Cuernavaca, within steps of its principal sights. The hotel has a café and plenty of parking space (not always the case in this city). $.

LAS MAÑANITAS
777-362-0000
www.lasmananitas.com.mx
Ricardo Linares 107, Col. Centro, Cuernavaca

One of only two properties in Mexico to be part of the prestigious Relais & Châteaux chain, Las Mañanitas has enjoyed a long-standing reputation as the premier hotel in Cuernavaca. This is the one destination just about everyone I spoke to in Mexico City recommended as the place to go. So I was understandably excited to check it out. And while I found hotels that were at least its equal, Las Mañanitas is certainly a classy place in an excellent location. The service is impeccable, the suites have all the under-stated opulence of colonial Mexico (rich wood furnishings, fireplaces, and large, comfortable beds), and the grounds are serene and beautiful. The Orlane Paris Spa is one of the more expensive ones around,

but it's got an extensive menu and a world-class reputation.

Perhaps Las Mañanitas is best appreciated in the early morning and at dusk; while it's early, you can stroll in the landscaped gardens with only peacocks, flamingos, and obsidian sculptures for company; and at night, the romantically lit hotel restaurant overlooking the gardens is truly picturesque. $$$-$$$$.

DINING

In addition to the restaurants mentioned below, I highly recommend dining at haciendas and spa resorts. In addition to the unique environment, the food I ate at these destinations was without exception of a high quality.

CASA HIDALGO
777-312-2749
http://casacolonial.com
Calle Hidalgo 6, Col. Centro, Cuernavaca

Juan Diego Pons knows what he's doing. The owner of the charming Casa Colonial has one of the city's better, and certainly best-located, restaurants in Casa Hidalgo. Across from the Palacio Cortés in the city center, this two-story haven with open-air rooftop terrace gets an enthusiastic nod for a few reasons. One, you get great views of the Palacio and the *zócalo,* which is especially pretty at night. Two, the balconies are perfect for a candle-lit romantic dinner for two. And three, the food is a delicious combination of local and international. For starters, try the shrimp *tacos sudados* (the horrible English translation is "sweaty tacos," but "moist" is the more apt description) or the deliciously refreshing cold mango soup with chunks of jicama (a type of turnip). Move on to the beef tongue, Veracruz style, a house specialty, or the *tampiqueña,* a hearty platter of steak, grilled strips of poblano chile, beans, and thick slices of white cheese. Seafood lovers will prefer rainbow trout cooked in white wine. Open Monday to Thursday 1:30–11 PM, Friday and Saturday 1:30 PM to midnight, Sunday 1:30–10 PM. $$.

EL FAISÁN

777-317-5281
Avenida Emiliano Zapata 1233, Col. Buenavista, Cuernavaca

The kindly old lady whose portrait hangs in this restaurant is Aurora Canto, the grand-mother of the owners of El Faisán (the Pheasant), on her 100th birthday. It is her legacy that lives on in one of Cuernavaca's most popular eateries. El Faisán specializes in cuisine from the Yucatán region of Mexico, offering a departure from typical Morelos fare like *cecina* and various cuts of meat. Among the most popular dishes here are the lime soup, *cochinita pibil* (slow-roasted suckling pig wrapped in banana leaves) and the namesake *faisán en pipián,* or pheasant in a pumpkin-seed sauce. Open daily 8 AM–11 PM. $$.

EL PATIO

777-101-0350; 800-002-5425
www.hotelescalinda.org.mx/cuernavaca/
At the Hotel Racquet Cuernavaca
Avenida Francisco Villa 100,
Fraccionamiento Rancho Cortés,
Cuernavaca

El Patio provides the same ambience and quality of food that you'll find when dining in a hacienda. Set inside the courtyard of the Hotel Racquet, its open-air, comfortable atmosphere is tough to beat, especially considering you can take a pleasant walk around the property after dinner. The food is pure Mexican, with the house specialty being— small surprise—*cecina*. This place also has a terrific breakfast menu, including local favorites like *huevos tirados* (scrambled eggs with frijoles) and *huevos sincronizados* (eggs, ham, and cheese smothered in mole sauce

on a tortilla). Open daily 7:30 AM–10:30 PM. $$–$$$.

GAIA

777-312-3656, 310-0031
www.gaiarest.com.mx
Boulevard Benito Juárez

Despite tough competition, Gaia wins my vote for favorite restaurant in Cuernavaca. It's simply got too many good things going for it. Located steps from the Cuernavaca Cathedral, the restaurant has an upscale elegance, stemming in part from its past life as a 19th-century colonial mansion. The dining rooms are interspersed throughout the old home, creating roman-tic niches and intimate spaces. It's got an interesting history as well. The house once belonged to a legendary actor by the name of Mario Moreno, better known and loved as Cantinflas. The magnificent pool fea-tures a Diego Rivera mural of Gaia, the earth and fertility goddess after whom the restaurant is named.

   And then there's the food, a sophisti-cated mélange of Latin and rest-of-the-world. It's not all fusion: the stuffed Brie hasn't got a chile anywhere near it and the delicious wild-mushroom cream soup is a classic recipe. For an entrée, try the lin-guine with shrimp in a cilantro sauce or the mahimahi marinated in miso and served with wasabi-flavored potatoes. For Mexican purists, there are the old standbys like *arrachera* tacos and more interesting con-coctions like adobo-crusted shrimp with tamarind sauce. Open Monday to Thursday 1–11 PM, Friday and Saturday 1 to midnight, and Sunday 1–6 PM. $$-$$$.

LA INDIA BONITA

777-312-5021, 318-6967
www.laindiabonita.com.mx
Morrow 15 B, Col. Centro, Cuernavaca

The oldest surviving restaurant in Cuernavaca, La India Bonita (the Beautiful

Indian) takes its name from Emperor Maximilian's lover. The restaurant pays full homage to Mexican décor; if you can, take a seat at one of the three patios. On Saturdays there are traditional dances here, and on Sundays there's a gut-busting buffet. The cuisine is typical Mexican fare, with Poblano specialties including mole *poblano* and *chiles en nogada*. The restaurant also has artifacts and traditional clothing for sale. Open Sunday and Monday 9 AM–5 PM, Tuesday through Friday 8 AM–10 PM, Saturday 9 AM–11 PM. $$.

LAS MAÑANITAS
777-362-0000
www.lasmananitas.com.mx
Ricardo Linares 107, Col. Centro, Cuernavaca

Even if you're not a guest at Las Mañanitas, dinner here is a special treat. The setting is incomparable; an open-air venue looking out onto the manicured, gently sloping gardens of the hotel; a wide terrace; and elegant, understated décor. The service is distinguished and professional. And the food is what you'd expect from a top-class institution. The award-winning menu is a combination of Mexican and international cuisine. The former includes indigenous delicacies like *escamoles* (ant eggs), *gusanos de maguey* (fried cactus worms), and traditional tortilla soup (in case the above two made you squeamish). The latter includes filet of red snapper in a curry sauce and the ridiculously decadent black-bottom pie. Open daily 8 AM–11 PM. $$$–$$$$.

LA PALAPA DEL VENADO
734-345-0252
www.elvenado.4t.com
Yautepec-Jojutla highway, no. 28, Tlaltizapán, Morelos

If you're traveling by car, I highly recommend this casual roadside eatery for its specialty: exotic meats, which range from the house special iguana soup to steaks made of venison, armadillo, skunk, possum, and even viper. It may sound frightening to the unadventurous palate, but the food here is hearty and well prepared, and very tasty. If you're the type who likes to "go where the locals go," La Palapa is well worth a visit. For more on La Palapa, see the sidebar under "Springs and Water Parks" in the next chapter. Open daily 11 AM–8 PM. $$.

TERRARIUM
777-512-6873
www.terrarium.com.mx
Avenida San Diego 1305, Cuernavaca

One of the fanciest dining destinations in the city, Terrarium offers a sophisticated setting and a creative menu. The restaurant occupies a two-story home that has been opened and transformed into a lovely dining space. Surrounded by a small but exotic garden, the dining room is both dramatic and intimate, with a staircase leading up one wall to a private dining area. The menu stays close to Mexican cuisine's traditional roots while blending in different flavors and textures. Try the fondue with *huitlacoche* served in a bread bowl or the delicious scallop carpaccio served with a chile and marinated onion dressing. The *chiles en nogada* is a specialty of the house (only available in August and September), and the *chiles en hojaldre* (poblano chiles filled with *huitlacoche* and wrapped in a phyllo pastry) is a classic worth tasting. $$–$$$.

TRATTORIA MARCO POLO
017-312-3484, 017-318-4032
www.marco-polo.com.mx
Hidalgo 30 Altos, Col. Centro, Cuernavaca

Walk by the Cuernavaca Cathedral at night and turn down Hidalgo Street, and you're bound to hear the pleasant chatter and clinking of silverware and glass coming from somewhere above you. Follow the

Carnivorous décor at Palapa del Venado

sound to Trattoria Marco Polo, a laid-back, charming Italian restaurant with a family atmosphere. The menu is simple and focuses on the food you know and love. You can't go wrong with homemade pasta options like fettuccine *alla salmonata* (made with a salmon and trout sauce) or spaghetti *alla vongole* (spaghetti with clams in tomato sauce). Its other strength is a range of thin-crust, topping-heavy pizzas baked in a wood-fired oven. For those who like quantity and quality, go for the *especial Marco Polo*, which has just about the entire antipasto menu on it. Open Monday through Thursday 1–10:30 PM, Friday and Saturday 1 PM to midnight, Sunday 1–10 PM. $-$$.

ATTRACTIONS, PARKS & RECREATION

One of the principal attractions in Cuernavaca is the spa experience, which brings thousands of Mexican and international tourists to the city every weekend. Apart from the spas, some of the best attractions can be found when you venture out of the city and explore the surrounding area. I've dedicated the next chapter to these excursions, but to give you a hint of what's to come, they include fabulous pre-Columbian ruins, water parks galore, and historic trails in the footsteps of friars and freedom fighters.

AERO DYNAMICO DE MEXICO

734-345-5487, 777-374-0860
www.ultraligeros-mexico.com
Calle de la Torre 20, San José Vista Hermosa, Morelos

Ever been in an ultralight? Know what an ultralight is? Well, think of it as a motorized hang glider, and Aero Dynamico, a bit of a trek from Cuernavaca but well worth it, is the place to go to try one out. The ultralight has two seats, one seat for your instructor, the other, forward seat, for you. It's probably the most gentle machine around to get you into the sky and give you a bird's-eye view of the area. You don't have to do anything but put your sunglasses on, sit back, and enjoy the scenery. Make sure to bring your camera to capture the vistas of the lake, the mountains, and the pastoral landscape below. In addition to four ultralights, Aero Dynamico has some nifty-looking gliders, which are available for longer trips, and a flight school. If you want to combine two experiences for a great day out, book a trip to Las Estacas Water Park, which has a mini runway specifically for ultralight landings. $$$-$$$$.

Ecotourism

Mountain climbing and ecotourism are popular pastimes in Morelos, thanks to its awesome mountain ranges and two nearby volcanoes. Note that the Popocatépetl volcano has been active recently and is naturally inadvisable for trekking. Also, it is strongly recommended that you go with a group or a guide on any of these excursions. Here are a few companies based in or around Cuernavaca.

ANGAMU TURISMO ALTERNATIVO

777-318-3737, 221-1573
www.angamu.com.mx
Priv. Club de Golf 12, Club de Golf Cuernavaca, Cuernavaca

Angamu offers a wide range of activities, including nature hikes, rappelling, and camping trips. Check to see when each service is offered, as not all are year-round. $$$-$$$$.

MEXICO OUTDOOR ADVENTURE

777-322-6555/800-728-4312
www.mexicooutdooradventure.com
Río Panuco 706, Col. Vista Hermosa, Cuernavaca

Mexico Outdoor conducts all kinds of excursions, including whitewater rafting, kayaking, subterranean river exploration, rappelling, hiking, rock climbing, and camping. The company's general director, Stephen MacDonald, organized Mexico's first national rafting team and has represented Mexico in world rafting competitions . . . so you know you're in good hands. $$$$.

MORELOS TRAILS

777-318-6480, 312-2279, 314-4018
www.morelostrails.com
Matamoros 11, Col. Centro, Cuernavaca

For a personal (and completely bilingual) guide to Cuernavaca's history, culture, natural surroundings, and eco-adventure, I can't recommend Rubén Cortés of Morelos Trails enough. My amiable and extremely knowledgeable guide through the state of Morelos is an accomplished mountain-climber and scuba diver, and knows where to take his guests. There's more on my journeys with Rubén in the next chapter, but if you're looking for an expert local guide to take you up into the mountains, beneath the waters, or around the town, he's the man to contact. $$$-$$$$.

Golf

Cuernavaca's climate is tailor-made for golf, and there are internationally acclaimed courses to be found in and around the city. The following are open for public play:

CLUB DE GOLF CUERNAVACA

777-314 0207, 314-0235
www.golfcuernavaca.com
Plutarco Elías Calles 31, Col. Club de Golf Cuernavaca

This nine-hole course just south of the city center is the most accessible to the city. It's been around since 1934, and has a clubhouse, restaurant and bar, meeting space, and pool. Private and group golf lessons are available. Open Tuesday to Thursday 7–7, Friday to Sunday 7–8. $$$$.

CLUB DE GOLF HACIENDA SAN GASPAR

777-319-4404, 319-4424
www.sangaspar.com
Avenida Emiliano Zapata, Col. Cliserio Alanis, Jiutepec

Club de Golf Hacienda San Gaspar is a par-72, 18-hole course designed by Joe Finger. With its dramatic views of the surrounding mountains and a 16th-century hacienda, it's considered one of the most beautiful golf retreats in the state. Visitors have access to a sauna, pool, tennis courts, restaurant, and bar. $$$$.

HACIENDA COCOYOC

735-356-2211, 356-1211; 800-504-6239
www.cocoyoc.com.mx
Carretera Federal Cuernavaca Km 32.5, Cocoyoc 62736

One of the farthest golf destinations from Cuernavaca proper, Hacienda Cocoyoc has two courses set amid its colonial surroundings: the nine-hole Club Deportivo Cocoyoc and the 18-hole Club Campestre Cocoyoc. Golfers have access to a bar, restaurant, pro shop, classes, and caddies; the latter course includes use of a pool, Turkish bath, and gym. Cocoyoc also charges very reasonable green fees. Open daily 7–6. $$$-$$$$.

TABACHINES GOLF CLUB AND RESTAURANT

777-314-3999
Km. 93.5, Carretera México-Acapulco

The most popular of the city's courses, Tabachines has an 18-hole course designed by Percy Clifford. It's also conveniently located right on the highway from Mexico City to Cuernavaca, and has a great restaurant on premises. Open Tuesday to Sunday 7–6, tee times 7–2. $$$$.

TREN TURÍSTICO

777-317-0421, 318-6045
Outside the Palacio de Cortés

Cuernavaca's Tren Turístico is a tourist trolley that takes you on one of four routes and covers 55 historical and cultural attractions. The train starts outside Cortés's Palace in

Cuernavaca's central plaza and is a good choice if you want to catch not only the main attractions but less-frequented stops like the Barranca de Amanalco Park. The trolley runs Monday to Thursday 11:50 AM—5:15 PM, with an extra trip at 7 P.M. on weekends. $.

Culture

JARDÍN BORDA
777-318-1044
www.arte-cultura-morelos.gob.mx
Avenida Morelos Sur 271, Col. Centro, Cuernavaca

Jardín Borda (Borda Garden) has an interesting history. José de la Borda was a silver tycoon from the nearby town of Taxco, Mexico's silver capital. In the 1700s he built a lavish retreat in Cuernavaca, valuing the region like so many others have done for its climate. His son Manuel converted the home to a botanical garden. In 1865 Maximilian and his wife, Carlota, made it their summer home, and it became the haunt of European nobles who came to be lavishly entertained by Mexico's ill-fated emperor. It became a cultural center in 1987, and today is a green oasis in the city center. The gardens are fashioned in the Andalusian style, with kiosks, fountains of Moorish design, and a small manmade lake where rowboats are available for rent. The lake is also an outdoor theater, with the stage across the water from the stone benches. The main building now houses a small museum of art. Open Tuesday to Sunday 10—5:30. $, free on Sundays.

LA CAPILLA DE LOS SANTOS REYES DE TETELA DEL MONTE
Calle León Salinas, Tetela del Monte

In the quiet neighborhood of Tetela del Monte, La Capilla de Los Reyes Santos, or the Chapel of the Saintly Kings, is one of Cuernavaca's hidden treasures that few visitors know about. This unique is linked, of all people, to Diana Spencer, aka Lady Di. John Spencer, Diana's uncle, came to Cuernavaca in 1967. A skilled artist, he chose a small, 16th-century chapel as his muse. Leaving the chapel itself intact, Spencer built an intricate and unusual border around the church. Designed to look like rolling waves, the stone walls were meant to symbolize the biblical Flood, with the chapel serving as the ark. The effect is quite beautiful. The grounds are peaceful and verdant, a fitting final resting place for Spencer, whose grave lies within the walls he built. Note also the Atrial cross in the courtyard: it's one of the few original ones left in Mexico. Atrial crosses, notable for the lack of a crucified Christ, were used by the church as a means to dissuade the practice of human sacrifices among the Indians. Open daily 8—2 and 4—7. Free.

IGLESIA DE SAN JOSÉ DE TLATENANGO
Avenida Emiliano Zapata, Tlatenango, Morelos
The little-known, nondescript Church of Saint Joseph of Tlatenango is actually the first church built in the Americas. It was commissioned by Cortés in 1521, right after the conquest of Tenochtitlán. Open daily 8—2 and 4—7. Free.

LA CATEDRAL DE CUERNAVACA
777-318-4590
At the corner of Hidalgo Street and Morelos Avenue

Fortress, monastery, and bastion of faith, the Cuernavaca Cathedral, formally known as the Catedral y Ex-Convento de Asunción de María, is easily the city's most impressive landmark. The cathedral was begun in 1529 and was completed in 1552, under the supervision of Cortés, and its open chapel is the oldest in the Americas. The era is important: it was the birth of New Spain, a time when indigenous rebellions were still very much a threat. This church was built with battlements and followed an austere design. The skull and crossbones above the entrance is the emblem of the Franciscan order, whose monks constructed the building with indigenous labor.

Once you pass through the gates, you'll notice an unusual contrast in the architecture. The almost garish pink and white walls are completely out of character with the dull gray stone of the bell tower and the monastery. The church was refurbished in 1960, and not all agreed with the updated look it was given. Inside, it is as bare and cavernous as it must have been in its heyday. Note the minimalist altar, the frescoes of the martyrdom of Saint Felipe de Jesús in the nave, and the faded ones in the courtyard. Note also the use of a certain shade of red paint. This was meant to help the indigenous people identify with their new, all-powerful God. Open daily 8–2 and 4–7. Free.

JARDÍN ETNOBOTÁNICO Y MUSEO DE MEDICINA TRADICIONAL Y HERBOLARIA
777-312-3108
www.inah.gob.mx/Museos/jardin_etnobotanico/index.html
Matamoros 14, Acapatzingo

Cuernavaca's botanical garden and museum of traditional and herbal medicine is set in a 19th-century summer home and ranch built by Emperor Maximilian. The home is known

John Spencer—designed border, Capilla de Los Santos Reyes de Tetela del Monte

Catedral de Cuernavaca Source: Morelos Tourism Board

as La Casa de la India Bonita (House of the Beautiful Indian Girl) after the indigenous young woman whom Maximilian took as his lover. Today the place is a monument to the native plants and flowers primarily of Morelos, but also other species that have become popular in Mexico. You can stroll through gardens of aromatic medicinal plants (the most impressive and important of the museum's collection), decorative plants, and a variety of orchids. Most plants are labeled in detail, including their original name in Nahuatl and, where appropriate, their medicinal purpose. Open daily 9–3, 4:30 for the gardens. Free.

MUSEO CASA ROBERT BRADY
777-318-8554
www.bradymuseum.org
Calle Netzahualcoyotl 4, Col. Centro, Cuernavaca

Casa Robert Brady is an incredibly diverse collection of art assembled by Robert Brady, an American who settled in the city in the 1960s. Brady was a dashing jetsetter, adventurer, painter, and socialite. He also had an exceptional eye for art, and collected more than 1,300 pieces from all over the world. These ranged from African masks by unknown artists to works by Diego Rivera and pre-Hispanic treasures, to a very kitschy Robert Brady doll that still lounges on his couch. As you roam through the house, which was a 16th-century Franciscan convent, you get to see it exactly as Brady left it. The museum's docent is tremendously knowledgeable, and if he offers to take you on a tour, don't pass it up. As he puts it, you can't put a value on the collection in the museum—it's a reflection of one man's eclectic tastes. Open Tuesday to Sunday 10–6. $.

MUSEO DE CUAUHNÁHUAC (PALACIO DE CORTÉS)

777-312-8171
Leyva 100, Col. Centro, Cuernavaca

When Hernán Cortés decided to build his residence in 1530, he chose a spot that was once a ceremonial center of the Tlahuica. His son finished the structure that now dominates the central plaza of downtown Cuernavaca. It was once the legislative headquarters for the state of Morelos (ironically, Morelos himself was once imprisoned here), and in 1974 was converted into the city's most complete museum (Cuauhnáhuac was the original name for Cuernavaca). It is also an excellent chronicle of Mexico's history from a regional point of view. Most everything in here comes from Morelos, including mammoth bones dating from 10,000 B.C., pre-Hispanic artifacts unearthed in the area, and colonial treasures. But the treasure of the museum is the fabulous murals painted by Diego Rivera from 1929 to 1930 titled *History of Cuernavaca and Morelos, Conquest and Revolution*. Dramatic scenes of feathered eagle warriors battling armored conquistadores, the subsequent enslavement of the Indians, the War of Independence, and the Mexican revolution—It's quintessential Rivera. There's a depiction of Zapata leading a white horse—Cortés's horse, in fact—symbolizing the return of the land to the people. Open Tuesday to Sunday 9–6. $.

LA TALLERA CASA ESTUDIO DE DAVÍD ALFARO SIQUEIROS

777-315-1115
Venus 52, Fraccionamiento Jardines de Cuernavaca

The modernist home and studio of Davíd Alfaro Siqueiros has been preserved as it was when the Mexican artist and muralist died here in 1974 at the age of 77. The studio has a work-in-progress feel to it: a scaffold set up at an incomplete mural, gallons of paint scattered on the steps. Siqueiros was a Stalinist and conspired in a plot to kill Leon Trotsky (who lived in Mexico City). During his incarceration, his wife used to write to him from this home. Open Tuesday to Sunday 10–6. $.

NIGHTLIFE

CASA HIDALGO

777-312-2749
http://casacolonial.com
Calle Hidalgo 6, Col. Centro, Cuernavaca

The newly remodeled rooftop lounge at Casa Hidalgo restaurant is a chic place to be at night. With fantastic views of the Palacio and the cathedral, a glass roof, and sophisticated black, white, and taupe décor, the lounge could be at home in Soho. The soft lighting system gives the place that extra touch of relaxed cool, and the live DJ on weekends keeps things lively. Open Thursday to Saturday 8 PM–3 AM. No cover.

EL ALEBRIJE

777-322-4282, 322-4183
www.elalebrijecuernavaca.com
Avenida Plan de Ayala 405, Col. Teopanzolco, Cuernavaca

Learn Spanish in Cuernavaca

Cuernavaca has become a center for Spanish-language schools, and many will help students coordinate lodging while they're in town, either at hotels or with local families. For those who want to spend time in Mexico and learn Spanish along the way, Cuernavaca is a terrific place to be. Among the schools in town are:

Cuernavaca Spanish Language School
777-311-8956
www.cuernavacalanguageschool.com
Azalea 3, Jardines de Reforma, Cuernavaca

Ideal Latinoamerica
777-311-7551
www.ideal-school.com
Privada Narciso Mendoza 107, Col. Pradera, Cuernavaca

UNIVERSAL
777-318-2904, 312-4902
www.universal-spanish.com
J.H. Preciado No. 171, Col. San Antón, Cuernavaca

Universidad Internacional
777-317-1087; 800-770-8646 (in Mexico); 800-574-1583 (from the U.S.)
www.spanishschool.uninter.edu.mx
San Jerónimo 304, Col. San Jerónimo, Cuernavaca

The most exclusive and largest club in the city has a huge dance floor that attracts Cuernavaca's hip-hopping elite. The building looks more like an auditorium than a club, but inside it's all lights, screens, and thumping music. Open Thursday to Saturday 10 PM–late. $$ for men, free for women.

EL SOLAR

777-100-1762
Avenida Plan de Ayala 505, Cuernavaca

This Cuban lounge, club, and late-night eatery is a smoky, steamy spot that's home to rhythmic music and a fun vibe. There's no cover unless there's a special event. Come early to ensure you get a seat, and take advantage of the large dance floor to try your salsa skills. If you get hungry, tacos and grilled meats highlight the menu. And the three-liter beer bongs should tide you over between snacks. Open Thursday to Saturday 7 PM–3 AM. No cover, $ for events.

ÈLYSEE SMART BAR

777-316-8714
www.elyseebar.com
Pabellón Vista Hermosa. Río Mayo 1207, Cuernavaca

A small, packed bar that is often stuffed with the young and the wealthy, Èlysee plays a mix of '90s pop, reggaetón, and dance music. There's no cover, but the bouncers are certainly selective of their clientele. The two-level space feels smaller than it is, thanks to the swarming crowds, and the booths lining the walls are the best seats in the house. You can buy sushi rolls at the entrance, which seems a bit chichi, but they're not a bad dietary option after you've been dancing for a while. The video screen is a pretty cool visual element. Open Wednesday, Friday, and Saturday 10:30 PM–5 AM. No cover.

EZENZA
777-312-2244, 312-1414
Yucatan 12, Col. Vista Hermosa, Cuernavaca
www.ezenza.net

You'll need a car or taxi to get here, and when you reach the street where it's located you'll swear you took a wrong turn. Hidden in a quiet neighborhood, Ezenza is a fantastic open-air bar and lounge set in a verdant, earthy space lit by flaming torches and lights. Because it's under the stars and nicely spread out, you won't feel claustrophobic even with the crowds—and if it rains, there is a retractable roof to keep you dry. There's often live music on Saturdays, but even absent live acts, the good music and chic décor (the white couches give it a South Beach feel) are alluring enough. Open weekends 9:30 PM–3 AM. $ for men (includes one drink), free for women.

JUÁREZ 4
777-312-7984
www.juarez4.com
Boulevard Benito Juárez 4, Col. Centro, Cuernavaca

A popular club just steps from Palacio Cortés and the main plaza, Juarez 4 is a two-floor disco set in a colonial home. A large dance floor dominates the main room, with high ceilings, lasers and lights, and giant screens. The second floor has a bar and balconies where you're likely to see patrons leaning out into the street and enjoying the night air. Juarez 4 plays hip-hop, house, and progressive music. Open Friday and Saturday 10 PM–5 AM. No cover.

LA PLAZUELA DEL ZACATE
Between Hidalgo and Galeana Streets
La Plazuela is one of the late-night hangouts that make Cuernavaca such a great nightlife destination. A cobblestone footpath around a fountain is home to a funky cluster of bars and small clubs. Your ears will catch a variety of music, from acoustic guitars to the latest hip-hop, and you have your pick of ambience. As you walk, smiling hawkers will tempt you into their particular spot, and you might want to visit a few different venues to keep the night interesting. Open Friday and Saturday (some on Thursday) 8 PM–3 AM. No cover.

MAMBO CAFÉ
777-313-5813, 313-4194
Avenida Vicente Guerrero, corner of Nueva Italia, Col. San Cristóbal, Cuernavaca
www.mambocafe.com.mx

A bit off the beaten path, this spacious club is like something out of a movie set about Cuba's heyday. Walk through a leafy bamboo entrance, then down a dimly lit hall and into a cavernous theater with vivid colors and décor, where you'll find outstanding live music every weekend. Ensemble bands play salsa, mambo, merengue, and cumbia, and a mixed crowd either sits at comfortable tables and enjoys the music or takes to the dance floor. The comfortable space, vibrant energy, and quality of the bands, which play multiple sets through the night, combine for a fun night out. Mambo Café is one of the few places open on Wednesdays, when there is no cover, and also has salsa classes from 8–10 PM on Wednesday, Thursday, and Saturday. Open Wednesday to Saturday 10 PM–5 AM. $$.

U.P. BARRA BAR
777-162-8323
Avenida Diana 18, Local 24, Gran Plaza Diana, Col. Delicias, Cuernavaca

This second-floor bar caters to a 30-plus crowd who come to lounge, drink, and scream at each other over the loud music. There are multiple TV monitors and 17 screens, which show either music videos or sporting events. The place has a retro feel heightened by the music, which ranges from 1970s to 1990s. No cover.

SHOPPING

GALERÍAS CUERNAVACA
777-322-9009; 800-221-5173
www.galeriascuernavaca.com.mx
Autopista Mexico-Acapulco Km. 87.85

Right off the highway from Mexico to Cuernavaca, this sprawling shopping center will compete with most neighborhood malls in the U.S. The stores are a mix of local brands and Western imports, with some high-end retailers like Hugo Boss and Tous Jewelry. Galerías also has a cinema, game room, and an activity center for kids. Open daily 11–9. $–$$$$.

IZCALLI
777-316-4264
www.izcallistores.com
Avenida San Diego 823, Plaza Caracol, Col. Vista Hermosa, Cuernavaca

A fashion boutique for the whole family, Izcalli has formal and casual clothing, shoes, jewelry, and accessories with distinctive Mexican flair. The products are made with all-natural fibers, and there's a great collection of *guayaberas* (comfortable, loose-fitting men's shirts). $$–$$$.

JORGE FENTON
751-348-0636, 348-0113
www.hacienda-sangabriel.com.mx
Km 41. 8 Carretera Federal Cuernavaca at Hacienda San Gabriel de Las Palmas, Chilpancingo, Amacuzac

Jorge Fenton is part of the family that owns Hacienda San Gabriel de las Palmas, and his is one of the most unusual jewelry shops you'll find. Fenton has developed a unique product using what the earth—or rather, the tree—gives him. Fenton takes leaves and, through a chemical process, treats them until they are delicate, hardened pieces that look like blown-glass masterpieces. Fenton then adds precious stones to create truly one-of-a-kind pieces. There is a workshop in the back where assistants carry out the process (each piece takes anywhere from 10 days to two months to complete), and Fenton himself is there to talk about his work (and his desire to ship the whole operation to China). Open daily 9–8. $$$$.

MERCADO DE ARTESANÍAS ZÓCALO
Next to Palacio Cortés

After you visit the Museo de Cuauhnáhuac, or Palacio Cortés, check out this indigenous market right next to the castle, located on the left as you exit. You'll find crafts, clothing, and artifacts from all over

Jorge Fenton jewelry creation

Mexico here, and the market specializes in semiprecious stones like onyx, quartz, and crystal, which are said to be sources of natural energy. Another popular item to look for is the huarache, a locally made sandal made of rubber and leather. Open daily 9–6, sometimes 7. $–$$$.

PLAZA CUERNAVACA
777-318-6182
www.plazacuernavaca.com
Av. Vicente Guerrero 110, Col. Lomas de la Selva, Cuernavaca

An open-air, two-floor mall complete with a Sears and a Sanborns, Plaza Cuernavaca has close to 200 stores within its faux-colonial walls. Brands you know (Lacoste, Dockers) compete with local products (Andrea Constantino for women's fashion, Boffi for cute children's clothing). Store hours vary, but generally open 10–9 daily. $-$$$.

VIVERO XOCHITLÁN
777-382-5698
Avenida Cuernavaca 2, Col. Ahuatepec, Cuernavaca

While there are obvious drawbacks to souvenir shopping in *viveros*, or nurseries, I have to mention at least one because Cuernavaca is so well known for its lovely flora. Vivero Xochitlán grows more than 800 varieties of plants and flowers, including begonias, orchids, poinsettias, and myriad other popular and exotic flowers. If you want something truly representative of this city, its flowers make the perfect symbol—even if they are ephemeral. $–$$$.

Weekly & Annual Events

CARNAVAL DE CUERNAVACA
Five days leading up to Ash Wednesday
The Cuernavaca Carnival is the big bash before Lent. Expect plenty of parties, excellent food accompanied by liberal amounts of alcohol, music, dancing and performances. Free.

Religious Festivals
There are religious festivals throughout the year all over Mexico. Typically, they are marked with traditional hymns, music, dances, and the general paraphernalia of the standard street fair: food kiosks, parades, sometimes rides and fireworks. Although they are deeply Catholic in nature, they also include distinctly Mexican elements. *Concheros* are ritual indigenous dances named for the musical instrument used (a Native lute made from the shell of an armadillo). *La Danza del Chinelo*, one of the region's most popular dances and a Morelos tradition for more than a hundred years, is characterized by people in outrageous costumes (velvet tunics, sombreros, capes, and costume masks) jumping and twirling around on their toes. And *jaripeo* is a musical bull-riding mini-rodeo. Look for one or more of them on these occasions:

Festival of the Wise Kings
January 5–6
At the Capilla de Los Santos Reyes de Tetela del Monte, Calle León Salinas

Festival of Saint Anthony of Padua
June 13
Chula Vista Street, San Antón

Festival of the Ascension of the Virgin Mary
August 15-17
At the Catedral de Cuernavaca, corner of Hidalgo Street and Morelos Avenue

Festival of Our Lady of Miracles
September 8
Avenida Emiliano Zapata in Tlatenango

Festival of Saint Michael
September–October (5 days)
Church of Saint Michael, at Matamoros and Degollado streets.

Festival of the Virgin of Guadalupe
December 12
Rayón Street

FERIA DE LA PRIMAVERA
March 21 to April 10

This being the City of Eternal Spring, the Festival of the Spring, or Spring Fair, is a pretty important event. This two-week celebration brings together a wide variety of entertainment, arts and crafts, and vendors, but the true stars are the magnificent floral expositions, which showcase the region's most colorful natural resource. Free.

NATIONAL ORCHID EXPOSITION
October
Typically at the Jardín Etnobotánico y Museo de Medicina Tradicional y Herbolaria, Matamoros 14, Acapatzingo
www.inah.gob.mx/Museos/jardin_etnobotanico/index.html

A must for orchid lovers, this annual weeklong event takes place in October, but exact dates vary. In addition to common and rare orchids, visitors can see and buy fruits, plants, and natural products. $.

DAY OF THE DEAD
November 1–2
Ocotepec
The Day of the Dead (el Día de los Muertos) is one of the most colorful, unusual, and distinctly Mexican festivals in the country. Despite the sinister name, this is a day of remembrance, when families gather to honor the spirits of the dead. In the town of Ocotepec, just north of Cuernavaca, the festival is one of the most important events of the year. People throw their doors open, inviting any and all to come in, admire the altars to the dead, and partake of homemade snacks (quite often tamales). It's typical for visitors to bring *veladores*, or small candles, to show respect for the recently deceased. The town cemetery is a focal point during this day, for obvious reasons. Free.

8

Touring Morelos

The previous chapter focused on Cuernavaca and its neighborhoods, but once you start exploring beyond the City of Eternal Spring, you'll realize that the state of Morelos is a fascinating destination, home to one of Mexico's most beloved folk heroes, two amazing pre-Hispanic ruins, and one town that is truly, officially, magical. Beyond the historic heritage of Morelos are its tremendous natural advantages. Sulfur springs and water parks, dramatic mountains and volcanoes, and a spectacular subterranean cave system are all within an hour or two's drive from Cuernavaca. And there is one special route that takes you on a pilgrim's journey to 16th- and 17th-century convents and churches, magnificent relics of Spain's colonial might and religious fervor.

Where prior chapters covered lodging, restaurants, and activities in depth, here I focus on each destination, and provide lodging, dining, and other recommendations when they represent something worthy of mention. Consider this a series of road trips exploring a Mexico that many tourists don't get to see.

XOCHICALCO

The sprawling ruins of Xochicalco are one of the wonders of Mexico. The name means "the place of the house of flowers" in Nahuatl, but it's more like the empire of flowers. This vast walled city-state was a mighty urban metropolis from A.D. 700–900. Interestingly, its rise to power occurred right after the fall of Teotihuacán and just before the ascent of Tula. As with other ancient strongholds, historians aren't completely sure why Xochicalco fell, but the prevailing theory is that it was destroyed from within.

Built on a series of adjacent hilltops, the city must have been an astounding sight during its zenith, but it is both formidable and fascinating even now—and that's with only about 15 percent of the ruins excavated. Visiting Xochicalco requires a full day, and you can opt to drive there yourself or take a tour. The tour will provide a lot more information, although the ruins themselves have plaques explaining the main sites.

Begin your day with a trip to the **Museo de Sitio de Xochicalco**. This solar-powered building is a pioneer of eco-technology, employing natural refrigeration and heating, and offers panoramic views of the ancient city. Every night at 7 PM from May to October, this is the place to be to catch a light and sound spectacle at Xochicalco. The museum houses relics and artifacts excavated from the city, with beautifully preserved pieces highlighting the exhibits. Chief among these is the *Señor de Rojo* (Red Man), a powerfully symbolic sculpture bathed in vermilion to give it its distinctive red hue.

After, drive or walk to the entrance of the site and enjoy the steep walk up to its main

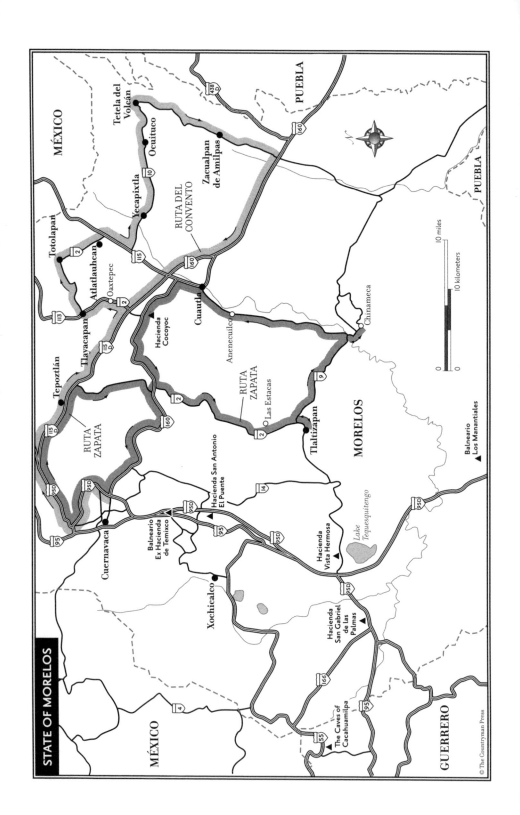

STATE OF MORELOS

MÉXICO

PUEBLA

PUEBLA

Tetela del Volcán

Ocuituco

Zacualpan de Amilpas

Yecapixtla

438 D

160

10

Totolapan

Atlatlauhcan

Oaxtepec

2

115

RUTA DEL CONVENTO

160

Tepoztlán

Tlayacapan

Hacienda Cocoyoc

Cuautla

Chinameca

2

115 D

RUTA ZAPATA

Anenecuilco

RUTA ZAPATA

Las Estacas

9

2

160

115 D

2

Tlaltizapan

MORELOS

95 D

95 D

Hacienda San Antonio El Puente

14

Balneario Los Manantiales

Cuernavaca

Balneario Ex Hacienda de Temixco

95 D

95

95 D

Hacienda Vista Hermosa

Lake Tequesquitengo

95 D

Xochicalco

95 D

Hacienda San Gabriel de las Palmas

MÉXICO

166

95

GUERRERO

55

The Caves of Cacahuamilpa

10 miles

10 kilometers

© The Countryman Press

buildings. The vastness of the ceremonial center will give you an idea of the city's former splendor. The most notable and intricate structure here is the Pirámide de la Serpiente Emplumada (Pyramid of the Feathered Serpent), where you'll find carvings and reliefs of twisting serpents, the symbol of Quetzalcoatl. The temple was reconstructed in 1909 by Don Leopoldo Batres. Nearby, keep your eyes on the floor for the Animal Ramp. A marvel in its time, this stone pathway to the main plaza was carved with animal reliefs. Xochicalco also has three ball courts, the most interesting of which is the northern court, or Teotlachtli, which has a unique shape that you'll probably miss unless you know a lot about ball courts.

The other treasure of this city lies beneath the surface: the ancient observatory. Xochicalco was a religious and economic powerhouse (it controlled the obsidian trade throughout Mexico), but it was also an important astronomical center. In AD 743, the first pre-Hispanic astronomical congress was held here, with scientists from all Mesoamerica attending. (The gathering is chronicled in reliefs on the walls of the Pyramid of the Feathered Serpent.) It was here that, after a total eclipse, all Mesoamerican calendars were synchronized.

Touring Morelos with Rubén

If you want to really see Morelos . . . and I mean explore it from the point of view of history, culture, ecotourism, and much more, give Rubén Cortés a call. Rubén runs Morelos Trails, a guide service that puts you in touch with a local expert (him) who can show you this area in a way few others can match.

Rubén Cortés of Morelos Trails

For one, he's been scaling the mountains around Morelos since he was a child, and he's an excellent guide for hikers and climbers. Second, he's a licensed scuba diver and can take you through the underwater catacombs of the state's myriad natural springs. Third, he's bilingual. And fourth (and not least), he's tremendous fun to be with, passionate about the land, knowledgeable about what he has to show you, and full of the kind of energy that will keep you going all day. For me, Morelos was one of Mexico's wonderful surprises, and that was in no small part due to Rubén.

Morelos Trails
777-318-6480, 312-2279, 314-4018
www.morelostrails.com
Matamoros II, Col. Centro, Cuernavaca

Observatory at Xochicalco Source: Morelos Tourism Board

Today, the practices of the ancients are preserved, thanks to a pre-Hispanic solar observatory still used to track the motion of the sun. A trip to this underground chamber is a must if you're visiting from the end of April to August 15, when you'll see a beam of sunlight shining through a roughly hewn opening, and a (modern-day) expert will be on hand to plot its course. During the equinox, when the sun is at its zenith, the entire chamber is brilliantly lit. On this day, Xochicalco draws spiritual pilgrims, dressed in white robes, from all over Mexico and beyond.

Xochicalco is an easy day trip from Cuernavaca, 22 miles southwest of the city and just off Highway 95 toward Acapulco. Open daily 9–5, observatory 10–5. $. Call 777-314-3920.

When you come down from the mountain and reach the Mexico-Acapulco highway, stop at **Nieves La Güera**, which makes some of the best *nieves,* or flavored ices, I've had. The most requested flavors are coconut and lemon, but you can also try cherry, guava, and vodka, among other concoctions. The ices are handmade in barrels, each barrelful taking one hour to make. La Güera is a roadside institution that's seen its share of celebrities over its 20-year existence, and it's a refreshingly cool ending to your Xochicalco excursion. Open daily 8–9. Located on the Mexico-Acapulco highway, Km. 100, Alpuyeca, Morelos. Call 777-391-5336. $.

TEPOZTLÁN

Mexico has a tourism initiative called *Pueblos Mágicos,* or Magical Towns, which is a designation given to small towns around the country that provide tourists with an otherworldly experience—either through their culture, environment, or history. Tepoztlán is the only *pueblo mágico* in Morelos, and it certainly has a mystical quality to it. With an ancient temple set high atop a cliff, a 16th-century former convent, striking mountain scenery, and a quaint, picturesque hamlet with winding cobblestone streets nestled in a green valley, Tepoztlán has a charm all its own.

The town was home to a temple to Ometochtli-Tepoztecatl, the god of pulque, which gives Tepoztlán a sort of Dionysian mythology. To this day, its mountains, specifically Tepozteco, are considered to have certain energies, and, perhaps not coincidentally, it's also famous for its prolific UFO sightings (there are plenty of places where you can pick up a UFO postcard).

Tepoztlán is only 12 miles from Cuernavaca, making it an easy day trip, but if you want to stay in town, it has one gem of a hotel. To get here, take the Mexico-Acapulco highway (95D) and get off at the Cuautla exit, which leads to the Milpa Alta–Cuautla highway. Get off at the Oaxtepec/Oacalco exit to reach the town.

The vast majority of tourists come here to climb Tepozteco and see the ruins of the small temple to Ometochtli. The entrance to this site is located at the end of Avenida del Tepozteco, the main road through the town. As you begin the climb up to the high bluff on which the temple sits, note the large stone cross on a round boulder by the river. This is the **Axitla Cross**, which marks the day (September 8, 1538) and place where Friar Domingo of the Dominican order baptized the Tepozteco, the lord of Tepoztlán.

Especially when one begins the walk up to the site, one can't help but wonder how the indigenous tribes built the temple (which they did between AD 1150 and 1350), perched as it is high above the town. But this mountain is said to have rejuvenating and invigorating properties. As the temple sits at an elevation of more than 6,500 feet and is quite a chal-

The ruins of Tepozteco

lenge to get to (there are no paved steps, making it a rugged hike), you'll need all the energy you can get . . . especially if you're here on weekends, when you might see a Mexican grandmother sprinting up the slope with a baby in her arms, outpacing you.

The temple is open from around 9 to 5. I say "around" because the custodian of the place will take his sweet time opening it up in the morning; I've seen tourists wait more than an hour for him to show. There's not a whole lot to see once you reach the site (the experience of the climb is the main attraction), and if you go with a guide like Rubén, ask to be shown the "alternate way." It's a tougher road, but features a lookout point with spectacular views of the valley, the town, and the temple. For those who want that perfect photo opportunity, this is the place to get it. As you climb, you'll also see a dome-shaped geographical feature atop a mountain on the other side of the valley. This is the Observatory, another popular hiking destination.

The temple at Tepozteco is a clear highlight of a trip to Tepoztlán, but it's not the only thing to see. After, head back down Avenida del Tepozteco to the *zócalo*. This is a pleasant plaza complete with a rather European-looking gazebo, and it's the heart of the town. Adjacent to the plaza is the Tepoztlán *tianguis*, one of the best markets in Morelos. During midweek it's primarily a food market, but caters more to tourists on weekends. A wide variety of ceramics, woodworks, puppets, clothing, and folk jewelry can be found here, along with delicious *antojitos* like quesadillas (Tepoztlán is known for them), *gorditas*, and *itacates* (cornmeal patties). Also try the *atole*, a flavored cornmeal drink, and the freshly made potato chips.

The market is next to the **Ex-Convento de La Natividad,** or Ex-Convent of the Nativity, and to get here you'll pass through an unusual gate, on which is depicted a mural made of sesame seeds, beans, and rice. This is an annual Tepoztlán project, remade each year. The theme is usually consistent, however, with the left side of the gate representing Mexico's pre-Hispanic roots and the right depicting its Catholic legacy. It's fitting that the arch should lie between the indigenous *tianguis* and the convent.

Construction of the convent began in 1550 by the Dominicans. Note the *almenas,* or battlements, atop the high walls; this convent was built, like many others during this period, as a defensive structure in addition to a religious one. Inside, make sure to visit the Sala de Profundis, which was the antechamber to the dining hall. Here you'll find the most beautiful murals in the convent, including reliefs of the Virgin Mother and Fray Dominic de Guzmán, the founder of the Dominican order. There's also a striking mural depicting Saint Catherine giving her heart to Christ, a very Aztec allusion.

One second-floor niche in the convent has a unique feature: the lookout. It offers another perfect photo opp, with the views of the hills all around you. In the cloister you'll find a small museum with dioramas of the area, exhibits on local life, commerce, and the famous "Chinelo" costumes used during Tepoztlán's carnival. Finally, make sure to visit the gift shop. Not only are the products here diverse (my favorite item is the miniature *coexcomate,* or thatch corn granary), but there is a well in one corner that was part of the original construction. Call 739-395-0225. The convent is open Monday to Friday, 8–2 and 4–7, Saturday and Sunday 7–7. The gift shop is open daily 10–6. Convent is free, $–$$$ for gift shop.

Before you leave the convent, stop by the courtyard for a look at the *cruz atrial,* or bare cross (i.e., one that does not show Christ), part of a conscious early effort by the monks to disassociate religion from human sacrifice. It wasn't until the end of the 16th century that crosses showing Christ crucified began to appear again in Mexico.

Ex-Convento de la Natividad

Your final sight-seeing stop in Tepoztlán is the small but well-appointed **Carlos Pellicer Museum,** located on Pablo A. González just behind the convent. The space is entirely devoted to pre-Hispanic art and artifacts, and while the majority are small pieces that won't immediately dazzle, they are so well arranged by origin and date that it's worth the visit (plus you can pick up your UFO postcard here). Call 739-395-1098. Open daily 10–6. $.

Before you head out (or head to your hotel), stop by **Tepoznieves,** where you'll find a dizzying array of delicious frozen flavored ices. You can get pretty much every fruit flavor you can imagine, plus a few concoctions like *oración del amor* ("oration of love"), a mix of almond, peach, and rose petal. Avenida Cinco de Mayo #21. Call 739-395-4839. Open daily 10:30–9.

LODGING

HOTEL REAL DEL VALLE

739-395-3264, 395-1610
www.hotelrealdelvalle.com
Avenida Prolongación Revolución 90, Tepoztlán, Morelos
On the road leading to the main center of Tepoztlán, the Real del Valle offers quite a few reasons to pull off and check in. It might not be in the heart of the city, but it's affordable, has plenty of open space, beautiful views, and amenities including a pleasant outdoor pool and rooftop spa with *temazcal* and Jacuzzi. The 14 rooms are brightly decorated and meticulously clean. Rates include a breakfast buffet, which should help you climb Tepozteco. $$.

POSADA DEL TEPOZTECO

739-395-0010, 395-2726
www.posadadeltepozteco.com
Paraíso 3, Tepoztlán, Morelos

Whatever mojo exists in Tepoztlán, the Posada del Tepozteco got a healthy dose of it. This is a serene sanctuary, an ivy-covered building with beautiful gardens, breathtaking views, and a *temazcal.* It's also an eco-friendly hotel, with a solar-heated pool and recycling (a true rarity in these parts). The hotel has 22 rooms, all differently decorated and all comfortably appointed. The junior suites, all in the newer building, have a terrace, and the two-room master suite is worth it just for the panoramic views you can wake up to. At the on-site **Sibarta** restaurant overlooking the terrace, you get the benefit of the mountain breezes as you dine on specialties like mole *tepozteco* (a house recipe), tilapia in tamarind sauce, and a delicious pear salad (all the salads are made with organic lettuce, another rarity). There's also a two-floor family guestroom, and a special-rate small room that's not listed on the Web site but can be had for a bargain, if you ask. The Posada also has quite the distinguished celebrity list. Angelina Jolie stayed here, and so did Antonio Banderas. $$–$$$.

POSADA SANTO DOMINGO

739-395-3294
Matamoros 35, Santo Domingo, Tepoztlán, Morelos

Posada del Tepozteco

The Posada Santo Domingo is a small, very basic hotel in an off-the-beaten path part of town. The rooms, while spotless, are nothing special. So why am I listing it? Two reasons. It is extremely cheap, and it offers some of the most affordable massage services around, including a proper *temazcal*. The masseuse is actually contracted out to other, bigger hotels, but you can get the same thing here for a fraction of the price. Even if you don't stay here, come for a massage. $.

Springs and Water Parks

There are more than 40 *balnearios,* or public swimming pools, in the state of Morelos, ranging from small thermal pools to sprawling water parks. The ones listed below are among the most popular and interesting.

BALNEARIO EX HACIENDA DE TEMIXCO

777-325-0355, 325-0197
www.temixcoacuatico.com
Carr. Federal México-Acapulco Km. 85

There are 22 pools here, but that's only half the story. The park has four waterslides, including one massive network of chutes called the Toborama, and a waterslide for kids only. There's also a wave pool, a river specifically for tubing, and an aquatic toboggan run. Not enough? Try the aquatic obstacle course or the water polo pools. In short, this place offers every type of aquatic excursion you can hope for in a water park, set amid the grounds of a former hacienda. When you've had enough of the water, there are basketball, volleyball, and soccer courts, along with mini golf. The park is only ten minutes from Cuernavaca on the Mexico-Acapulco highway. Open daily 9–6. $$.

BALNEARIO LOS MANANTIALES

734-349-8263; 555-760-4776
www.losmanantiales.com.mx
Tlaquiltenango, Morelos off Carr. Federal México-Acapulco Km. 149 in Xicatlacotla

The great benefit of Los Manantiales is not its number of pools but its proximity to nature. There are two natural pools and a number of springs around the park. Among its most pleasant attractions are its waterfalls, which are again a product of the environment rather than manmade artifice. Feel free to dive under these cascades for a delicious rush of fresh water. To get here, take the Mexico-Acapulco highway to exit 149, and turn right. Open daily 9–6. $.

LAS ESTACAS

743-345-0077; 553-004-5300
www.lasestacas.com
Km. 6, Carr. Tlaltizapán-Cuautla S/N, Ejido Bonifacio Garcia, Tlaltizapán, Morelos

Balneario Las Estacas Source: Morelos Tourism Board

Las Estacas is not your conventional water park; that is to say, the tubes, chutes, and rides you see in other places are absent here. Instead, you get a huge sprawl of a place that takes full advantage of its tremendous natural bounty. The early black-and-white *Tarzan* TV series used to be filmed here, which gives you an idea of the property's rustic bounty.

Once you enter and pass the 18-hole mini-golf course, walk along the banks of the winding Green River, whose crystal-clear water (except for June to September, when the churning silt turns it a brownish hue) leads to a beautiful bubbling spring-fed pool (which stays clear year-round). The river, incidentally, is 10,000 years old. There are Tyrolean zip-lines stretching from wooden planks through the dense foliage around you, should you care to take to the trees.

Crossing the river, you'll come to a large *palapa* hut that's the main hub of the park, where you'll find lockers, a restaurant, and, nearby, lodging. The accommodations here are among the best bargains you'll find. The master suite alone is a gem, quite unexpectedly luxurious with flat-panel TVs,

A Meal to Remember at La Palapa del Venado

On the way to Las Estacas, La Palapa del Venado (the Deer Hut) is a highly recommended pit stop on your Morelos tour. A rustic roadside eatery, it isn't much to look at from the outside, or the inside. But it's likely to offer one of the most authentic meals you'll partake of on your vacation.

How authentic, you ask? Well, most of the signature dishes aren't even printed on the menu, which includes typical Mexican specialties. Go ahead and ignore the menu and ask for the real deal: the exotic meats. The iguana soup, a tomato broth with a spicy kick and hunks of iguana meat (if you've ever tried alligator, it's not far off), is an almost-mandatory starter. Then move on to the main course: deer, skunk, viper, possum, and armadillo are among the exotic entrées you'll find here. They're not on the menu because hunting these species for commercial purposes is technically illegal, but the owners of La Palapa get a pass from the local authorities, who are among the establishment's loyal patrons.

Speaking of the owners, they're a talkative, pleasant couple, and the proprietor is something of a prankster. But while the banter is good, the food is better. Vegetarians will hate this place (one look at the animal skins hanging on the wall should do the trick), but the average carnivore is in line for a very tasty meal. You can order your choice of meat grilled plain, with a garlic butter sauce, or in a green or red chile sauce. The grilled venison steak I had was perfectly cooked, juicy, and filling, and came with a side of grilled chiles and rice.

This is a tremendously popular place for Mexican families from all walks of life. The food is reasonable, the ambience rustic and completely informal, and the owners even sell a few home remedies that have, according to them and their clients, miraculous medicinal properties. Iguana blood, for example, is a good treatment for anemia. Skunk blood works wonders on asthma and skin defects such as acne. Viper blood is said to be effective against certain types of cancer. These can be drunk either straight, in a glass, or in a broth. Of course, my recommendation is limited to the restaurant; experiment with the local remedies at your own risk. Oh, and if you feel tired (the iguana soup in particular is a heavy dish), you're welcome to use the hammock at one end of the restaurant. Many patrons do.

La Palapa del Venado is located on the Yautepec-Jojutla highway, no. 28, in Tlaltizapán. Call 734-345-0252. Web site: www.elvenado.4t.com. Open daily 11–8.

A waitress shows off one of the specials at La Palapa del Venado

private pool, and comfortable, modern furnishings. For those who don't want to spring for the suite, the other rooms are quite comfortable.

Beyond this area are the first of the park's four pools, as well as a large, shallow man-made lake for kids, equipped with slides and obstacle courses. And still, we've only covered about half of the park. Besides swimming, other activities here include scuba diving, basketball, volleyball, and fishing. And then there's the Bamboo Fort, a walled enclosure that's the camping section of the park. Finally, there is also a ranch with a stable of horses available for riding, and petting zoo with cows, rabbits, ostriches, and pigs . . . all the elements of a working farm (except for the ostriches).

Las Estacas is about 50 minutes by car from Cuernavaca. Take the Mexico-Acapulco highway to the Civac-Cuautla exit, heading toward Yautepec. When you reach Yautepec, turn right on the Jojutla-Tlaltizapán intersection, and follow the signs. The park is about 10 miles from Yautepec. Open 8–6 daily, until 9 if you're spending the night. $$–$$$.

CENTRO VACACIONAL OAXTEPEC (OAXTEPEC VACATION CENTER)
www.imss.gob.mx
735-356-0101, 356-0202; 800-523-5008
Mexico-Cuautla highway, Km. 27, Yautepec, Morelos

Oaxtepec is more like an aquatic community than a park. This gigantic complex can easily keep you busy for a weekend, and that's when it sees the most action. The center's various lodging facilities include: a campground (you can rent tents, sleeping bags, and accessories); two basic hotels; a youth hostel; a tiny neighborhood of pink-and-white cabins, each with their own private pool; and even three-bedroom, three-bathroom homes for rent. But as large as Oaxtepec is, it's filled to capacity on weekends, when hordes of Mexicans descend on it; if you can, try to come midweek.

As for the park, its sheer size is so staggering that a cable car runs from one end to the other (from Thursday to Sunday). The pools include natural mineral pools and five swimming pools, including an Olympic-size pool with multilevel diving boards, spread out over two zones. And that doesn't include the water park, which is the largest in Latin America. The center also boasts a stadium, auditorium, several restaurants, and fast-food kiosks. But its visual centerpiece is its great geodesic dome, home to pungent sulfur springs and a botanical garden where you'll find three petroglyphs from the Olmec era half-buried in the ground. Near the dome (you'll have to ask where precisely, as its not labeled), is what remains of an ancient staircase that once marked the entrance to Montezuma's gardens. Finally, try to make it to *la Torre* (the Tower), not just for the cable car but for the panoramic park views.

Oaxtepec is located a half hour by car from Cuernavaca. Take the Mexico-Acapulco highway to the Cuautla exit, and get on the Milpa Alta–Cuautla highway. The center is located at Km. 27, in Yautepec. Open daily, hours vary depending on activity, most facilities open 10–6. $–$$$.

ZAPATA'S ROUTE

It is hard to wander far in Morelos without encountering traces of Emiliano Zapata Salazar, the dour, taciturn folk hero with the drooping moustache, sombrero, and glaring eyes. Zapata fought for the rights of Mexican farmers and laborers against the establishment, and while he's a national hero, he occupies a special place in the hearts of Morelos citizens. Zapata was born here, formed his army here, and fought his many skirmishes against hacendados whose homes you can still visit. Many buildings claim to have a Zapata-inspired bullet-hole lodged somewhere in the walls. And Morelos was where Zapata died, betrayed and ambushed . . . although what happened to him remains a subject of speculation to this day.

There is a fascinating trail through Morelos that chronicles Zapata's life. From what remains of his humble home to the scene of his final showdown with the government troops, you can track Zapata's life through small-town Mexico. In the process, you'll visit museums, monuments, and murals that depict the man who became a legend.

As mentioned in Chapter 1, it was Francisco Madero who began the movement to get rid of the Porfiriato in 1910, which bloomed into the Mexican Revolution. Maderos, however, was an intellectual, as well as an hacendado. He enlisted the help of Torres Burgos to build his resistance, but the military was never Burgos's strong suit. And so he turned to Zapata.

Zapata was a skilled horseman who brought control to an unruly and undisciplined fighting force in the early years of the revolution. But he also butted heads with the aristocratic Madero. Zapata was always for the people, while Maderos never bought into Zapata's land-redistribution dreams. Their ideological split led Zapata to plot his own course through the war—participating in 160 battles from 1910 to 1917—galvanizing and sustaining the revolution through its hardest years, but ultimately leading to his death.

The Route

If you retrace Zapata's footsteps chronologically, you'll be backtracking all over the state. Rather, I suggest taking the following route:

As you come into Cuernavaca from Highway 95 onto Avenida Emiliano Zapata, one of the first landmarks you'll notice, dominating a roundabout, is a statue of Zapata on horseback in full gallop, sword drawn. Let this be the beginning of your journey. From here, you'll travel to the small town of **Tlaltizapán,** where Zapata chose to establish his headquarters in 1914. To get here, follow Highway 95 (Mexico-Acapulco) south until you get to the junction of Route 138 toward Yautepec. When you reach Yautepec, you'll come to the intersection of Route 138 and Route 2. Turn right to head south on Route 2, which will take you to Tlaltizapán. A stern-faced statue of Zapata holding a copy of his famous *Plan de Ayala* greets you as you enter the town, on your way to the Cuartel de Zapata (Zapata Barracks) and a mausoleum where the general's soldiers are interred.

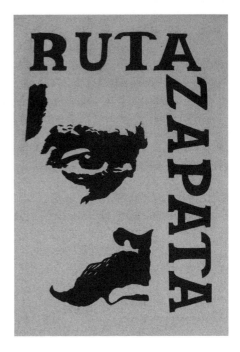
Ruta de Zapata marker

From Tlaltizapán, head back north on Route 2 until you come to the junction of Route 2 and Route 9. Take a right on Route 9 to reach **Chinameca** (head straight past the four-way stop), where Zapata was gunned down. After, retrace your step to the Y intersection, with Route 9 on your left heading back to Cuernacava. Take a right and head north to **Anecuilco** and Zapata's home. Finally, continue north on Carretera a la Villa until you get to Pasaje a Montes de Oca. Make a right, and then a quick left on Avenida Insurgentes to get to **Cuautla,** where an imposing monument stands guard over Zapata's final resting place. Finish your tour with a well-deserved lunch in this charming town. To return to Cuernavaca, follow Insurgentes to Avenida Interoceánico, which will take you back to Route 138, which in turn leads you straight back to Cuernavaca. As you travel, keep on the lookout for the Ruta de Zapata markers, which feature a graphic of Zapata's face staring determinedly back at you.

CUARTEL DE ZAPATA

734-345-0020, 345-0022
Vicente Guerrero 57, Tlaltizapán, Morelos

The Cuartel de Zapata, or Zapata's Barracks, is also the (Spanish-only) Museum of the Revolution of the South. When Zapata came here, it was a rice mill, but he made it his headquarters from 1914–18, and the people of Tlaltizapán hid their beloved hero from troops hunting him throughout the state. The museum catalogs Zapata's involvement in the revolution from his early days to the zenith of his fame. Among the exhibits are the clothes Zapata wore when he was killed (complete with bloodstains), various types of money that the different warring factions produced during the war to pay for goods, and a copy of Zapata's famous *Plan de Ayala*. After drafting it, he said, "El que no tenga miedo que pase a firmarlo" (Let he who is not afraid step forward to sign it). It was, essentially, a declaration of war. The museum also has no shortage of depictions of Zapata, along with photos of some of the key figures in the revolution. Open Tuesday to Sunday 10–6:30. $.

EX-CONVENTO DE SAN MIGUEL ARCÁNGEL DE TLALTIZAPÁN AND ZAPATA MAUSOLEUM

Vicente Guerrero and Leona Vicario, Tlaltizapán, Morelos

In the atrium of this 16th-century Dominican church is a light-blue-and-white mausoleum that Zapata ordered built for himself and his most faithful soldiers while he was still alive. Zapata didn't get his wish, as he was buried in Cuautla, but many of his generals are entombed here. You can see the bullet holes along the church walls and especially the bell tower, evidence of skirmishes between Zapata's men and the army. Free.

EX-HACIENDA CHINAMECA

Chinameca, Ciudad Ayala, Mor., Col. Chinameca

On April 10, 1919, Emiliano Zapata rode up to the front gate of Hacienda Chinameca. He was there at the behest of one Colonel Jesus Guajardo, who said he had defected from Venustiano Carranza's forces and wanted to join Zapata's army. But Guajardo was a double agent planted by Carranza's men to lure Zapata into an ambush.

By this time, the revolution had become a protracted, bitter affair and was taking its toll on the Mexican people. In 1917 Carranza became the president of the republic. He had successfully fought against Pancho Villa in the north, and had cornered Zapata in Morelos. The war was going badly for the everyman-hero. Some say Zapata knew he was riding into an ambush when he accepted Guajardo's offer. Either way, he traveled to the hacienda with only one companion. As soon as he crossed the threshold, Carranza's soldiers opened fire. Zapata fell, riddled with some 200 bullets. He was 39 years old. Soldiers tied his corpse to a horse and rode the three hours to Cuautla, where Zapata's body was displayed to the public before burial.

Today, all that stands of the Hacienda Chinameca is the archway through which Zapata rode into what was once the courtyard of the property. Beneath the gate is a statue of Zapata astride his white horse, which is depicted as rearing up as though preparing to gallop away from the imminent onslaught. It captures the last seconds of the general's life. Walk to the other side of the entrance into the bare plaza and turn around; you'll see the walls peppered with bullet holes, and you can imagine the barrage that flew at Zapata.

On the walls behind the gate are sayings from famous Mexican leaders from 1810 to 1970. And you'll almost always find an old soul reclining by the foot of the statue. These individuals are here to recount the legend of Emiliano Zapata. For a token tip, they will wax eloquent, their eyes misting over, about their beloved hero. They might not be entirely sober, but they're terrific storytellers, and if you speak Spanish it's worth it to engage them in conversation. One thing they will surely bring up is whether or not Zapata truly died. Many Morelians contend that the general sent a body double to the meeting. This belief is supported by the fact that the body in question, already battered by gunfire, suffered so much abuse from the jolting horseback ride to Cuautla that it wasn't recognizable by the time it reached its final resting place. To this day, some say, the general is alive and well in some other part of the world.

Whether it was Zapata or someone else who died that day in 1919, Zapata's army fell apart thereafter, and Colonel Jesus Guajardo's name passed into infamy. The revolution would live on, as others took up the mantle after Zapata. But none fought so hard, and with such single-minded dedication, for Mexico's agrarian lower class. Free, $ for a story from a salty old devotee.

ZAPATA'S HOME AND MUSEUM
777-314-3920
Emiliano Zapata S/N, Col. Anecuilco, Ayala, Morelos

Zapata was born in the tiny town of Anecuilco, in a modest adobe dwelling. Its remains still stand, but the home itself is not much to look at. Rather, come for the museum and the powerful mural, which is an artistic time line. The first half covers Xochicalco, the subjugation of the Indians, and Zapata as a child witnessing injustice. The centerpiece is a striking portrait of Zapata breaking the chains of corruption (note the wealthy aristocrat, the monk, and the soldier representing the corrupt). The mural ends with Zapata's ambush at Chinameca and a candlelight vigil around his corpse. The small museum has a jumble of artifacts that date from pre-Hispanic times to Zapata's era. Every piece in here has been donated by the townspeople, from colonial artifacts to pieces of Cuahuixtla, the first hacienda Zapata destroyed.

ZAPATA'S GRAVE
Plaza Revolución del Sur, Cuautla, Morelos

Zapata was buried in Cuautla on April 12, 1919. Today, in Plaza Revolución del Sur (Revolution of the South), you'll find a large statue of the general marking his final resting

Mural of Zapata at his home and museum in Anecuilco

place. The poncho-clad figure clutches a rifle in one hand and a scroll in the other on which are written the words *Tierra y Libertad* (Land and Liberty), Zapata's mantra.

From here, walk across the street to the town's *zócalo,* where you'll see the beautiful building of the municipal presidency on one side and the brightly colored, 16th-century Dominican Ex-Convent of Santo Domingo on the other. Walk under the arches of the municipal presidency to its far end, where you'll find a plaque commemorating the spot where Zapata's body was brought from Chinameca. Here it was displayed to the public for two days, on April 11 and 12, so the people could verify that it was their hero who had fallen. Free. Open 24/7.

THE CONVENT ROUTE

La Ruta del Convento is also known as *La Ruta del Volcán,* because it ends at the foot of the mighty Popocatépetl volcano. Similar to Zapata's Route, the Convent Route takes you deep into small-town Mexico, to rural communities where the largest and most important structure for hundreds of years was clearly the church. As you visit these former convents, you'll notice how large they were in comparison to the towns in which they reside. This was no accident. When the Spanish conquered the lands outside the Aztec capital, religious orders moved in quickly to convert the Indians to Catholicism. One way to do so was to build impressive temples to the Christian God that could be seen for miles around, clear symbols of power and position. It is these early bastions of Spanish spiritual superiority in the New World that mark this route.

To visit all of the convents on the *Ruta* requires two days. However, in a day trip you can comfortably visit the majority of them (there is no entrance fee and generally they are open from 8–2 and 4–7 on weekdays, 8–8 on weekends). You'll also traverse some of the same territory covered in the other destinations in this chapter, which will help you pick out lodging and dining options as needed. Finally, enjoy the scenic geography of Morelos as you travel, from its pastoral fields to its rugged mountains.

Las Golondrinas

Nicolas Catalán is a pedestrian-only street lined with shops and eateries leading away from the *zócalo*. Walk down this road until you get to Las Golondrinas (the Swallows), where you can give Zapata a final sendoff by indulging in an excellent meal. The restaurant is set in the courtyard of a 17th-century building, and beneath its white canopy lies a pleasant open-air dining area. The specialty here is *molcajete*, a dish named for the stone bowl in which it is prepared and served. There are several varieties to choose from, from *cochinita pibil* (slow-roasted pork) to barbecued rabbit. You can also sample regional classics like *tampiqueña* or chicken in mole *pipián*. The restaurant has an extensive cocktail menu, if you feel like toasting the good general, or merely honoring the end of La Ruta de Zapata. Los Golondrinas is located at Nicolas Catalán 19-A, Centro Cuautla, Morelos. Call 735-354-1350 or visit www.las-golondrinas.com.mx.

Open 8–midnight daily. $-$$.

The excellent molcajete at Las Golondrinas

The Route

From **Cuernavaca**, take the Mexico-Acapulco highway (95D) to the Cuautla exit, which leads to the Milpa Alta–Cuautla highway (Route 115D). Follow the road to the Oaxtepec/Oacalco exit, which will take you to **Tepoztlán** and the Ex-Convento de La Natividad. After, return to the Milpa Alta–Cuautla highway and continue east toward Cuautla until you veer left onto Route 113, to **Oaxtepec**. The road becomes Avenida Romulo F. Hernandez and leads to the Ex-Convento Santo Domingo de Guzmán.

From here, take a left to get on Avenida Nacional, which will take you to Carretera Tlayacapan-Yautepec (Route 2). Take a right and head to **Tlayacapan** and the Convento de San Juan Bautista. After, you'll continue what is essentially a loop, following Route 2 (Carretera Tlayacapan-Atlatlahucan) to the small towns of **Totolapán** and **Atlatlahucan**, before Route 2 rejoins Route 115D. Turn right here and head south to the junction of Route 10. Take a left to head toward **Yecapixtla**. Keep on Route 10, heading east and then south, to get to the remaining ex-convents in **Ocuituco, Tetela del Volcán**, and **Zacualpan de Amilpas**. To return to Cuernavaca, follow Route 10 south and then take a right on Highway 160, which eventually becomes the Milpa Alta–Cuautla highway. The convents below are listed chronologically according to this route.

LA CATEDRAL DE CUERNAVACA

777-318-4590
At the corner of Hidalgo Street and Morelos Avenue, Cuernavaca, Morelos

Since your starting point is Cuernavaca, begin at the Cuernavaca Cathedral, or Catedral y Ex-Convento de Asunción de María. In the convent, make sure to check out the early murals, which can be found in the cloister and include an afterlife genealogy of Saint Francis. There's also a wooden statue of Saint Christopher revering Christ. Free.

EX-CONVENTO DE LA NATIVIDAD

739-395-0225
Off the main plaza between Avenida Revolución and Avenida Zaragoza, Tepoztlán, Morelos

As mentioned above, this convent in Tepoztlán is noted for its murals, especially the ones in the Sala de Profundis, which was the antechamber to the dining hall. Most every convent on this route has at least one unique distinguishing feature, and this one has the lookout. An arched niche on the upper floor, it has breathtaking views of the hills. Don't miss the small museum in the cloister, and the gift shop, which stocks Mexican music, clothing, and artifacts, and is built around the convent's old well.

EX-CONVENTO SANTO DOMINGO DE GUZMÁN

On Avenida Romulo F. Hernandez adjacent to the Centro Vacacional Oaxtepec, Yautepec, Morelos

Begun in 1535, this was the first convent established by the Dominicans in the Americas. At the time, Oaxtepec was the most important city of the Tlahuica tribe, and this structure played a key role in fulfilling the church's evangelical mission in the region. Visitors will be struck by the incredibly detailed black-and-white murals that can be found throughout the convent and especially in the cloisters. Many saints are depicted, and their names and stories are well labeled in Spanish. Also take note of the cloister's domed roof, with its intricate blue, black, and red hexagonal pattern. The convent's other distinguishing feature is its round stained-glass window in the chapel, which floods the chapel in warm light during the day, resembling a miniature sun. The convent was used as a school in the 1920s, and there is still a public library here with free Internet access.

CONVENTO DE SAN JUAN BAUTISTA
Avenida Juárez and Plaza de la Corregidora, Tlayacapan

Montezuma I himself laid out the town of Tlayacapan, which is worth a visit even if you're not on the convent route. It's famed for its clay works, and you can visit small pottery workshops that have been family businesses for generations. There's also a small but excellent museum near the picturesque red-and-white municipal building. But first we must cover the Convento de San Juan Bautista.

One of the convent's distinguishing features is the absence of a bell tower. It's the only convent on the route without one, which makes it the most original; all the convents were originally built without

Saint Paul mural, Ex-Convento Santo Domingo de Guzmán

towers, which were added in later centuries. San Juan Bautista also has the largest atrium of any church in Morelos. The convent is more noted for its construction and dimensions than its artistic merits. It's the third-tallest in Morelos, and you'll feel the height once you look up at the high vaulted ceilings. The interior is quite bare, painted a uniform white with traces of the original work on the roof. Make your way to the portico of the pilgrims to see the convent's most well-preserved frescoes.

Finally, check out the small museum located in the convent's Sala De Profundis. The collection includes Tlahuica artifacts, beautiful murals, religious paintings and ornaments, and, most bizarrely, a series of desiccated mummies, including eight children, that was uncovered during an excavation and date back to the 1500s. In 1996 San Juan Bautista was declared a UNESCO World Heritage Site, one of only 11 to receive the designation in Mexico.

Next, cross the *zócalo* to visit **La Cerreria** (the Waxworks), the town's museum and cultural center. The building was once used by Zapata as a barracks, though it's not on the Zapata Route. Today it contains Tlahuica Indian artifacts as well as a detailed exposition on the *barra*, or clay, for which Tlayacapan artisans are renowned. (On weekends there is an artisan market from 10–6 in town where you can find well-made and affordable pieces.) The cultural center also coordinates trips to local workshops during the week. The building

Convento de San Juan Bautista

is named for its use as a candle factory, another Tlayacapan tradition represented in the museum. Finally, check out the small display of unusual pink and zebra-striped animals and figurines, each tied to a firework. These are made as amulets to cure sickness. The museum is located at the Plaza de la Corregidora.

EX-CONVENTO DE SAN GUILLERMO
Along the Carretera a Totolapán, off the *zócalo*, Totolapán, Morelos

The small town of Totolapán is home to the only church in Morelos where there is an order of monks still in residence. The convent is unique for the XPS and IHS circular designs covering its front wall. Much of the architecture is neoclassic, dating from the 18th century, but the cloister has remnants of the original 16th-century structure, including murals done by the St. Augustine Order, which built the church. The interior has an updated look, with red-and-white sheets decoratively draped from the chandelier and a crucified Christ behind a glass enclosure. You can still see monks in brown and gray robes working in the yard and orchards. The order has been here since the 1500s, and to this day members dispense medicine to the community.

TEMPLO Y EX CONVENTO DE SAN MATEO APÓSTOL
Carretera Atlatlahucan-San Juan Texcalpán off the *zócalo,* Atlatlahucan, Morelos

In the tiny town of Atlatlahucan, the Augustine church of Saint Matthew Apostle, dating from 1533, is a prime example of traditional Catholicism in Mexico. For one, it's the only one in Morelos with an outer wall and an inner wall, and an open-air chapel to one side that's used for processions. The front façade boasts a 1903 clock, a gift from Porfirio Díaz, and an interesting depiction above the front door combines pre-Hispanic and Catholic imagery. If you visit during mass, you'll see that the old ways are honored here. Men still sit on the left, women—veiled and wearing long skirts—on the right. The interior is quite attractive, with white sheets with embroidered angels extending from the ceiling in long sweeping arcs. The cloister has very well-preserved geometric designs visible on the roof. Finally, note the distinctive painting of Christ, which shows his followers trying to save souls trapped in hell, including—interestingly—bishops, kings, and even a pope.

EX-CONVENTO Y PARROQUÍA DE SAN JUAN BAUTISTA DE YECAPIXTLA
At the *zócalo* along the Carretera Yecapixtla-Tetela del Volcán, Yecapixtla, Morelos

The former convent and parish church of Saint John the Baptist in Yecapixtla was built in 1535. It was originally Franciscan but was later given to the Augustine order. It is a huge and imposing structure, almost the size of the Cuernavaca Cathedral, and similarly built as a fortress church. The church is an excellent example of gothic architecture, visible in the large rosette above the front doors and the ancient stone pulpit to the right, which dates from the 16th century and bears the Augustine symbol (a heart pierced with three arrows). The former convent is also one of the few in Morelos in which a priest is still in residence in the cloister.

TEMPLO Y EX-CONVENTO DE SANTIAGO APÓSTOL DE OCUITUCO
Carretera Ocuituco-Los Alacranes, off the *zócalo,* Ocuituco, Morelos

The former convent of Saint James the Apostle in Ocuituco is the first convent built by the Augustine order in the Americas. Construction was begun in 1534. The crowning glory of

---

The *Cecina* of Yecapixtla

While on the Convent Route, there is a good reason to wait until you reach Yecapixtla before you break for lunch. This town is famous for its *cecina*, the signature dish of Morelos, and **El Portón** is an excellent place to find out why. The no-frills restaurant may scare you away with its bareness: a few rustic tables, its proprietor sporting Wellington boots at all times, and the general air of a butcher's shop rather than a restaurant, may not be what you had in mind. But ignore any misgivings and walk right in. After ordering (the sausages are also excellent), ask to go check out how they make it. Behind the dining area you'll see workers stripping thin strips of beef, salting and stitching them, and then hanging them on bamboo rods to dry under the sun.

The quality of *cecina* depends on the cut, the saltiness, and the drying. At El Portón, the process takes all day, but the final product is tender and tasty. Try a few tacos *de cecina* with cheese, cream, and beans, together with an *ensalada de nopales*. The other reason to trust in this restaurant is its reputation for good hygiene. Those Wellingtons the owner has on? They're to keep him dry during the frequent cleansing of the area where they make their *cecina*. El Portón is located on Sufragio Efectivo 5, Col. Centro, Yecapixtla, Morelos. Call 731-357-2453. Open daily 9–5. $.

---

this building is the 16th-century *Fuente de los Leones* (Fountain of the Lions), which dominates the church's courtyard. The hexagonal fountain is a typical design of Spanish churches with Moorish influence. At its edges are stone figurines of lion heads (giving it its name), frogs, and angels. Also to be found here is a replica of the tiny chapel of the church of Calvario in downtown Cuernavaca. This convent has also been declared a UNESCO World Heritage Site.

TEMPLO Y EX-CONVENTO DE SAN JUAN BAUTISTA DE TETELA DEL VOLCÁN
Carretera Tlalmimilulpán-Tetela del Volcán, at the zócalo, Tetela del Volcán, Morelos

The easternmost of the convents along the Ruta del Convento, the church and former convent of Saint John the Baptist is located at the foot of the Popocatépetl volcano. Because of its location, this town is subject to much colder weather than the other stops along the route, but the trade-off is the magnificent scenery. The convent was built by the Dominicans between 1571 and 1581. This was also the site of the first secular parish in the state of Morelos. Its yellow painted façade and red border makes a pleasant contrast to the buttresses that mark it as another defensive structure. Inside, check out the colorful murals and passageways lined with murals of crosses. In the cloister, look for a very unusual mural of the resurrection of a native Indian at the hands of Friar Domingo of the Dominican order of Tepoztlán.

TEMPLO Y EX-CONVENTO DE LA INMACULADA CONCEPCIÓN DE ZACUALPAN DE AMILPAS
Plaza de la Constitución, Amilpas, Morelos

Set against the dramatic backdrop of Popocatépetl, the last stop on the Ruta del Convento brings you to the church and former convent of the Immaculate Conception. Begun by the Augustines in 1535, the church wasn't finished until 1567. This is a classic representation of 16th-century architecture, which mixes Spanish style (arched columns, depictions of

Augustinian saints) and indigenous influences. Of particular note is the ornate, 19th-century altarpiece in the open-air chapel, representative of the baroque school and considered one of the most beautiful in Morelos. Also look for a painting of the genealogical tree of the Augustine order.

THE CAVES OF CACAHUAMILPA

I'm cheating a bit with this one, because Las Grutas de Cacahuamilpa are actually in the neighboring state of Guerrero, but they're such a fixture of Morelos tourism that they deserve mentioning here.

Cacahuamilpa, roughly translated, means "the place where peanuts are planted," but don't let the simple name diminish your expectations. This underground cave system is among the largest in the world and has an eerie, almost alien beauty.

Pre-Hispanic tribes used to think the yawning cave mouth was the entrance to the underworld. During the Mexican War of Independence and the revolution, troops used to hide here, including Vicente Guerrero and Emiliano Zapata. Porfirio Díaz held banquets in its underground halls, but since 1936, it's been a national park.

The only way to see the caves is by guided tour, and the site's guides are Spanish-speaking. For an English version, go with an outside tour group. The way to the caves takes you across the lip of a lush green valley. In fact, for 50 pesos, you can test your mettle with a Tyrolean (you hang from a cable and zipline across a very deep chasm; it's a short ride and a long way down).

Once inside the caves, you'll encounter a world combining human imagination with nature's random artistry. The walk through is easy, thanks to a well-lit, broad path through

Las Grutas de Cacahuamilpa Source: Mexico Tourism Board

the system. Multicolored lights throw the towering stalagmites, ponderous stalactites, and odd sculptures into sharp relief, and the various minerals found here lend their own hues to the subterranean landscape.

The two-hour, 2.5-mile roundtrip tour takes you into caverns of absolutely jaw-dropping size. Along the way, your guide will flash his light here and there, pointing out some of the more distinctive figures. Particularly impressive is the monolithic, 81-meter Champagne Bottle (Beer Bottle, to some), perhaps the most photographed structure in the caves; the natural auditorium; and the Throne Room. From February to March, Cacahuamilpa also offers an overnight caving excursion to two subterranean rivers running beneath the system.

The caves are located 50 miles from Cuernavaca, and the drive takes you through an agricultural heartland. From the city, take Highway 95 toward Acapulco. Turn right at Alpuyeca toward the caves, and follow the signs. Call 721-104-0155/104-0156 or visit http://cacahuamilpa.conanp.gob.mx. Open 10–5 daily. $, overnight excursion. $$$.

A Traveler's Dictionary

Basic Spanish

If you travel to Mexico without ever having taken a single Spanish class, you'll be well served by at least attempting to gain a modicum of facility with the language. While English is spoken in tourist areas, some basic Spanish will go a long way to improving your experience in Mexico City and beyond.

Bare Necessities
Yes—*Sí*
No—*No*
Please—Por favor (a slangy version is *¡porfa!*)
Thank you—*Gracias*
Thank you very much—*Muchas gracias*
You're welcome—*De nada*
I don't know—*No sé*
I'm sorry—*Lo siento*
Good—*Bueno*
Better—*Mejor*
Bad—*Malo*
Worse—*Peor*
Okay/Fine—*Está bien*
And—*Y*
But—*Pero*
English—*Inglés*
Spanish—*Español*
I don't speak Spanish—*No hablo español*
I don't speak Spanish well—*No hablo bien el español*
I don't understand Spanish—*No entiendo español*
Do you speak English?—*¿Usted habla inglés?* (formal)/*¿Hablas inglés?* (informal)
Is English spoken here?—*¿Se habla ingles aquí?*
How do you say . . . —*¿Cómo se dice . . . ?*
Where is . . . ?—*¿Dónde está . . . ?*
How much is . . . ?—*¿Cuánto es . . . ?/ Cuánto cuesta . . . ?*
I want . . .—*Yo quiero . . .*
Excuse me?—*¿Perdón?*
Excuse me (to get by)—*Perdóneme*
Excuse me (to ask a question/get attention)—*Discúlpeme* (Mexicans also say *¿mande?* or, informally *¿cómo?*)

Greetings and Goodbyes
Hello—*Hola*

Good morning—*Buenos días*
Good afternoon—*Buenas tardes*
Good evening—*Buenas noches*
How are you?—*¿Cómo estás?* (informal)/*¿Cómo está?* (formal)
How are you (informal)?—*¿Que tal?*
Good/Very good, thanks—*Bien/Muy bien, gracias*
And you?—*¿Y usted?*
Pleased to meet you—*Mucho gusto*
Goodbye—*Adiós*
See you later—*Hasta luego*
See you soon—*Hasta pronto*
Be seeing you—*Nos vemos*
Take care—*Cuidate*
Have a good day—*Que tenga un buen día*
Hope all goes well for you—*Que le vaya bien*

Numbers

0—*Cero*
1—*Uno/Una*
2—*Dos*
3—*Tres*
4—*Cuatro*
5—*Cinco*
6—*Seis*
7—*Siete*
8—*Ocho*
9—*Nueve*
10—*Diez*
11—*Once*
12—*Doce*
13—*Trece*
14—*Catorce*
15—*Quince*
16—*Dieciseis*

17—*Diecisiete*
18—*Dieciocho*
19—*Diecinueve*
20—*Veinte*
30—*Treinta*
40—*Cuarenta*
50—*Cincuenta*
60—*Sesenta*
70—*Setenta*
80—*Ochenta*
90—*Noventa*
100—*Cien*
150—*Ciento cincuenta*
200—*Doscientos*
500—*Quinientos*
1,000—*Mil*
1,000,000—*Un millón*

Days and Months

Monday—*Lunes*
Tuesday—*Martes*
Wednesday—*Miércoles*
Thursday—*Jueves*
Friday—*Viernes*
Saturday—*Sábado*
Sunday—*Domingo*
Day—*Día*
Today—*Hoy*

Tomorrow—*Mañana*
Yesterday—*Ayer*
Day after tomorrow—*Pasado mañana*
Day before yesterday—*Antes de ayer*
The next day—*El día siguiente*
Week—*Semana*
Month—*Mes*
Year—*Año*

Time

Time—*Tiempo*
Hour—*Hora*
Minute—*Minuto*
Second—*Segundo*
What time is it?—*¿Qué hora es?*
It's one o'clock—*Es la una*
It's two o'clock—*Son las dos*
It's three o'clock in the afternoon—*Son las tres de la tarde*
At nine o'clock in the morning—*A las nueve de la mañana*

At two thirty—*A las dos y media*
It's ten past seven—*Son las siete y diez*
At quarter to five—*A las cinco menos cuarto*
Noon—*Mediodía*
Afternoon—*La tarde*
Midnight—*Medianoche*
Night—*La noche*
Last Night—*Anoche*
Dawn—*La madrugada*

Pronouns and Terms of Address

I—*Yo*
You—*Usted* (formal)/*Tú* (informal)
He/Him—*Él*
She/Her—*Ella*
We/us—*Nosotros*
They—*Ellos/Ellas*

You all—*Ustedes*
Mr.—*Señor*
Mrs.—*Señora*
Miss (young)—*Señorita*
Sir/Mr. (formal)—*Don*
Sir/Mrs. (formal)—*Doña*

Friends and Family

Husband—*Esposo*
Wife—*Esposa*
Son—*Hijo*
Daughter—*Hija*
Brother/Sister—*Hermano/Hermana*
Father—*Padre*
Dad—*Papá*

Mother—*Madre*
Mom—*Mamá*
Grandfather/Grandmother—*Abuelo/abuela*
Boyfriend/Fiancé—*Novio*
Girlfriend/Fiancée—*Novia*
Friend—*Amigo/Amiga*

The Five W's

Who—*Quién/Quiénes* (for more than one)
What—*Qué*
When—*Cuando*
Where—*Dónde*
Why—*Por qué* ("Because" is also *porque*, but it's one word instead of two)

Sizes and Amounts

Big—*Grande*
Small—*Pequeño/chico*
More—*Más*
Less—*Menos*
A lot—*Mucho*
A little—*Poco*
Nothing—*Nada*
Everything—*Todo*

Getting Around

Here—*Aquí*
There—*Allá*
From . . . to . . .—*De . . . a . . .*
Neighborhood—*Colonia*
Road—*El camino*
Street—*Calle*
Little street—*Callejón*
Avenue—*Avenida*
Highway—*Carretera/Autopista*
Block—*Cuadra*
Kilometer—*Kilómetro*
North—*Norte*
South—*Sur*
West—*Oeste/Poniente*
East—*Este/Oriente*
Left—*Izquierda*
Right—*Derecha*
Straight ahead—*Derecho, adelante*
Back—*Atrás*
Behind—*Detrás*
In front of—*En frente a*
Airport—*Aeropuerto*
Bus—*Autobús/Bus* (In Mexico City, the small, boxy public buses are called *peseros*)
Bus stop—*Parada*
Bus terminal—*Terminal de autobuses*
Where does this bus go?—*¿A dónde va este autobús?*
Taxi—*Taxi*
What do I owe you—*¿Cuanto le debo?*

Getting a Room

Do you have a room?—*¿Hay cuarto?*
Rate/Tariff—*Precio/Tarifa*
Room—*Habitación*
A single room—*Un sencillo*
A double room—*Un doble*
Air-conditioning—*Aire acondicionado*
Key—*Llave*
Bed—*Cama*
Bathroom/toilet—*Baño/el baño*
Shower—*Ducha*
We offer . . .—*Contamos con . . .* (Used to describe what is included, especially amenities in a hotel)

Emergencies

Help—*Ayuda*
Watch out!—*¡Cuidado!*

I need help—*Necesito ayuda*
Please help me—*Ayúdeme por favor*
Police—*Policía*
Ambulance—*Ambulancia*
Doctor—*Médico*
Firefighters—*Bomberos*
Emergency—*Emergencia*
Medicine—*Medicina*

Mexican Spanish and Slang

Mexican slang, especially *chilango* slang, is rich, varied, at times vulgar, and often quite hilarious. I regret that I can only give you a taste of it here, but I'll throw in a general observation. Slang in Mexico is all about double meanings. Innuendos, double-entendres, and not-so-subtle allusions make up the backbone of any decent bar conversation, and if you find your friend or compadre giggling away at the seemingly most innocuous comments, it's because he or she has found some way to interpret them in a less politically correct (and often phallic) way. It's all in good fun, and it certainly makes for lively discussions!

¡Aguas!—Literally "waters," it means "Watch out!"
Antro—Nightclub
¿Bueno?—Hello, when answering the phone
Bronca—Issue/problem/fight
Carajo—Not just limited to Mexico, this is an all-purpose mild expletive a few degrees south of "drat!"
Chamaco/Chamaca—A child
Chavo/Chava—Guy/girl
Chela—Beer
Chilango—A term used to describe Mexico City residents
Chingar—A vulgar way of saying to screw (in both senses) a person
Chingón—Awesome
¿Cómo ves?—Literally "How do you see?," it means "What do you think?"
Cuate—Friend, pal, or guy
Fresa—Literally "strawberry," it's used to describe someone as a rich or obnoxious brat
Gabacho—slang for "American"
Güey—Dude
Güero—Light-skinned person (not an offensive word)
Lana—Literally "wool," slang for cash
Licenciado/a—A term of respect, like Doctor, given to those who are college graduates
No mames—No way/No fooling
¿Qué onda?—What's up?
Órale—A sort of general utterance that's like saying "right on"
Pachanga/Pachangear—Party/to party
Padre—Literally "father," it means "cool" and it's a word you'll hear everywhere, as in *que padre* (how cool), *está padre* (it's cool), or *padrísimo* (the coolest)
Pinche—A very rude and vulgar expletive
Ratero—Thief

DINING IN MEXICO: WHAT TO ORDER

Dining in Mexico is one of my favorite pastimes, but it should come with this caveat: be prepared to not understand the menu, no matter how good your Spanish is. That's because many Mexican culinary terms have Nahuatl roots and therefore do not exist in your Spanish class (or in Spain, for that matter).

The Basics

To eat—*Comer*
To drink—*Beber*
Restaurant—*Restaurante*
Inn/Tavern—*Fonda*
Breakfast—*Desayuno*
Lunch—*Comida*
Dinner—*Cena*
Menu—*La carta; el menú*
Plate—*Plato*
Glass—*Taza*
Knife—*Cuchillo*
Spoon—*Cuchara*
Fork—*Tenedor*
Napkin—*Servilleta*
Drinking water—*Agua pura/potable*
Bottled water—*Agua mineral*
Bottled carbonated water—*Agua mineral con gas*
Beer—*Cerveza*

Wine—*Vino*
Juice—*Jugo*
Tea—*Té*
Coffee—*Café*
Milk—*Leche*
Straw—*Popote*
Meat—*Carne*
Chicken—*Pollo*
Fish—*Pescado*
Shellfish—*Mariscos*
Shrimp—*Camarones*
Soup—*Caldo*
Bread—*Pan*
Fruit—*Fruta*
Beans—*Frijoles*
Bon appétit!—*¡Buen Provecho!*
The check—*La cuenta*
Cheers!—*¡Salud!*

Items on the Mexican Menu

Antojitos—The name given to a host of finger food and snacks found at taquerías and restaurants
Birria—A stew made with lamb, goat, or mutton, chiles, and dried roasted peppers, among other spices and herbs
Cajeta—Caramel
Camote—Mexican sweet potato

The Many Uses of "Mother"

Mothers are incredibly important in Mexican society, but so is the word "mother," or *madre*, because it has seemingly endless applications in the local vernacular. *Un madre*, for example, is a general failure. *Un desmadre* is a complete disaster. A *madrino* is a bouncer or thug. *Tu madre* is, literally and figuratively, "Your mama." And then there's the ever popular *me vale madre*, literally "It's worth mother to me," which is a way of saying I could give a hoot (but slightly more powerful). And the funny thing is, this is just a sampling of the many uses of "mother" in Mexico.

Cecina—A thinly sliced, salted, and cured meat that is dried in the sun before being cooked

Chapulines—Grasshoppers, typically toasted in lemon juice and garlic

Chilaquiles—Fried, crispy tortilla chips mixed with a red or green chile sauce and typically served with chicken and cheese; it's also a popular breakfast food

Chile—Chile peppers are the most ubiquitous ingredient in Mexican cuisine, offering a tremendous variety, cooking style (dried, roasted, ground, charred), and dating back to the earliest Mesoamerican tribes. Here are just a few of the more popular chiles you'll find in Mexican cuisine:

> *Arbol*—Thin, dry, and spicy
>
> *Chilaca*—A long, thin, dark green or brown chile that ranges from mild to medium in heat; when dried, it's called a chile pasilla
>
> *Guajillo*—A dried, pointy, deep red chile that can be very spicy
>
> *Habanero*—A plump orange chile that is among the hottest around
>
> *Jalapeño*—One of the more famous chiles in the U.S., these are medium to large green chiles (red when mature) that are relatively spicy and named after the town of Xalapa, where they were traditionally grown; dried and smoked jalapeños are called chipotle
>
> *Poblano*—A typically mild, large green pepper from Puebla (when dried, it is called chile ancho)
>
> *Serrano*—A small, hot, and thin chile that is green, red, or yellow depending on its maturity

Chile relleno—A roasted fresh poblano pepper (sometimes ancho or pasilla peppers are used instead) stuffed with cheese, and/or meat (typically a mix of pork, raisins, and nuts), covered in egg batter and fried, and usually smothered in a tomato sauce.

Chipotle—A dried and smoked jalapeño pepper

Cochinita pibil—A Yucatán specialty, this is slow-roasted pork that's been marinated in citrus juice and wrapped in banana leaves

Comida corrida—An inexpensive, "express" set menu usually featuring soup, entrée, and dessert

Cuitlacoche or *huitlacoche*—A truffle-like fungus found on corn

Elote—Roast corn

Epazote—A green, leafy herb similar to licorice

Escamoles—Ant eggs (they have a nutty taste and a soft consistency)

Fideos—Noodles

Flor de calabaza—Squash blossom

Guajolote—Turkey (the more common *pavo* is also used)

Gusanos de maguey—Cactus worms (typically fried and served with tortillas)

Huachinango—Red snapper

Jaiba—Crab

Jamaica—Hibiscus

Jicama—A type of Mexican turnip

Jitomate—Tomato

Mixiote—An oven-cooked or pit-barbecued meat dish (usually mutton, rabbit, or chicken), seasoned with pasilla and guajillo chiles and other seasonings, and wrapped in the outer skin of the maguey plant

Molcajete—A variety of meats, vegetable, or cheeses cooked and presented in the stone bowl that gives the dish its name

Mole—A general name given to a variety of sauces, the most typical of which combines ground chiles with onion, charred tortilla, nuts or seeds, and unsweetened chocolate

Mollete—A Mexican take on a grilled-cheese sandwich, *molletes* are grilled sandwich rolls stuffed with frijoles and cheese.

Nopales—The fleshy oval pads of the cactus (sometimes called cactus leaves)

Pozole—A stew typically made with hominy, pork or chicken, lime, salt, chiles, onions, and avocado

Rajas—Roasted and peeled strips of poblano chile

Róbalo—Sea Bass

Tamales—A pre-Hispanic classic, tamales are made from cornmeal dough (*masa*) or ground corn, often filled with meat, seafood, insects, vegetables, and other ingredients, then wrapped in a corn husk and steamed

Tlacoyo—A flat, torpedo-shaped cornmeal cake toasted and stuffed with a variety of fillings, including *flor de calabaza*, *huitlacoche*, and beans and cheese

Torta—A Mexican sandwich, with a choice of fillings served on a crusty white roll, also called *cemita*

What to Drink

Aguas frescas—Literally "fresh waters," this is a blend of water, sugar, and either fruits, cereals, or seeds

Atole—A hot, thick drink made with cornmeal, crushed fruits, and sugar or honey

Barrilitos—Mexico's popular fruit-flavored soft drink brand

Jarritos—Another popular brand of fruit-flavored carbonated soft drinks

Mezcal—A liquor distilled from the agave plant (not tequila, which is only made from blue agave)

Michelada—A Mexican take on the Bloody Mary, made with beer instead of vodka

Tequila—The classic liquor made by fermenting and distilling the sap of the blue agave plant

Pasita—A liquor made from raisins

Pulque—An alcoholic, often flavored beverage fermented from the juice of the agave plant

How It's Cooked

Adobo/Adobado—Marinated in a spicy vinegar and chile sauce

A la parrilla—Grilled

A la talla—Fish rubbed with spices and grilled on a rack over hot coals

Al carbon—Charbroiled

Al pastor—Meat (almost always pork) roasted on a vertical spit, like a gyro

Al vapor—Steamed

Asado—Roasted

Barbacoa—Slow-roasted in a pit or over an open fire

Empanizada—Breaded

Encebolladao—Cooked with onions

Frito—Fried

Guisado—Stewed

Horneado—Baked

Rostizado—Roasted

What to Order at the Taquería?

The first time I checked out a menu at a local taquería, I almost got up and walked away. Besides the familiar references to tacos and enchiladas, I couldn't understand a thing. In fact, even the stuff I recognized, like chalupas, was invariably different from the Tex-Mex versions I was familiar with. And what the heck was a *huarache* doing on a menu? I thought it was something you wore on your feet. What about *alambre*? Here's a little clarification so you don't feel as lost as I initially did:

Alambre—A flavorful mix of steak, bacon, onion, green pepper, and cheese

Carnitas—Braised, tender, sliced pork

Curtido—A garnish of pickled carrots and onions served at most taquerías

Chalupa—An elongated oval tortilla, resembling the *chalupas*, or canoes, that give them their name, topped with shredded meat, cheese and other ingredients

Chimichanga—A deep-fried burrito, often served with salsa and guacamole

Enchilada—A corn tortilla placed briefly in hot oil and often dipped in a chile sauce, wrapped around a filling, and baked. Enchiladas are usually garnished with more sauce and cheese; other varieties include *enfrijoladas* (dipped in refried beans instead of chile) and *entomatadas* (dipped in tomato sauce)

Flauta—A corn tortilla rolled around a filling, usually shredded beef or chicken, and then deep fried

Gordita—A thick tortilla, sometimes made with *pan Árabe* (pita bread) stuffed with a filling, usually beans or spicy shredded meat and cheese

Huarache—A large, flat, oval-shaped tortilla (*huarache* means "sandal") topped with fried meat and chiles

Pancita—Sheep's stomach cooked with spices

Quesadillas—Corn or flour tortillas folded over a filling of cheese and sometimes other ingredients, and cooked until the cheese is melted and the tortilla is slightly crisp.

Sope—Another name for *gordita*

Taco—Quite simply, a tortilla wrapped around a filling

Tacos al pastor—Tacos made with sliced roast pork marinated in adobo off a vertical spit

Tacos al carbón—A taco filled with charbroiled meat

Tacos de cabeza—Tacos made with meat from the goat's head

Tinga—Spicy, shredded pork

SHOPPING IN MEXICO: WHAT TO BUY

Mexico has an incredibly rich and varied arts and crafts industry that combines ancient techniques and artistry, colonial European touches, religious inspiration, and rustic beauty. It's also an indication of the riches that the land provides: materials include onyx, wood, clay, and silver. Souvenir shopping in Mexico can be both rewarding and fun, especially in Mexico City, where you'll find items from all over the country. Most souvenirs are self-explanatory (handwoven baskets, silverware, and hammocks, for example), but here are a few typical items you may want to look out for:

Alebrijes—Brightly colored papier-mâché or wood figurines of fantastical creatures combining elements of both real and mythical animals

Árbol de la vida—The tree of life, one of the most iconic folk art products of Mexico, is the

La Calavera de la Catrina

The world of Mexican arts and crafts is rich and varied. From fine Talavera pottery to onyx figures to colorful textiles and much, much more, Mexico has a far-reaching tradition of craftsmanship and artistry. One of my favorite souvenirs, and one that exemplifies the country, is the myriad skull and skeleton figurines that are associated with the Day of the Dead. The most famous of these is *la Calavera de la Catrina* (the Elegant Skull), the iconic figure of a female skeleton in a long gown and a feathered hat, often sporting an umbrella. The image, first created by engraver José Guadalupe Posada in 1913, has become a popular national symbol, and makes for a wonderfully original and authentic keepsake.

most famous product of Metepec; it's a clay sculpture of a tree, varying in size, adorned with leaves, flowers, and biblical or folkloric figures, and usually symbolizes birth or renewal

Calaveras—A variety of festive skeletons and skull figurines that stem from the Day of the Dead festival

Canastas—Handwoven baskets

Coexcomate—Miniature replicas of pre-Hispanic thatch corn granaries

Guayabera—A traditional loose-fitting linen or cotton shirt, usually white with embroidery

Huarache—A popular local sandal traditionally made from recycled tire soles and woven leather

Huipil—A traditional embroidered woven blouse that dates to the Mayan civilization

Jorongo—A poncho

Papel amate—Art and stationery made from the bark of the Amate tree

Papel picado—Colorful punched paper, perforated with elaborate designs and used as a common folkloric decoration

Rebozo—A traditional woven shawl made of cotton or silk, featuring string ends and intricate designs

Retablos—Religious paintings typically on wood or tin

Serape—A traditional shawl or blanket

General Index

Lodging by Price

Inexpensive   Up to $100 per night
Moderate $102-$200 per night
Expensive $201 to $300 per night
Very Expensive   more than $300 per night

Inexpensive

Inexpensive-Moderate

Inexpensive-Expensive

Inexpensive-Very Expensive

Moderate

Moderate-Expensive

Moderate-Very Expensive

Expensive

Expensive-Very Expensive

Very Expensive

Dining by Price

Inexpensive	Up to $10
Moderate	$11-$25
Expensive	$26 to $35
Very Expensive	more than $35

Inexpensive

Antojitos Acapulco (Puebla), 219
Café el Jarocho (Coyoacán), 155
Cemitas las Poblanitas (Puebla), 220
Churrería el Moro (Colonia Centro), 76
El Califa (Condesa), 130
El Chupacabras (Coyoacán), 157
El Güero (Condesa), 130
El Huequito (Colonia Centro), 77
El Rey del Suadero (Polanco), 107
El Turix (Polanco), 107
Italian Coffee Company (Atlixco), 257
Karma Bagels (Cholula), 245
La Pérgola (Cholula), 245
Los Gueros (Colonia Centro), 77
Mercado Benito Juárez (Atlixco), 258
Mercado Insurgentes (Juárez), 144
Mercado San Juan Arcos de Belén (Colonia Centro), 79
Mi Taco Yucateco (Colonia Centro), 77
Plaza Hidalgo (Coyoacán), 157
Si No Le Gusta Me Voy (Colonia Centro), 77
Tacuqui (Cuauhtémoc), 143
Taquería los Parados (Polanco), 107

Inexpensive-Moderate

Adonis (Polanco), 106
Bistrot 61 (Roma), 128
Charlie Pacaya's (Atlixco), 257
El Bajío (Polanco), 106
El Fogoncito (Anzures), 107
El Greco (Condesa), 130
El Mural de los Poblanos (Puebla), 220
El Ranchito (Puebla), 220
Fonda de Santa Clara (Puebla), 221
Hostería Santo Domingo (Colonia Centro), 78
Jardín del Pulpo (Coyoacán), 156
La Fonda de Con Chon (Colonia Centro), 78-79
La Ópera (Colonia Centro), 79
La Tecla (Roma), 131
Los Tulipanes (Cholula), 245
Mi Ciudad (Puebla), 223
Restaurante Cocoyotla (Cholula), 245-246
Saks (San Ángel), 157-158
Salón Corona (Colonia Centro), 77
Trattoria Marco Polo (Cuernavaca), 280-281

Inexpensive-Expensive

Café Tacuba (Colonia Centro), 75-76
Danubio (Colonia Centro), 76

La Casa de Las Sirenas (Colonia Centro), 78

Moderate

Cantina la Guadalupana (San Ángel), 155
Casa Hidalgo (Cuernavaca), 278-279
Casa Reyna (Puebla), 219
Como (Polanco), 106-108
El Faisán (Cuernavaca), 279
Fonda de Santa Clara (Insurgentes Sur), 130-131
Fonda el Morral (Coyoacán), 156
Fonda el Refugio (Juárez), 143
Fonda Garufa (Condesa), 130
La Cantina de los Remedios (Puebla), 221-222
La India Bonita (Cuernavaca), 279-280
La Palapa del Venado (Morelos), 280
La Quinta Luna (Cholula), 245
Los Girasoles (Polanco), 108
Spuntino (Polanco), 110

Moderate-Expensive

Capicua (San Ángel), 155-156
Casa Lamm (Roma), 128
Contramar (Roma), 128-129
El Cardenal (Colonia Centro), 76-78
El Lobby (Polanco), 108
El Patio (Cuernavaca), 279
Gaia (Juárez), 279
Izote (Polanco), 108
La Purificadora (Puebla), 222-223
La Taberna del León (San Ángel), 158
Les Moustaches (Cuauhtémoc), 143-144
Ligaya (Condesa), 131
Los Danzantes (Coyoacán), 156
Los Girasoles (Colonia Centro), 79
Mesón Puerto Chico (Tabacalera), 144-145
Restaurante la Compañía (Puebla), 223
Rosato (Santa Fe), 169
Terrarium (Cuernavaca), 280
Thai Gardens (Condesa), 131

Moderate-Very Expensive

Ekos (Puebla), 221
Evita (Tabacalera), 142-143
Paxia (San Ángel), 157
Paxia (Santa Fe), 169

Expensive

Solea (Polanco), 110

Expensive-Very Expensive

El Patio (Condesa), 129
Jaso (Polanco), 109
Las Mañanitas (Cuernavaca), 280
Puerto Madero (Polanco), 109
Pujol (Polanco), 109-110
Tezka (Juárez), 145
Zhen Shanghai (Polanco), 110

Dining by Cuisine